The Big Book

of

Dramatized Classics

Other titles in the "Big Book" series

THE BIG BOOK OF FOLKTALE PLAYS
THE BIG BOOK OF HOLIDAY PLAYS
THE BIG BOOK OF COMEDIES
THE BIG BOOK OF CHRISTMAS PLAYS

The Big Book

of

Dramatized Classics

25 adaptations of favorite novels, stories, and plays for stage and round-the-table reading

Edited by

Sylvia E. Kamerman

Publishers   PLAYS, INC.   *Boston*

Library of Congress Cataloging-in-Publication Data

The Big book of dramatized classics : 25 adaptations of favorite novels, stories, and plays for stage and round-the-table reading / edited by Sylvia E. Kamerman.
    p.   cm.
    Summary: Presents stage adaptations of "A Tale of Two Cities," "The Wizard of Oz," "Wuthering Heights," "Treasure Island," "Alice in Wonderland," "Anne of Green Gables," "Moby Dick," "Great Expectations," and others.
    ISBN 0-8238-0299-X
    1. Children's plays, American. 2. Literature--Adaptations. [1. Plays. 2. Stage adaptations.] I. Kamerman, Sylvia E.
PS625.5.B54 1993
812.008'09282--dc20   93-3387
                                         CIP
                                         AC

Manufactured in the United States of America

CONTENTS

ROUND-THE-TABLE READING PLAYS

The Big Book

of

Dramatized Classics

▣▣A Tale of Two Cities

by *Charles Dickens*
Adapted by *Walter Hackett*

Characters

NARRATOR
JUDGE
PROSECUTOR
JURYMAN
MADAME THÉRÈSE DEFARGE
ERNEST DEFARGE
SYDNEY CARTON, *Lucie's friend*
CHARLES DARNAY, *Marquis St. Evrémonde*
LUCIE, *his wife*
DR. MANETTE, *Lucie's father*
JARVIS LORRY, *a banker and friend of Dr. Manette*
MISS PROSS, *nursemaid*
JAILER
JOHN BARSAD
RAMBEAU
SEAMSTRESS
GUARD
JURORS ⎫
SPECTATORS ⎭ *extras*

SCENE 1

TIME: *1793.*
SETTING: *Courtroom. Judge's bench is on a diagonal down cen-*

3

*ter, with five chairs facing it, jurors' bench at one side, specta-
tors' bench at the other. Played in front of curtain.*

BEFORE RISE: JUDGE *sits at bench.* JURORS, *including* JURYMAN,
sit at jurors' bench. CHARLES DARNAY, MADAME THÉRÈSE DE-
FARGE, ERNEST DEFARGE, *and* PROSECUTOR *sit facing* JUDGE.
LUCIE, DR. MANETTE, SYDNEY CARTON, JARVIS LORRY, *and*
MISS PROSS *sit in spectators' bench, along with as many other*
SPECTATORS *as desired.* JAILER *stands off to the side. Stage
is dim. All remain still as* NARRATOR *enters, crosses center,
addresses audience.*

NARRATOR: The French Revolution drew into its grasp thousands of victims, many of them innocent. Among these was
Charles Darnay, of the aristocratic French family of St.
Evrémonde. Some years earlier, young Darnay had taken up
residence in London, where he met and married Lucie Manette, daughter of Dr. Alexandre Manette, a Frenchman who
had spent many years as a political prisoner in the Bastille.
Returning to France, Darnay had been seized and falsely accused of acts against the Republic of France, and specifically
against Ernest Defarge, wine vendor, and his wife, Thérèse,
a ruthless minor figure in the Revolution. (NARRATOR *exits.
Lights up.*)

JUDGE (*Droning loudly*): The prisoner, Charles St. Evrémonde,
called Darnay, will rise. (CHARLES *rises.*) Prosecutor, inform
this court by whom the prisoner has been openly accused.
(PROSECUTOR, MADAME DEFARGE, *and* ERNEST DEFARGE *rise.*)

PROSECUTOR: By Ernest Defarge and Thérèse Defarge, his wife.

JUDGE (*To* JURYMAN): How votes the jury?

JURYMAN: The jury finds the prisoner . . . guilty. (LUCIE *cries
out;* DR. MANETTE *comforts her.* SPECTATORS *react loudly;
many cheer.* JAILER *crosses to* CHARLES, *takes his arm.*)

JUDGE: Charles St. Evrémonde, called Darnay, this court con-
demns you to death by the guillotine! (LUCIE *springs to her
feet, cries out again.* JUDGE *and* JURYMAN *exit.* DEFARGES
smile, self-satisfied, shake PROSECUTOR'S *hand, then all three
exit.* JAILER *starts to lead* CHARLES *out.*)

LUCIE: No! No! (DR. MANETTE *rises, puts his arm around her as she sobs.*) Oh, Charles, how can I live without you? What shall we do?

CHARLES (*In comforting tone*): Don't worry, Lucie. All will be well.

CARTON (*Loudly*): You, jailer! Hold!

JAILER (*Snarling*): What do you want, Englishman?

CARTON: Let them have a few seconds together.

JAILER: Nothing was said to me about it.

CARTON: It can do no harm. Please, just a few seconds.

JAILER (*Growling*): Well, just a few. And hurry. (*Releases* CHARLES, *steps aside*)

DR. MANETTE (*Gently*): Go ahead, Lucie. (LUCIE *approaches* CHARLES.)

LUCIE (*Gratefully; to* CARTON): Thank you, Sydney. (CARTON *smiles, nods.*)

CARTON: We'll wait in the corridor. Dr. Manette, Miss Pross, Mr. Lorry, please come with me. (CARTON, DR. MANETTE, MISS PROSS, MR. LORRY *exit.*)

LUCIE (*Falling into* CHARLES's *embrace*): Oh, Charles!

CHARLES: Lucie, my dearest. (*Pause*) I—what can we say?

LUCIE: Nothing, except to remember how much we love each other.

CHARLES: We must take comfort in that!

LUCIE: *We* know you're not guilty. It was not even a proper trial. You were doomed before you stepped into the prisoner's box.

CHARLES: No need to think about that now.

LUCIE: Perhaps it is not too late. Father will try everything in his power to save you. And Sydney is shrewd. Perhaps he can help.

CHARLES: Kiss our child for me. If ever you need help, lean on our friends—Lorry and Pross and Carton.

JAILER: You've had long enough. Come along. (*Takes* CHARLES *roughly by the arm*)

LUCIE: Please, jailer, one more minute. (JAILER *ignores her, starts off with* CHARLES.)

CHARLES: Goodbye, Lucie.

LUCIE (*Screaming*): Charles! Charles! No!

CHARLES: Think of me often. (*They exit.* LUCIE *begins to weep, walks slowly off stage as lights dim to blackout. Benches and chairs are removed. After a short pause, spotlight comes up on* DR. MANETTE *and* JARVIS LORRY, *who are engaged in worried conversation.*)

DR. MANETTE: I still have some influence. The judges, the jury, all these men in power knew me many years ago. They know that I am not an enemy, Mr. Lorry.

LORRY (*Troubled*): That is true, Dr. Manette. It is well worth trying, but there is not much time—only twenty-four hours. If only I could be of help. . . .

MANETTE: You're a kind friend, Mr. Lorry. (CARTON *enters.*) Mr. Carton, how is Lucie? Where is she?

CARTON: Miss Pross is with her.

MANETTE: My poor Lucie! I must go quickly to ask the Prosecutor and the President to rescind the harsh sentence. There's no time to lose.

LORRY: Do you wish me to accompany you, Dr. Manette?

CARTON: That is not a good idea, Mr. Lorry. As an Englishman, you would only be a drawback.

MANETTE (*Helplessly*): Perhaps you are right, Sydney. Your advice is always sound.

CARTON: Go at once, Doctor. And godspeed.

MANETTE: Thank you, Sydney. Farewell. (*He exits.*)

LORRY (*Hopefully*): Mr. Carton, do you think the officials will look favorably upon Dr. Manette's appeal?

CARTON (*Sighing; shaking head*): Did you not see the reaction of the court spectators?

LORRY (*Sadly*): Yes, I heard the fall of the ax in that sound.

CARTON (*Gently*): Don't despair. It will be some consolation to Lucie to know we tried to save Charles for her. (*Abruptly*) Well, I'm off.

LORRY: Where are you going?

CARTON: To walk and think.

LORRY (*Seriously*): Life sometimes takes a peculiar twist.

CARTON (*Musing*): Yes, Mr. Lorry, life is of little worth when we misuse it, but it is always worth the effort to save. (*Blackout*)

* * * * *

SCENE 2

BEFORE RISE: NARRATOR *enters, addresses audience.*

NARRATOR: Sydney Carton's steps were aimless as he walked along the Paris streets. Jumbled thoughts tugged at his mind. (CARTON *enters, walks in front of curtain, stops center to muse to himself.*)

CARTON: Shall I show myself? Yes, I think so. It is well that these people should know that such a man as I am here. But I must take precautions. Let me think it out. (*Still deep in thought, he exits.*)

NARRATOR: Carton turned his steps toward the Saint Antoine suburb and the wine shop of the Defarges, the pair who had testified against Charles Darnay. (*Exits as curtain rises*)

* * *

SETTING: *Defarges' wine shop, represented by counter, barrels, wine bottles, a few small tables. May be played before curtain.*

AT RISE: ERNEST *stands behind counter, and* MADAME DEFARGE *sits nearby, knitting.* CARTON *enters briskly.*

CARTON: Good evening, madame, monsieur.

ERNEST: Good evening, monsieur. Some wine?

CARTON: Yes, thank you. (*He sits at table.* ERNEST *serves* CARTON *a glass of wine.*)

MME. DEFARGE: You are English?

CARTON: Yes, madame, I am English.

ERNEST: Are you in Paris on business?

CARTON (*Agreeing*): Yes, on business. I drink to the Republic. (*Drinks wine*) Ah, fine wine.

MME. DEFARGE: Have you attended our great spectacle, the aristocrats' meeting with Madame Guillotine?

CARTON (*Slowly*): My French, madame, it is not the best. I do not quite understand.

MME. DEFARGE: Small matter, Englishman. Before you leave, you will see the tumbrils rolling through the streets, the old ladies knitting, and the heads rolling in the basket. (CARTON *finishes wine.*)

CARTON: I do not quite understand. (*Lifts empty wine glass*) Another glass of wine, please.

ERNEST: That you understand. (*Serves* CARTON *more wine*)

CARTON (*Raising glass*): Your health, Citizen and Citizeness. (*Smacking lips*) Excellent wine. (*Drowsily*) Excellent! Been up since daybreak ... so tired, sleepy. (*Yawns*) I'll close my eyes for just a ... few seconds. ... (*Puts head on arms as if asleep*)

ERNEST: Pig of an Englishman. I should toss him into the gutter.

MME. DEFARGE: Let him sleep. We have more important things to discuss. Did you observe Dr. Manette's face today?

ERNEST: He has suffered much.

MME. DEFARGE (*Knitting rapidly*): His face is not that of a true friend of the Republic. Let him take care of his face.

ERNEST: And you have observed his daughter, as well.

MME. DEFARGE: I have observed his daughter, today and every day, on the street and walking by the prison.

ERNEST: We shall be avenged tomorrow afternoon, when her husband's head rolls into the basket.

MME. DEFARGE (*Angrily*): Vengeance is what I wish. Do away with all the St. Evrémondes, I say—or Darnays, as they are called. His family persecuted mine, and so I say, vengeance for all Evrémondes.

ERNEST: Of course, Charles Darnay himself had nothing to do with the wrong done your family.

MME. DEFARGE (*Unyielding*): No matter. He is going to suffer, even though we had to swear falsely in court. And now—

ERNEST (*Timidly*): Are you also going to conspire against Dr. Manette, and Darnay's wife?

MME. DEFARGE (*With increasing fury*): Yes, and against their child. When I am done, none will survive.

ERNEST: What do you propose to do?

MME. DEFARGE: You and I will swear that we saw Lucie Darnay signaling her husband in jail. We will produce other witnesses who also have seen this happen, not once but twice. We will produce a note she wrote to him.

ERNEST (*Nervously, looking at* CARTON): Not so loud. This Englishman will hear.

MME. DEFARGE: He is asleep. Besides, he does not understand French. Lucie Darnay, her child, and father will follow Charles Darnay to the guillotine. (*Cackling*) That Lucie has such a fine, blonde head. I can see the executioner holding it aloft for all to see. (*Suddenly,* CARTON *stirs.* ERNEST *shoots a warning glance at* MME. DEFARGE, *who continues to knit rapidly.*)

ERNEST: Monsieur, did you have a nice nap? (CARTON *looks up, shakes head in disbelief.*)

CARTON: I'm sorry. I have not had much sleep in the past two days. (*Rises, takes coin from pocket*) Thank you, monsieur (*Hands coin to* ERNEST, *bows to* MME. DEFARGE), madame. Good day. (*He exits. Curtain*)

* * * * *

SCENE 3

TIME: *A short while later.*

SETTING: *Dr. Manette's house, simply furnished.*

AT RISE: LORRY *is anxiously hovering above* DR. MANETTE, *who is slumped wearily in chair.* CARTON *enters.*

MANETTE (*Whimpering in childlike manner*): Where is my bench? I cannot find my bench. What have you done with my work? I must finish those shoes.

CARTON (*Concerned*): Mr. Lorry, what is wrong with Dr. Manette?

LORRY (*In low voice; shaking his head*): The strain has been too much for him. He thinks he is back in the Bastille.

MANETTE: These shoes must be done tonight.

CARTON (*In an undertone*): I suppose he was unsuccessful in trying to free Darnay?

LORRY: The officials would do nothing. One of them brought him here in this condition. There is nothing to be done.

CARTON (*Trying to get* MANETTE *to rise*): Dr. Manette, you must go to bed. You need rest.

MANETTE (*Protesting*): But my shoes . . .

CARTON: Tomorrow will be time enough to finish the shoes. Go to bed, Doctor, please. (MANETTE *rises, exits slowly left.*)

LORRY (*Shaking head*): Poor man. He is broken.

CARTON: There is no time to lose. Now, Mr. Lorry, I want you to listen closely. Don't ask me why I make the stipulations I am going to make, and exact the promise I'm going to exact. I have a good reason.

LORRY (*Listening intently*): I do not doubt it. Go on.

CARTON (*Taking paper from his pocket and handing it to* LORRY): First, take this. It's the certificate that allows me to leave Paris. (*Points to paper*) You see—Sydney Carton, Englishman.

LORRY: What am I to do with it?

CARTON: Keep it for me until tomorrow. I am going to the prison tomorrow to see Charles.

LORRY (*Anxiously*): But the prison officials won't allow it.

CARTON: I shall see John Barsad and work through him.

LORRY: The spy?

CARTON: Yes. I'll grease a few palms. Leave it to me, but it is better for me not to take my pass with me into prison.

LORRY: What good will your seeing Charles Darnay do?

CARTON: I owe it to him and the others. (*Takes another paper from pocket*) Now, also take this paper. It belongs to Dr. Manette. (*Hands it to* LORRY) It's the certificate that will enable him and Lucie and her child to leave France at any time. Put it with mine and your own.

LORRY: I'll guard it with my life.

CARTON: These passes are good until recalled, and I have good reason to think that the doctor's and Lucie's may soon be canceled.

LORRY (*Alarmed*): Are they in danger?

CARTON: Great danger. They are in danger of denunciation by Madame Defarge. I heard it from her own lips. (LORRY *registers alarm.*) Don't look so horrified. You will save them all.

LORRY: *I?* But how?

CARTON: Tomorrow you and the others are to hurry to the seacoast by private coach. Have your horses ready, so that you can leave by two in the afternoon.

LORRY: But what if Lucie objects to leaving before her husband goes to the guillotine?

CARTON: Tell her it was his last wish. Impress that upon her.

Tell her more depends upon her leaving than she dares believe or hope. Be ready here, taking your own seat in the carriage as you wait. The moment I come to you, let me into the coach, and drive away.

LORRY: Then I am to wait for you, under all circumstances?

CARTON: Yes! As soon as I am in the coach, nothing is to stop you until you touch foot in England. I must have your solemn word on this.

LORRY: I swear it.

CARTON (*Tensely*): And remember, if you change your course one bit, a number of lives will be lost.

LORRY (*Suddenly*): You've forgotten Miss Pross.

CARTON: I'll see her now and make arrangements. She will travel in a lighter carriage, leaving one hour later than you and the others, at three o'clock. She will overtake your coach at the first stop.

LORRY (*Worried*): I wish you would tell me more.

CARTON: There is nothing more to tell. I am depending on you, Mr. Lorry.

LORRY: Let us hope everything goes well tomorrow. I don't know what we would have done but for you, Sydney. (*Quick curtain as they exit*)

* * * * *

SCENE 4

TIME: *The next afternoon; one o'clock.*

SETTING: *Prison, a divided stage: at right is jail cell, with stool and small table. Pen and paper are on table. At left is prison anteroom. Backdrop shows drab, gray walls, window with bars on it.*

AT RISE: CARTON *and* JOHN BARSAD *are onstage.* BARSAD *is pacing anxiously.*

BARSAD: I don't like this, Mr. Carton. It is too dangerous.

CARTON (*Gruffly*): You're being well paid, Barsad.

BARSAD: No matter; it still is dangerous business. And speaking of money, Mr. Carton, we'll need a bit more.

CARTON: I paid you last night.

BARSAD: Rambeau, the head jailer—he'll want more.

CARTON: How much have you told him?

BARSAD (*Shrugging*): Oh, nothing more than I was supposed to tell. I said that you wished a few minutes alone with Darnay.

CARTON (*Sternly*): See that you say no more.

BARSAD (*Looking off left*): Here comes Rambeau now. (RAMBEAU *enters*.)

RAMBEAU (*Gruffly*): Well, Barsad, what do you wish?

BARSAD: Monsieur Rambeau, this is the gentleman I spoke to you about. Sydney Carton, the Englishman. Last night you said you would allow him to visit his friend Darnay for a few minutes.

RAMBEAU: That was last night.

BARSAD: Just for a few minutes.

RAMBEAU: St. Evrémonde or Darnay or whatever his name is— he has an appointment in less than an hour. It is too late to see him now.

BARSAD: But it is a simple favor.

RAMBEAU: If I were caught, it might mean *my* head.

CARTON: Monsieur Rambeau, I appreciate the delicacy of your position, but I am wondering if perhaps a small offering might not be well received. Say, ten gold louis.

RAMBEAU (*Considering*): Twenty would be more like it.

CARTON: Twenty, then. (*Takes coins from pocket, hands them to* RAMBEAU) Here you are.

RAMBEAU: If you are caught, I know nothing about it, not a thing.

CARTON: We understand.

RAMBEAU: Follow me. (RAMBEAU *starts to cross right, followed by* CARTON *and* BARSAD. *Lights dim almost to blackout; spotlight comes up on* CHARLES DARNAY, *right, sitting on stool in jail cell.* RAMBEAU *pulls keys from pocket, mimes unlocking cell door.*) Here you are. Only a few minutes, now. I'll be up the corridor waiting. Call for me when you need me. (*Exits right.* CARTON *approaches* CHARLES. BARSAD *stands, as if outside cell door.*)

CHARLES (*Faintly*): Who is it?

CARTON: It is I, Charles.

CHARLES: Sydney?

CARTON: Yes.

CHARLES: Are you a prisoner?

CARTON: No, Charles. Lucie sent me to you with a most earnest, emphatic entreaty. You must obey it.

CHARLES: Of course. I will do anything Lucie asks.

CARTON: There is no time to ask me what it means. Here, then, put on my boots. (CARTON *takes off his boots, pushes them over to* CHARLES.)

CHARLES: Sydney, what are you doing?

CARTON (*Tensely*): Just do as I say, Charles! (*Swiftly removing cravat, hat and coat, handing them to* CHARLES, *who is putting on* CARTON's *boots*) Change your cravat for mine. Put on my coat and hat. And be swift about it.

CHARLES (*In despair, as he struggles to put on* CARTON's *boots, clothes*): Sydney, there is no escaping from this place. It can't be done!

CARTON (*Ignoring* CHARLES): There are pen and paper on this table. Write what I shall dictate. (*Pushes* CHARLES *into chair*) Quick!

CHARLES (*Picking up pen*): To whom do I address it?

CARTON: To no one. Just write this. (*As* CARTON *stands behind him, dictating,* CHARLES *writes.*) "If you remember the words that passed between us long ago, you will readily comprehend this. . . ." (CARTON *surreptitiously removes vial from pocket.*)

CHARLES: Is that all?

CARTON: No, keep on . . . (*Moves vial close to* CHARLES' *face*)

CHARLES: What do you have in your hand, Sydney? Is that a weapon?

CARTON: Never mind! Write on. "I am thankful that the time has come when I can prove them. That I do so, is no subject for regret or grief. . . ."

CHARLES (*Looking up, sniffing air*): What is that odor . . . a vapor?

CARTON: It is nothing. Take up the pen and finish. Hurry! "If it had been otherwise, I should have so much the more to answer for."

CHARLES (*Groggily*): That vapor . . . my head.

CARTON: I have to do it, Charles. (*Struggling with* CHARLES, *holding vial to his nose*) Have to . . . a few more whiffs and you'll. . . . (*Pauses.* CHARLES *slumps in chair.*) There. Just enough to make you sleep soundly. This note, Charles, I'll leave inside your coat. (*Folds paper, puts it inside* CHARLES' *coat*) There! (*Calls off left*) Barsad! Barsad!

BARSAD (*Stepping forward*): Here I am. Is he all right?

CARTON: Unconscious. No hazard now.

BARSAD: Not if you keep to your bargain.

CARTON: If they do discover the trick, you and he and the rest will be many miles from here. Now, call the jailer and take Darnay to the coach. Leave by the same gate we entered.

BARSAD (*Nervously*): But if we're caught—what then?

CARTON: You won't be if you do exactly as I say. Get Darnay to the coach in the courtyard. Turn him over to Mr. Lorry, and make sure they depart immediately. Here, let's get him to his feet. (*They struggle to pull* DARNAY *up.*) There. I'll sit at the table, my back to the door, my head in my hands. (*He does so.*)

BARSAD (*Calling out*): Monsieur! Monsieur Rambeau! (RAMBEAU *enters.*)

RAMBEAU (*In surly tone*): You took long enough. This is a busy day for me. There are fifty-two visitors to the guillotine today. Fifty-two! (*Suddenly*) What has happened to Monsieur Carton?

BARSAD: This has been too much for him to bear. He has fainted. We must get him outside into the air at once.

RAMBEAU (*Mockingly*): So afflicted to find his friend, Darnay, has drawn a prize in the lottery of the guillotine.

BARSAD: I will support him. You open the door. (RAMBEAU *mimes opening cell door.* BARSAD *and* CHARLES *cross left, then exit.* RAMBEAU *mimes locking cell door, then crosses left.*)

RAMBEAU (*Laughing*): A pair of unconscious men. (*Looks back at cell, where* CARTON *remains at table, head in hands as if asleep*) Never worry, Monsieur Darnay, I shall be back for you soon. Meanwhile, rest well. (*Exits left*)

CARTON (*Rising after short pause*): God be with you, Darnay, and you, too, my dearest Lucie. (*Short pause, then spotlight dims, and curtain slowly closes.* NARRATOR *enters before curtain, addresses audience.*)

NARRATOR: Minutes later, a prison guard led Carton out into the shadows of the damp prison corridor. He was led to a large and windowless room already crowded with other victims, where he awaited his fate. Meanwhile, in the courtyard a few miles away, Mr. Lorry paced nervously back and forth, occasionally consulting his watch. (LORRY *enters, paces, looks at watch.*) Inside the waiting coach were Lucie Darnay, her child, and Dr. Manette. Suddenly, a small cart driven by Barsad, the spy, approached. (NARRATOR *exits.* BARSAD *enters.* LORRY *hurries toward him.*)

LORRY: Thank heaven you're here!

BARSAD: I hurried as fast as I could. I didn't want to attract too much attention.

LORRY: We must be leaving in a few minutes. (*Tensely*) Where is he?

BARSAD: Just a few yards away, in the back of my cart. Give me a hand with him.

LORRY: What happened?

BARSAD: He's overcome.

LORRY: I can well understand. (*They go off and quickly reenter, one on each side of* DARNAY.)

BARSAD (*Grunting*): Easy, now.

LORRY (*Surprised*): Hold on! This isn't Carton. It's—it's—

BARSAD: Yes, it's Darnay.

LORRY: But how—

BARSAD: There's no time to explain. Get him into your carriage.

LORRY (*Anxiously*): Where's Carton? (*Pause*) I say, where's Carton? (*Suddenly*) Barsad, you mean Carton changed places with Darnay?

BARSAD: Yes.

LORRY (*Upset*): But we can't allow him to do it.

BARSAD: He told me to tell you that you're to keep your promise to depart immediately. (*Sound of clock striking twice is heard off.*) There's your signal. Be off! (*They exit with* DARNAY.)

* * * * *

SCENE 5

TIME: *An hour later.*
SETTING: *Last checkpoint outside of Paris. Guardhouse is right.*
AT RISE: GUARD *stands in front of guardhouse.* LORRY *enters, carrying papers.*
GUARD: Who goes here? (*Points off*) Who is in that coach?
LORRY: Travelers.
GUARD (*Demanding*): Your papers.
LORRY (*Handing papers to* GUARD): Here you are, Captain.
GUARD (*Reading*): Alexandre Manette. Physician. French. (*Looks off*) Which is he?
LORRY: The old gentleman.
GUARD (*Calling off*): Are you Alexandre Manette?
MANETTE (*From off; in childlike voice*): My shoes, I must fix them. It is getting late.
GUARD (*Roughly*): Apparently the citizen-doctor is not in his right mind. Perhaps the Revolution fever has been too much for him.
LORRY: He is not well.
GUARD: Many suffer from it. (*Reads again*) Lucie St. Evré-monde, called Darnay. His daughter. French. (*Quizzically*) St. Evrémonde . . . Darnay! Ah, so this is the wife of the gentleman who has an engagement with the guillotine.
LORRY: Yes.
GUARD: Let her show her face.
LORRY: Please, captain, she is asleep.
GUARD (*Grumbling*): Very well. And her child. (*Looks off*) Ah, yes, I see her.
LORRY: Yes.
GUARD: Sydney Carton. Advocate. English. Which is he?
LORRY (*Pointing off*): He is the one in the corner.

GUARD: Apparently the Englishman is in a swoon. (*Calls out*) You there, Englishman.

LORRY (*Quickly*): He is overcome. At best his health is not good.

GUARD: A sleepy group of companions you have.

LORRY: We have been through much anguish these past few days. It is understandable.

GUARD: It is none of my worry. And the last—Jarvis Lorry. Banker. English.

LORRY: I am Lorry.

GUARD: This is your whole party?

LORRY: Except for a servant, who is following in another coach.

GUARD: Wait here while I stamp and countersign your papers. I shall be back. (*Exits. After a moment,* LUCIE *enters.*)

LUCIE (*Softly*): Mr. Lorry.

LORRY: Sshh! Lucie, quiet, please. The guard will hear you.

LUCIE (*Trembling with excitement*): He's—he's here. Mr. Lorry, it's Charles, my Charles. Am I dreaming?

LORRY: No, I'll explain later.

LUCIE (*Holding up paper*): This paper tucked into Charles' coat is in Charles' hand, but it's—the message is not from him. It says, (*Reads*) "If you remember the words that passed between us long ago, you will readily comprehend this when you see it—" (*Pause*) It's (*Sobbing*) it's from Sydney!

LORRY (*Gravely*): He's a brave man, Lucie.

LUCIE: He did this for us.

LORRY: For you, Lucie. (*Sharply*) Get back into the coach. The guard is returning. (LUCIE *exits quickly.* GUARD *reenters.*) Is all in order, Captain?

GUARD (*Handing papers to* LORRY): Here are the papers— stamped and countersigned. You may pass on, Citizen.

LORRY: Thank you.

GUARD: By the way, Citizen Lorry, how many?

LORRY: I do not understand you.

GUARD: How many to the guillotine today?

LORRY: Fifty-two.

GUARD: A good number. The guillotine goes on handsomely. And so a pleasant journey, Citizen. (GUARD *returns to guardhouse. Curtain closes as* LORRY *exits.*)

* * * * *

SCENE 6

BEFORE RISE: NARRATOR *enters, addresses audience.*

NARRATOR: As three o'clock approached, a lighter coach that was to take Miss Pross and the luggage arrived at Lucie St. Evrémonde's home. The coach was loaded quickly, and the driver left to buy some additional straps with which to secure the load, promising to return shortly. Within the house, Miss Pross busied herself with some last-minute details. And as she did, a mysterious figure entered the house. (NARRATOR *exits as curtain rises.*)

* * *

SETTING: *Lucie's home. Clothes are strewn about on bed, chairs. There is a window in backdrop.*

AT RISE: MISS PROSS *is alternately straightening up and looking out window.* MME. DEFARGE *enters quietly.*

MISS PROSS (*Startled*): Who are you, and what do you mean by bursting into a private residence?

MME. DEFARGE: This wife of St. Evrémonde, where is she?

PROSS: You shall not get the better of me. (*Proudly*) I am an Englishwoman.

MME. DEFARGE (*Boldly*): And I am Thérèse Defarge. Does that mean anything to you?

PROSS: Yes, it means the cause of all our trouble. If it were not for you and your husband, none of this would have taken place.

MME. DEFARGE (*Mockingly*): In the square my friends are reserving my place for me. We shall knit, without losing a stitch, as we watch the heads fall. I shall see my hated enemy, St. Evrémonde, and shall gloat as the knife falls. And now produce your mistress. I wish to pay my compliments to her.

Pross (*Firmly*): I know your intentions are evil, and you may depend upon it, I'll hold my own against them. (*Stands in front of exit*)

Mme. Defarge: Imbecile! I take no answer from you. Stand out of the way!

Pross: No!

Mme. Defarge (*Suddenly*): The confusion here. Odds and ends on the floor. She's—she's gone! Escaped—isn't she?

Pross: You cannot touch her.

Mme. Defarge: Charges are to be brought against her and her child and father.

Pross: Preferred by you and your worthy husband, no doubt.

Mme. Defarge: Where are they? If they have escaped, they can be pursued and brought back.

Pross: I don't care a tuppence for myself. I know the longer I keep you here, the greater hope there is for my dear Lucie.

Mme. Defarge: Stand back from that door. Let me out.

Pross: Make a move toward me and I'll tear out your hair.

Mme. Defarge: I'll give the word, and still have time to see her husband's head roll.

Pross (*Steadily*): I'll not budge.

Mme. Defarge (*As she pulls a gun from her pocket*): I'll rip you to pieces.

Pross: Madame Defarge, put away that gun.

Mme. Defarge: This is your last chance. Get away from that door. (*Advances on* Pross, *tries to push her aside*)

Pross (*Struggling*): You're not strong enough, Madame Defarge. Every minute you are here is worth a . . . hundred . . . thousand guineas to . . . my darling Lucie.

Mme. Defarge: I'll . . . I'll—

Pross: But you won't. (*In a final desperate effort,* Pross *pushes* Mme. Defarge. *Gun goes off, and* Mme. Defarge *slumps to floor.*)

Mme. Defarge (*In disbelief*): I'm . . . I'm shot.

Pross (*Breathing heavily*): You shot yourself, Madame Defarge, right through your heart. Your eyes are glazed. You're dying. And I can't say I feel sorry. Now you know what it is like, you who have heaped so much sorrow and anguish on innocent people. Before you close your eyes, let me tell you something. (*She whispers.*) Charles Darnay escaped. Right now he is riding away from you and your Revolutionists toward England and freedom. (*Pause*) You do understand, don't you? (MME. DEFARGE *whimpers.*) Good! (PROSS *rushes over to window, looks out*) Ah, the driver is just returning. (*Calls out*) I'm on my way! (*As she exits*) Goodbye, Madame Defarge. You will not take your place with the other knitters. (*Exits quickly as curtain closes*)

* * * * *

SCENE 7

SETTING: *Prison corridor. There are two chairs center. May be played before curtain.*

AT RISE: *Spotlight comes up on* SEAMSTRESS, *who is sitting in chair, head bowed. After a moment,* JAILER *leads in* CARTON.

JAILER: Well, mademoiselle, you will have company as you wait your turn with Madame Guillotine. This is Charles St. Evrémonde, like you a traitor to the Republic of France! (*Exits*)

SEAMSTRESS (*Shyly, after a pause*): Citizen St. Evrémonde. (*Pause*) Or perhaps I should address you as Monsieur Darnay. I am a poor seamstress who was tried the same day as you. Do you remember?

CARTON: Of course I do. I forget what you were accused of.

SEAMSTRESS: Plots. Though heaven knows I am innocent.

CARTON: I believe you.

SEAMSTRESS (*Bravely*): I am not afraid to die, but I have done nothing. Monsieur, if I may ride with you, will you let me hold your hand? I am not afraid, but I am so small and weak, and it will give me more courage.

CARTON: Of course, my dear.

SEAMSTRESS: Oh, thank you. (*Astonished*) But you're . . . you're not Charles St. Evrémonde, called Darnay!

CARTON (*In low tone*): Please, mademoiselle. Don't say it.

SEAMSTRESS: Are you willing to die for him?

CARTON: Yes, for him and his wife and their child.

SEAMSTRESS (*With a smile*): Now I can face it with more courage. You are a brave man. (JAILER *enters.*)

JAILER: It is time.

CARTON (*To* SEAMSTRESS): Hold my hand ... to the last. (*He takes her hand; they rise.* CARTON *speaks quietly as they exit.*) It is a far, far better thing that I do, than I have ever done; it is a far, far better rest that I go to, than I have ever known. (*Quick curtain*)

THE END

Production Notes

A Tale of Two Cities

Characters: 7 male; 4 female; 6 male or female; as many male and female extras as desired for Jurors, Spectators.

Playing Time: 30 minutes.

Costumes: Late eighteenth-century French.

Properties: Knitting; wine glasses; coins; documents; keys; vial; toy gun.

Setting: Scene 1, courtroom: Judge's bench is on diagonal down center, with five chairs facing it, jurors' bench at one side, spectators' bench at the other. This scene may be played in front of curtain. Scene 2, Defarges' wine shop. There are barrels, wine bottles, a few small tables. May be played before curtain. Scene 3, Dr. Manette's house, simply furnished with chairs, tables. Scene 4, prison, a divided stage: At right is jail cell, with stool and small table. Pen and paper are on table. At left is prison anteroom. Backdrop shows drab, gray walls, window with bars on it. Scene 5, checkpoint: Guardhouse is right. Scene 6, Lucie's home. Clothes are strewn about on bed, chairs. There is a window in backdrop. Scene 7, prison corridor: There are two chairs center. May be played before curtain.

Sound: Clock striking twice; gunshot.

▣▣Wuthering Heights

by Emily Brontë
Adapted by Lewy Olfson

Characters

ELLEN DEAN, *housekeeper*
CATHERINE EARNSHAW
HINDLEY EARNSHAW, *her brother*
HEATHCLIFF
EDGAR LINTON

SCENE 1

TIME: *Late eighteenth century.*
SETTING: *Kitchen at Wuthering Heights, large manor on the English moors.*
AT RISE: *Sound of thunder and rain is heard off and on throughout scene.* CATHERINE EARNSHAW *hovers over* ELLEN DEAN, *who is preparing tea tray.*
CATHY (*Anxiously*): You won't forget the jam, will you, Nelly?
ELLEN (*With a touch of sarcasm*): How am I to forget it, Miss Catherine, with you reminding me of it every five minutes?
CATHY (*Nervously*): It's just that Edgar—Mr. Linton, that is—is so very fond of your blackberry jam.
ELLEN (*Smiling*): You're taking a particular interest in pleasing Mr. Linton.
CATHY (*Flustered*): Nonsense, Nelly. Whatever are you hinting at?

23

ELLEN (*Blandly*): I wasn't hinting at anything, miss.

CATHY: Just because I ask you to be sure to serve blackberry jam . . .

ELLEN (*Pointedly*): Just because you've asked me seven times to be sure to serve blackberry jam.

CATHY (*Sharply*): Don't be impertinent, Nelly. Remember that I am the mistress of this house.

ELLEN (*Coldly*): I beg your pardon, miss.

CATHY (*Remorsefully*): Oh, Nelly, Nelly, I'm sorry I spoke so. I didn't mean it. My tongue ran away with me. I'm so nervous today. Oh, you *do* forgive me, don't you?

ELLEN (*Smiling*): Of course, Miss Catherine. (*Puts jam jar on tray*) Now, *there's* your jam. See that your precious Mr. Edgar Linton doesn't eat it all. I want to have some for Heathcliff's supper. Heathcliff likes my jam *too,* you know.

CATHY (*Anxiously*): Heathcliff won't be here, will he? Nelly, you must be sure not to let Heathcliff into the drawing room while Mr. Linton is here—not for anything in the world!

ELLEN (*Reprovingly*): Miss Cathy! How can you say such things? Heathcliff is the dearest friend you have in the world.

CATHY (*Impatiently*): Oh, I know that, but surely you can understand. Heathcliff's so—so wild—so untamed. And Mr. Linton is such a gentleman. You know they don't get on together! And I want everything this afternoon to be perfect—just as Edgar would like it. (*Wheedling*) Promise you won't let Heathcliff into the drawing room this afternoon, Nelly, please.

ELLEN (*Annoyed*): But this is Heathcliff's home!

CATHY: Wuthering Heights is *not* Heathcliff's home. He was not born here, and he does not belong here. He lives here, but he's a gypsy, a foundling—no better than a servant.

ELLEN (*Upset*): Miss Catherine, your father loved Heathcliff as though he were his own son—ever since he found the boy as a very young child and brought him here to Wuthering Heights.

CATHY (*Coldly*): My father may have found Heathcliff, as you say, and brought him here, and loved him, but my father is dead. My brother Hindley is master here now. You know how Hindley hates Heathcliff; he's always hated him. And I—

ELLEN (*Interrupting hotly*): You wouldn't dare to say that *you* hate Heathcliff, too.

CATHY (*Weakening*): Perhaps I don't *hate* him, but Heathcliff and I belong to different worlds now. Surely you see that, Nelly. It was different before when we were *children*. Naturally, we clung to each other—particularly when Hindley was so brutal, and hated us both. But we are not children any more.

ELLEN (*Softly*): I know.

CATHY (*Aloof*): Heathcliff is a servant, and I am a lady. We can no longer be—what we once were to one another. You must see that, Nelly, and Heathcliff must be made to see it, too.

ELLEN (*Seriously*): You know Heathcliff loves you, Miss Catherine.

CATHY (*Petulantly*): He has no business doing so. I have never invited him to love me.

ELLEN (*Sighing*): Perhaps you know best, miss. But when I think of all those times, with the two of you running along the moors, laughing, so happily . . .

CATHY (*Pained*): Stop it, Nelly. I don't want you to remind me of those times.

ELLEN: But they are part of the truth about Heathcliff, too.

CATHY (*Softly*): Yes. His tenderness with me, his affection, are part of the truth.

ELLEN (*Gently*): And your affection for him?

CATHY (*Sternly again*): Yes, we *were* close—once. We are so no longer. (HINDLEY, *a crude, loutish man of about twenty, enters left.*)

HINDLEY: Have you nothing better to do, Ellen Dean, than stand and gossip with your mistress? Is there no work to be done?

ELLEN (*Subdued, curtsying*): I'm sorry, Mr. Hindley. It will not happen again. (*Busies herself with tea things*)

HINDLEY: See that it doesn't. And, Catherine, mind that you don't give her an excuse for not working. There's no need for you to be in the kitchen.

CATHY (*Timidly*): I—I'm sorry, Hindley. I just wanted to remind Nelly—to remind Mrs. Dean that she was to serve jam with the tea.

HINDLEY: Does she need reminding after all the years she's been housekeeper at Wuthering Heights? No, I know the real reason you're here, my girl. Looking for that precious Heathcliff of yours, I'll warrant.

CATHY (*Flushed, but with dignity*): I have no concern with Heathcliff, brother. You have ordered me to have nothing to do with him, and I have obeyed your wishes.

HINDLEY: I'm glad to hear it. Not that I'll have much longer to worry about the two of you.

CATHY (*Surprised*): What do you mean, Hindley?

HINDLEY: I've just been talking with that (*Sneering*) sweet young gentleman of yours—Mr. Linton of Thrushcross Grange.

CATHY (*Excitedly*): Edgar? Is he already here?

HINDLEY: He is. The young man's taken with you, Catherine, there's no doubt of it. You play your cards right, and the Linton fortune will leap into your lap, you'll see. (*Thunder sounds far off.*)

CATHY: Is Edgar in the drawing room? I must go to him!

HINDLEY (*Laughing*): Look at her, Ellen Dean. How the blood comes to my sister's pretty young cheeks, just at the thought of Edgar Linton's fortune.

ELLEN (*Quietly*): I am sure you do your sister an injustice, sir.

HINDLEY (*Laughing, to* CATHY): You'd best compose yourself, my girl. You wouldn't want that poor fool to see you in this state. I'll go and amuse him for a few minutes. But see that you come along quickly.

CATHY: Thank you, Hindley. I will. (HINDLEY *exits.* CATHY *runs to mirror; anxiously*) Oh Nelly, do I look all right? Is my hair neat? I wonder—should I have a sprig of heather in it?

ELLEN: You look beautiful, Miss Catherine. You'll capture the man, sure enough.

CATHY (*Horrified*): Surely you don't think it's the *money* I'm after, Nelly!

ELLEN (*Blandly*): I? I think nothing, Miss Catherine. (HEATH-CLIFF *enters, carrying large armload of wood. He does not see* CATHY, *but goes to* ELLEN.)

HEATHCLIFF: I've fetched you enough wood for a winter, Nelly.

And just in time, too. Ten minutes more, and the storm would have caught me.

ELLEN: Thank you, Heathcliff.

HEATHCLIFF: A bad rain is headed this way. (*Seeing* CATHY) Cathy! I didn't see you.

CATHY (*Coolly, turning to door*): I am just leaving, Heathcliff.

HEATHCLIFF (*Putting wood on hearth*): You can't run off like that, Cathy, without a word. It's been so long since I've seen you.

CATHY (*Evasively*): I know. Hindley . . .

HEATHCLIFF (*Laughing*): Cathy, when were we ever frightened of Hindley before?

CATHY: Please, Heathcliff, I must go.

HEATHCLIFF: But you can't be busy this afternoon. You're not going out, are you? You didn't order a carriage.

CATHY (*Evasively*): No, I—of course I'm not going out. It's raining.

HEATHCLIFF: Then why have you that silk frock on?

CATHY (*Helplessly*): Nelly . . .

ELLEN (*Gently to* HEATHCLIFF): Guests are expected, Heathcliff. Mr. Linton is calling on Catherine.

HEATHCLIFF (*Scornfully*): So you'd turn me out for that silly friend of yours, eh, Cathy? I suppose he's a fine gentleman, and I'm no longer good enough for you.

CATHY (*Indignantly*): Edgar Linton is not silly—though he *is* a gentleman.

HEATHCLIFF (*Desperately*): But it's raining, Cathy. Surely he won't come in this storm.

CATHY (*Coolly*): He's—he's already here. And that's quite enough about it, Heathcliff.

HEATHCLIFF (*Angrily*): Then go to him! Fly! I shouldn't dream of holding you from your pleasure, my lady. (*With a mocking bow*)

CATHY (*Hotly*): I am going. It gives me great satisfaction to do so. (*Turns in doorway*) Mrs. Dean, you will bring the tea when I ring for you.

ELLEN (*Taken aback; coldly*): Indeed, miss. (*Curtsies*) When did

I ever not do so? (CATHY *exits left and slams door. Both stare after her.*)

HEATHCLIFF (*Tensely*): Nelly, what has happened to her? Why has she changed? She was never this way before.

ELLEN (*Shaking her head*): Time passes, Heathcliff, and you have both changed.

HEATHCLIFF (*Hotly*): It is she who has changed. Not I! (*Sadly*) She cares nothing for me—while I care everything for her.

ELLEN: I would not say that she cares nothing for you. Do you remember the other day when Hindley struck you with his riding crop?

HEATHCLIFF (*Rubbing his arm*): It's not likely I could forget it.

ELLEN: She cried for you, Heathcliff. She tried not to let me see, but I did.

HEATHCLIFF: *I* have cried for *her*, Nelly, and I have had more reason to cry than she. (*Sounds of storm grow louder, then subside.*) How the wind whistles! And the drumming of the rain. . .

ELLEN: It will be the worst storm of the season.

HEATHCLIFF (*Contemptuously*): I do wonder that our fancy Mr. Linton dared to brave the weather and come to the Heights.

ELLEN: Do you dislike him so much, Heathcliff?

HEATHCLIFF: I do—and yet, to tell the truth, I envy him. I'm always trying to settle how I shall pay them back—Hindley *and* Edgar—for robbing me of Cathy's love. I don't care how long it takes, if I can only do it at last.

ELLEN: For shame, Heathcliff!

HEATHCLIFF: I only wish I knew the best way! But I shall plan it out. (HINDLEY *enters left.*)

HINDLEY (*Gruffly*): Mrs. Dean, we shall need no tea. The young man's flown.

ELLEN (*Puzzled*): I do not take your meaning, sir.

HINDLEY (*Laughing*): He just went off in his carriage. I watched from the upstairs window. I'll wager he thought he'd be drowned if he waited another moment. (*Scornfully*) No doubt my good sister will be down to tell you all about it, foolish child!

HEATHCLIFF (*Sternly*): Do you speak of Miss Catherine in that tone, sir?

HINDLEY (*Aggressively*): And if I do? Do not forget for a moment, Heathcliff, that I am master here.

HEATHCLIFF (*Firmly*): I forget nothing.

HINDLEY (*Backing down a bit*): You have forgotten your chores. You were told to fill the woodbox. It is yet half empty.

ELLEN (*Protesting*): But Mr. Hindley, in such rain—

HEATHCLIFF (*Calmly staring at* HINDLEY): Never mind, Nelly. I am not afraid of a bit of water, as some are. And the air is fresher in the stables than here. (*He turns and strides out.*)

HINDLEY (*Raging*): Insolent puppy! Mrs. Dean!

ELLEN: Sir?

HINDLEY: I shall have my dinner in my room tonight. Alone.

ELLEN (*Curtsying, as he exits*): Very good, sir. (*She shakes her head and begins putting cups away. Sighs; to herself*) I know not which is worse—the storm outside or the one beneath the roof of Wuthering Heights! (CATHY *enters left.*)

CATHY (*Timidly*): Nelly? Are you alone?

ELLEN: Yes, miss.

CATHY: Where's Heathcliff?

ELLEN: About his work in the stable, I suppose.

CATHY (*Tearfully*): Oh, Nelly, I am very unhappy.

ELLEN (*Dryly*): A pity. You're so hard to please—so many friends, and so few cares, and yet you can't make yourself content.

CATHY: Will you keep a secret for me?

ELLEN: Is it worth keeping?

CATHY: Yes, and it worries me. I want to know what I should do. Edgar Linton has just asked me to marry him, and I've given him an answer.

ELLEN (*Taken aback*): What was it, Miss Catherine?

CATHY: Before I tell you whether it was a consent or a refusal, tell me which it should have been.

ELLEN: Really, miss, that's not for me to say.

CATHY: I accepted him, Nelly. Be quick, and say whether I was wrong.

ELLEN (*Coldly*): If you have accepted him, what good is it discussing the matter? Now that you have pledged your word, you cannot retract it. (*Door opens and* HEATHCLIFF *enters, thoroughly drenched and carrying another armload of wood. Others do not see him. When he sees* CATHY, *he tiptoes behind settle, out of sight.*)

CATHY: But say whether I should have done so!

ELLEN: There are many things to be considered. First and foremost, do you love Mr. Edgar?

CATHY: Of course I do.

ELLEN: Why do you love him?

CATHY: Well—because he is handsome, and pleasant and rich.

ELLEN: Poor enough reasons. Do you love Mr. Heathcliff?

CATHY (*Starting*): Heathcliff?

ELLEN: Be honest, Miss Catherine. Do you love Mr. Heathcliff?

CATHY (*After a pause*): Sometimes I think I love him more than life itself. I have only to look into Heathcliff's eyes, and I know his every thought. Those black eyes burn into the very core of my being. Sometimes I think he'll end by driving me mad.

ELLEN: I should say you loved Heathcliff more than you will ever love Mr. Linton.

CATHY: Perhaps. In my deepest heart, I feel I have no business to marry Edgar Linton, but don't you see, Nelly? It would degrade me to marry Heathcliff; so I mean never to let him know how much I love him. Oh, Nelly, he's more myself than I am. Whatever our souls are made of, his and mine, they are the same. Edgar's is as different as a moonbeam from lightning, or frost from fire. But (*Firmly*) Edgar Linton is the man I will marry, because Heathcliff is a gypsy—a stranger. I—I'm almost afraid of him. And what we fear, they say we come to hate. Deeply as I love Heathcliff, I think a part of me shall always hate him. (HEATHCLIFF *drops pile of wood behind settle and darts swiftly off right.* CATHY *jumps, startled.*) What was that?

ELLEN (*Looking about*): Perhaps a shutter banging in the wind.

CATHY (*Running to window*): Oh—Nelly! Someone is running down the road. Someone was listening!

ELLEN: Who is it, miss? Not—not Heathcliff!

CATHY (*Pained*): Oh, Nelly, it is! It *is* Heathcliff! He must have been listening all the while. I must stop him!

ELLEN (*Holding her fast*): Are you mad, Miss Catherine? Think of the storm!

CATHY (*Trying to pull free*): But he heard me, Nelly, he heard. I must stop him. I must explain. Heathcliff! (*She breaks free and runs to door.*) Heathcliff! Stop! (*She pulls door open and darts out.*) Heathcliff!

ELLEN (*Standing in doorway, calling out*): Miss Catherine! Come back!

CATHY (*From off right, her voice trailing off, as sounds of wind and rain become stronger*): Heathcliff! Heathcliff! (*Curtain*)

* * * * *

SCENE 2

TIME: *Three years later.*

SETTING: *The same.*

AT RISE: EDGAR LINTON *is pacing up and down before fire.*

EDGAR (*Agitated*): It is madness, Mrs. Dean, sheer madness.

ELLEN (*Consolingly*): Come, come, Mr. Linton, surely you exaggerate. Can it be such a terrible thing for Miss Catherine—I mean to say, Mrs. Linton—to wish to come back here to visit Wuthering Heights, after so long an absence? She has been away for three years.

EDGAR: The doctors have ordered her to have complete rest—nothing must be allowed to upset or excite her. It is only a month since Catherine has been allowed to leave her bed. Undertaking the journey from Thrushcross Grange to the Heights has been too much of a strain on her.

ELLEN: But it's such a little distance, sir. And she seemed so well when she arrived . . . and so happy to see the house once more. Why, she has not been here since the day you and she were married.

EDGAR: But does it not seem odd to you that Catherine should wish to come back to a home where she had been so unhappy as a girl?

ELLEN (*Thoughtfully*): It is true that Catherine endured many unhappy hours here, but there were happy times, too, Mr. Linton. Do not forget that it was in this house that you proposed to her.

EDGAR (*Smiling*): How well I remember that night. Such an awful storm there was! That was also the night Heathcliff disappeared, was it not?

ELLEN (*Softly*): Yes.

EDGAR: He was never heard of again, was he? Odd—his disappearing like that, with no reason.

ELLEN (*Quietly*): I would not say there was no reason.

EDGAR: But it *was* a mystery of sorts, wasn't it? Catherine used to speak of him quite often during the first few months of our marriage. But when our little girl was born, she never mentioned him again. (*Shrugging*) She must have forgotten all about him. (*Thunder is heard off.*)

ELLEN (*Pointedly*): There is little that Miss Catherine forgets, Mr. Linton.

EDGAR: She seems to have forgotten her old hatred for Hindley. When I left them together in the drawing room just now, Catherine was behaving as though there had never been so much as a cross word between them.

ELLEN: Miss Catherine always had strange ways of showing her feelings.

EDGAR: Catherine does indeed behave in a contrary manner at times. One never can be sure what she is thinking. It is as though her mind were miles and miles away. Sometimes I fear for her sanity. It is not her bodily health alone that has been shattered, I fear.

ELLEN (*With genuine concern*): I hope that you exaggerate, sir.

EDGAR (*Looking off*): Hush—I think she is coming. (CATHY *enters left, followed by* HINDLEY.)

HINDLEY: I tried to make her rest, Linton, but she will have none of it. (*Crash of thunder is heard off.*)

CATHY (*Running to* ELLEN): Oh, Nelly, darling Nelly!

ELLEN (*Embracing her*): Welcome back to Wuthering Heights, Miss Catherine.

CATHY: It's hard for me to realize that I'm really here once again—here in our own snug kitchen. It all seems so long ago. (*Moves about, touching furniture and objects*) Everything is just as I remembered it.

ELLEN: Nothing has changed here, miss, in the past few years.

CATHY: But the settle—the settle has changed! Surely the one we had was not so large, Nelly—no, not by half.

HINDLEY: Of course it's the same settle, Cathy.

CATHY (*With an odd look at* ELLEN, *as she runs her hand along the settle*): But this one is so tall—so broad. Someone might hide behind it, even, and we would not know he was there. Someone might be standing behind it now, listening to every word we say.

EDGAR (*Worried*): Cathy, my love, you must sit down. You promised me you would rest.

HINDLEY: Linton is right, Catherine. You have had enough excitement for one day.

EDGAR: Come, darling, let me take you home.

CATHY: But I haven't had a proper visit with Nelly, Edgar darling. *Do* let me stay a little longer—just to talk to Nelly.

EDGAR: Will you promise to be good, and sit quietly by the fire? Remember what the doctors have said.

CATHY: Yes, yes, I promise. You and Hindley must go and fetch the carriage. I want to be alone with Nelly for a few minutes.

HINDLEY: Come along, then, Linton. Ten minutes more will do no harm, I'm sure.

EDGAR (*Moving toward door*): Very well. But no more than ten minutes. See that she doesn't exert herself, Mrs. Dean.

ELLEN: I will indeed, sir. (*Men exit left.*)

CATHY (*After a slight pause, in low voice*): Oh, Nelly, can you guess what it means to me to be here again?

ELLEN: Of course, Miss Catherine. This was your home.

CATHY (*Sharply*): That is not why I came. My home! The misery I endured here, the pain, the suffering. For that I would never have set foot in this house again. No, no. I had to come— because he is here.

ELLEN (*Looking at her, sharply*): What do you mean, Miss Catherine?

CATHY: He is here. In every corner, on every stair, at every window, I see Heathcliff.

ELLEN: Heathcliff!

CATHY: Oh, Nelly, you cannot guess what torture these past three years have been. There has never been an hour, never a moment, when his face was not before me. The torment of it, the agony! To know he is gone, but not to know where. To know that he ran away, and that he was driven away by me. And to know I love him—that I always have, and that I always will.

ELLEN (*Alarmed*): You must not think such thoughts, miss. Come sit down. You are feverish.

CATHY: Open the window, Nelly. I want to hear the wind again. Such a wind as blows across the moors!

ELLEN: I dare not open it, Miss Catherine. You'd catch your death!

CATHY (*Laughing suddenly*): Hindley thought I did not remember the settle! He believed me, Nelly. But you knew better, didn't you? (*Thunder, off right, then a loud knocking at door.* CATHY *jumps up.*) There is someone at the door, Nelly.

ELLEN: Yes, Miss Catherine, I'll just see who it is.

CATHY (*Frightened*): No, no. I'm afraid. I don't wish to see anyone.

ELLEN: But, miss, I must open the door.

CATHY: Wait just a moment, till I leave.

ELLEN: Very well, miss, as you wish.

CATHY (*Imploringly*): But send him away quickly—whoever it is. I must leave soon, and I want to come back to kiss you goodbye.

ELLEN (*Gently*): Very well, Miss Catherine. (*There is pounding on door.*)

CATHY (*Whimpering*): I'm so frightened—I'm frightened! (*She runs out left.* ELLEN *shakes her head and turns to open door right. It bursts open, and* HEATHCLIFF *enters. He is finely dressed in a dark suit and riding cloak.* ELLEN *does not recognize him.*)

ELLEN: What, sir, do you walk into a house without being invited?

HEATHCLIFF (*Smiling*): Is it my old nurse, Nelly Dean?

ELLEN (*Taken aback*): No! No! Can it be . . . Heathcliff?

HEATHCLIFF: Have I altered so much that you know me not?

ELLEN: Why, sir! You are a gentleman. Your clothes—your manner—I should not have known you.

HEATHCLIFF (*Smoothly*): Oh, yes, I have come up in the world since I left Wuthering Heights. I left this house a gypsy beggar, and I come back a wealthy gentleman. Who would have dreamed that night . . .

ELLEN (*Interrupting, quickly*): Oh, let us not speak of that night!

HEATHCLIFF (*Ironically*): To think that I owe all this (*Indicates his finery*) to her. She led me to wealth, did Cathy—but she led me to misery, too.

ELLEN (*Somewhat frightened*): Is it really you, Heathcliff?

HEATHCLIFF: It is really I. Are you not glad to see me, Nelly?

ELLEN (*Anxiously*): Oh, for myself, gladder than I can say. (*Sighs*) I have missed you, Heathcliff, and worried for you, too. But Miss Catherine . . .

HEATHCLIFF (*Eagerly*): Miss Catherine—yes, yes, tell me about her.

ELLEN (*Intensely*): No, you must not see her. It would be too cruel.

HEATHCLIFF (*Harshly*): She has been cruel enough to me in my time, has she not, Nelly? And it is to see her that I have come. They told me at Thrushcross Grange that she is here. Will you go and fetch her?

ELLEN (*Upset*): Do not ask it of me. I could not answer for the consequences.

HEATHCLIFF (*Determinedly*): If you will not bring her to me, then I must find her for myself. (*He starts toward door, as it opens, and* CATHY *enters.*)

CATHY: May I come—(*She stops when she sees* HEATHCLIFF. *They stand quite still, staring at each other.*)

ELLEN (*Crying*): What madness this is! (*She runs off calling.*) Mr. Linton! Mr. Hindley!

CATHY (*Quietly*): Is it really you, Heathcliff?

HEATHCLIFF (*Rushing to her and embracing her*): Oh, Cathy! Oh, my life! How can I bear it?

CATHY (*Pushing him away gently*): Are these tears on your cheek, Heathcliff? What now? You have broken my heart. And yet you bewail the deed, asking for pity. I shall not pity you—not I!

HEATHCLIFF (*Holding her by the arm*): You were never one to pity, Catherine.

CATHY: How strong you are! How many years do you mean to live after I am gone?

HEATHCLIFF: Do not speak, Cathy. Only let me hold you.

CATHY (*Harshly*): I wish I could hold *you*—hold you till we were both dead. I shouldn't care for your suffering. I care nothing for your suffering. (*Pushes him firmly away*) Why shouldn't you suffer? I do. Will you forget me, Heathcliff? Will you say, twenty years hence, "That's the grave of Catherine Earnshaw Linton. I loved her, long ago, and was wretched to lose her; but it is past." Will you say so?

HEATHCLIFF: Don't torture me till I'm as mad as you.

CATHY: No, no—*you* could never suffer as *I* do.

HEATHCLIFF (*Angrily*): You speak of suffering, after what you did to me? You drove me away, Cathy!

CATHY (*Simply*): Yes. I drove you away.

HEATHCLIFF: You admit, then, that you caused me this grief, this pain, this aching loneliness! Did you love me so little, Cathy?

CATHY (*Proudly*): I loved you so much.

HEATHCLIFF: You loved me? I fear you are mad indeed.

CATHY: You doubt . . . that I loved you? That I love you still? Heathcliff, don't you understand that we would have destroyed each other, you and I? Torn each other to bits? Yes, I loved you then. Why else would I have torn the very heart from my bosom, if not to save you? Look at what you have become for leaving me—a gentleman! And *this* is your thanks, your understanding? I am dying, Heathcliff—and you have broken my heart!

HEATHCLIFF: No, *I* have not broken your heart. *You* have broken it, and in so doing you have broken mine. (*Bitterly*) So much the worse for me, that I am strong. Do you think I want to live when you are in the grave?

CATHY (*Sobbing*): If I've done wrong, I'm dying for it. It is enough. Forgive me!

HEATHCLIFF: It is hard to look at those eyes and not forgive. I forgive what you have done to me.

CATHY (*In anguish*): Oh, why on earth did you ever return?

HEATHCLIFF: I had to see you once more. But now I must go.

CATHY (*In anguish*): Don't go, Heathcliff! Don't go!

HEATHCLIFF: I must, Cathy. But from this hour, I know that our souls are forever intertwined. I will be alone no more!

CATHY (*Stretching out a hand to him*): Heathcliff! (*He turns swiftly and exits.* CATHY *stands as if transfixed. After a pause, in an altered voice*) Heathcliff? Heathcliff? (*Pause*) Let us go out on the moors. (*She walks slowly to door and opens it.*) Is my hair neat, Nelly? Do I look all right? (ELLEN *and* EDGAR *rush in left.*)

EDGAR: Cathy! (CATHY *does not seem to hear him.*)

CATHY: I wonder, Nelly—should I have a sprig of heather for my hair?

ELLEN (*Putting her arm around her, gently*): There, there, miss. Everything is all right now.

CATHY (*Without hearing her or looking at her*): Heathcliff? Heathcliff? (*Pause*) Open the window, Nelly. I want to hear the wind. (*Lights dim. In the darkness wind and rain are heard, and* CATHY's *voice calling, "Heathcliff! Heathcliff! Curtain*)

THE END

Production Notes

WUTHERING HEIGHTS

Characters: 3 male; 2 female.

Playing Time: 30 minutes.

Costumes: Appropriate dress of the period. Cathy's gown in Scene 1 is pretty and elaborate. In Scene 2, she wears a coat and hat. Ellen wears simple, dark dress and apron. Edgar is dressed in an elegant suit of the period, and Hindley wears riding clothes. Heathcliff wears rough work clothes in Scene 1, changes to suit and riding cloak for Scene 2.

Properties: Firewood, tea tray with cups, saucers, etc., pot of jam.

Setting: The kitchen at Wuthering Heights, a large manor on the English moors. Door down right leads outside; another door left, to the rest of house. Window is right center, fireplace is up center. Mirror hangs on wall to left of fireplace. The room is furnished with a high-backed settle, which stands by fireplace, and a table, chairs, cupboards, etc.

Lighting: The room is dimly lit for Scene 1, brighter for Scene 2.

Sound: Thunder, rain, and wind, as indicated in text.

◨◨The Wonderful Wizard of Oz

by *L. Frank Baum*
Adapted by *Frances Mapp*

Characters

DOROTHY
TOTO, *her dog*
WITCH OF THE NORTH
MUNCHKINS
SCARECROW
TIN WOODMAN
COWARDLY LION
GUARDIAN OF THE GATE
THE WIZARD OF OZ
WICKED WITCH OF THE WEST
GLINDA THE GOOD, *Witch of the South*
FLORIA, *her lady-in-waiting*

SCENE 1

SETTING: *The Country of the Munchkins, in the Land of Oz.*
AT RISE: DOROTHY, *with* TOTO *beside her, is sitting center on a low platform. Down center are pair of silver slippers and nearby is* SCARECROW *half-hidden by straw, propped up against fence.*
DOROTHY (*Looking around*): Toto, this place doesn't look familiar

39

to me at all. That cyclone must have carried us far away from home! (*She stands, walks about, confused. After a moment, she shakes her head and sits again.*) Toto, I believe we're lost. (WITCH OF THE NORTH *enters right, as several* MUNCHKINS *run in left.*)

WITCH OF THE NORTH: Welcome, most noble sorceress, to the Country of the Munchkins in the Land of Oz.

DOROTHY (*Jumping up, somewhat frightened*): Why, who are you?

WITCH: I am the Witch of the North, a friend of these Munchkins, whose country you are now in. We are all very grateful to you for killing the wicked Witch of the East, and desire to serve you in any way possible. (MUNCHKINS *make bobbing curtsies.*)

DOROTHY: You are very kind. But . . . but I didn't kill anyone.

WITCH: *You* didn't, but your house did. You see, your farmhouse was picked up by the cyclone and landed here in Munchkin, right on top of the wicked Witch of the East, killing her and freeing us from her hateful reign. (*Points to silver slippers*) See, there are the silver slippers that she wore! She was so old and mean that after she was killed, she just dried up and blew away. Please accept the shoes as a token of our thanks for freeing us from the Witch. 'Tis said they have magic powers, but I know not what they are. (*She sits on platform.*)

DOROTHY (*Puzzled*): Dear me, what a strange place. Are you a *real* witch? (*She sits beside the* WITCH.)

WITCH: Yes, indeed, but I am a good witch, and the people love me.

DOROTHY: But I thought all witches were wicked.

WITCH: Oh, no. That is a great mistake. There were only four witches in the Land of Oz, and two of them, those who live in the North and South, are good witches, those in the East and West are wicked witches. Now that the Witch of the East is dead, there is but one wicked witch in all the Land of Oz— the one who lives in the West.

DOROTHY: Perhaps you can tell me, Witch of the North, how I can get back to Kansas and Aunt Em. She'll be dreadfully worried, you know. And my dog Toto always gets upset in a strange place. (TOTO *sits up and barks furiously.* MUNCHKINS *laugh heartily.*)

WITCH: I do not know where Kansas is, Dorothy. But there is one person in Oz who will surely know. All ways of magic are known to him.

DOROTHY (*With excitement*): Who is he? And where can I find him?

WITCH: Our mighty wizard, the Wizard of Oz—he will tell you how to get back to Kansas. I myself have never seen him, for he lives in the Emerald City of Oz, a wondrously beautiful city, whose gates are studded with jewels.

DOROTHY (*Anxiously*): Is he a good man?

WITCH: He is a good *wizard*. Whether he is a man or not, I do not know.

DOROTHY: We'll go right away. How can I get there? (*She rises.*)

WITCH: Follow the yellow brick road through the Great Forest, and that will lead you to the Emerald City. But wear the silver slippers, for they will keep you from harm. One more thing I can do for you. I will give you my magic kiss, and no one will dare injure a person who has been kissed by the Witch of the North. (*She rises, kisses* DOROTHY *on the fore-head.*) And now goodbye. We in Munchkin will always be ready to welcome you back. A safe journey! (WITCH *exits left, followed by* MUNCHKINS, *who wave cheerfully as they leave.*)

DOROTHY: Come, Toto. (*Puts on slippers*) Oh! They fit! (TOTO *jumps up and down excitedly.* DOROTHY *walks a few steps, then notices* SCARECROW.) Oh, my gracious, Toto, look—a funny stuffed man. (*Bends over him*) Why, it's a scarecrow. But such a mournful-looking face! (*Brushes straw off him.* SCARECROW *moves slightly, then grins at her.*)

SCARECROW: Good day.

DOROTHY (*Jumping back in alarm*): Oh, I didn't know you were alive, Mr. Scarecrow. (*Helping him up*) I never knew scarecrows *could* be alive.

SCARECROW (*Testily*): Of course I'm alive. (*He looks at* TOTO *curiously.*) But what is that odd little animal? And who are you, and where are you going?

DOROTHY: My name is Dorothy. This is Toto, my dog. We live in

Kansas, but a cyclone picked up our house and when the wind died down we found ourselves in Oz. The good Witch of the North told us to go to the Emerald City and said that the Wizard of Oz would tell us how to get back to Kansas.

SCARECROW (*Puzzled*): Where is the Emerald City? And who is the Wizard of Oz?

DOROTHY (*Surprised*): Why, you don't know?

SCARECROW (*Sadly*): No, indeed. You see, I am only stuffed with straw so I have no brains at all.

DOROTHY: No brains at all?

SCARECROW (*Shaking his head*): None at all. I don't mind my legs, arms, and body being stuffed because I can't get hurt. But with my head stuffed with straw instead of brains, how am I ever to know anything? (*Sadly*) I'm really just a fool.

DOROTHY (*Sympathetically*): You're not a fool! But I understand how you feel. If you come with me, I'll ask the Wizard to do all he can for you. Perhaps he will give you some brains.

SCARECROW: Oh, thank you, Dorothy.

DOROTHY: Well, come on, then. Let's be off! (*They exit right. Curtain*)

* * * * *

SCENE 2

SETTING: *The Yellow Brick Road, in the Great Forest.*

AT RISE: TIN WOODMAN *stands motionless down left, arm upraised, holding his ax over a pile of logs.* DOROTHY, TOTO, *and* SCARECROW *enter right.*

DOROTHY (*Noticing* TIN WOODMAN): Oh, look! (*Rushing over to him*) It's a Tin Woodman, but he's only half finished his wood chopping. And see—he's been crying!

SCARECROW (*Going to* TIN WOODMAN): So he has, so he has. (*Studying him*) I've never seen anyone like him before. (TIN WOODMAN *groans.*)

TIN WOODMAN (*Haltingly*): Don't stand there staring at me. Help me! Do something! You don't suppose I *want* to stand here like this, do you?

DOROTHY (*Amazed*): I've never heard of such a thing as a *live* tin woodman! (*To* TIN WOODMAN) What shall we do? How can we help you?

TIN WOODMAN: Send that straw-stuffed creature to my cottage over there and bring me my can of oil. I was caught in the rain while chopping wood, and my joints are rusted. Hurry!

SCARECROW: My, my, such a bother.

DOROTHY: Oh, go ahead, Scarecrow. It won't take a minute. (*He exits, grumbling.*)

TIN WOODMAN: Thank you. What's your name? (TOTO *exits.*)

DOROTHY: My name is Dorothy, and this is my dog, Toto. (*She looks about for* TOTO, *calls him.*) Toto! Toto! Oh, well, he'll be back soon. We're from Kansas but got lost in a storm. (*Looking off*) Here comes the Scarecrow! (SCARECROW *reenters, holding can of oil. He and* DOROTHY *oil* TIN WOODMAN, *who slowly lowers his arm and stretches cautiously.*)

TIN WOODMAN (*Smiling*): That's much better. You have no idea how tiresome it is to stand there for two days, helpless, waiting for someone to save you.

SCARECROW: Dorothy is a kind little girl. She saved me and now she's saved you. Hooray for Dorothy! (*He starts to dance, falls clumsily.* DOROTHY *and* TIN WOODMAN *set* SCARECROW *on his feet, brush him off.*) Thank you. I'm all right now. Let's go, Dorothy.

TIN WOODMAN: Where are you going?

DOROTHY: To the Wizard of Oz. He's going to tell me how to get back to Kansas, where I live.

SCARECROW: And he's going to give me some brains.

TIN WOODMAN (*Wistfully*): Do you suppose he would give me a heart? The tinsmith forgot to give me one when he made me, and I would like to be able to have feelings.

DOROTHY (*Doubtfully*): Well—I don't know, but if he can give the Scarecrow some brains, he can surely give you a heart. Why don't you come with us?

TIN WOODMAN: I believe I will. (*Sound of lion roaring is heard off.*)

DOROTHY: What's that? (TOTO *runs in, pursued by* COWARDLY LION. TOTO *hides behind* DOROTHY, *who smacks* LION *on the nose.* LION *sits on his haunches, howling and rubbing his nose.*) What do you mean, chasing a little dog that's so much smaller than you? You ought to be ashamed of yourself.

LION: I can't help it. I'm afraid to chase anyone as big as I am.

SCARECROW: Who ever heard of a cowardly lion?

TIN WOODMAN (*Scornfully*): And you're supposed to be the King of the Beasts!

LION (*Weeping*): I know, but I've always been afraid to fight, and now no one respects me. What can I do?

DOROTHY: I know! Why not come with us to the Wizard of Oz, and see if he can give you some courage!

LION: Do you think he can? Really?

DOROTHY: I'm sure he'll try! I want to go back to Kansas. The Scarecrow wants some brains, and the Tin Woodman wants a heart, so you might as well come with us and get some courage.

LION: I might as well. At least it won't be any worse than staying in the forest and being laughed at for being so cowardly. (*Wipes tear from his eye*)

SCARECROW: Good! That's settled. Let's go! (*They exit right. Curtain*)

* * * * *

SCENE 3

SETTING: *Throne room of palace in the Emerald City.*

AT RISE: GUARDIAN OF THE GATE *is standing beside throne, polishing spectacles. A box of spectacles is on small table near throne.* DOROTHY, TOTO, SCARECROW, LION *and* TIN WOODMAN *enter.*

GUARDIAN (*Noticing them*): What ho! Who might you be? Stop where you are this instant! No one enters the throne room without my permission.

DOROTHY: Please, sir, we are strangers who have come to the Emerald City hoping to see the Wizard of Oz.

GUARDIAN: Indeed! And how do I know you're not conspirators come to kill the Wizard?

TIN WOODMAN: We're not enemies. We want help from the mighty Wizard.

DOROTHY: You see, we heard that Oz was a good and powerful wizard and that he could work all kinds of magic.

GUARDIAN (*Doubtfully*): It has been many years since anybody asked to see Oz. But since you are here, I may as well tell him. But first you must put on a pair of spectacles. (*Points to box*)

DOROTHY: Why?

GUARDIAN: Because if you do not wear spectacles, the brightness of the Great Oz would blind you. (*He fits spectacles on everyone, including* TOTO, *then goes behind the screen in back of throne. Lights dim, gong sounds.*)

OZ (*Loudly from behind screen*): I will talk to them. The girl first. (GUARDIAN *reenters from behind screen.*)

GUARDIAN (*To* DOROTHY): Stand in front of the throne! (DOROTHY *hesitantly goes center.*)

OZ: I am Oz the Terrible. Who are you, and what do you want?

DOROTHY (*Timidly*): I am Dorothy the Meek and Small. The Witch of the North told me that you would be able to help me find the way back to Kansas.

OZ (*From behind screen*): Do you not like it here in Oz?

DOROTHY: Oh, yes, sir, but . . .

OZ (*Loudly from behind screen*): Why should I do this for you?

DOROTHY: Because you are strong and powerful, and I am small and weak.

OZ (*From behind screen*): Well, then, here is your answer. You cannot expect to get back to Kansas without doing something for me. Help me, and I will help you.

DOROTHY: What is it you wish me to do?

OZ (*From behind screen*): Kill the Wicked Witch of the West.

DOROTHY (*Upset and frightened*): But I cannot do that!

OZ: You killed the Witch of the East.

DOROTHY: That was an accident. And if you are a wizard and cannot kill her, how can I?

OZ (*From behind screen*): That I do not know, but you must do it, and then I will see you again. Now go, and do not come back until you have completed your task. (*Gong sounds.* DORO-

THY *goes back to her companions. They push* SCARECROW *center stage, then retreat down right.*) I am Oz, the Great and Terrible. Who are you and why do you wish to see me?

SCARECROW: I am only a scarecrow stuffed with straw, and I have no brains. So I have come to you hoping that you will give me brains like other people.

Oz (*From behind screen*): I never grant favors, but this I will do. Help Dorothy kill the Wicked Witch, and when you return, I shall give you brains as good as any other man's. (*Gong sounds.* SCARECROW *goes back to others.* TIN WOODMAN *moves center.*)

TIN WOODMAN: Oz the Great, I am made of tin and have no heart, so I cannot love anybody. Will you give me a heart so that I may be like other people?

Oz (*From behind screen*): If you desire a heart, you must earn it. Help Dorothy kill the Witch of the West. When that is done, return and you shall have a heart that is the finest of any in Oz. (*Gong sounds.* TIN WOODMAN *returns to others.*)

DOROTHY: It's your turn, Cowardly Lion. Go on.

LION (*Meekly*): But I'm afraid to. I'm leaving! (*He starts to exit, but others push him center. He stands before throne, trembling, hiding his face between his paws.*)

Oz (*From behind screen, in a loud and terrible voice*): You wish to see me? (LION *runs back to* DOROTHY, *who pushes him center again.*)

LION: Oh gracious, gracious me! Great Wizard, I am a cowardly beast. Give me courage so that I may truly be the King of the Beasts.

Oz (*From behind screen*): Bring me proof of the Witch's death, and you shall be made brave. Now go, all of you. (*Gong sounds, lights come up.*)

LION: What shall we do? (*Others join him center.*)

SCARECROW: If we don't go, I shall never have any brains.

TIN WOODMAN: Nor I a heart.

DOROTHY: And I shall never see Aunt Em and Uncle Henry again. I suppose we must try it, but I do not want to kill anybody.

LION: Nor I, but I will go with you although I haven't the courage to kill the Witch.

TIN WOODMAN: I haven't the heart to kill the Witch but I shall certainly go with you.

SCARECROW: I would not know how to kill the Witch but I certainly am not going to stay here.

DOROTHY (*To* GUARDIAN): Which road leads to the Wicked Witch of the West?

GUARDIAN: There is no road. No one ever wishes to go to the country of the Winkies where the Wicked Witch lives. But if you keep toward the West, where the sun sets, you cannot fail to find her. Take care, for the Witch is wicked and fierce, and will try to make you her slaves.

DOROTHY (*Bravely*): Thank you for your warning, but we must find the Wicked Witch and destroy her. (*She starts to exit right with others, as* GUARDIAN *begins to polish spectacles again.*) Goodbye.

GUARDIAN (*Waving, as they exit*): Goodbye, and good luck. (*Curtain*)

* * * * *

SCENE 4

SETTING: *Kitchen of the Wicked Witch of the West. Pail of water is on the floor.*

AT RISE: WICKED WITCH OF THE WEST, *muttering incantations, is stirring cauldron center, in front of large screen.*

WICKED WITCH: I have torn the Scarecrow to pieces, I have broken the Tin Woodman, and starved the Cowardly Lion. (*She stops stirring.*) But I can do no harm to Dorothy, because she bears the charmed kiss of the good Witch of the North. Now she will try to destroy me. (*Walks about, thinking*) What shall I do? I have used up all the power of my Golden Cap. If I had the silver slippers that Dorothy wears, I could regain all my power. But she never takes them off, except when she takes a bath—and I can't go near her then, because water will melt me. (DOROTHY *and* TOTO *enter left.*)

DOROTHY (*Angrily, to* WITCH): You wicked creature! What have you done to the Scarecrow and the Tin Woodman and the Lion?

WICKED WITCH: They came here with you to harm me, so I turned the Scarecrow into a pile of straw, and I made tin cans from the Woodman. I starved the Lion until he grew so thin, he disappeared.

DOROTHY (*Tearfully*): Oh, my poor friends! How terrible! (WITCH *suddenly takes hold of* TOTO.)

WICKED WITCH (*With an evil laugh*): And now I have Toto, and you will never have him back—(*Slyly*) unless you give me your silver slippers. (DOROTHY *starts toward* WICKED WITCH, *who moves one hand as if casting a magic spell.*) Now, my pretty one, invisible bars will keep you away from me! (DOROTHY *seems to stumble, losing one of her slippers, which* WICKED WITCH *quickly snatches, letting go of* TOTO *as she does so.*) I have it! I have the slipper! (*She dances around stage, waving slipper.* DOROTHY *tries to catch her.*) Now I must have the other one!

DOROTHY: Give me back my shoe, you wicked creature!

WICKED WITCH: Never! It is mine now. And someday I shall get the other slipper, too.

DOROTHY (*Angrily*): No, you won't! (*She picks up pail of water and throws it on* WICKED WITCH.)

WICKED WITCH (*Crying out*): Oh-h-h! You have destroyed me. Now I shall melt away. (*She stumbles about.*)

DOROTHY (*Concerned*): Oh, I'm very sorry.

WICKED WITCH (*Weakly*): Didn't you know water could kill me?

DOROTHY: Of course not.

WICKED WITCH: In a few minutes I shall melt away. All my power is gone, all my evil undone. (*Sadly*) The Lion will become fat again, and the Tin Woodman will be mended, and the Scarecrow back in shape. (*Angrily*) And to think one small girl should be the end of me! (*She stumbles to screen.*) I'm melting. (*With a final cry, she disappears behind screen, dropping her hat and the silver slipper.*)

DOROTHY (*Astonished*): She really has melted! (*Goes to screen and looks at hat*) Now we are all free and can go back to Oz.

(*Calling*) Tin Woodman! Scarecrow! Lion! (*They all enter from behind screen.*)

TIN WOODMAN (*Shaking leg*): What a relief! I was afraid I'd never walk again!

SCARECROW (*Flexing arms*): I'm all in one piece again! What happened?

LION: How did you set us free, Dorothy?

DOROTHY: The old witch melted when I threw a pail of water on her.

TIN WOODMAN: Melted! Then the Witch is gone forever!

DOROTHY: Yes. All that is left is my silver slipper. (*Picks up slipper and* WITCH's *hat*) And here is the Wicked Witch's Golden Cap.

LION: Let us go back to the Emerald City at once. We'll take the Witch's Golden Cap, and we can claim our promises from the Wizard. (DOROTHY *puts on slipper, and all exit right. Curtain*)

* * * * *

SCENE 5

SETTING: *Same as Scene 3.*

AT RISE: GUARDIAN *is dusting throne, as* DOROTHY, TOTO, SCARE-CROW, LION, *and* TIN WOODMAN *enter right.*

DOROTHY: Excuse me, sir—

GUARDIAN (*Startled*): Bless my soul, if it isn't the little girl from Kansas! I must tell the Great Oz at once. (*Goes behind screen. Lights dim; gong sounds.*)

OZ (*From behind screen, in loud and terrifying voice*): What? Back again?

DOROTHY (*Going center*): Yes, Great Oz. We killed the Wicked Witch, and now we have come to claim our reward.

OZ (*From behind screen*): Goodness gracious! How did you do that?

DOROTHY: I threw a pail of water on the Witch, and she melted away right before my eyes. Here is her Golden Cap to prove it.

LION: I want some courage! (*He dashes to throne, growls, and knocks over screen, revealing* THE WIZARD OF OZ, *a small, meek man, dressed in an ordinary suit.* LION *looks at him astonished.*) Why, you're only a man!

TIN WOODMAN (*Amazed*): Are you the Wizard of Oz, the Great and Terrible Oz?

OZ (*Meekly*): Yes, I'm afraid I am.

SCARECROW (*Sadly*): But you're no magician. (*He sits dejectedly on floor.*) Now I won't get my brains!

DOROTHY (*Angrily; to* OZ): I should think you would be ashamed of yourself. How could you pretend to be a great magician?

OZ (*Hurriedly*): I'm a very good magician.

SCARECROW: You're only a fake.

OZ (*Turning imploringly to* SCARECROW): You won't tell anyone, will you? All my subjects fear me, and if you tell them the truth, I will have no power over them at all.

DOROTHY (*Thoughtfully*): Well, we won't tell them about you, if you tell me how I am going to get back to Kansas.

TIN WOODMAN: And how shall I ever get a heart?

OZ: Now let me see. (*He paces up and down.*) Yes, that's it. I will make you a heart! Just come with me. (OZ *and* TIN WOODMAN *exit left.*)

SCARECROW (*Hopefully*): If he is able to give the Tin Woodman a heart, perhaps he really can give me some brains. (OZ *and* TIN WOODMAN *reenter.* TIN WOODMAN *has a large gold heart pinned to his chest.*)

OZ: There now—you see, you have a heart of the finest gold.

LION (*Curiously*): How do you feel?

TIN WOODMAN: About the same, except for a curious sensation in my chest.

SCARECROW: That is your first feeling. And now, Oz, can you help me?

OZ: You do not really need brains, Scarecrow. All you have to do is to think hard. That is all anybody with brains does.

SCARECROW: But I will never know if I *can* think. It will only be make-believe.

OZ: Perhaps if I should stuff your head with bran and needles and pins, you would be able to think. Yes, I believe that combination would make an exceptionally good brain. Come, follow me. (*Both exit.*)

TIN WOODMAN: It's really a most curious feeling. I do believe I am beginning to like you, Cowardly Lion.

LION: Thank you, Tin Woodman. (Oz *and* SCARECROW *reenter.*)

SCARECROW: I can feel my brains starting to work already.

Oz: And how about you, Cowardly Lion? What was it that you wanted?

LION: Courage—so that I may be King of Beasts.

Oz: If you tried very hard to be brave, I am sure you would never be cowardly again.

LION (*Meekly*): Oh, but I would. Why, I'm afraid of my own shadow.

Oz: Just a minute. (*He goes out left, comes back carrying a glass of dark-colored liquid.*) Drink this, and it will make you brave.

DOROTHY (*Nervously*): It won't hurt him, will it, Oz?

Oz: Of course not, my dear. (*He hands drink to* LION, *who gulps it down after a momentary hesitation. Others watch him curiously.*)

TIN WOODMAN: How do you feel?

LION: Why, very brave indeed.

DOROTHY (*Disappointedly*): But you can't help me, can you, Oz?

Oz (*Gently*): I'm afraid not, my dear. I have no magic powers that can carry you back to Kansas. (*Suddenly*) But I know someone who does.

ALL: Who?

Oz: Glinda the Good, the Witch of the South. She lives at the edge of the desert and can certainly tell you how to reach Kansas.

DOROTHY: I must start at once.

TIN WOODMAN: I shall go with you, for now that I have a heart I cannot let you go unprotected.

LION: I am brave enough to keep you from danger. I, too, shall go.

SCARECROW: I will be lonesome without you, my friends, so I'm going, too.

DOROTHY: Goodbye, Oz. Thank you for helping us.

Oz: Goodbye. Be sure to come back to the Emerald City for a visit when you can. (*They exit. Curtain*)

* * * * *

Scene 6

Setting: *Throne room of palace of Glinda the Good.*

At Rise: Glinda *is seated on throne center.* Floria *stands right of throne. A loud chime is heard off.*

Glinda: Floria, see who wishes entrance.

Floria: Yes, mistress. (*She exits and returns with* Tin Woodman, Scarecrow, Lion, Toto, *and* Dorothy, *who carries the Golden Cap.*)

Glinda: Welcome, my friends. What brings you to the Land of the South?

Dorothy: The Wizard of Oz directed me to you in hopes that you could show me how I can return to Kansas.

Glinda: What are you carrying in your hand?

Dorothy: This is the Golden Cap that belonged to the Wicked Witch of the West.

Glinda: If you will give me the Golden Cap, I can work its magic spell, and call the Winged Monkeys. They will take you wherever you wish to go. (Dorothy *hands the Cap to* Glinda.)

Dorothy (*To others*): And what will happen to you, my good friends?

Tin Woodman: Now that the Wicked Witch of the West is dead, the Winkies were kind enough to ask me to be their ruler. I shall go back there and rule until you come again.

Lion: The great beasts of the Great Forest want me for their King. Now that I have my courage I shall rejoin them until such time as we meet again.

Scarecrow: And I shall go back to the Emerald City as King. The idea of having a stuffed man as ruler seemed to appeal greatly to the people of the city.

Glinda: Good! Then my first command to the Winged Monkeys shall be to carry the Scarecrow to the Emerald City. My second command shall be to take the Tin Woodman to the Land of the Winkies, my third to carry the Lion to the Great Forest.

SCARECROW: But what about Dorothy?

GLINDA: You had the power to return to those you love all the time, Dorothy. But first you had to be sure of your heart's desire. Are you sure now?

DOROTHY: Oh, yes, yes! More than anything else in this whole world. I want to see Aunty Em and Uncle Henry again!

GLINDA (*Smiling*): Then you are ready. Clap your heels together three times and the silver slippers will carry you back to Kansas.

DOROTHY (*Taking hold of* TOTO): Thank you, Glinda. I shall try to come back again next year. And now goodbye, dear friends. I shall never, never forget you. (*Others crowd around, embracing her warmly. They step aside, and* DOROTHY *and* TOTO *come down center. Closing her eyes and clapping her heels together three times*) I wish to be back in Kansas! (*Softly*) I wish to be back in Kansas! I wish to be back in Kansas! (*Blackout*)

ALL (*Ad lib*): Goodbye! Don't forget us! Come back soon! (*Etc. Curtain*)

THE END

Production Notes

THE WONDERFUL WIZARD OF OZ

Characters: 1 male for wizard; 5 female; 5 male or female for Scarecrow, Tin Woodman, Lion, Toto, and Guardian. As many extras as desired for Munchkins.

Playing Time: 30 minutes.

Costumes: Dorothy wears simple dress and pinafore. Witch of the North is dressed in white, with white pointed hat. Munchkins wear blue tunics and trousers and blue pointed hats. Toto and Lion wear appropriate animal costumes. Scarecrow is dressed in baggy trousers, loose tunic, floppy hat, stuffed with straw. Woodman's costume is silver, and he wears a funnel for a hat, and carries a large cardboard ax. Guardian wears a uniform. Wizard wears an ordinary suit, and Wicked Witch wears traditional black costume and a golden cap. Glinda and Floria wear appropriate court costumes. Glinda has a wand and wears a crown.

Properties: Silver slippers, oilcan, box of spectacles, large golden heart, glass of dark liquid.

Setting: Scene 1: The Country of the Munchkins. A low platform is at center, and at right is a fence with a pile of straw beside it. Scene 2: The Yellow Brick Road in the Great Forest. A path of yellow cloth or paper goes across stage. Down left is a pile of logs, and a backdrop of trees may be used to represent forest. Scenes 3 and 5: The throne room of the palace in the Emerald City. A throne, covered with emeralds, is placed on a low platform at left, and behind it is a large screen. A small table with box of spectacles is at right. Scene 4: The kitchen of the Wicked Witch. A large cauldron is at one side. Scene 6: The throne room of Glinda the Good. A throne, covered with rubies, is at center. There are exits right and left in all scenes.

Lighting: Lights dim in Scenes 3 and 5, as indicated. Blackout at end, as indicated.

Sound: Offstage gong, loud chime, as indicated in text.

🉐 Moby Dick

by *Herman Melville*
Adapted by *Adele Thane*

Characters

ISHMAEL, *narrator*
QUEEQUEG, *harpooner*
PELEG, *owner of the whaleship* Pequod
ELIJAH, *a strange man, "prophet of doom"*
STARBUCK, *first mate*
STUBB, *second mate*
FLASK, *third mate*
SAILORS, *crew of the* Pequod
PIP, *cabin boy*
AHAB, *captain of the* Pequod
VOICE OF MASTHEAD
VOICE OF CAPTAIN OF THE BACHELOR
GARDINER, *captain of the* Rachel

SCENE 1

TIME: *1842.*

SETTING: *The whaleship* Pequod, *in Nantucket harbor. Divided stage, representing a section of deck and captain's cabin. A ship's rail extends across back of stage. Mainmast is at center, encircled by pinrail holding coils of rope. Near pinrail is a barrel holding harpoons. A tool box is on top of hatch, and a*

55

wooden keg down left. Captain's cabin down right has table and chair, wall map, and rolled maps on desk.

AT RISE: ISHMAEL *enters down left, carrying carpetbag. He walks center, tips cap and bows to audience.*

ISHMAEL: Call me Ishmael. I am a schoolmaster by profession, but every so often I get the urge to leave my quiet existence and go to sea. Whenever I grow grim about the mouth; whenever it is damp November in my soul; and especially when I feel like knocking people's hats off—then it is high time to get to sea. (*Takes cap off with a flourish*) Now, don't think I go to sea as a passenger. Oh, no! I go as a sailor. That's the life! (*Pause, while* ISHMAEL *puts cap on*) Some years ago, I decided to sign onto a whaling ship. The giant whale is such a mysterious monster! So I set out for the port of Nantucket. (QUEEQUEG *enters from rear, and walks down aisle through audience, carrying a harpoon.*) In Nantucket I made the acquaintance of an expert harpooner named Queequeg from the South Sea Islands. (ISHMAEL *walks left, points to* QUEEQUEG.) Queequeg looked frightening and bizarre, but he was one of the kindest and most courageous people I've ever known. (QUEEQUEG *mounts steps to stage and clasps* ISHMAEL'S *hand.*) We decided to sign on the same whaling ship—the *Pequod.* (PELEG *enters, sits at table down right.* ISHMAEL *crosses to* PELEG, *followed by* QUEEQUEG.) Is this the captain of the *Pequod?*

PELEG: Supposin' it be?

ISHMAEL: I was thinking of shipping out with you.

PELEG: Ye were, were ye? Ye know nothin' at all about whalin', I daresay.

ISHMAEL: Nothing, sir, but I shall soon learn.

PELEG: Have ye met Cap'n Ahab?

ISHMAEL: Who's Cap'n Ahab?

PELEG: Captain of this ship.

ISHMAEL: I thought you were the captain.

PELEG: I'm Mister Peleg, owner of the *Pequod.* But if ye want to know what whalin' is, I can put ye in the way of findin' out. When you see Cap'n Ahab, ye'll see that he has only one leg.

ISHMAEL: Was the other lost by a whale?

PELEG: Young man, it was chewed up and crunched by the most monstrous whale that ever was! Still feel inclined for whalin'?

ISHMAEL: I do, sir.

PELEG (*Holding out paper and pen*): Very well. Sign this paper. What's your name?

ISHMAEL: Ishmael. (*Signs paper*) My friend, a harpooner, wants to sign on, too. His name is Queequeg. (*Beckons* QUEEQUEG *forward*)

PELEG: Has he ever killed any whales?

QUEEQUEG: I kill hundred whales.

PELEG (*Delighted*): Ye don't say! All right, I'll take ye on. Can ye sign your name, or do ye make your mark?

QUEEQUEG (*Opening shirt, pointing to tattoo on chest*): Queequeg sign like this bird—kokovoko-bird of my island. (*He draws on paper.*)

PELEG: Very good. Report on board tomorrow morning. We sail with the tide. (ISHMAEL *and* QUEEQUEG *start left.* PELEG *exits down right. As* ISHMAEL *and* QUEEQUEG *reach steps, they are stopped by* ELIJAH, *who enters at rear and calls to them.*)

ELIJAH: Shipmates, are ye sailin' on the *Pequod*?

ISHMAEL: Yes, we've just now signed the articles.

ELIJAH (*Walking to stage*): Anything in the articles about your souls?

ISHMAEL: About *what?*

ELIJAH (*Mysteriously*): Your souls. Mebbe ye haven't got any— but no matter. He's got soul enough for an entire crew.

ISHMAEL: Let's go, Queequeg. This fellow is mad.

ELIJAH (*Blocking their way*): Stop! Ye haven't seen Captain Ahab yet, have ye?

ISHMAEL: No, we haven't.

ELIJAH: Ye'd better jump when he gives an order. (*Secretively*) Do ye know about the leg he lost according to the prophecy?

ISHMAEL: Yes, I know about his leg.

ELIJAH: *All* about it? Are ye sure?

ISHMAEL: Pretty sure. Now, if you'll step aside—

ELIJAH (*Backing out of their way*): Certainly. (ISHMAEL *and* QUEEQUEG *go down steps.*) What's signed is signed, and what's to be will be. *Some* sailors go with him, I guess. Heaven pity 'em!

ISHMAEL (*Impatiently*): Look here, if you have anything important to tell us, out with it!

ELIJAH (*Clapping* ISHMAEL *on the shoulder*): I like to hear a chap talk up that way! You're just the man for Captain Ahab—the very man! Goodbye to ye. I shan't see ye again very soon, I reckon—unless it be at the bottom of the sea. (*Chuckling to himself,* ELIJAH *turns to exit.*)

ISHMAEL: Wait a minute! What is your name? (ELIJAH *stops and faces* ISHMAEL.)

ELIJAH (*Speaking portentously*): It's Elijah—Elijah, the prophet of doom! (*Goes up aisle and exits*)

ISHMAEL: Well, I don't need a prophet to tell me my stomach is empty. Come along, Queequeg, let's get some breakfast. (*Exit up aisle. Lights dim to blackout to denote passage of time. During blackout, voices of shipmates are heard off.*)

STARBUCK: Make ready to sail! Weigh anchor!

STUBB: Man the mastheads!

FLASK: Man the capstan!

STARBUCK: Cast off! (*When lights come up,* SAILORS *are gathered at ship's rail, waving as if to shore. They turn and sing "Cape Cod Girls" or another sea chanty.* ISHMAEL *reenters at end of song.*)

ISHMAEL (*Indicating* SAILORS): Those are the sailors of the *Pequod,* picked by destiny to sail our ship. (SAILORS *cheer and exit.* ISHMAEL *stands down right.*) The anchor is up, the sails are set, and off we plunge like fate into the lone Atlantic. (STARBUCK, STUBB, *and* FLASK *enter left and stand talking. When* ISHMAEL *speaks to audience, mates talk in pantomime.*)

STARBUCK: I don't much fancy shipping on so long a voyage with a captain I've never met.

ISHMAEL (*To audience*): That's Starbuck, first mate of the *Pequod,* an honest, God-fearing man—the only voice of sanity on the ship.

STUBB: Captain Ahab came aboard last night and he's stayed inside his cabin since. They say he has a pegleg made of whalebone.

ISHMAEL: That's Stubb, the second mate—good-natured, happy-go-lucky. The other fellow is the third mate, Flask.

FLASK: I've heard the tales about a mad captain. Who knows?

STUBB (*Laughing*): If Ahab be mad, whatever comes, I'll go to it laughing, for a laugh is the easiest, wisest answer to all that's strange.

STARBUCK (*Calling out as he exits left*): Eight bells there, forward!

FLASK (*Following* STARBUCK *off*): Eight bells there, bellboy!

STUBB (*Following* FLASK *off*): Strike the bell eight, little Pip! (*Sound of ship's bell is heard.*)

ISHMAEL (*To audience*): Pip is both bellboy and cabin boy. Poor little Pip, a boy from Alabama, beating his tambourine and singing his songs. (PIP *enters up left, singing a few lines of a sea chanty and striking tambourine as he dances across stage and exits.*) For several days after leaving Nantucket no one saw Captain Ahab. Then one morning, as I entered upon my noon watch, there he stood on deck. (ISHMAEL *turns to deck as* AHAB *enters, carrying megaphone. One of his legs is a white peg.*)

AHAB (*Calling through megaphone*): All hands on deck! Everybody aft! (*Calls overhead*) Mastheads there, come down!

SAILORS *and* MATES (*As they enter; ad lib*): Aye, aye. It's the captain! It's Captain Ahab! (*Etc.* ISHMAEL *joins* SAILORS *as they assemble.*)

AHAB: Tell me, men. What d'ye do when ye see a whale?

SAILORS: Sing out for him!

AHAB: And what d'ye do next, men?

1ST SAILOR: Lower away and after him!

AHAB: And what tune is it ye pull to?

2ND SAILOR: A dead whale or a stove boat!

AHAB: Aye, that's the tune! (*Holds up big, bright coin*) Look ye, my hearties! D'ye see this ounce of Spanish gold? It is a sixteen-dollar gold piece. (*Eager exclamations from* SAILORS) Mr. Starbuck, hand me that sledge hammer and a nail. (STARBUCK *gives* AHAB *hammer and nail from tool box.*) Hark ye now! Whoever of ye raises me a white-headed whale—*white,* mind ye—with a wrinkled brow and a great crooked jaw—he gets this big gold ounce, my boys! (SAILORS *cheer as* AHAB *nails gold piece to mast.*) It's a *white* whale, I say. Skin your eyes for him! Look sharp for white water, and if ye see but a bubble sing out for him!

FLASK: Cap'n Ahab, is this white whale the one some call Moby Dick?

AHAB (*With a triumphant shout*): Aye! Moby Dick!

STARBUCK: Was it Moby Dick that took off your leg, sir?

AHAB (*Furiously*): Aye, Mr. Starbuck, it was that cursed white whale that made a peggin' lubber of me! (*Slapping his peg-leg*) I'll chase him round Good Hope, and round the Horn, and round perdition's flames before I give him up! (*Pointing his finger at* SAILORS) That's what ye've shipped for, men! Ye've shipped to chase the white whale over every sea until he spouts black blood! What say ye, my hearties? Will ye swear death to Moby Dick?

SAILORS (*Together*): Death to Moby Dick!

AHAB: Steward, go draw some grog for the men! (*Delighted reaction from* SAILORS. *All except* AHAB, STARBUCK, *and* ISHMAEL *exit.* ISHMAEL *goes down left, sits on keg.* AHAB *turns to* STARBUCK, *who stands apart, brooding.*) What's the long face for, Mr. Starbuck? Are ye not game for Moby Dick?

STARBUCK (*Sharply*): I'm game for his crooked jaw, and for the jaws of death, too, if it comes fairly in the way of our ship's business. But I signed on to hunt whales, not to avenge my captain. How much will your vengeance fetch in the Nantucket market?

AHAB: Nantucket market! Bah! My vengeance will fetch me a premium—*here!* (*He pounds his chest.*)

STARBUCK: Vengeance on a poor dumb creature that struck you blindly, out of instinct? It's madness! It's blasphemy!

AHAB: Don't talk to me of blasphemy! (*Shaking his fist at the sky*) I'd strike the sun if it insulted me! Beware of Moby Dick, Mr. Starbuck!

STARBUCK: Beware of Ahab, captain—beware of yourself!

AHAB: If we hunt not Moby Dick—heaven hunt us all.

STARBUCK: Heaven keep us all! (AHAB *strides to cabin, sits at table, unrolls maps and studies them intently.* STARBUCK *exits left. Spotlight on* ISHMAEL.)

ISHMAEL (*Standing; to audience*): I learned more about Moby Dick from the crew. He was distinct because of his whiteness and immense size, and he traveled alone, whereas most whales traveled in herds. Yes, there was something unusual about Moby Dick, and, to Ahab, all the evils in the world were embodied in the great white whale, and so he must be destroyed if Ahab was to survive. (*Offstage, sound of lively jig and* SAILORS' *boisterous laughter*) That is the crew carousing, drinking, and dancing to the destruction of Moby Dick. It's as if Ahab's hate is theirs, and the white whale their foe as much as his. (*Looking toward* AHAB) And there Ahab sits, poring over his sea charts, plotting the place where Moby Dick might be found. (*Pauses, turns to audience*) The *Pequod* sailed southward peacefully—then, turning to the East, the Cape winds began to blow. (*Stage darkens. Sound of thunder and rising wind is heard.*) Cape of Good Hope, do they call it? Rather Cape Torment, as it was called in days of yore. For we found ourselves in a wild and tormented sea. (*Sound of wind gets louder. Thunder and lightning*) The winds howled around us and the sky was split by thunder and lightning. (*Moves down right, as* STARBUCK *enters left. Storm effects continue during dialogue in following scene.*)

STARBUCK (*Shouting through megaphone*): Hands by the halyards! Stand by to reef all sails! Double-lash the whaleboats! (SAILORS *and* FLASK *run on, crisscross deck, then run off.* STARBUCK *stops* FLASK.) Flask! See to the anchors—lash them down securely! (FLASK *exits left as* STUBB *and* QUEEQUEG *enter right.*)

STUBB (*Pointing off right*): Queequeg, get ye aloft to the mizzen tops'l yard, and lash the sail against the wind.

QUEEQUEG: Too much thunder up there. (*Exits right*)

STUBB (*Turning to* STARBUCK): Nasty work, this—but the sea will have its way. (*Sings a few bars of "Blow the Man Down"*)

STARBUCK: Stubb, let the storm sing in our rigging, but you hold your peace!

STUBB: But I sing to keep my spirits up. (PIP *enters, terrified, and throws himself at foot of mast.*)

PIP: Have mercy on this small boy down here! (STARBUCK *seizes* STUBB *by shoulder and turns him upstage, facing the ship's rail.*)

STARBUCK (*Pointing out over rail*): Look there, Stubb! See how the gale comes from the East where Ahab is heading for Moby Dick? (AHAB *leaves cabin, steps out on deck.*) If we could persuade the captain to turn the ship to leeward and sail back around Good Hope, that would be the shortest way home to Nantucket.

STUBB: He'd never do it—never! Quiet. Here he comes. (AHAB *crosses to* STUBB *and* STARBUCK. SAILORS *gather on deck.*)

STARBUCK (*To* AHAB): We must send down the main tops'l yard, sir. The band is working loose. Shall I strike it, sir?

AHAB: Strike nothing! Lash it!

STARBUCK: But the fore tops'ls are in rags, sir, and the job sheet is fouled. Shall I slash it free, sir?

AHAB: Slash nothing and strike nothing! I've weathered a lifetime of gales in square riggers. Only cowards take down sails in bad weather. (*Sudden repeated flashes of lightning and crashes of thunder.* PIP *shrieks and runs to* AHAB, *crouching at his feet.*)

STARBUCK (*Grasping* AHAB'S *arm*): God is against you, Ahab! 'Tis an ill voyage—ill begun, ill continued. Turn the ship about, and sail home.

OTHERS: Aye, aye!

AHAB: *No!* All your oaths to hunt the white whale are as binding as mine—and heart, soul, and body, old Ahab is bound.

1ST SAILOR (*Shouting to others*): Mates! Shall we let this crazy old man drag us all down to doom with him?

SAILORS: No, no! (AHAB *snatches harpoon from barrel and threatens* SAILORS *with it. They fall back, petrified.*)

AHAB (*In thunderous voice*): There is one captain that is lord over the *Pequod*. What I have willed, I will do! Moby Dick, I shall clutch thy heart at last! (AHAB *hurls harpoon over ship's rail. Blackout. Curtain. Recorded sea chanty may be played to bridge interval to Scene 2.)*

* * * * *

SCENE 2

TIME: *1843.*

SETTING: *Same as Scene 1.*

AT RISE: AHAB *is in cabin, studying maps. Megaphone is on table.* ISHMAEL *enters, walks down left.*

ISHMAEL: The *Pequod* weathered the storms and entered the serene Pacific Ocean. But for Ahab there was no serenity in the Pacific. He knew that somewhere in its deep lurked the great white whale—Moby Dick. (*Crossing left*) The *Pequod* sailed on. Days went by. (*Stops and looks out front*) Then in the Sea of Japan, another ship was sighted. It was the *Bachelor,* heading for home. (STARBUCK *enters.*)

VOICE OF MASTHEAD (*Offstage*): Sail ho! Sail ho! (AHAB *looks up.*)

STARBUCK (*Shouting up to* MASTHEAD): Where away?

MASTHEAD: Three points on the starboard bow, sir! (AHAB *picks up megaphone, hurries onto deck.*)

VOICE OF CAPTAIN OF BACHELOR (*Calling from rear of auditorium*): Ahoy the *Pequod!* This the *Bachelor,* a whaling ship out of Nantucket. Come aboard!

AHAB (*Speaking through megaphone*): Have ye seen the white whale?

BACHELOR CAPTAIN: No, only heard of him, but don't believe in him at all! Come on aboard! We're a full ship homeward bound.

AHAB: A full ship homeward bound, eh? Call me an empty ship outward bound. (*Turning to* STARBUCK) Forward there! Set all sail, Mr. Starbuck, and keep her to the wind! (STARBUCK *exits left.* AHAB *exits up right, calling out.*) Up helm! Keep her off round the world!

ISHMAEL (*To audience*): Soon after this encounter with the *Bachelor,* one of Stubb's oarsmen in the whaleboat hurt his hand, and Pip was chosen to take his place. You remember Pip—the boy who was so frightened of the storm. Pip loved the kindly side of life; he didn't belong in the harsh world of the whaler. On Pip's third trip in the whaleboat, a harpooned whale lurched against the boat and the terrified Pip leaped into the sea, and was left there. Several hours later, the *Pequod* rescued him, but by this time Pip had lost his mind. Pip's madness drew him closer to Ahab. (ISHMAEL *sits on keg.* AHAB *enters up right, carrying harpoon.* PIP *enters, his tambourine hanging from his belt.*)

PIP (*Dreamily*): Cap'n? Master Ahab?

AHAB: Ah, Pip! Have you come to help me?

PIP: Who do you call Pip? Pip jumped from the whaleboat. Pip's missing.

AHAB (*Placing harpoon in barrel*): Then who are you, boy?

PIP: Bellboy, sir—ding, dong, ding! (*Calls out*) Who's seen Pip, the coward?

AHAB (*Looking upward*): Are there no hearts in heaven? Look down here! Ye created this luckless child, and now ye have abandoned him—as ye have abandoned me. (*Laying his hand on* PIP's *head*) There is a kinship between us, lad.

PIP (*Woefully*): Oh, master, when Pip was drowning, he was terribly afraid.

AHAB (*Offering his hand*): Come, lad, take my hand. (PIP *does so.*)

PIP (*Holding* AHAB's *hand*): Ah, now, if poor Pip had felt so kind a hand as this, perhaps he'd never have been lost. I will not let this hand go.

AHAB: Nor will I let go your hand. Come along. (*They exit off right.*)

ISHMAEL (*Rising*): There go two daft ones—one daft with strength, the other daft with weakness. (*Pause*) The next day, a large ship, the *Rachel*, was seen bearing down upon the *Pequod*. Ahab knew the captain of the *Rachel*—Captain Gardiner.

CAPTAIN GARDINER (*Calling from rear of auditorium*): Ahoy, there, *Pequod!* (SAILORS *and mates enter, gather on deck.*

AHAB *enters and looks out through binoculars.* GARDINER *calls again, walking down aisle toward stage.)* Ahoy, the *Pequod!*

AHAB (*Cupping hands and shouting*): Ahoy, Captain Gardiner! Have ye seen the white whale?

GARDINER: Aye, yesterday.

AHAB (*Excitedly*): Yesterday? Come aboard! (GARDINER *climbs to stage.*) Where did you see him?

GARDINER: Several miles to leeward. Suddenly a huge white head and hump rose out of the water.

AHAB (*Hopefully; rubbing his hands*): He's not killed, is he?

GARDINER: No, the harpoon is not yet forged that will do that.

AHAB: Not forged! (*Snatching harpoon from barrel*) Look ye, Gardiner. Here in this hand I hold his death!

GARDINER: Then heaven help you. Have you seen a whaleboat adrift?

AHAB: No, have you lost one?

GARDINER: Aye. When Moby Dick was sighted, one of our boats gave chase and fastened onto him.

AHAB: Go on, go on! What happened?

GARDINER: The boat disappeared like lightning. Moby Dick ran off with it in tow. (*In despair*) My son, my own boy, is in that boat. I beg you, Ahab, search for him—just for forty-eight hours. I'll pay you roundly for it. (AHAB *is silent.*) He's my only son, Ahab—not twelve years old. (*Silence.* GARDINER *grabs* AHAB's *arm and shakes it frantically.*) I'll not go until you say "aye" to me!

AHAB (*Jerking his arm free*): Brace forward, Mr. Starbuck. Let the ship sail as before. (SAILORS *murmur angrily.*)

GARDINER: You have a child, too, Ahab. Do to me as you would have me do to you if your son was lost. (*To* SAILORS) Run, men! Stand by the square in the yards! (SAILORS *start to obey* GARDINER, *but* AHAB's *voice freezes them.*)

AHAB: Avast! Do not touch a single rope! (*Turns to* GARDINER) I must catch up with Moby Dick. Your boy probably drowned with the rest of them. I must go. Brace forward, Mr. Starbuck! (*Calling out*) Mastheads, skin your eyes for Moby Dick! (SAILORS *disperse.* GARDINER *sorrowfully descends steps and exits at back.* AHAB *stands alone, staring out front.*) He's out there somewhere, Old Moby Dick is, swimming in these seas. (*Exits right*)

ISHMAEL (*Coming forward*): Soon the two ships were far apart, but as long as the *Rachel* was in sight, she could be seen winding her woeful way, her masts thick with men looking for survivors. (*Pause.* AHAB *enters up right and leans over ship's rail at rear of deck.*) As Ahab sought Moby Dick, there came a clear, steel-blue day when the air seemed to dispel the canker in his soul. (ISHMAEL *sits on keg.* STARBUCK *enters left.*)

AHAB: Starbuck, it was on such a day as this that I struck my first whale, as a boy harpooner of eighteen. Forty years ago! Forty years of continual whaling, whole oceans away from that young girl I married when I was past fifty. I sailed for Cape Horn the morning after we wed, and I've made the son she bore me a fatherless child. Oh, Starbuck, what a forty years' fool old Ahab has been!

STARBUCK (*Compassionately*): Then end it now, Captain! Why should you or anyone give chase to Moby Dick? Let us fly these deadly waters—let us sail away home! Come, Ahab, we'll head back to Nantucket. (STARBUCK *starts off right, but stops when* AHAB *does not follow.*)

AHAB (*Crying out*): What nameless, inscrutable thing is it that commands me? Why is it that I keep pushing myself on to do what in my heart I would not dare to do?

MASTHEAD (*Offstage*): There she blows!

AHAB (*Calling up to* MASTHEAD): Where? *Where?*

MASTHEAD (*Off*): Leeward, sir—two miles off! (AHAB *and* STARBUCK *hurry downstage and look off,* AHAB *using binoculars.*)

AHAB: It's Moby Dick! (*Sound: low tympani roll.* SAILORS *and mates crowd onstage.*)

1ST SAILOR: There she blows!

2ND SAILOR: Glory, what a spout!

STARBUCK: He's heading straight to leeward, sir, and dead away from us.

STUBB: He can't have seen the ship.

FLASK: He's going to sound! (*Tympani roll louder*) There go the flukes!

3RD SAILOR: See the suds he makes, and what a hump!

AHAB: Set all sails! Stand by the boats! Mr. Starbuck, stay on board, and keep the ship. (SAILORS *scatter;* STARBUCK *remains behind.*)

STARBUCK: Ahab, it's not too late, even now, to stop. Moby Dick does not seek you. It is *you* who madly seek him!

AHAB: And I'll girdle the unmeasured globe ten times, if need be, but I'll slay him yet!

STARBUCK (*Pleading*): Ahab, I beg you, think of your wife and child!

AHAB: Nothing can change the course of my destiny. I am fate's lieutenant; I act under orders. (*Pause, then quietly*) For the last time, my soul's ship starts upon this voyage, Starbuck.

STUBB (*Entering*): All is ready, Captain.

AHAB: Good! Have the crew stand by to lower the boats. (*Takes harpoon from barrel*)

STUBB (*Pointing*): Look, sir! Moby Dick is rising—he breaches.

AHAB: Aye, breach your last to the sun, Moby Dick! Your hour and my harpoon are at hand. Mr. Starbuck, the ship is yours. (*Shouting as he exits*) Crew, stand by! Make ready to lower away!

STUBB: Blow on, and split your spout, old whale—the crazy fiend himself is after ye! (*Exits*)

STARBUCK: Heaven keep us all, but already my bones feel damp within me. (*Lights dim to blackout. Curtain closes. Spotlight up on* ISHMAEL *standing down left*)

ISHMAEL (*To audience*): Soon all the boats were lowered, and we began rowing to leeward. I was an oarsman in Ahab's boat, which was in the lead. (*Following lines may be heard over loudspeaker.*)

AHAB (*On mike*): Oars! Oars! Grip your oars, men. Pull!

STUBB (*On mike*): *Pull, pull!* Break your backbones—*pull!*

FLASK (*On mike*): Pull, will ye? Pull! That's the stroke!

SAILORS (*Chanting*): *Pull—pull—pull—*(*Continues softly under* ISHMAEL's *next speech*)

ISHMAEL: We raced forward noiselessly toward the unsuspecting prey. Moby Dick seemed to be swimming with a gentle joyousness. As we neared him, he suddenly turned and charged the boats. By skillful maneuvering, we avoided him, and all three boats hurled harpoons into his sides.

STUBB (*On mike*): Look out, boys, he's going to sound! There he goes! (*Sound of tympani roll*)

ISHMAEL: Slowly, Moby Dick rose from the water; his marble white body arched high, and warningly waving his bannered flukes in the air, revealed himself, sounded, and went out of sight. (*Tympani stops.*) Ahab stood in the prow of his boat, waiting for Moby Dick to surface again. (*Spotlight up on* AHAB, *standing in bow of boat before curtain, center, holding his harpoon*)

AHAB (*Staring down*): He's down there, but he'll breach quickly.

ISHMAEL: We all held our breaths as Moby Dick boomed his entire bulk into the air in an act of defiance, then fell back into the sea.

AHAB: Beach me! Beach me there on that white back!

ISHMAEL: The boats darted forward to attack. Moby Dick turned and met our charge. With open maws and lashing tail, all heedless of our darting lances, Moby Dick crossed and recrossed, snarling the lines so that the boats were pulled every way.

AHAB: I grin at thee, thou grinning whale! His heart—I'll have his heart! (*Drumbeat is heard, and continues under following speeches.*)

ISHMAEL: Starbuck steered the *Pequod* toward Moby Dick in the hope of saving us. Moby Dick caught sight of the advancing ship, pointed his massive forehead at it and in a rush crashed its bow. (SAILORS *give wild cries.*)

AHAB (*Shouting*): The whale! The ship! Starbuck, save my ship!

ISHMAEL: Moby Dick smote the *Pequod* again and again with his mighty forehead. Men and timbers reeled, and we heard the waters pour into the broken bow of the ship.

AHAB: The ship, where is the ship? Must it perish then, and without me? (*Spotlight on* ISHMAEL *out, up on* AHAB *as he raises his harpoon*) Now, Moby Dick—I turn my body from the sun and face everlasting darkness. For hate's sake I spit my last breath at thee! From hell's heart I stab at thee! (*As* AHAB *aims to throw out his harpoon, there is a blackout.*

Sound of a sharp, metallic chord is heard. Drumbeat stops. Light appears on ISHMAEL. *Boat and* AHAB *have disappeared.*)

ISHMAEL: Ahab's harpoon darted true. But the harpoon rope caught Ahab around the neck and jerked him from the whale-boat. Ahab was gone! Moby Dick, in a final gesture, turned to face the setting sun, and died. The *Pequod* sank from sight in a whirling vortex that sucked everything down with it— and the vast shroud of the sea rolled on as it rolled five thousand years ago. (*Pause.* ISHMAEL *moves forward into another light, center.*) The drama is done. Why, then, does anyone now step forward? Because one did survive the wreck. I, and I alone, escaped to tell you the tale. On the second day, a ship drew near and picked me up. It was the *Rachel,* that in her search after her missing children, found only another orphan. (ISHMAEL *exits. Recorded chanty may be played as he exits.*)

THE END

Production Notes

MOBY DICK

Characters: 15 or more male (female actors may take any parts, if desired).

Costumes: Mid-eighteenth-century dress. Ishmael wears jacket and trousers, string tie, cap with visor. Peleg wears tail coat, trousers, bowler hat. Elijah is shabbily dressed in faded jacket and patched trousers with ragged scarf tied around neck. Ahab and Gardiner wear pea jackets, white trousers, string ties, caps with visor. Ahab also has white peg leg, white scar on side of his face, and binoculars around his neck. Sailors wear white or blue trousers, striped jerseys, cummerbunds; some wear stocking caps or bandanas, and most are barefoot. Queequeg's arms, face are tattooed; he also has bird tattoo on chest, and his hair is disheveled. Pip wears overalls cut off at knees, and shirt.

Properties: Carpet bag; tambourine; megaphone; large gold coin.

Setting: The whaleship *Pequod*. Divided stage, representing section of the deck and captain's cabin. Ship's rail extends across back of stage. Mainmast is at center, encircled by pinrail holding coils of rope. Near pinrail is barrel holding harpoons. Left of mast, a low platform represents hatch. On top of hatch is tool box. Wooden keg is down left. Captain's cabin is suggested by table and chair down right. On table are maps, log book, papers, pen-and-ink stand. In final scene, cutout of bow of a boat is set flush against curtain and actor stands forward in it.

Lighting: Lightning; blackouts; spotlights, as indicated in text.

Sound: Ship's bell; storm sound effects; tympani roll; drumbeat; recorded music of sea chanties.

꧁The Scarlet Pimpernel

by *Baroness Orczy*
Adapted by *Michael T. Leech*

Characters

MR. JELLYBAND, *English innkeeper*
SALLY, *his daughter*
MR. HEMPSEED, *a customer*
OTHER CUSTOMERS, *extras*
CHAUVELIN, *French government agent*
CHAUVELIN'S COMPANION, *an extra*
LORD ANTHONY DEWHURST
COUNTESS DE TOURNAY
SUZANNE, *her daughter*
VICOMTE, *her son*
SIR ANDREW FFOULKES
LADY MARGUERITE BLAKENEY
SIR PERCY BLAKENEY, *her husband*
LORD GRENVILLE
BUTLER
BALL GUESTS, *extras*
SERVANT
FRENCH INNKEEPER
FRENCH OFFICER

SCENE 1

TIME: *1792, during the Reign of Terror after the French Revolution.*

71

SETTING: *The Fishermen's Rest, an English inn. Fireplace, chairs, and tables holding coffee cups, mugs, and cider jugs complete setting. Window is in right wall; right exit leads outside, left exit leads to other rooms.*

AT RISE: MR. JELLYBAND *is standing with his back to the fireplace.* SALLY, MR. HEMPSEED, *and* OTHER CUSTOMERS *are standing about, or sitting at tables.*

MR. JELLYBAND: Bring in some more cider, Sally! They're a thirsty lot tonight!

CUSTOMERS (*Ad lib*): Aye! That we are! Right you are, Jellyband. (*Etc.*)

SALLY: Right away, Father. (*She exits left, briefly, reentering with a large jug of cider.*) Here's the cider, Father. (*Fills mugs and exits*)

MR. JELLYBAND (*Proudly*): Now tell me, gentlemen, if that isn't the best British cider you've ever tasted!

1ST CUSTOMER (*Raising his mug*): From one of the best inns of old England!

MR. HEMPSEED: Your guests tonight will be coming over from France, will they not?

MR. JELLYBAND: Yes, with Sir Andrew Ffoulkes. They'll be glad to see the lights of Dover, poor souls.

MR. HEMPSEED: Terrible times they're having in France, what with their revolution and all.

MR. JELLYBAND: Well, what can they expect, Mr. Hempseed? Rising up and murdering their nobility as though they were cutting off the heads of cabbages. The three Royalist refugees from France who are arriving here tonight have been helped in their escape by the Scarlet Pimpernel.

ALL (*Ad lib*): The Scarlet Pimpernel! A fine fellow! Clever man! (*Etc.*)

MR. HEMPSEED: They say he's like a shadow. No one knows who he is, except that he's English. He steals into Paris and rescues the prisoners from under the very knife of the guillotine!

MR. JELLYBAND: A toast! A toast, gentlemen, to that brave Englishman, the Scarlet Pimpernel!

ALL: To the Scarlet Pimpernel!

(CHAUVELIN *rises from a table at rear, where he has been sitting with* COMPANION.)

CHAUVELIN (*To* MR. JELLYBAND): You seem very proud of the exploits of this gentleman, sir.

MR. JELLYBAND (*Enthusiastically*): He's a true-blooded Englishman. And being one myself, I'm proud of him!

CHAUVELIN: Does anybody—er—have any idea who the Scarlet Pimpernel is?

MR. HEMPSEED (*Shaking his head*): Not a soul. (LORD ANTHONY *enters right.* CHAUVELIN *sits again.* OTHER CUSTOMERS *exit.*)

MR. JELLYBAND: Ah, Lord Anthony! (CHAUVELIN *leans forward to listen.*)

LORD ANTHONY: Evening, Jellyband, old chap. Evening, Mr. Hempseed. (SALLY *enters left.*) Sally! You grow prettier every time I see you!

SALLY (*Embarrassed*): Oh, your lordship! Father, why don't you see if the wine is cooled for the guests? (MR. JELLYBAND *smiles, motions to* MR. HEMPSEED, *and both exit.*)

LORD ANTHONY (*Urgently*): Sally, will you give Sir Andrew a message when he comes in? Tell him privately, mind you, that I'll meet him here in the coffee room at ten o'clock tonight on urgent business.

SALLY (*Nodding*): You can rely on me, Lord Anthony.

LORD ANTHONY (*Moving closer*): I'm sure I can, Sally. (*He and* SALLY *talk aside.* CHAUVELIN *and his* COMPANION *quietly rise and exit.* SALLY *exits.*)

MR. JELLYBAND (*At door*): This way, Countess. (*He enters and steps aside as* COUNTESS DE TOURNAY, SUZANNE, *and the* VICOMTE *enter with* SIR ANDREW.)

LORD ANTHONY: Welcome to old England, Countess. (*Bowing to them*) Mademoiselle Suzanne, Monsieur le Vicomte.

COUNTESS (*Sighing in relief*): Ah, messieurs, what can I say? I am so deeply grateful. I cannot believe we are safe at last. What a frightful journey!

SUZANNE (*Animatedly*): We were taken out of Paris in a filthy market cart full of vegetables!

VICOMTE: The cart was driven by a fearful old hag who said

her family had the plague, (*Laughs*) and the sergeant was so terrified that he let us through.

SIR ANDREW: Do you know who the old hag was, my friends? The Scarlet Pimpernel!

SUZANNE (*Astonished*): Is it true?

SIR ANDREW (*Bowing*): I have it on excellent authority!

COUNTESS: A true hero—whoever he is!

SUZANNE: Why does he call himself the Scarlet Pimpernel?

SIR ANDREW (*Enthusiastically*): The Scarlet Pimpernel is the name of a humble English flower, and now the name that conceals the identity of the bravest man in all of Europe!

SUZANNE (*Quietly*): We have heard that he has promised to save my father, who is still in hiding in France.

COUNTESS (*Fervently*): I pray with all my heart that he succeeds.

LORD ANTHONY: So do we all, Countess. (*Turns to* MR. JELLY-BAND) Tell me, Jellyband, is anyone else staying here at the inn?

MR. JELLYBAND: No, milord—that is, no one your lordship would object to. Sir Percy and Lady Blakeney will be here presently, but they won't stay.

COUNTESS: Lady Blakeney? Was she not once Marguerite St. Just—an actress at the Comedie Française?

LORD ANTHONY: She was indeed, madame. A beautiful and witty woman, who now is married to the country's richest and most elegant man, Sir Percy Blakeney.

COUNTESS (*Coldly*): I know her well. She sent my cousin's family to the guillotine.

SUZANNE (*Vehemently, to* COUNTESS): Marguerite and I were at school together in Paris. She is one of my dearest friends— how can she be so wicked?

COUNTESS (*Sharply*): Suzanne! That woman's brother is an enemy to the Royalist cause. (*The clatter of coach wheels is heard offstage.* SALLY *enters.*)

SALLY (*Excitedly*): Sir Percy and Lady Blakeney are here! (*She curtsies and exits, followed by her father.*)

COUNTESS: I refuse to be in the same room as that woman!

SIR ANDREW (*Indicating exit*): Let us go in to dinner, Countess.

(*They start toward exit left but pause as* LADY MARGUERITE BLAKENEY *enters right, carrying a fan.*)

MARGUERITE (*Brightly*): Good evening! (*She recognizes* SUZANNE *and sweeps across to her.*) Suzanne! What are you doing here? How good to see you! And your mama, too! (*Turns to* COUNTESS)

COUNTESS (*Ignoring* MARGUERITE): Suzanne, I forbid you to talk to that woman!

MARGUERITE (*Stunned, then regaining control*): Ah, Countess! Pray tell me, what bothers you?

COUNTESS (*Coldly*): We are no longer in France, madame, and I am at liberty to forbid my daughter to touch your hand in friendship. Come, Suzanne! (*She sails past* MARGUERITE *and exits left.*)

SUZANNE: Oh, Marguerite—(*She rushes to* MARGUERITE *and embraces her.*)

COUNTESS (*From offstage*): Suzanne! (SUZANNE *gives* MARGUERITE *a parting look and exits.* MARGUERITE *turns to* SIR ANDREW.)

MARGUERITE (*Dryly*): I hope little Suzanne doesn't grow old like her mother! (VICOMTE *quietly turns to fireplace to warm himself.*)

SIR ANDREW: Suzanne is very lovely.

MARGUERITE (*Softly*): She is indeed. (*Spiritedly*) But, what an old dragon the Countess is! (*Mimicking her*) "Suzanne! I forbid you to talk to that woman!"

LORD ANTHONY: How they must miss you at the Comedie, Lady Blakeney! The Parisians must hate Sir Percy for marrying you and taking you away!

MARGUERITE (*Warmly*): Ah, but it would be hard to hate Sir Percy! His wit would disarm even the Countess!

SIR PERCY (*At doorway*): I say—is some impudent upstart talking about me?

MARGUERITE (*Laughing*): It is your wife, my dear. You have nothing to fear.

SIR PERCY (*Entering*): Nothing to fear? If it's my wife, I may have everything to fear! (*All laugh.* SIR PERCY *turns to* SIR

ANDREW *and* LORD ANTHONY.) How are you, Ffoulkes? And you, Tony? Did you ever see such beastly weather?

SIR ANDREW: Yes—it is—er—rainy. (*There is an awkward pause.*)

SIR PERCY (*Puzzled*): What's got into you all?

MARGUERITE: Oh, it's nothing, Percy. Only an affront to your wife.

SIR PERCY (*To* MARGUERITE): Who was the brave man who dared tackle you, my dear?

VICOMTE (*Turning quickly to face* SIR PERCY): Monsieur, it is my mother who has angered your wife. I cannot ask pardon for my mother. To me, she is right. (*Pauses; brazenly*) And I am ready to challenge you to a duel.

SIR PERCY (*Unmoved*): My good man, I never fight duels. Frightfully uncomfortable things, duels—aren't they, Tony?

MARGUERITE: Play the peacemaker, I pray you, Lord Tony.

LORD ANTHONY: Sir Percy is right, Vicomte. It would hardly be fitting for you to start your stay in England with a duel. You know duels are illegal here.

VICOMTE (*Bowing to* SIR PERCY; *curtly*): If monsieur is satisfied, I withdraw.

SIR PERCY (*Aside to* LORD ANTHONY, *sharply*): If he's the sort you and your friends bring over from France, Tony, then I think you should drop 'em in the sea halfway over.

LORD ANTHONY: Come, Sir Percy, let's find Jellyband and forget the whole thing over some good hot food.

SIR PERCY: Good idea, Tony. Come along, Sir Andrew. (*To* VICOMTE) Do join us, Vicomte. (*To* MARGUERITE) If you'll excuse us, my dear—(MARGUERITE *nods and turns to look out window.* LORD ANTHONY, SIR ANDREW *and* VICOMTE *exit.* SIR PERCY *pauses at door, looks back at* MARGUERITE, *then exits.*)

CHAUVELIN (*Entering quietly, unnoticed by* MARGUERITE): Ah! The beautiful Lady Blakeney!

MARGUERITE (*Turning quickly*): Oh! How you startled me! Chauvelin! Is it really you?

CHAUVELIN: Chauvelin himself, *citoyenne,* at your service.

MARGUERITE: I am pleased to see you. But what brings you to the shores of England?

CHAUVELIN (*In official tone*): I am the representative of the Revolutionary Government of France to King George's England.

MARGUERITE (*Teasingly*): You are climbing up in the world!

CHAUVELIN (*Bowing*): Thank you, madame. And how is your brother Armand?

MARGUERITE: Quite well, thank you. He returns to France tomorrow.

CHAUVELIN: He is a good servant of the Republic, and of France, is he not?

MARGUERITE: Of course! (*Suspiciously*) What do you imply? Armand loves France.

CHAUVELIN (*Calmly*): I do not doubt it. (*Pauses*) You have heard, perhaps, of the Scarlet Pimpernel?

MARGUERITE: And who has not?

CHAUVELIN (*Intensely*): Then you must know that this mysterious person is one of France's bitterest enemies, and therefore the enemy of brave men like your brother Armand.

MARGUERITE (*Cautiously*): France has many enemies these days.

CHAUVELIN (*Sternly*): Surely you'll agree, Lady Blakeney, that as daughter of France, it is your duty to help your country?

MARGUERITE (*Surprised*): I? But I don't see how, Chauvelin.

CHAUVELIN (*Ingratiatingly*): As Lady Blakeney, you are the center of London society. You see and hear everything. You can unmask the Scarlet Pimpernel.

MARGUERITE (*Firmly*): It's only fair to tell you, Chauvelin, that although I fully support the Revolution, I abhor its bloody murders. They are a blot on the name of France.

CHAUVELIN (*Persistently*): You must help me find the Scarlet Pimpernel for France, *citoyenne!*

MARGUERITE (*Taken aback*): Where can *I* find such an elusive creature? Besides, there is little you could do even if you knew his identity. He is English.

CHAUVELIN (*Fiercely*): I would take a chance on that. He will go to the guillotine first, and we will apologize later.

MARGUERITE (*Shuddering*): You would send to the guillotine a brave man whose only crime is to save women and children, old and young men from a horrible death? (*Fiercely*) I'll have none of your dirty work.

CHAUVELIN: Then I assume you prefer to be insulted by every French aristocrat who escapes to this country.

SIR PERCY (*Calling offstage*): Marguerite? Marguerite? (*He enters.*) It's time to return home. (*Looking about*) My, it's dark as a tomb in here.

MARGUERITE (*Lightly*): Chauvelin and I were just having a little chat, Percy.

SIR PERCY (*Surprised*): Is that you, Chauvelin, here from Paris? (*Teasingly*) Good evening, little fellow!

CHAUVELIN (*Coldly*): Good evening.

SIR PERCY: Marguerite, we must start back (*He goes toward door.*)

MARGUERITE (*To* CHAUVELIN): Goodbye, monsieur.

CHAUVELIN: Farewell for now, Lady Blakeney—until we meet in London! (MARGUERITE *ignores last remark and sweeps out, followed by* SIR PERCY. *Sound of clock striking ten is heard offstage.* CHAUVELIN *moves to hide in dark corner.*)

LORD ANTHONY (*Entering*): Ah, good, the place is deserted. (SIR ANDREW *follows, carrying papers.*)

SIR ANDREW: I have the papers here—instructions from the Scarlet Pimpernel. (*He puts them on table and they bend over them.*)

LORD ANTHONY: I understand there are special orders for me.

SIR ANDREW: Yes. Armand St. Just will be on his way to Paris tomorrow. There's a letter here from him. No one suspects Armand yet, but he wants us to watch out for a clever man named Chauvelin who is determined to find the Scarlet Pimpernel and to crush the League. (*As they pore over letters,* CHAUVELIN *goes to exit and motions off left.* COMPANION *enters quickly and both men sneak up on* LORD ANTHONY *and* SIR ANDREW. *After brief scuffle, Englishmen fall to the floor, unconscious.*)

CHAUVELIN (*Grabbing papers*): Hm-m-m—Armand St. Just a traitor to the Revolution after all! (*He holds up letter.*) Now,

Lady Blakeney, I think you *will* help me find the Scarlet Pimpernel! (*Curtain*)

* * * * *

SCENE 2

TIME: *Three days later; the evening of Lord Grenville's ball.*

SETTING: *The supper room of Lord Grenville's London home. Easy chair and other chairs are included in furnishings. Exit left leads to ballroom; exit right leads to other rooms.*

AT RISE: LORD GRENVILLE *stands right, greeting his guests.* CHAUVELIN *lurks in background.* COUNTESS, SUZANNE, VICOMTE, LORD ANTHONY, *and* SIR ANDREW *stand together left, conversing quietly.* BUTLER *stands by door.*

SUZANNE (*To* SIR ANDREW): What a delightful ball! It's so good to be dancing again, though I wonder at my having such a good time when poor Papa is in such danger in Paris!

SIR ANDREW: Dear Suzanne, if the Scarlet Pimpernel has sworn to help him escape from France, then you have nothing to fear!

BUTLER (*Announcing*): Sir Percy and Lady Blakeney! (SIR PERCY *and* MARGUERITE *enter.*)

LORD ANTHONY (*Bowing to* MARGUERITE): My dear Lady Blakeney, how good to see you.

MARGUERITE: And you, Lord Tony.

CHAUVELIN (*Aside to* MARGUERITE): Lady Blakeney, a word with you please.

MARGUERITE (*To others, reluctantly*): Excuse me. (*She and* CHAUVELIN *move to one side, while others remain center.*)

COUNTESS (*Loudly*): You see, Suzanne, your dear Marguerite is already a faithful ally of revolutionary spies, consorting with Chauvelin! (COUNTESS *exits in a huff, and* SUZANNE, *distressed, follows.*)

SIR ANDREW (*Following after them*): Really, I must protest, Countess . . . (*All exit, except* MARGUERITE *and* CHAUVELIN.)

CHAUVELIN: Now, Lady Blakeney, I think you would be wise to listen.

MARGUERITE (*Calmly*): Is that a threat, monsieur?

CHAUVELIN: Just a note of caution, madame. (*He pauses.*) Your brother is in deadly peril. (*She starts, then calms herself.*)

MARGUERITE: Come, now! Armand in danger? I don't believe it.

CHAUVELIN: When I asked your help for France three days ago, you refused. Perhaps now you will change your mind. (*Pause*) A letter from your brother to Sir Andrew Ffoulkes came into my hands recently.

MARGUERITE: Well? What of it?

CHAUVELIN (*Slowly*): That letter showed him to be the arch enemy of France. He is in league with the Scarlet Pimpernel.

MARGUERITE (*Trying to hide her terror*): It's not possible! Armand would never help the aristocrats he so despises!

CHAUVELIN: Armand is guilty beyond the slightest hope of pardon, and as soon as we catch him (*Draws his finger across his throat*), it is goodbye to your dear brother—unless you help me find the Scarlet Pimpernel! (*Ingratiatingly*) If you find him for me, the compromising letter will be returned to you and your brother will be spared.

MARGUERITE (*Grimly*): You would force me to spy for you in return for Armand's life—is that it?

CHAUVELIN: Madame, do not waste my time. (*Smiles*) Among the other papers carried by Sir Andrew was a note indicating that the Scarlet Pimpernel himself would be at this ball tonight. Find out who and where he is, and your work is done. *Au revoir!* (*Exits*)

MARGUERITE (*Starting after him*): Wait—oh, wait! (*She stops.*) Oh, how can I do such a thing? Yet if I do *not,* my dear brother Armand will be—guillotined! (*She exits left as* SIR PERCY, LORD GRENVILLE, LORD ANTHONY, *and other* BALL GUESTS *enter right, carrying punch glasses. They stop center.*)

SIR PERCY (*To* LORD GRENVILLE): And we poor, ordinary men have had to stand by while the ladies worship a cursed shadow!

LORD GRENVILLE (*Raising his glass*): To the shadowy Pimpernel—whoever he is! (*They all raise their glasses.*)

SIR PERCY: In his honor, I've made up a little verse.

LORD GRENVILLE: Let's hear it, Sir Percy!

LORD ANTHONY: Yes, come on, old chap, let's hear it.

SIR PERCY: Since you insist, gentlemen. (*Pauses, then recites*)
We seek him here, we seek him there,
The French have sought him everywhere.
Is he in Heaven? Is he in Hell?
That old elusive Pimpernel!

LORD ANTHONY: Hurrah for the poet! Let's have it again! (*All except* SIR PERCY *exit left, repeating the Pimpernel verse.* SIR PERCY *looks after them, smiles, settles into chair, right, and dozes off.*)

CHAUVELIN (*Entering quietly*): That old elusive Pimpernel, eh? We shall see how elusive he is! (MARGUERITE *enters, distracted, and starts as she sees* CHAUVELIN.)

MARGUERITE: Oh! You startled me!

CHAUVELIN: Shhh! (*He indicates the sleeping* SIR PERCY *and draws her downstage; whispering*) Do you have news for me?

MARGUERITE (*Haltingly*): I stole a note from Sir Andrew.

CHAUVELIN (*Eagerly*): What was in it?

MARGUERITE: It was from the Pimpernel. It said, "I start for Calais tomorrow. If you wish to speak to me, I shall be in the supper room at one o'clock precisely."

CHAUVELIN: Good. It is almost one o'clock, and we are in the supper room now.

MARGUERITE: What will you do?

CHAUVELIN: When I find out who the Scarlet Pimpernel is, I shall have him followed. I myself will leave for France tomorrow. The papers I acquired spoke of a certain Blanchard's hut at Calais. I shall go there and unmask the Scarlet Pimpernel—at last!

MARGUERITE (*Anxiously*): And Armand?

CHAUVELIN: I have already promised you that when I lay my hands on the Scarlet Pimpernel I will return Armand's letter, and I assure you, your precious Armand will be in England, safe with his charming sister. (MARGUERITE *withdraws as* CHAUVELIN *sits. A clock chimes one.*) It's one o'clock. I'll soon have my hands on the Scarlet Pimpernel. (*Impatiently*) I wonder what can be keeping him. (*Curtain*)

* * * * *

SCENE 3

TIME: *A few hours later.*

SETTING: *The garden of the Blakeneys' home at Richmond. At right are table and chairs; Sir Percy's ring is under table.*

AT RISE: MARGUERITE *and* SIR PERCY, *still wearing ball clothes, enter.*

MARGUERITE (*Urgently*): Percy—I need to speak with you.

SIR PERCY (*Pausing*): What can I do for you, my dear?

MARGUERITE: Percy, Armand is in grave danger. He is so rash—and one of his letters, a very compromising one, has fallen into the hands of a fanatic. Armand may face the guillotine. Can you do anything?

SIR PERCY (*Dryly*): Perhaps you should seek the help of the Frenchman—Chauvelin.

MARGUERITE (*Aghast*): I cannot ask him, Percy!

SIR PERCY (*Studying her a moment; sincerely*): I pledge my word that Armand will be safe. Now, I must be off.

MARGUERITE (*Urgently*): One more moment, please, Percy. I have something I have wanted to explain to you for a very long time.

SIR PERCY (*Gently*): What is it, my dear?

MARGUERITE: It concerns us—and the Countess. (*Haltingly*) The Countess de Tournay believes I am responsible for sending her cousin and his family to the guillotine. I swear I am innocent, but so-called friends have told you and the Countess otherwise—and I know you have believed them, though you are still so kind to me. Until now, I have been too proud to tell you *my* story, since you listened to others first.

SIR PERCY (*Moved*): I have waited almost a year to hear the story from your own lips.

MARGUERITE (*Linking arms with him, as they start toward left exit*): Up until the very morning her family members were executed, I was doing all I could to save them—(*They move offstage. Lights may dim briefly and come up again to indicate the passage of time.* MARGUERITE *reenters, alone, wearing a shawl over her shoulders. To herself*) He must believe I am innocent. He seemed so different in the hour we just spent in the garden. Oh, I *do* love him. (SIR PERCY *enters, wearing long cloak.*) Percy! Where are you going?

SIR PERCY: I have urgent business to attend to in London. It has to do with Armand.

MARGUERITE: Oh, Percy! Promise me you'll come back soon. (*She gazes at him intently.*)

SIR PERCY (*Tenderly*): Yes, I will come back very soon. (*He holds her hand a moment, then exits quickly.*)

MARGUERITE: Farewell! (*She waves.* SERVANT *enters.*)

SERVANT: Madame, a young lady is here to see you.

MARGUERITE: It must be Suzanne! (*To* SERVANT) Ask her to come into the garden.

SERVANT: Yes, madame. (*He exits.*)

MARGUERITE: How furious the old Countess was when I invited Suzanne here!

SUZANNE (*Running on*): Marguerite, my dear friend!

MARGUERITE: Oh, Suzanne. (*They embrace.*) It's so good of you to come. (SUZANNE *sits, then notices ring under table.*)

SUZANNE (*Picking up ring*): Have you lost a ring, Marguerite? (*Handing ring to* MARGUERITE)

MARGUERITE (*Looking at it*): It must be Percy's. (*Examining it more closely*) How very strange—

SUZANNE: What is it?

MARGUERITE: Nothing, really—but it's odd. Percy *sets* the fashion as a rule. I didn't expect him to be following one!

SUZANNE: What do you mean?

MARGUERITE: As you know, the Scarlet Pimpernel is the toast of England! Everyone is wearing clothing and jewelry adorned with flowering scarlet pimpernels, in honor of our mysterious hero. And here is my foolish husband with a pimpernel ring! (*Shows ring to* SUZANNE, *then puts it into her pocket*) Now, tell me, Suzanne—what is the latest news of your father?

SUZANNE: Oh, I have no fear now, Marguerite. The Scarlet Pimpernel himself has gone to save Papa! He is to be in London this morning, and Calais by tonight.

MARGUERITE (*Thoughtfully*): In London this morning? And then Calais? (*Pauses; suddenly*) Oh, no!

SUZANNE (*Alarmed*): What is it, Marguerite?

MARGUERITE (*Weakly*): It's nothing, really nothing. You did say that the Scarlet Pimpernel has gone *today*?

SUZANNE: Yes, but what has upset you so?

MARGUERITE (*In distress*): I must be alone for a moment.

SUZANNE: Whatever you say, Marguerite. (*She embraces* MARGUERITE *and then exits, troubled.*)

MARGUERITE: How could I have been so blind? My own husband is the Scarlet Pimpernel! Now I understand everything. He wore a mask of stupidity to throw dust in everyone's eyes. Oh, Percy, what a fool I've been! (*Suddenly*) And I've betrayed him to Chauvelin! Now Percy has gone to Calais with that monster at his heels. Have I sent my own husband to his death?

SERVANT (*Entering, holding letter*): A letter just arrived by special runner, your ladyship.

MARGUERITE (*Taking letter and reading it*): It is Armand's letter returned by Chauvelin! Heaven help me—that means Chauvelin is on the track of the Scarlet Pimpernel! (SERVANT *exits, as* SUZANNE *enters.*)

SUZANNE: Is it bad news, Marguerite? Can I do anything?

MARGUERITE: Yes—yes, Suzanne. I will come back to London with you. I must see Sir Andrew, and then I must go to Calais! Come, Suzanne, I have not a moment to waste! (*They exit. Curtain*)

* * * * *

SCENE 4

TIME: *That evening.*

SETTING: *An inn at Calais. The stage is divided into two rooms, with foyer at right, and a private room at left. Scrawled on wall of foyer are words,* LIBERTÉ, ÉGALITÉ, FRATERNITÉ. *A chair stands left; tables and chairs, in main room, at right. A screen and curtained doorway may divide the set.*

AT RISE: FRENCH INNKEEPER, *carrying valise, enters private room left, followed by* MARGUERITE *and* SIR ANDREW. INNKEEPER *puts down valise.*

SIR ANDREW (*Handing money to* INNKEEPER): Here you are, Innkeeper. (INNKEEPER *takes money, nods, and exits.*)

MARGUERITE (*Taking off her cloak, shuddering*): What a dreadful place this is, and oh, what a frightful journey! The delay in crossing from Dover was unbearable. Do you think Sir Percy managed to cross before us in his yacht?

SIR ANDREW (*Soothingly*): It is almost certain.

MARGUERITE: Oh, Sir Andrew, I'm terrified that Percy will walk straight into a trap. I just pray that we are not too late. Did you say Percy will be here for supper?

SIR ANDREW: That was the plan, Lady Blakeney. Chauvelin and his men may be on the way here already. He followed our boat from Dover, less than an hour later. He knows of this inn and will make straight for it.

MARGUERITE (*Hopefully*): Still, I'm sure that by the time Chauvelin arrives, we shall be at sea again with Sir Percy safe aboard.

SIR ANDREW: You are forgetting one thing—the Count de Tournay and your brother Armand are at Blanchard's hut waiting for the Scarlet Pimpernel. Percy will not leave without them.

MARGUERITE (*Alarmed*): You are right. Whatever the risk, he *must* save them. But he has to be told that Chauvelin is on his track. Do you think you can find Sir Percy in time to warn him? I could stay here and watch the foyer without being seen myself.

SIR ANDREW (*Considering a moment*): Very well. But I beg you, madame, do nothing rash. The place is infested with spies. If I do not find Sir Percy, and he comes here first, do not reveal yourself to him unless you are positive that you are alone.

MARGUERITE (*Grimly*): I would do nothing to jeopardize my husband's life more than I have already.

SIR ANDREW: Very well. I will return as soon as I can. (*He exits. She stands at one side of doorway, opens curtain, and watches. Knocking is heard.*)

CHAUVELIN (*Thrusting open door*): Innkeeper! Innkeeper!

INNKEEPER (*Running in*): Ah, monsieur—

CHAUVELIN: Quick, get me some soup and something to drink.

INNKEEPER: At once, *citoyen!* (INNKEEPER *exits.*)

CHAUVELIN (*To himself, as he paces*): So, Scarlet Pimpernel, at last I have you cornered. Every road is guarded! I shall soon find out where those fugitives are hidden—and then the tall stranger cannot possibly get away. With luck I shall get him alive! (*Laughs maliciously*)

MARGUERITE (*To herself*): Every road guarded! Oh, what can I do? Percy, oh Percy, where are you? (*Offstage* SIR PERCY *is heard loudly singing "God Save the King."*) There he is! And he is walking straight into a trap! (SIR PERCY *enters inn, stops singing as he sees* CHAUVELIN.)

SIR PERCY: I say, it's Monsieur—er, Chauvelin. I never thought to find you here!

CHAUVELIN (*Evilly*): My dear Sir Percy, what a pleasant surprise! (*Curtain*)

* * * * *

SCENE 5

TIME: *Later that night.*

SETTING: *A lonely cliff, with a large bush off center. Sound of pounding surf may be heard in background. Scene may be played before curtain.*

AT RISE: MARGUERITE *enters hurriedly. Her dress is torn.*

MARGUERITE: Oh, I can't go on. I am exhausted (*Pauses to catch her breath*), but somehow I must get to Blanchard's hut to warn Sir Percy and the others before Chauvelin comes. (*Footsteps and voices are heard offstage.*) Who can that be? (*She hides behind bush as* CHAUVELIN *enters with an* OLD MAN, *who carries lantern.*)

CHAUVELIN (*Angrily*): The Pimpernel may have gotten by me at the inn, but I'll make him pay for it now! (*To* OLD MAN) How much farther do we have to go?

OLD MAN (*Fearfully*): Not far, your honor, I promise you.

CHAUVELIN: Are you sure of the road?

OLD MAN (*Greedily*): As sure as I am of the presence of the gold pieces in your excellency's pocket.

FRENCH OFFICER (*Entering*): *Citoyen* Chauvelin!

CHAUVELIN (*Impatiently*): Yes. Do you have news? Have you seen the stranger?

OFFICER: No, but a few moments ago we saw two men, one old, the other young, go into a fisherman's hut just over the cliff from here. By creeping close to the hut I overheard them. There is no doubt that the old man is the Count de Tournay, and they are here to slip across the sea to England.

CHAUVELIN (*Eagerly*): Where is the hut?

OFFICER: Nearby. You can see it if you look over the cliff top.

CHAUVELIN: Good. Where are your men?

OFFICER: All about. Every path is covered.

CHAUVELIN: Here are my orders. (MARGUERITE *creeps forward to listen.*) Listen carefully. Creep up to the hut again to see if a tall Englishman has joined the other two. If he has, you will signal with a sharp whistle. The hut will be surrounded immediately, and the men inside taken prisoner. On no account is the Englishman to be hurt. I want him alive—understand?

OFFICER: I understand, *citoyen.*

CHAUVELIN: If the two men are still alone, we will wait for the arrival of the leader, and your signal will then be the hoot of an owl. No one—*no one*—is to move until the leader arrives. He is the one we *must* capture tonight!

OFFICER: Your orders shall be carried out exactly, *citoyen.*

CHAUVELIN (*To* OLD MAN, *roughly*): You will stay here. We shall need you to carry back the wounded.

OLD MAN (*Fearfully*): But I am terrified of being alone in the dark, excellency. What if I should cry out and the fugitives should hear me—?

CHAUVELIN (*Impatiently*): Very well. (*To* OFFICER, *as he thrusts* OLD MAN *toward him*) Here, take this old fool with you and make sure he keeps quiet. (OFFICER *pushes him off.* CHAUVELIN *looks out to sea, and* MARGUERITE *moves up cautiously.*)

MARGUERITE (*Urgently; to herself*): Somehow I must get to the hut to warn them. . . . (*Exits unnoticed by* CHAUVELIN)

CHAUVELIN (*Peering off*): If only the moon would stay out for a moment, I could see. That looks very much like a British schooner standing off there. It is—with all sails set! But I cannot see her landing boat. (OFFICER *reenters, leading* MAR-GUERITE, *who is gagged.*)

OFFICER: Look what I found by the cliff—this dainty little creature. I gagged her before she could make a sound. (*He sits* MARGUERITE *down and exits.*)

CHAUVELIN (*Coming over*): A woman! Imagine that... (*He bends to take a closer look.*) Dear me, Lady Blakeney, this *is* a pleasant surprise! (*Sternly*) Before I remove this handkerchief, it is only fair to tell you that the slightest shout from you to warn the fugitives, and my men will seize the Count and your dear brother and shoot them before your eyes. (*Unties gag*)

MARGUERITE (*Faintly*): I will remain quiet, monsieur.

CHAUVELIN (*Suspiciously*): What brings you to Calais, Lady Blakeney?

MARGUERITE (*Breathlessly*): I had to see for myself that Armand was safe.

CHAUVELIN (*Studying her a moment, then aside*): Her own husband, the Pimpernel, and she doesn't know! (*To* MARGUERITE) I knew you would see it my way. Believe me, your brother will be quite safe. It is the Pimpernel I am after and his time has almost run out. (*Hoot of an owl is heard.*) Ah, the signal. Very well, we must sit here and wait until the Scarlet Pimpernel arrives! (*He turns to face offstage. Both freeze in their positions. Lights may also dim to indicate the passage of time. Shortly,* CHAUVELIN *turns back to* MARGUERITE.) A whole hour and he has not come. He must arrive soon.... (*Suddenly,* SIR PERCY *is heard loudly singing "God Save the King."* CHAUVELIN *draws gun from belt and takes aim.*)

MARGUERITE (*Screaming*): Armand! Armand! For God's sake, fire! Your leader is near—he is betrayed! (*She dashes off, calling out*) Fire!

CHAUVELIN (*Calling to his men*): Stop that woman! (*To himself*) I must go into the hut. Not one of them shall escape alive. (*He runs off. Shouting and shots are heard off.* CHAUVELIN *calls from offstage.*) After them! (*He reenters with* OFFICER, *who leads* MARGUERITE. *She collapses.* CHAUVELIN *turns angrily to*

OFFICER.) You fool! You let them get away! You and your men will pay for this blunder with your lives!

OFFICER: But, sir, you ordered us not to move until the Englishman arrived.

CHAUVELIN: I ordered you to let no one escape!

OFFICER: The men in the hut had been gone some time . . .

CHAUVELIN (*In disbelief*): You mean—(*Furiously*) you *let* them go?

OFFICER (*Nervously*): You ordered us to wait, and not to move, on pain of death. We waited. The men had left long before the woman screamed.

CHAUVELIN (*Peering off, anxiously*): Which way did they go?

OFFICER: I could not tell. They descended the cliff and then vanished.

CHAUVELIN: Wait—what's that I see near the schooner?

OFFICER (*Straining to see*): Could it be the landing boat—returning?

CHAUVELIN (*Angrily*): With the fugitives aboard! (*Suddenly*) Yet, wait a minute! We heard the voice of the Scarlet Pimpernel only a few moments ago. He has contrived to send the fugitives ahead, but he himself cannot have gotten away. Was there anything left in the hut?

OFFICER (*Taking note from his pocket*): Just this note, dropped in a corner.

CHAUVELIN (*Grabbing it*): Give it to me! Fetch a lantern! (OFFICER *exits briefly and returns with lantern.* CHAUVELIN *examines note.*) Instructions to the fugitives, it appears, stamped with the seal of the Pimpernel! (CHAUVELIN *reads.*) "When you receive this, wait for two minutes and then creep out of the hut one by one. Keep to the left. A mile away a boat awaits you." (CHAUVELIN *looks up.*) Aha! (*Reading again*) "Tell my men to send the boat back to the creek at Calais, the one in a direct line from the Inn of the Chat Gris. I shall be there." (CHAUVELIN *folds note.*) This is good news. Perhaps the enigmatic Pimpernel is going to pay for this adventure after all! We must go at once.

OFFICER: What about the lady?

CHAUVELIN: We will leave her here. (*To* MARGUERITE, *slyly*) Au *revoir,* Lady Blakeney. Remember me to Sir Percy! (*Smiling cynically, he bows and exits.*)

MARGUERITE (*Tearfully, as she tries to gather her strength*): Oh, what have I done? Oh, Percy, my dear husband, where are you?

OLD MAN (*Entering very slowly*): Bless my soul, m'dear, I'm right here!

MARGUERITE (*Startled; crossing to him*): Percy, is that you? You disguised yourself as the old man! Oh, Percy, Percy!

SIR PERCY (*Embracing her*): There, there, m'dear. It's all right.

MARGUERITE: Oh, Percy, how could I have treated you so badly? If you only knew—

SIR PERCY (*Removing wig and beard; softly*): I know everything, Marguerite.

MARGUERITE: And can you forgive me?

SIR PERCY: I have nothing to forgive, dearest. Your heroism and devotion have more than atoned for that episode at the ball.

MARGUERITE: Then you knew, all the time?

SIR PERCY: All the time. Had I but known what a noble heart yours was, Marguerite, I would have trusted you as you deserved.

MARGUERITE: Is Armand safe?

SIR PERCY: Safe with the Count de Tournay and Sir Andrew aboard the yacht.

MARGUERITE: How did they get there?

SIR PERCY: I'll tell you the whole story. Back at the inn, I shook off Chauvelin by offering him a pinch of snuff—but I gave him a whiff of pepper instead!

MARGUERITE (*Amused*): So that's what sent Chauvelin into his sneezing fit! I was watching from behind the curtain!

SIR PERCY (*Chuckling*): Is that so, my dear? Well, then as you know, that's how I was able to make my escape! I went to an old friend in Calais and borrowed this disguise. Then I offered to help Chauvelin find the hut.

MARGUERITE: Percy, how clever of you!

SIR PERCY: Fortunately, I was able to creep up to the hut in the dark and leave a note for Armand and the Count. The soldiers paid no attention to the dirty old man from Calais! They were terrified of Chauvelin. I waited until I was sure my friends had escaped, and then I gave the signal!

MARGUERITE: And no one suspected you. (*Suddenly*) But, Percy, we are lost! The note you left at the hut with orders for the boat to return—Chauvelin found it! He has gone to surround the creek!

SIR PERCY (*Laughing merrily*): Have no fear. Along with the first note I sent a second, a fake one, to be left in the hut. Our friend Chauvelin will wait for hours, but no boat from the yacht will go to Calais! Armand has the real instructions.

MARGUERITE (*Relieved*): I'm so glad, Percy.

SIR PERCY: Come, dear one, I shall not be happy till we are safe in England again! (*They embrace and start off, as the curtain falls.*)

THE END

Production Notes

THE SCARLET PIMPERNEL

Characters: 12 male; 4 female; males and females for Servant and Other Customers and Guests.

Playing Time: 45 minutes.

Costumes: Appropriate late 18th-century dress. Countess de Tournay wears black in Scene 1. All wear ball clothes for Scene 2. Scene 3, Marguerite adds shawl to ball gown; gown has pocket in it. Sir Percy wears cloak. Scene 4, Marguerite and Sir Andrew wear cloaks over clothes. In Scene 5, Marguerite's dress is torn; Chauvelin has gun tucked in belt; Sir Percy is dressed as old man, with wig and beard.

Properties: Coffee cups and mugs, jugs of cider, tray, fan, punch glasses, ring, letter, valise, money for Sir Andrew, kerchief gag for Marguerite, lanterns, note for Officer.

Setting: Scene 1: English inn. Fireplace, tables, chairs complete setting. Window is in right wall; right exit leads outside, and left exit leads to other rooms. Scene 2: supper room of Lord Grenville's London home. Easy chair and other chairs are included in furnishings. Left exit leads to ballroom; right exit leads to other rooms. Scene 3: garden of Blakeneys' Richmond home. At side of stage are table and chairs; Sir Percy's ring is under table. Scene 4: inn at Calais. Stage is divided, with entrance to inn at right, and private room at left. Screen and curtained door may divide set. Scrawled on wall of inn are words, LIBERTÉ, ÉGALITÉ, FRATERNITÉ. Exits are left and right. Chair is in room at left; tables and chairs, in main room, at right. Scene 5: a lonely cliff, with bush large enough to hide Marguerite. May be played before curtain.

Lighting: Lights dim, as indicated.

Sound: Coach wheels on cobblestones, clock striking, carriage and horse hooves, sound of surf, hooting owl, gun shots.

▣▣ The Inexperienced Ghost

by *H. G. Wells*
Adapted by *Paul T. Nolan*

Characters

PINK, *a ghost*
MRS. SANDERSON, *an elderly matron*
BEATRICE WINCHELSEA, *her ward*
SIR CHARLES HEPPLEWHITE, *a suitor*
DICKIE, *another suitor*

TIME: *1890.*

SETTING: *The richly furnished drawing room of the Sanderson home in London. Room is paneled and hung with drapery. Table, center, holds small hand mirror. Up left is a hidden exit, unlit, through which Pink and Sir Charles may disappear unseen. Up right is a door leading to rest of house.*

AT RISE: *Stage is dimly lit.* PINK *enters up left. His hair, hands, and face are a ghostly white and he carries a lit candle, moving about room as if searching for something. Now and then he thumps walls and floor.*

PINK (*Almost in tears*): There must be one somewhere. A room like this is just bound to have a secret passage. (*Door up right opens halfway; light floods in.* MRS. SANDERSON, BEATRICE, SIR CHARLES, *and* DICKIE *enter, without noticing* PINK. BEATRICE

93

carries lit candelabra. During the following exchange, PINK *seeks frantically for hiding place upstage while others move about downstage.*)

DICKIE (*Crossing down center*): Really, Aunt Dorothy, I do think you are being dreadfully unfair. I do so love Beatrice.

MRS. SANDERSON: Dickie, I think you are an absolutely wonderful house guest. But as a husband for my ward, Beatrice, you are not my choice.

BEATRICE (*Tearfully*): Don't I have anything to say about whom I'll marry, Aunt Dorothy?

MRS. SANDERSON (*Coolly*): Nothing at all, my dear.

BEATRICE: But, Aunt Dorothy, Sir Charles is impossible.

SIR CHARLES (*Simpering*): Now, really, Beatrice, is that kind?

MRS. SANDERSON: Impossible men make the very best husbands. When a woman enters marriage expecting anything very much from a husband, she is bound to be disappointed. Sir Charles, you must admit, will never be a disappointment.

SIR CHARLES: Thank you, Aunt Dorothy.

MRS. SANDERSON: Sir Charles, when and *if* you become my ward's husband, I'll permit you to call me *aunt* during the yule season. Until then, remember your place.

SIR CHARLES (*Fawning*): Oh, of course, Mrs. Sanderson, I meant no familiarity.

MRS. SANDERSON: Now, you two men run along. I want to speak to Beatrice alone.

SIR CHARLES: Oh, of course. Come, Dickie.

DICKIE (*Entreatingly*): Beatrice, plead for me.

BEATRICE: Of course I will, Dickie. (DICKIE *and* SIR CHARLES *exit.* BEATRICE *places candelabra on table.* PINK *blows out his candle and flattens himself against back wall.*) If you say I am to marry Sir Charles, I suppose I shall, Aunt Dorothy. (*Sighs deeply*) It's just that Sir Charles is such a ninny.

MRS. SANDERSON: I agree, my dear. But I have more important things to do just now than discuss Sir Charles. (*Pauses*) There's a ghost in this room.

BEATRICE (*Alarmed*): A what?

MRS. SANDERSON (*Matter-of-factly*): A ghost, I'm sure of it.

BEATRICE: How do you know?

MRS. SANDERSON: I have an instinct for such things. (*Looks around, spies* PINK, *points at him accusingly*)

PINK (*Mustering up his courage*): Boo! (*Pause; louder*) Boo!

MRS. SANDERSON (*Unperturbed*): And boo to you, too. (*Turning to* BEATRICE) You see, he really is a ghost, Beatrice.

BEATRICE (*Uncertainly*): I suppose so, but he looks half scared to death.

MRS. SANDERSON: Most unfortunate for a ghost, but at least he *is* a ghost. And to think that I haven't believed in ghosts for a moment during the last five-and-twenty years.

PINK (*Desperately*): Boo-o-o!

MRS. SANDERSON (*Gesturing dismissively*): Oh, do be quiet. Are you a guest here? (*Haughtily*) I don't recall issuing you an invitation.

PINK: No, I'm not a guest, I'm a ghost.

MRS. SANDERSON: Well, that doesn't give you the run of my home.

BEATRICE (*To* PINK): What are you doing here?

PINK: I'm haunting.

MRS. SANDERSON: You haven't any business doing that.

PINK: Of course, I have. I'm a ghost.

MRS. SANDERSON: That may be, but you have no business haunting here. This is a respectable home. Many of my friends bring their children when they come to call, and some poor little mite could easily come upon you and be scared out of her wits.

BEATRICE (*Reproachingly*): I suppose you didn't think of that.

PINK (*Weakly*): No, I didn't.

MRS. SANDERSON: You should have. You have no claim on this place, have you? That is, you weren't murdered here, or anything of that sort?

PINK: No, madam. I just thought—

MRS. SANDERSON: Your coming here is a mistake. And if I were you, I'd vanish right away.

PINK (*Timidly*): Well, the fact is, madam—

BEATRICE (*Breaking in*): Aunt Dorothy is right. You should vanish.

PINK: Well, to be quite honest . . . I can't.

MRS. SANDERSON: You *can't?*

PINK: There's something I've forgotten. I've been here since midnight last evening, hiding in cupboards of the empty bedrooms and closets, and. . .

MRS. SANDERSON (*Nodding her head vigorously*): I knew it! I sensed it!

PINK (*Miserably*): It's not my fault. I've never haunted before, and I don't seem to be much good at it.

MRS. SANDERSON: Oh, come, come. Show a little courage.

PINK: I can't.

BEATRICE: Maybe, if you would just try harder.

PINK: I've tried several times, and I just can't haunt.

MRS. SANDERSON: Well, let's sit down and talk about it. (*She attempts to take* PINK'*s arm, but her hand seems to pass right through it.*) What's wrong with your arm? It's like touching a puff of smoke.

BEATRICE: He's a ghost, Aunt Dorothy, remember?

MRS. SANDERSON: Of course. (*Puzzled*) But we can see him, can't we?

BEATRICE: I think so. (*To* PINK) We do see you, don't we?

PINK: I think so. But I don't have a real body, you know.

MRS. SANDERSON: Of course. Well, I do hope news of this doesn't get out.

BEATRICE: It wouldn't do to have people think your house is haunted, Aunt Dorothy.

MRS. SANDERSON (*With a wave of her hand*): Oh, I shouldn't mind that. But what would people say if they knew we were entertaining a *no*body in our drawing room?

PINK (*Upset*): I don't think that's a very nice thing to say.

MRS. SANDERSON (*Softening*): Perhaps not. But do let's sit down. It's so uncivilized to carry on a conversation standing up. (*Sits*) It's rather tiring, too. (BEATRICE *sits.* PINK *paces about room.*)

PINK: Besides, I'm no more of a nobody than Sir Charles.

BEATRICE (*Surprised*): You know Sir Charles?

PINK: I knew him.

MRS. SANDERSON: Is Sir Charles a ghost? I should have suspected it!

PINK: I don't think he's a ghost. He's just a nobody. I should imagine he would be very pleased to be a ghost. Then it wouldn't be so bad to be a nobody.

BEATRICE (*Cheerfully*): You see, Aunt Dorothy, I really can't marry Sir Charles. Everybody knows he's a nobody. Even the spirits.

MRS. SANDERSON: We are not here to discuss your suitors, Beatrice. We are here to discuss the problem of how to make Mr. . . . . (*To* PINK) What *is* your name?

PINK: I'm called Pink. And please don't tell me I don't look in the pink.

MRS. SANDERSON: I have no intention of saying any such thing. (*Aside*) Though I must admit there is some justice in the observation. (*Abruptly*) Now enough of this chitchat. It seems to me, my dear Pink, that you have put yourself into a most awkward position.

PINK (*Woefully*): It's not the first time.

BEATRICE (*Interestedly*): Oh?

PINK: I was once the senior English master at Clayton, you know.

MRS. SANDERSON: Oh, you're *that* Pink. Sir Charles has spoken of you.

PINK: Sir Charles is really responsible for my present condition.

MRS. SANDERSON: He invited you here? (*With irritation*) Really, that man is impossible. I am almost sorry that I have selected him for your husband, Beatrice.

BEATRICE (*Hopefully*): It's not too late to change your mind, Aunt Dorothy.

MRS. SANDERSON: I *never* change my mind.

PINK: Sir Charles didn't invite me here. He . . . he really caused me to be sent . . . (*Piously*) there. (*Points upward*)

BEATRICE: How sad!

PINK (*Quickly*): I didn't really mind once I got used to it. Life was always uncomfortable for me.

BEATRICE: You poor boy.

PINK: Everyone was always mean to me—my father and mother, my teachers at school, my schoolmates. Perhaps I was too sensitive.

MRS. SANDERSON (*Dryly*): Perhaps you were.

PINK: Nobody ever really appreciated me or understood me. I never had a real friend in the world. I never succeeded in anything.

BEATRICE: Weren't you good at rugby?

MRS. SANDERSON: Or painting?

BEATRICE: Or poetry?

PINK (*Firmly*): I was never any good at anything. Even in examinations. Whenever I got into an examination room, I quickly forgot everything I studied.

BEATRICE: What you needed was a girl who understood you.

PINK: I found one. But she was exactly like me. We made each other miserable.

MRS. SANDERSON: What are things like—on the Other Side?

PINK: It's very peaceful. I like it. But the other ghosts tell me I don't really understand. That's how I came to be here.

BEATRICE: Because you didn't understand?

PINK: Yes. Whenever I met a nice group of kindred spirits, the ghosts of young men of my own age, someone would mention haunting. They seemed to think it was great fun. (*Shrugging*) I didn't really want to come back, but finally I realized that I just had to—if I wanted to take part in a conversation, you understand.

MRS. SANDERSON: Yes, I see.

BEATRICE (*Delicately*): But, how was Sir Charles responsible for you . . . for your journey to the Other Side?

PINK: He asked me to look into his petrol tank to see if we had enough to drive down to the river.

MRS. SANDERSON: I don't see how that—

PINK: He even gave me the matches.

MRS. SANDERSON (*Alarmed*): What?

PINK: Of course, he didn't do it on purpose. But he's responsible nevertheless. (*Quickly*) I don't hate him or anything like that. In fact, I don't really feel anything about Sir Charles. He's a nobody, and it's really very difficult to feel anything about a nobody.

BEATRICE (*Sympathetically*): I know just what you mean, Mr. Pink. (*Looks imploringly at* MRS. SANDERSON)

MRS. SANDERSON (*Brusquely*): Well, this is all very well, and I am very sorry for you, Pink. But our problem is how to get you back to the Other Side.

PINK (*Tearfully*): I'll never make it back. I'll just wander around through all eternity, and everyone I meet will be impatient with me.

MRS. SANDERSON: We're not impatient with you, Pink.

PINK (*Pouting*): You are, too.

MRS. SANDERSON (*Firmly*): Young man, I'm not used to being contradicted.

PINK: I'm sorry.

BEATRICE: Perhaps if you told us how you came here.

PINK: I can't. It's against the rules. Besides, I don't know anything.

MRS. SANDERSON: Well, just tell us what you are supposed to do to return.

PINK: Well . . . maybe that would be all right. (*Turns*) The spirit stands and faces west. (*Points*) That's west, isn't it?

BEATRICE (*Standing*): No, it's east.

PINK (*Turning to face the other way*): Perhaps that has been my trouble. Then he places the tips of his fingers on his eyes and says, "East is East and West is West; Now take this ghost home to rest." And then he puts his fingers in his ears and off he goes. (*He does so, but nothing happens. Mournfully*) See, it doesn't work.

MRS. SANDERSON: Well, try again. Maybe you're leaving something out.

PINK (*Taking a deep breath*): "East is East and . . ." (*Suddenly*) No, I can't do it.

MRS. SANDERSON: Why not?

PINK (*Embarrassed*): I'm shy.

BEATRICE (*Helpfully*): We'll turn our backs.

PINK: You won't peek?

MRS. SANDERSON: Certainly not.

BEATRICE: Of course not.

PINK: Well, I'm going to go in the corner so you can't see me.

MRS. SANDERSON (*Rising*): You may do as you please, but hurry.

I don't have all evening to spend on this sort of foolishness. (*Knock on door is heard.*)

PINK: Now I'll never get out of here.

MRS. SANDERSON: Be quiet. I shall take care of this. (*Calling*) Yes?

SIR CHARLES (*From off*): It is I, Mrs. Sanderson. May I come in?

MRS. SANDERSON (*Calling*): One moment, Sir Charles. (*To* PINK) Shall I have Sir Charles join us?

PINK (*With a sigh*): Let him in. Maybe when he sees me, it will frighten him to death.

BEATRICE: I don't think so. Sir Charles has no imagination.

PINK: I suppose you're right. (*Wryly*) He'll probably want me to pay for his petrol tank.

MRS. SANDERSON (*Loudly*): Sir Charles, go back and talk to Dickie. I shall want to talk to both of you presently.

SIR CHARLES (*Off; whining*): Dickie won't talk to me. He says I'm dull.

MRS. SANDERSON: Tell him not to be stupid, Sir Charles. If one didn't talk to dull people from time to time, one would never have time to think.

SIR CHARLES (*Off*): Very well.

MRS. SANDERSON (*To* BEATRICE): When you are married to Sir Charles, I may forbid him admittance to my home.

BEATRICE: That doesn't seem fair, since you are making him marry me.

MRS. SANDERSON: It will give you a sanctuary from him. (*Turning to* PINK) Now, go ahead with your disappearing.

PINK: All right, but don't look. (*He goes to shadowy corner of room.*)

MRS. SANDERSON (*Turning her back on* PINK): We are not looking.

PINK: You, too, Miss Beatrice. Look the other way.

BEATRICE (*Reluctantly*): Well, all right. (*She picks up hand mirror from table, turns her back to* PINK, *holding mirror up so she can see him behind her.*)

PINK: Well, here goes. But I just know it won't work. "East is East and West is West; Now take this ghost home to rest."

(*Sound of a loud rush of wind escaping, as if air was let out of a balloon.* PINK *exits unseen by audience.*)

BEATRICE (*Watching in mirror*): It worked!

MRS. SANDERSON: Are you sure? (*She walks left and looks about.*)

BEATRICE (*Triumphantly*): I saw it in the mirror. There he was, and there he wasn't. I'm sorry you missed it, Aunt Dorothy.

MRS. SANDERSON (*Haughtily*): I don't care for that sort of vulgar entertainment. It's too much like opera—all noise and spectacle, no understanding.

BEATRICE: But it wasn't like that at all. He didn't do it right the first time. He was supposed to put his thumbs in his ears, not his fingers.

MRS. SANDERSON (*Intrigued*): That does seem much more reasonable. (*Knock on door is heard. Calling off*) Just a moment! (*She surveys room*) You are sure he's gone, aren't you, Beatrice?

BEATRICE: Absolutely.

MRS. SANDERSON: All right, if you're sure. (*Calling off*) All right, gentlemen, you may enter. (DICKIE *and* SIR CHARLES *enter.*)

DICKIE: It just won't work, Aunt Dorothy. Try as I may, I just can't like Charles.

MRS. SANDERSON: I didn't say that you had to *like* him, Dickie. I just said that you should *talk* to him.

SIR CHARLES: I thought you said he should like me. (*To* DICKIE) I'm sorry, Dickie. Apparently, you may dislike me if you wish.

DICKIE: I don't *dislike* you, Charles. I can't stand you.

SIR CHARLES: Nobody seems able to stand me. (*Sighs*) I guess Pink was the last friend I had.

BEATRICE: It's odd that you should mention Pink. He was just here.

DICKIE: Isn't Pink the one who died?

SIR CHARLES: Yes, blew up my car doing it, too. (*Magnanimously*) But I don't hold it against him.

DICKIE: What in heaven's name was he doing here if he's dead?

BEATRICE: I should have said his *ghost* was here.

SIR CHARLES: That's odd. What would Pink's ghost be doing here? He didn't say, I suppose?

MRS. SANDERSON: As a matter of fact, he did. He was out haunting.

SIR CHARLES (*Guffawing*): Haunting? I didn't imagine that old Pink would go in for that sort of thing. Although it's hard to say what a man will do after he goes Over There.

DICKIE (*Amazed*): There really was a ghost in here? (*Reproachfully, to* BEATRICE) Why didn't you call me, Beatrice? I would like to have seen him.

BEATRICE: Aunt Dorothy thought it better if you didn't.

DICKIE: Why's that, Aunt Dorothy?

MRS. SANDERSON: Well, actually, Dickie, it had nothing to do with you. It was Sir Charles.

SIR CHARLES: I?

MRS. SANDERSON: Yes, you and Pink had been . . . er . . . associates, he told us. So naturally, we thought it might be rather unpleasant for you to see his ghost.

SIR CHARLES: Nonsense! I should have liked to see old Pink— even if he was no longer in the pink. (*Laughs*) That's a rich one, isn't it? Old Pink not in the pink anymore. (*Laughs again*)

BEATRICE (*Dryly*): He said you would say that.

SIR CHARLES (*Suddenly serious*): He did, eh? Imagine that. One must know a frightful lot when one is a ghost. Did he say anything about paying me for my motor car? He blew it up, you know.

BEATRICE: He didn't do it on purpose. In fact, he rather suggested that you were responsible.

SIR CHARLES (*Upset*): Why would he think that?

BEATRICE: He said you gave him matches to look into the petrol tank.

SIR CHARLES: Well, I did. But I thought anyone would have better sense than to do anything I suggested.

MRS. SANDERSON: I hope that you keep that in mind, Beatrice, when you and Sir Charles are married. To have a husband who is always wrong is really a blessing. It gives one a sense of certainty.

DICKIE (*Pleading*): You are not really going to let Charles marry my Beatrice, are you, Aunt Dorothy?

MRS. SANDERSON: She is not *your* Beatrice. She is *my* Beatrice. And I certainly do intend that she should marry Sir Charles.

DICKIE: But she loves me.

BEATRICE (*Going to* DICKIE *and taking his arm*): That's true, Aunt Dorothy. (*Affectionately*) I love Dickie.

MRS. SANDERSON (*Stepping between them*): I have made up my mind that you are to marry Sir Charles, and that's the end of it.

DICKIE: But why did you make up your mind that it should be Charles? Why not me?

MRS. SANDERSON (*Stumped*): I've quite forgotten the reasons now, but I'm sure they must have been good ones. I always have good reasons for what I do.

DICKIE: If Charles weren't in the picture, would you have chosen me?

MRS. SANDERSON: I suppose so. (*Kindly*) I am really quite fond of you, Dickie. (*Sighs*) But Sir Charles is in the picture.

DICKIE: Charles, I think you should bow out.

SIR CHARLES (*Stomping his foot*): Why should I? I want to marry Beatrice.

DICKIE: But she loves *me*.

BEATRICE: I really do, Sir Charles.

SIR CHARLES: That may be your opinion, Beatrice, but quite frankly, I don't see what that has to do with me. If I were to wait for a young lady to come along who preferred me to Dickie, I should never marry. And now that Pink is gone, I need a wife. I do so miss old Pink. I wish that you had told me he was here, Mrs. Sanderson.

MRS. SANDERSON: My only concern with your Mr. Pink was in getting him to return to wherever it was he came from.

SIR CHARLES: Didn't he want to go back? That doesn't sound like Pink. He always wanted to go home when he was alive.

MRS. SANDERSON: He didn't know how to go back. There's some sort of mumbo jumbo about it, and he had forgotten it.

SIR CHARLES (*Shaking his head*): That's old Pink, all right. It must be frightfully hard for him Over There without me. I was the one who explained things to him.

DICKIE (*Wryly*): Like looking into a petrol tank with a lighted match?

SIR CHARLES: I don't imagine they have petrol tanks Over There.

BEATRICE (*Boasting*): I saw him disappear.

SIR CHARLES (*Impressed*): You did! I wish I had seen that. How did he do it?

BEATRICE: It's really very simple. He walked up here. (*She goes to position from which* PINK *disappeared.*) He stood facing west. Then he put his fingers on his eyelids, and said, "East is East and West is West; Now take this ghost home to rest." Then he—

MRS. SANDERSON (*Breaking in*): That's quite enough, Beatrice.

BEATRICE (*Returning downstage*): I was just explaining how Pink disappeared.

MRS. SANDERSON: *Explaining* it is one thing. *Doing* it is quite another. How do you know that you won't suddenly be transported to the Other Side?

BEATRICE (*Simply*): Because I'm not a ghost. I am very much alive.

MRS. SANDERSON: That may be very well, but I don't feel it is altogether safe to involve oneself in this sort of thing. It's rather like going into politics. It may seem to be great fun, but then the first thing you know, you find yourself elected, and then where are you? Best not to take chances.

SIR CHARLES: I say, Mrs. Sanderson. I should like to know how to transport myself Over There. It must be great fun, haunting and all that sort of thing.

BEATRICE: There's nothing to it, Sir Charles. After Pink finished speaking, he put his thumbs in his ears and off he went.

SIR CHARLES: I'd like to try that.

MRS. SANDERSON: I shouldn't advise it.

DICKIE: Nor should I, Charles.

SIR CHARLES (*Sulking*): You just don't want me to have a good time. I'm going to try it. I face west. (*Faces right*) I put my fingers on my eyelids and I say, "East is East and West is West; Now take this ghost home to rest." I take my thumbs and put them into my ears. (*He does so.*) It didn't work.

DICKIE: Of course, it didn't work. You're not a ghost. You're a living person.

BEATRICE: Besides that, you were standing facing east, not west.

SIR CHARLES: I'll try it again.

MRS. SANDERSON: Please, Sir Charles, this is most annoying.

SIR CHARLES: I'll go up here so that I'll be out of the way. (*He goes to dark corner, up left, from which* PINK *disappeared.* MRS. SANDERSON, BEATRICE, *and* DICKIE *continue to talk with their backs to him.*)

MRS. SANDERSON: Charles is really a most impossible man.

BEATRICE (*Exasperated*): I can just see myself as his wife, while he spends years and years trying to disappear. What will I tell the children?

SIR CHARLES: "East is East and West is West; Now take this ghost home to rest." (*Sound of wind escaping and* SIR CHARLES *exits, unseen by audience, unnoticed by other actors.*)

DICKIE: I suppose I shall go on hearing that the rest of my life when I come to call.

BEATRICE: You won't be coming to call after I marry Sir Charles. (*Upset*) You'll . . . you'll . . . be marrying someone else.

DICKIE (*Staunchly*): Never! I shall remain faithful to your memory forever.

MRS. SANDERSON (*Thoughtfully*): I wonder why I did decide on Sir Charles rather than you, Dickie. You are such a nice boy. (*Calling back*) Sir Charles, why did I decide on you rather than Dickie? (*Turns*) Sir Charles! Sir Charles! (*They rush to spot where* SIR CHARLES *was last seen.*)

DICKIE (*Looking around*): He must be here someplace.

BEATRICE: He's gone!

MRS. SANDERSON: He's disappeared. I knew that he shouldn't have mixed with that spiritual business.

DICKIE (*Incredulous*): But it couldn't have worked.

BEATRICE: What do you mean, Dickie?

DICKIE: Do you remember when Charles' car blew up?

MRS. SANDERSON (*Excitedly*): That's it! That's why I picked Sir Charles. I liked his motorcar. But, of course, the car's gone now; so my reason is, too. (*Pause; decidedly*) Dickie, you may

marry Beatrice. (*Calling*) Sir Charles—wherever you are—
the engagement is off.

DICKIE (*Overwhelmed*): Why, thank you, Aunt Dorothy.

BEATRICE (*Puzzled*): I still don't understand about Sir Charles.

DICKIE: Charles was in the car when it blew up.

BEATRICE: I know he was, but Sir Charles wasn't hurt.

DICKIE: Yes, but that was the odd part. His car was blown to
bits.

MRS. SANDERSON (*Sorrowfully*): Couldn't even find so much as
a piece of tin. It was such a nice motorcar, too.

DICKIE: And yet Charles sitting behind the wheel wasn't even
touched. He must have been a ghost ever since that accident.
It's the only answer.

MRS. SANDERSON: Why didn't he say something about it? How
terribly inconsiderate. I'm no snob, but actually coming to
one's home as a guest when one is a ghost does seem to me to
be a breach of good manners.

DICKIE: He probably didn't even know he was dead. Charles has
always looked rather ghastly.

BEATRICE: Yes, Aunt Dorothy, when one is like Sir Charles, how
does one know whether he is alive or dead? (*Taking* DICKIE's
arm; beaming at him) And does it really matter?

MRS. SANDERSON: Well, I find it all highly unconventional, and
I am glad the whole business is over. Come, we will go and
make arrangements for you two to be married at once. Ghosts
in any form are an inconvenience, but inexperienced ghosts
are worse than inexperienced servants. I shall probably sell
the house just to be sure that I never have to deal with business of this nature again. (MRS. SANDERSON *exits, followed by*
DICKIE *and* BEATRICE, *walking arm-in-arm. Lights dim, and*
PINK *and* SIR CHARLES, *whose hair, face, and hands are now
ghostly white, step from shadows and come downstage.*)

PINK (*Crossly*): I'm sorry I ever let you join me. I should have
known that coming here to haunt would bring me trouble.

SIR CHARLES: It's all your fault. *You're* the one that blew us up.

PINK: But you're the one who talked me into coming back on
this haunting expedition. I should have known better after

my first experience. I had just gotten back, and along you came.

SIR CHARLES: Oh, come on, I remember the instructions Beatrice gave me. It worked for me the last time. It will work again. Now let's try. We stand facing north.

PINK: South!

SIR CHARLES: North! (*They continue to bicker. Curtain*)

THE END

Production Notes

THE INEXPERIENCED GHOST

Characters: 3 male; 2 female.

Playing Time: 30 minutes.

Costumes: Appropriate dress of the late nineteenth century. Pink's hair is powdered, and he wears heavy white makeup on his face and hands. When Sir Charles returns as a ghost, his hair is also powdered, and he wears white makeup.

Properties: Battery-operated candle and candelabra.

Setting: The drawing room of the Sanderson Home in London. It is paneled and hung with drapery and is richly furnished. Table, center, holds small hand mirror. Up left is a darkened corner with exit concealed from audience. Up right is door leading to rest of the house.

Lighting: Lights are raised and dimmed to match movement of candles and for appearance and disappearance of ghosts.

Sound: Rush of wind, as indicated in text.

▣▣Anne of Green Gables

by *Lucy M. Montgomery*
Adapted by *Jamie Turner*

Characters

MARILLA CUTHBERT
MATTHEW CUTHBERT
ANNE SHIRLEY
MRS. RACHEL LYNDE
MRS. BARRY
DIANA BARRY
PEDDLER
REVEREND ALLAN
MRS. ALLAN

SCENE 1

TIME: *Early 1900s.*

SETTING: *Kitchen in Green Gables, a farm on Prince Edward Island. Door left leads outside. Dining table and chairs are center; rocking chair, footstool, easy chair and lamp are left. Cupboard or long table across back of stage holds dishes, kitchen utensils, etc. Stove with pots on it stands right. A large window is set into back wall. Exit right leads to rest of house.*

AT RISE: MARILLA CUTHBERT *sits in rocking chair, sewing.*

MARILLA (*To herself*): Where is that brother of mine? He should be back from the station by now. (*Rises and crosses to stove*)

This stew will be cold if he doesn't come soon. (MARILLA *turns as* MATTHEW CUTHBERT *and* ANNE SHIRLEY *enter.* ANNE *carries a battered suitcase and wears a worn straw hat.* MARILLA, *puzzled, points to* ANNE.) Matthew Cuthbert, who's *that?* Where's the *boy* we sent for? (*During following conversation,* ANNE *looks back and forth at* MARILLA *and* MATTHEW.)

MATTHEW: There wasn't any boy at the train station, Marilla. Just this girl.

MARILLA (*Upset*): But there must be a mistake. We sent word to Mrs. Spencer at the orphanage to send us a *boy.*

MATTHEW (*Matter-of-factly*): Well, she didn't. She sent *her,* and I couldn't very well leave her at the station, mistake or not.

MARILLA (*Upset*): Well, this is a pretty state of affairs. How is a *girl* going to be able to help us with our work on the farm?

ANNE (*Bursting in, spiritedly*): You just don't want me! You don't want me because I'm not a boy! (*Dramatically*) I might have expected it! Nobody ever did want me! I should have known all this was too good to last. (*Tearfully*) Oh, what shall I do? (*Throws herself into chair, buries head in her arms, and sobs loudly*)

MARILLA (*Sharply*): Well, well, there's no need to cry about it.

ANNE (*Looking up*): Yes, there *is* need. You would cry, too, if you were an orphan and had come to a place you thought was going to be home and found they didn't want you because you're not a *boy.* (*Dramatically*) Oh, this is the most *tragical* thing that ever happened to me! (*More sobs*)

MATTHEW (*Gently*): Marilla, we'd best let her get a night's sleep. She's had a hard day.

MARILLA (*To* ANNE, *soothingly*): Now, now. Don't cry anymore. We're not going to turn you out of doors tonight. What's your name?

ANNE (*Wiping eyes*): Well . . . I wish my name were *Cordelia.* It's such an elegant name. But my real name is Anne—with an e on the end. A-n-n-e looks so much more distinguished than plain old A-n-n, don't you agree?

MARILLA (*Tartly*): I don't see what difference it makes. (*Shakes head, puzzled*) Come, let's have our supper, and then you can get to bed.

ANNE: Oh, I couldn't possibly eat, thank you anyway.

MARILLA (*Sternly*): And why not?

ANNE (*With a deep sigh*): Because I am in the depths of despair.
Can *you* eat when you're in the depths of despair?

MARILLA: I've never been in the depths of despair, so I can't say.

ANNE: Well, it's a very uncomfortable feeling indeed. When you
try to eat, a lump comes right up in your throat and you can't
swallow a thing, not even a chocolate caramel. (*Looks at pot
on stove*) Everything looks extremely nice, but I still cannot
eat. I hope you won't be offended.

MATTHEW: I guess she's too tired to eat, Marilla. (*Gently*) Come
on, Anne, let me show you your room. (*Exits*)

MARILLA: Good night, Anne.

ANNE (*Starting to exit*): I'm sorry, Miss Cuthbert, but I can't
bear to say *good* night when I'm sure it's the very worst night
I've ever had! (*Exits.* MARILLA *ladles stew from pot to bowl,
sets it on table.* MATTHEW *reenters, sits at table, and begins to
eat.*)

MARILLA: Well, Matthew, this is a pretty kettle of fish! The girl
will have to be sent back to the orphanage, of course.

MATTHEW (*Sighing*): Well, yes, I suppose so.

MARILLA (*Sharply*): You *suppose* so? Don't you *know* it?

MATTHEW (*Uneasily*): Well, she's a nice little thing, Marilla.

MARILLA (*Sharply*): Matthew Cuthbert! You don't mean to say
you think we ought to keep her! We need a boy to help out on
the farm. What good would she be to us?

MATTHEW (*Firmly*): *We* might be some good to *her,* Marilla.

MARILLA (*Crossing arms*): I can see as plain as plain that you
want to let her stay.

MATTHEW: It does seem kind of a pity to send her back when
she's so set on staying. (*Chuckling*) She's quite an interesting
little girl, Marilla. You should have heard her talk coming
home from the station.

MARILLA: Oh, she can talk, all right, but talk is . . .

MATTHEW (*Interrupting*): I can hire a boy to help out with the
farm, Marilla.

MARILLA: Well, I . . . (*Exasperated*) Matthew! You're a stubborn one, for sure. (*Sighs heavily*) I can fight forever, but I may as well give in now as later. All right, Matthew. She can stay.

MATTHEW (*Smiling*): You won't regret this decision, Marilla. It will be nice to have a lively little girl on the farm.

MARILLA (*Shaking head; to herself*): Marilla Cuthbert, did you ever suppose you'd see the day when you'd be adopting an orphan girl? (*Curtain*)

* * * * *

SCENE 2

TIME: *Next morning.*

SETTING: *Same.*

AT RISE: MARILLA *is setting food for breakfast on table, at which* MATTHEW *is seated.*

MARILLA (*Calling off*): Anne! Time to be up and dressed for breakfast! (ANNE *enters.*)

ANNE: Oh, aren't mornings a wonderful thing? Though my heart is still aggrieved, I'm not in the depths of despair anymore. I'm glad it's such a sunshiny morning; it's easier to bear up under afflictions when the sun is shining, isn't it?

MARILLA (*Grumpily*): Never mind all your talk now. Let's sit down to eat. (ANNE *and* MARILLA *join* MATTHEW *at table. They start to eat.* MARILLA *puts down fork and speaks to* ANNE *in businesslike tone.*) I suppose I might as well tell you that Matthew and I have decided to keep you (MATTHEW *smiles.*)—that is, if you will try to be a good little girl. (ANNE *looks disturbed.*) Why child, whatever is the matter?

ANNE (*Bewildered*): I'm crying—and trembling. I can't think why. I'm as glad as glad can be. But *glad* doesn't seem the right word at all. I was glad when I saw that wild cherry tree blooming outside my window, but this—oh, Miss Cuthbert, this is something more than glad! (*Sobs loudly, wipes eyes*)

MARILLA (*Briskly*): Well, there's no sense in getting so worked up. You are really too emotional. And you must not call me Miss Cuthbert. We'll be just Marilla and Matthew.

ANNE: Oh, Miss—I mean, Marilla—I'll try ever so hard to be good—*angelically* good.

MARILLA (*Looking out window*): Well, here comes your first opportunity. Our neighbor Mrs. Rachel Lynde is headed up the path to pay us a visit.

MATTHEW (*Standing*): I'm going to plant the rest of my turnips. (*Exits right. Sound of knock at door.* MARILLA *rises, goes to door, and lets in* MRS. RACHEL LYNDE, *who brushes past her to sit at table.*)

MARILLA (*Dryly*): Why, Rachel, you're out early this morning. (*Joins her at table*)

MRS. LYNDE (*With a groan*): I must be coming down with a terrible case of the rheumatics. I can just feel myself stiffening up something fearful! (*Sighs heavily*) Well, well, life is full of suffering. (*Turns to peer over her glasses at* ANNE) Well! And who is *this*, Marilla?

MARILLA: This is Anne Shirley, Rachel. Mrs. Spencer sent her to us from the orphanage. Anne, this is Mrs. Lynde.

MRS. LYNDE: I thought you said you were getting a boy from the orphanage. (*Stares at* ANNE *disapprovingly*) She's very homely and skinny, Marilla. And did anyone ever *see* such freckles—or hair as red as carrots?

ANNE (*Jumping to feet; angrily*): Carrots! How dare you call me homely and skinny! You are a rude, impolite woman! How would you like to be told that you are fat and clumsy? You've hurt my feelings *excruciatingly,* and I shall never forgive your unkindness! Never! (*Stamps foot and runs from stage, crying.* MARILLA *and* MRS. LYNDE *sit in stunned silence.*)

MRS. LYNDE: Well! What a temper! I don't envy you your job of bringing *that* up, Marilla!

MARILLA (*Tersely*): What Anne just did was very naughty, Rachel, but what you said was very unkind. (*Sighs*) I'll have to give her a good talking to. (*Rises*)

MRS. LYNDE (*Sharply*): Take my advice and do that "talking to" with a good-sized hickory switch. You'll have trouble with that child, mark my words! (*Rises and goes to door*) Goodbye, Marilla! I'm going to look around in your garden for a few minutes before I go, if you don't mind. I want to have a word with Matthew, too. (*Exits.* MARILLA *turns, shakes head, and sighs.*)

MARILLA (*Calling*): Anne, come here. (ANNE *enters, head down.*) Now, aren't you ashamed of the way you spoke to Mrs. Lynde?

ANNE: She had no right to say those things.

MARILLA: True, but you had no right to fly into such a fury. You must ask her forgiveness.

ANNE (*Stubbornly*): I can *never* do that, Marilla. (*Dramatically*) You can shut me up in a dark, damp dungeon inhabited by snakes and toads, but I *cannot* ask Mrs. Lynde to forgive me.

MARILLA (*Sternly*): Disrespect in a child is a terrible thing, Anne. I'm disappointed in you. (ANNE *hangs her head. Pause*) You did tell me that you would try to be good, didn't you?

ANNE (*Looking up*): Now that my temper has died down, I suppose I *am* sorry for speaking so to Mrs. Lynde.

MARILLA: And you will tell her so?

ANNE: Yes, Marilla. I will. (MARILLA *goes to door.*)

MARILLA (*Calling*): Rachel! Anne has something to say to you. Will you please come back in for a minute? (ANNE *is mouthing words to herself.*) What are you doing, Anne?

ANNE: I'm practicing what I must say to Mrs. Lynde. (MRS. LYNDE *enters, and* ANNE *approaches her, falling down on her knees and extending her hands.*) Oh, Mrs. Lynde, I am *so* extremely sorry. (*In a quivering voice*) I could never express all my sorrow, no, not if I used up a whole dictionary. You must just try to *imagine* the extent of my grief. I have been dreadfully wicked and ungrateful. Oh, Mrs. Lynde, *please, please* forgive me. (MRS. LYNDE *and* MARILLA *exchange surprised glances.*)

MRS. LYNDE (*Embarrassed*): There, there, child. Get up. Of course I forgive you. I guess I was a little too harsh.

ANNE (*Rising*): Oh, thank you, Mrs. Lynde. Your forgiveness is like a soothing ointment to my heart.

MRS. LYNDE (*Patting* ANNE *on head*): Good day, Anne. Good day, Marilla. (*Aside, to* MARILLA) She's an odd little thing, but you know, on the whole I rather like her. (*Exits. Curtain*)

* * * * *

SCENE 3

TIME: *Next day.*

SETTING: *Same.*

AT RISE: MARILLA *is sweeping floor, while* ANNE *dries dishes.*

MARILLA: Anne, the Barrys are coming over this morning. Mrs. Barry is going to return a skirt pattern she borrowed. You can get acquainted with her daughter, Diana. She's about your age.

ANNE (*Dropping dish towel*): Oh, Marilla, what if she doesn't like me?

MARILLA: Now, don't get into a fluster. I'm sure Diana will like you well enough. Just be polite and well behaved, and don't make any of your startling speeches.

ANNE: *You'd* be flustered, too, Marilla, if you were going to meet a little girl who might become your best friend. I've never had a best friend in my whole life. My nerves are absolutely *frazzled* with excitement! (*Knock at door is heard.*)

MARILLA (*Exasperated*): Calm yourself, child. (*Opens door, and* MRS. BARRY *and* DIANA *enter.*) Hello, Margaret. Hello, Diana.

MRS. BARRY: How are you, Marilla?

MARILLA: Fine. I'd like you both to meet the girl we've adopted. (*Gestures*) This is Anne Shirley.

ANNE: That's "Anne" spelled with an *e.*

DIANA: Hello, Anne, I'm Diana.

MRS. BARRY (*Taking* ANNE's *hand*): How are you, Anne?

ANNE: I am well in body although considerably troubled in spirit, thank you, ma'am. (*Aside, to* MARILLA) There wasn't anything startling in that, was there?

MARILLA: Anne, why don't you take Diana outside and show her the flower garden, while Mrs. Barry and I talk? (*Women sit.*)

ANNE: All right, Marilla. (*Girls exit through door and walk round to stage front, sit on edge of stage, and look at each other shyly.*)

MRS. BARRY (*To* MARILLA): I'm glad for the prospect of a playmate for Diana. She spends too much time straining her eyes over books. (*Women then mime conversation during following exchange.*)

ANNE (*Fervently*): Diana, do you think . . . do you think you can like me well enough to be my best friend?

DIANA (*Laughing*): Why, I guess so. I'm glad you've come to live at Green Gables. It'll be fun to have somebody to play with.

ANNE (*Seriously*): Will you swear to be my friend for ever and ever?

DIANA (*Gasping*): Why, it's wicked to swear!

ANNE: *My* kind of swearing isn't wicked. There are two kinds, you know.

DIANA: I've heard of only one kind.

ANNE: My kind just means promising solemnly.

DIANA (*Uncertainly*): Well, I guess it wouldn't hurt to do that. How do you do it?

ANNE: First, we stand up. (*Girls stand.*) Then we join hands— so. (*They join hands.*) I'll say the oath first, and you repeat after me. (*Closes eyes*) I solemnly swear to be faithful to my best friend, Diana Barry, as long as the sun and the moon shall endure. Now you say it and put my name in.

DIANA: I solemnly swear to be faithful to my best friend, Anne Shirley, as long as the sun and moon shall endure. (*Laughs*) I can tell we're going to have lots of fun together, Anne Shirley! Will you go with me to the Sunday School picnic next week? It's going to be ever so much fun! Everyone takes a picnic basket, and we eat our lunch down by the lake and go for boat rides—and then we have *ice cream* for dessert!

ANNE: Ice cream! Oh, Diana, I would be perfectly *enraptured* to go, if Marilla would let me. I'll go ask her right now. Come on. (*Girls reenter left and approach* MARILLA *and* MRS. BARRY.) Oh, Marilla! Diana has invited me to go to the Sunday School picnic with her next week! I've never been to a picnic, though I've dreamed of them often. Oh, and Marilla—think of it— they are going to serve *ice cream! Ice cream,* Marilla! And there will be boats on the lake and everyone will take a picnic basket—and, oh, dear Marilla, may I go, *please,* may I? I would consider my life a graveyard of buried hopes—I read that in a book once, doesn't it sound pathetic?—if I couldn't go to the picnic! *Please* say that I can go, Marilla.

MARILLA (*Shaking head and clicking tongue*): Anne, I've never seen the likes of you for going on and on about a thing. Now, just try to control yourself. As for the picnic, I'm not likely to refuse you when all the other children are going.

ANNE (*Throwing her arms around* MARILLA): Oh, you dear, good Marilla! You are so kind to me.

MARILLA (*Flustered*): There, there, never mind your hugging nonsense. I'll make you up a nice lunch basket when the time comes.

MRS. BARRY: Anne may ride over to the picnic with Diana if you like, and we'll bring her home, too. (*Rises*) We must be going home now, Diana. Maybe you can play together tomorrow. Thank you, Marilla, for the nice visit.

DIANA: Goodbye, Anne. (DIANA *and* MRS. BARRY *exit.*)

ANNE: Oh, Marilla, looking forward to things is half the pleasure of them, don't you think? I do hope the weather is fine next week. I don't feel that I could endure the disappointment if anything happened to prevent me from getting to the picnic. (*Curtain*)

* * * * *

SCENE 4

TIME: *Several days later.*

SETTING: *Same. There is a brooch on floor, under chair. Loose flowers and vase are on table.*

AT RISE: ANNE *sits with patchwork in lap, daydreaming.* MARILLA *enters.* ANNE *begins stitching vigorously.*

ANNE: I've been working steadily, Marilla, but it's ever so hard when the picnic is *this very afternoon.* I keep trying to imagine what it will be like.

MARILLA (*Looking around, puzzled*): Anne, have you seen my amethyst brooch? I thought I put it right here in my pin cushion, but I can't find it anywhere.

ANNE (*Nervously*): I—I saw it last night when you were at the Ladies Aid Society. It was in the pin cushion, as you said.

MARILLA (*Sternly*): Did you touch it?

ANNE (*Uncomfortably*): Yes. I pinned it on my dress for just a minute—only to see how it would look.

MARILLA (*Angrily*): You had no business touching something that didn't belong to you, Anne. Where did you put it?

ANNE: Oh, I put it right back. I didn't have it on but a minute. I'll never do it again. That's one good thing about me. I never do the same naughty thing twice.

MARILLA (*Sternly*): You did not put it back, or else it would be here. You've taken it and put it somewhere else, Anne. Tell me the truth at once. Did you lose it?

ANNE (*Upset*): Oh, but I *did* put it back, Marilla. I'm perfectly certain I put it back!

MARILLA (*Angrily, her voice rising*): If you had put it back, it would be here, Anne. I believe you are telling me a falsehood. In fact, I know you are.

ANNE: Oh, but, Marilla . . .

MARILLA (*Harshly*): Don't say another word unless you are prepared to tell me where the brooch is. Go to your room and stay there until you are ready to confess. (*Downcast,* ANNE *starts toward exit.*)

ANNE: The picnic is this afternoon, Marilla. You *will* let me out of my room for that, won't you? I *must* go to the picnic!

MARILLA: Anne Shirley, you'll go to no picnic nor anywhere else until you've confessed! Now, *go!* (ANNE *exits.*)

MATTHEW (*Entering*): Where's Anne? I wanted to show her the new geese down at the pond.

MARILLA (*Coldly*): She's in her room. The child has lost my amethyst brooch and is hiding the truth from me. She's *lied* about it, Matthew.

MATTHEW: Well, now, are you certain, Marilla? Mightn't you have forgotten where you put it?

MARILLA (*Angrily*): Matthew Cuthbert, I'll remind you that I have kept the brooch safe for over fifty years, and I'm not likely to lose track of it now.

MATTHEW: Don't be too hasty to accuse Anne. I don't think she'd lie to you. (*Exits.* MARILLA *begins to arrange flowers in vase on table as* ANNE *enters.*)

ANNE: Marilla, I'm ready to confess.

MARILLA: Well, that was mighty quick. What do you have to say, Anne?

ANNE (*Speaking quickly, as if reciting from memory*): I took the amethyst brooch, just as you said. I pinned it on my dress and then was overcome with an irresistible temptation to take it down by the Lake of Shining Waters to pretend that I was an elegant lady named Cordelia Fitzgerald. But, alas, as I was leaning over the bridge to catch its purple reflection in the water, it fell off and went down—down—down, and sank forevermore into the lake.

MARILLA (*Staring at* ANNE *in anger*): Anne, you must be the wickedest girl I ever heard of to take something that wasn't yours and to lose it and then to lie about it and now to show no sign of sorrow whatever!

ANNE (*Nervously*): Now, I've confessed, Marilla. Will you please punish me so that I can go to the picnic?

MARILLA (*Incensed*): Picnic, indeed! You'll go to no picnic! That will be your punishment, and it isn't half severe enough either for what you've done!

ANNE (*Sobbing*): Not go to the picnic! But, Marilla, that's why I confessed! Oh, Marilla, you promised! Think of the ice cream, Marilla! How can you deny me the ice cream and break my heart?

MARILLA (*Stonily*): You needn't plead, Anne. You are *not* going to the picnic, and that is final. (ANNE *flings herself into chair, sobbing and shrieking wildly.*) I believe the child is out of control. (MARILLA *walks around, wringing her hands. She suddenly catches sight of brooch under chair and picks it up with a startled cry. To herself*) What can this mean? Here's my brooch, safe and sound! And I thought it was at the bottom of the lake! (ANNE *looks up.*) Anne, child, whatever did you mean by saying you took it and lost it?

ANNE: Well, you said you'd keep me in my room until I confessed, so I thought up an interesting confession so I could go to the picnic. But then you wouldn't let me go after all, so my confession was wasted.

MARILLA (*Trying to look stern, but finally laughing*): Anne, you do beat all! But I was wrong—I see that now. I shouldn't have doubted your word when you'd never told me a lie before. Of course, you shouldn't have made up that story, but I drove you to it. So if you'll forgive me, I'll forgive you. Now, go upstairs and wash your face and get ready for the picnic.

ANNE: It isn't too late?

MARILLA: No, they'll just be getting started. You won't miss a thing—especially the ice cream. That's always last.

ANNE (*Squealing happily*): Oh, Marilla! Five minutes ago I was in the valley of woe, but now I wouldn't exchange places with an angel! (*Exits*)

* * * * *

SCENE 5

TIME: *Next day.*

SETTING: *Same, but there are various cooking implements, mixing bowl, can of flour, sugar, etc., on table.*

AT RISE: MARILLA *is dusting furniture.* ANNE *enters.*

ANNE: When I woke up just a while ago, Marilla, I spent a good ten minutes at my window just remembering yesterday's splendid picnic. I could hardly bear to face a plain old ordinary day after such a romantic experience. Words fail me to describe the ice cream, Marilla. I assure you it was *scrumptiously sublime.*

MARILLA: I'm glad you had a pleasant time, Anne, but you must come back down to earth. I've invited the new minister, Mr. Allan, and his wife for tea this afternoon.

ANNE (*Clasping hands*): Oh, Marilla! How divine! I think Mrs. Allan is perfectly lovely. I've watched her during sermons every Sunday since they've come here. She wears such pretty hats and has such *exquisite* dimples in her cheeks!

MARILLA: Humph! You'd do better listening to the sermon instead of studying hats and dimples.

ANNE: Marilla, will you let me make a cake for the Allans? I'd love to do something special for them.

MARILLA: Well, I suppose you can—if you'll be very careful to measure properly and clean up afterward.

ANNE: Oh, I will, I will—I promise! Thank you, Marilla! (ANNE *goes to table and starts to measure, stir, etc. As she works, she alternately hums and talks.*) I do hope the minister and Mrs. Allan like layer cake. Diana says she has a cousin who doesn't even like ice cream. Can you *imagine,* Marilla? (*Pause*) I wonder if Mrs. Allan will ask for a second piece of cake? She's probably a dainty eater, judging from her waistline. (*Pours batter into pan*) I eat quite a bit, and I'm awfully skinny, but Diana eats hardly anything and is ever so plump. (*Puts pan into oven*) There, now. The cake's in the oven, Marilla. Oh, I don't see how I can ever wait till this afternoon. I'm bound to *explode* before the Allans arrive.

MARILLA: Goodness, child, let's hope not. That would be quite a spectacle. Now, why don't you go outdoors and run off a little of your excitement? I'll keep a close eye on your cake and take it out when it's done.

ANNE: Thank you, Marilla! (*Exits left and comes round to stage front, and sits on edge of stage as* PEDDLER *enters right, pushing cart on floor before stage.* MARILLA *works at kitchen table during following exchange.*)

PEDDLER (*Stopping center; calling up*): Hello there, miss. Would you be interested in buying some of my wares?

ANNE (*Leaning over to look down at* PEDDLER): Uh—well—what kinds of things do you have?

PEDDLER (*Peering up at* ANNE, *shaking his head*): Well, right here in my cart, miss, I have a bottle of Mr. Roberts' Magic Hair Potion that is guaranteed to turn you into the raven-haired beauty of Prince Edward Island. (*Takes bottle from cart*) One simple application will give your hair a glossy, ebony sheen.

ANNE (*Touching her hair*): My red hair *is* a sore affliction to my soul. And I *have* always dreamed of having beautiful black hair. But I have only fifty cents. (*Fishes in pocket*)

PEDDLER: Well, now, I'll tell you what, miss. The regular price of Mr. Roberts' Magic Hair Potion is seventy-five cents, but just for today I'll give it to you for only fifty cents. (*Takes her money and gives her the bottle; exits quickly*)

ANNE: What a kind-hearted man! (*Excited*) Now I can be the dark-haired beauty I've always wanted to be! I'll go home right now and put the magic potion on before the Allans come.

With my cake and my beautiful new hair, I'm sure to impress them! (*Exits.* MARILLA *takes cake from oven, rearranges flowers in vase, straightens napkins at table.*)

MARILLA: The Allans will be here any minute. Where has Anne gone off to? (*Calls off*) Anne! Time for tea! (MATTHEW *enters.*)

MATTHEW: I didn't see Anne outside, Marilla. (*Knock on door is heard.*)

MARILLA: Oh, dear. That must be the Allans. Now, where could Anne be? (*Goes to door and opens it.* REVEREND *and* MRS. ALLAN *enter.*) Hello, Reverend Allan. Mrs. Allan. Do come in! We're so glad you could come.

MRS. ALLAN: How lovely of you to invite us for tea, Marilla.

REV. ALLAN: We've been looking forward to it. (*To* MATTHEW) Hello, Matthew.

MATTHEW (*Shaking hands with* ALLANS): Welcome to our home.

MARILLA (*Gesturing to chairs*): Please have a seat. Anne will be right here to greet you. (ANNE *enters, wearing large, floppy hat, head down.*) Here I am, Marilla.

MARILLA (*Startled*): Why, Anne, what in the world are you doing with that hat on?

ANNE: Uh—my head feels a little chilly, Marilla. Good day, Reverend and Mrs. Allan. It's an honor to have you come for tea. (*Curtsies with a flourish. Her hat falls off, and* ANNE's *hair, bright green, tumbles down.*)

MARILLA (*Stepping back; covering mouth*): Anne Shirley! What have you done to your hair?

MATTHEW (*Amused*): It looks *green!*

ANNE (*Miserably*): Oh, please don't scold me. I'm utterly wretched as it is, and scolding would only make it worse. (*Covers face with hands*) I wanted to have beautiful raven hair—the peddler promised—but . . .

MARILLA (*Sternly*): Peddler? What peddler?

MATTHEW: I did see a traveling peddler pass by this morning. . . .

MARILLA (*Sharply*): Anne, what did you buy from the peddler?

ANNE: Mr. Roberts' Magic Hair Potion. My hair was supposed to turn glossy black, but it turned . . . (*Holding up a strand*) green.

MARILLA (*Shaking head*): You get yourself into such scrapes,

Anne! Will you ever run out of ideas for mischief? (MATTHEW *chuckles quietly, then all but* ANNE *join in, laughing heartily.* ANNE *frowns.*)

REV. ALLAN (*Smiling, holding hand out to* ANNE): I don't believe we've ever been greeted in such a unique fashion, Anne. We're pleased to be here.

MRS. ALLAN (*Shaking* ANNE's *hand*): Hello, Anne. Don't be upset. I like little girls with imagination and an adventurous spirit. (ANNE *brightens.*)

MARILLA: Well, I do hope you'll pardon us. I certainly hadn't expected to greet you in such a fashion. Anne, we'll have to see what we can do with your hair after tea. But for now, let's all sit down. Everything's ready. *(All sit.)* Let me serve the cake first. Anne made this all by herself.

MRS. ALLAN: What an accomplished girl to bake such a lovely cake!

REV. ALLAN: Yellow layer cake is my favorite, Anne. (*Each takes a bite of cake and makes a face. All cough, take quick sips of tea, gasp, etc.*)

MARILLA: Anne Shirley! What did you put into that cake?

MATTHEW: Well, now, it does taste a mite peculiar.

ANNE (*Forlornly*): I put in what the recipe said. Maybe it was the baking powder!

MARILLA: Baking powder, fiddlesticks! What flavoring did you use?

ANNE: Only vanilla.

MARILLA: Go and bring me the bottle of vanilla you used. (ANNE *gets up and brings back small brown bottle from cupboard, which she hands to* MARILLA. MARILLA *looks at bottle, startled.*) Anne Shirley, you've gone and flavored our cake with Matthew's cough medicine! (ANNE *cries out in distress and runs off. All look at one another, stunned, as curtain closes.* ANNE *enters before curtain and sits, crying dejectedly.* MRS. ALLAN *enters and stands quietly while* ANNE *talks aloud to herself.*)

ANNE (*Crying*): Oh, I'm disgraced forever and forever. I shall never live this down, not if I live to be a hundred years old. I can never look the Allans in the face again. First my hair and then the cake. (*Sighs*) How can I ever tell Mrs. Allan that the cake was an innocent mistake? What if she thinks I tried to *poison* her?

MRS. ALLAN (*Stepping closer*): Oh, I doubt that she'll think that. (ANNE *looks up and rises quickly, wiping eyes.*) You mustn't cry like this, Anne. It's only a funny mistake that anybody might make.

ANNE (*Sniffing*): Oh, no, it takes me to make such a mistake, Mrs. Allan. And I so wanted to have that cake perfect for you.

MRS. ALLAN: In that case, I assure you I appreciate your kindness and thoughtfulness just as much as if it had turned out all right. Now, you mustn't cry anymore, but come down to the flower garden with me. Miss Cuthbert tells me you have a flowerbed of your own. I want to see it, for I love flowers. (*They begin walking across stage together.*)

ANNE: Well, I suppose there's one encouraging thing about making mistakes. There *must* be a limit to the number one person can make, and when I get to the end of them, then I'll be through with them for good. (*They exit.*)

THE END

Production Notes

ANNE OF GREEN GABLES

Characters: 6 female, 3 male.

Playing Time: 25 minutes.

Costumes: Turn-of-the-century attire. Women wear floor-length cotton skirts or dresses, high-necked blouses, hair on top of head. Girls wear dresses and pinafores. If actress playing Anne is not a redhead, she may wear a wig or two braids of rust-colored yarn, then green wig for hair-dyeing episode. Matthew wears overalls. Reverend Allan wears dark suit. Peddler wears baggy pants and jacket.

Properties: Fabric, needle, thread; small battered suitcase; worn straw hat; broom; dish towel; brooch; pin cushion; loose flowers and vase; feather duster; wooden peddler's cart, from which hang pots, pans, and is filled with odd items, including a bottle of hair dye; coins; cake; large, floppy hat.

Setting: Farmhouse kitchen/sitting room, with dining table and five chairs; rugs, lamp; rocking chair, footstool, and another chair stage left; small table between two chairs; cupboard or long table across back on which to set dishes, kitchen utensils, cake pans, etc. A "stove" made from a large appliance box is near cupboard. Large window is cut into back wall. Working door is left.

Lighting: No special effects.

Pride and Prejudice

by *Jane Austen*
Adapted by *Olive J. Morley*

Characters

ELIZABETH BENNET
JANE BENNET
MARY BENNET
KITTY BENNET
LYDIA BENNET
MRS. BENNET, *their mother*
MR. BENNET, *their father*
MAID
MR. BINGLEY
MR. DARCY
LADY CATHERINE DE BOURGH

SCENE 1

TIME: *Early nineteenth century.*
SETTING: *The Bennet parlor, in rural England. Sofa is up center, and chairs, small tables, etc., are placed around stage. There is a window left, and an exit right. Cabinet upstage holds small bottle.*
AT RISE: JANE *and* ELIZABETH *are sitting on sofa.* JANE *is working on embroidery, and* ELIZABETH *is sketching.* MARY *sits apart, reading.*

JANE (*Gently, leaning over* ELIZABETH's *shoulder*): That's good, Lizzie. (*Looks carefully at sketch*) Why, it's Sir William Lucas to the very life!

ELIZABETH (*Sprightly; laughing*): Yes, Jane, it's Sir William breathing the air on his estate, where he has retired to think with pleasure on his own importance!

JANE: Lizzie! Do you ever cease from laughing at people?

ELIZABETH: I hope I never ridicule what is wise and good, but follies and nonsense *do* divert me, and I laugh at them whenever I can.

MARY (*Primly*): An unbridled sense of humor can sometimes lead to great trouble. (*Shrill laughter and talking are heard offstage.*)

JANE: Lydia and Kitty are here at last! What can have kept them so long at Aunt Philips's? (KITTY *and* LYDIA *enter, excitedly.*)

LYDIA: Mary, Lizzie, Jane! You will never guess what news we have! The Devonshire regiment is stationed in Meryton!

ELIZABETH (*Bored*): What, all that excitement over a few regimentals?

LYDIA: *You* can turn up your nose if you like, Lizzie. There'll be all the more partners at the Assembly Balls for Kitty and me! We've met and spoken to half a dozen already! There was a charming Mr. Wickham.

JANE (*Roused at last*): But, Lydia, Kitty! Surely you don't mean you have spoken to these gentlemen without a proper introduction!

KITTY: Oh, Aunt Philips introduced us to Wickham.

LYDIA: He's simply delightful! So dashing! (*Rambles on*) And he introduced us to a whole group. And they're coming to the next Assembly. I've never been so complimented in my life and if it goes on like this, I do believe Kitty and I will be married before any of you three!

ELIZABETH (*With sarcasm*): That *would* be a triumph, indeed!

LYDIA (*Not noticing the sarcasm*): Yes, wouldn't it! And you can't think what Mr. Wickham said to me, Kitty. (*She whispers. They both go into loud giggles.* MRS. BENNET *enters left, in a great flurry.*)

MRS. BENNET: Girls, girls, what do you think! Netherfield Park is to be taken on a lease, by a gentleman called Mr. Bingley, with an income of five thousand pounds a year!

JANE: How very pleasant to have a new neighbor! And a rich one!

MARY: And a gentleman!

KITTY: Is he married, Mama?

MRS. BENNET: Of course not, child. What would be the point of my being so interested if he were already settled? Just think of it, girls—five thousand a year, Netherfield, and unmarried! I declare, I feel quite unnerved at the thought of it! Bring me my smelling salts, Jane. (*She sinks into chair.* JANE *quickly fetches bottle from cabinet.* ELIZABETH *fans her mother.* MARY *returns to her book.*)

JANE (*Administering the salts*): Dear Mama, how sweetly solicitous you are for our welfare!

MRS. BENNET: I've good reason to be, with five daughters, and your father required by law to leave his estate to that odious clergyman, Mr. Collins. And all of you without husbands!

ELIZABETH (*Smiling*): But, Mama, we are all still reasonably young. There is surely no need for any of us to consider spinsterhood as permanent yet!

JANE: Do not be anxious on our account, Mama.

MRS. BENNET: But it behooves me to be anxious! Go to your father, Jane, and tell him that he must call on Mr. Bingley immediately.

JANE: But would it not seem that we were pushing ourselves?

MRS. BENNET: Nonsense. It is your father's duty as a neighbor to call, and if we don't push ourselves, Lady Lucas will be there before us. I know her, the designing woman! She has her daughter Charlotte still on her hands at twenty-seven. There is not a moment to lose. Go, Jane, quickly! (*Reluctantly* JANE *exits.*)

MARY: Think of it!

LYDIA: Unmarried!

KITTY: And five thousand a year!

ELIZABETH: But Mr. Bingley might not be attracted to any of us, and in any case, he cannot marry us all!

MRS. BENNET: If he marries one of you, I'd be quite satisfied. And as to not being attractive to him, Elizabeth, you know perfectly well a sensible girl can marry whom she chooses.

ELIZABETH: But *we* might not like him.

MRS. BENNET: It would be your duty to like a man with an income that size. You are being very selfish, Lizzie. (*Pauses*) What is taking Jane so long? (*Calls*) Jane! Jane! (JANE *enters.*) Well, tell us. When is your father going to call on Mr. Bingley?

JANE: My father says that he sees no occasion for calling, but that *you* may go, and take us all.

MRS. BENNET (*In disbelief*): I—I go! But that is impossible! What reason did he give?

JANE (*Puzzled*): I think he must have been joking, really. He sent this strange message: "You can all go by yourselves if you like, and I will send him a few lines to assure him of my hearty consent to his marrying whichever of my daughters he chooses, though I must throw in a good word for my Lizzie!" (ELIZABETH *bursts out laughing.*)

MRS. BENNET (*With indignation*): Then he will not call! Oh, have you ever heard of such a thing! That Fate could have sent me such a husband as Mr. Bennet! Here I have been planning and striving to introduce you to gentlemen of prospects, and the moment one comes into the neighborhood, he will not call! Oh-h! It's too vexatious!

KITTY *and* LYDIA (*Ad lib*): Then we shan't even meet him! And any one of us might have lived at Netherfield Park! (*Etc.*)

MRS. BENNET: I will go myself and talk your father into reason. (*She rises and bustles to door, then stops midway.*) Elizabeth, you can always get round your father. Do, do, my love! Tell him *you* particularly wish to meet Mr. Bingley.

ELIZABETH: Indeed, Mama, I do not, but I will go if you wish. (ELIZABETH *exits left.* MRS. BENNET *paces back and forth, fanning herself.*)

MRS. BENNET (*Tearfully*): Always in his library reading. I declare, such selfishness passes all bounds! (*She bursts into loud sobs.* JANE, KITTY, LYDIA *and* MARY *gather round, comforting her.* ELIZABETH *appears at doorway.*)

ELIZABETH (*Coming downstage*): Indeed, there is no need for this grief, dear mother. (MR. BENNET *enters behind* ELIZABETH.)

MR. BENNET: Indeed not, Mrs. Bennet. Your concern is certainly unnecessary, since I called on Mr. Bingley yesterday.

MRS. BENNET (*Recovering; wildly excited*): You called on him?

LYDIA: Yesterday?

KITTY: Really *called,* Papa?

MARY: On Mr. Bingley? (*To each of these questions,* MR. BENNET *nods, smiling.*)

MRS. BENNET: Heaven be praised! Dear, dear Mr. Bennet! (*To girls*) Girls, whoever had such a husband! Have not I always told you how unselfish your father is!

LYDIA (*Excitedly*): Tell us, Papa, what is Mr. Bingley like?

MR. BENNET: Lydia, my dear, Mr. Bingley is a thoroughly likable, upstanding young man, and I dare say, he will be very glad to see you all. Now that this confusion seems to be sufficiently cleared up, I will return to the library. (*Exits*)

MRS. BENNET (*Overjoyed*): Dear Mr. Bennet! Always planning for your welfare! (*To* JANE) Jane, we must arrange a dinner party. (*Sound of horses' hooves is heard offstage.* BENNETS *look questioningly at one another.*)

ELIZABETH: Who could that be? (*They rush to window.*)

MRS. BENNET: It must be Mr. Bingley!

MARY (*Looking out window*): And who is that with him?

ELIZABETH: Papa said that he has a friend from Derbyshire staying with him, a very tall man with a proud bearing. Mr. Darcy, I think he is called.

MRS. BENNET: Not Mr. Darcy of Pemberley! Girls, we are made! Why, he has ten thousand a year!

MARY, KITTY, *and* LYDIA (*Craning necks eagerly to look out window; ad lib*): Ten thousand! My goodness! (*Etc.*)

ELIZABETH (*Disdainfully*): If he had double ten thousand, I should not fancy such an arrogant-looking man.

MRS. BENNET: Don't be ridiculous, Lizzie.

ELIZABETH: But, Mama, Papa told me that he was eaten up with pride of family. He had a haughty, disdainful manner, and would scarcely speak to him.

MRS. BENNET: All I can say is, Lizzie, if you give way to so much prejudice, you'll never get a husband.

KITTY (*Pushing* LYDIA *aside*): Don't push so, Lydia. Let me see.

JANE (*Restraining her*): Kitty, don't pull the curtain. They may see us watching.

MRS. BENNET: Girls, do you realize they will be here any moment? There, they are dismounting. Kitty, go instantly and do your hair. You, Mary, go and change into something prettier. Lydia, pick up those bonnets and go tidy yourself (*All scramble to pick up needlework, settle cushions, etc. Finally* MRS. BENNET, MARY, KITTY *and* LYDIA *bustle out in a flurry.*)

JANE (*Looking again through window*): Do you like the looks of him, Lizzie?

ELIZABETH: Who? Mr. Bingley? He has an easy, well-bred carriage. Yes, I think I shall like him.

JANE: And Mr. Darcy?

ELIZABETH: I wish he were not so proud.

JANE: They are being shown in. (*She turns from window.*) Lizzie, is my hair tidy? (*Smooths hair with her hands*)

ELIZABETH: Jane, you are blushing! I shall begin to think that Mama's hopes may be realized!

JANE: Lizzie! Why, I have not even met him! And *you* looked with some interest at Mr. Darcy!

ELIZABETH: He looks very intelligent, and is certainly handsome. I *might* have looked with interest at him, if he were not so proud. (*Deliberately and clearly*) I do not like proud men. (MAID *opens door wide, and enters.*)

MAID (*Announcing*): Mr. Bingley! Mr. Darcy! (ELIZABETH *and* JANE *turn toward open door, making deep curtsies, as curtain falls.*)

* * * * *

SCENE 2

TIME: *A few weeks later.*

SETTING: *An Assembly Ball. Scene may be played before curtain.*

BEFORE RISE: *Dance music is heard from off.* JANE *and* MR. BINGLEY *enter, start to cross stage, stop center.*

MR. BINGLEY: Miss Bennet, I am delighted that I have come to make Netherfield Park my home. I never expected to find such beauty here in the country!

JANE (*Embarrassed*): Why, Mr. Bingley, I dare say all our lives will be enriched by your presence here. (*They continue left and exit. After a moment,* ELIZABETH *and* MR. DARCY *enter from right talking.*)

ELIZABETH (*Archly*): It is *your* turn to say something now, Mr. Darcy. I talked about the dance, and you ought to make some kind of remark on the size of the room, or the number of couples.

DARCY: Do you talk by rule only, at balls such as this, Miss Elizabeth?

ELIZABETH: Sometimes. One must speak a little, you know. It would look odd to be entirely silent for half an hour together, and yet for the advantage of *some,* conversation ought to be so arranged that they may say as little as possible.

DARCY: Are you consulting your own feelings in the present case, or do you imagine that you are gratifying mine?

ELIZABETH: Both, for I have always seen a great similarity in the turn of our minds. We are both of an unsocial, taciturn disposition, unwilling to speak, unless we expect to say something that will amaze the whole room. But I shouldn't compare us. Perhaps you just do not enjoy the company of ladies.

DARCY: Miss Elizabeth, in the whole range of my acquaintance, I cannot boast of half a dozen ladies who are really accomplished.

ELIZABETH: Then, Mr. Darcy, you must expect a great deal in your idea of an accomplished woman.

DARCY: Yes, Miss Elizabeth, I do. A woman must have a thorough knowledge of music, singing, drawing, dancing, and all the modern languages to deserve the word "accomplished." Besides all this she must possess a certain something in her air and manner of walking, the tone of her voice, her address and expressions.

ELIZABETH (*With some amusement*): I am no longer surprised at your knowing *only* six accomplished women, Mr. Darcy. I rather wonder now at your knowing any. I must say, I don't have in my character the vanity and pride that you do.

DARCY: Ah, vanity is a weakness, indeed. But, pride—where there is real superiority of mind, pride will always be a good regulation. (*Pauses*) Miss Elizabeth, as I have pride in my intellectual powers, so too do I have pride in my feelings for you.

ELIZABETH (*Puzzled*): Your feelings for me, Mr. Darcy? Whatever do you mean?

DARCY: In vain have I struggled to keep them restrained, but I can no longer. (*Pauses*) Miss Elizabeth, you must allow me to tell you how ardently I love you.

ELIZABETH (*Astonished*): Mr. Darcy!

DARCY: You are surprised. Yes, I confess, so am I. I realize that there will be obstacles—you are inferior to me, and in a sense, such a marriage would be beneath me. I have considered your background fully, and I am aware of much that is lacking. But I love you. I wish to marry you in spite of this.

ELIZABETH: Mr. Darcy, in cases such as this the usual custom is to express gratitude for the sentiments avowed. If I could feel gratitude, I would now thank you. But I cannot. From the very beginning of my acquaintance with you, your manners impressed me with the fullest belief of your arrogance, your conceit, and your selfish disdain of the feelings of others. Mr. Darcy, you are the last man in the world whom I could ever be prevailed upon to marry.

DARCY (*Stung by her remarks*): I perfectly comprehend your feelings, madam, and have now only to be ashamed of what my own have been. Forgive me for taking up so much of your time, and accept my best wishes for your health and happiness. Good day. (ELIZABETH *watches as he exits left. Then she exits right.*)

* * * * *

SCENE 3

TIME: *Some months later.*
SETTING: *Same as Scene 1. Small bottle is on table.*

AT RISE: MRS. BENNET *is lying on sofa.* JANE *and* MARY *are fanning her.* ELIZABETH *stands by window, alternately looking out and pacing.*

ELIZABETH: If only we knew something! If Papa would only write to say where he is, if there has been any sign of them!

MRS. BENNET: It's just like your father *not* to write. He has no consideration of my nerves—none.

JANE (*Gently*): Mama dear, he was distracted with grief and anxiety, like you, when he heard of Lydia's elopement with Mr. Wickham. His silence means there is no news.

MARY: Has Mr. Wickham any prospects at all?

MRS. BENNET: You *know* Mr. Wickham has no prospects—a penniless ne'er-do-well.

ELIZABETH: And a thousand pounds deep in debt!

MRS. BENNET (*Moaning*): Oh, my poor Lydia! What is to be done?

ELIZABETH (*Hopelessly*): Nothing can be done. Unless Father discovers their whereabouts in time.

MRS. BENNET: My darling Lydia! Eloping to Gretna Green, with no family standing by and no proper clothes for her wedding! No money! Oh, my poor baby!

ELIZABETH (*Sharply*): Lydia is far from a baby, Mama, and she has been selfish and thoughtless to us all.

MARY (*Primly*): Alas, yes! But we may draw from the event this useful lesson—that one false step from a female involves her in endless ruin.

ELIZABETH: Oh, Mary, stop moralizing at such a moment! (*Paces again*) Kitty should have told us what she knew.

MRS. BENNET: Kitty may know more. (*Sitting up abruptly and calling*) Kitty! Kitty! Come here this minute! (KITTY *enters sulkily, holding a book.*)

KITTY: What is it, Mama? (*Looks around*) How you all take on so! I wish I were with Lydia. We'd be having fun.

MRS. BENNET: Kitty, put down that novel, you heartless girl! Did you know of this and say nothing?

KITTY: How could I? Lydia said I wasn't to tell.

MRS. BENNET: You wicked girl, not to tell your parents! (*Sitting up*) Oh, that I had not such a husband, such children! Here's Jane deserted in her prime by that fellow Bingley, when I had all but ordered the wines for the engagement party. And now Lydia runs off with a penniless soldier and disgraces the whole family. This will be all over the neighborhood, and it will give that stuck-up Mr. Darcy even more cause to look down his nose at us. (*She lies back.*)

ELIZABETH: Mr. Darcy—yes. (*Goes to window*) He certainly will have cause *now* to consider our family beneath contempt. And I have always suspected that he persuaded Mr. Bingley to leave here to keep him from you, Jane.

JANE: Do not let it worry you, Lizzie.

ELIZABETH (*Facing* JANE): The trouble with Mr. Darcy is that he is all arrogance and pride, and his possessions and inheritance have given him a sense of his own importance far exceeding its worth. (*Looks out window*)

MRS. BENNET: It's just as well you *don't* admire him, Lizzie, now that all this has happened.

ELIZABETH (*Suddenly excited*): Why, there is a carriage coming up the drive, with a lady in it! Who can it be? (JANE, KITTY *and* MARY *join her.*) Lady Catherine de Bourgh! Mr. Darcy's aunt! What can bring her here?

MRS. BENNET (*Starting up*): Good gracious me! Girls, girls, come and set this sofa to rights. Mary, take away those medicines. Jane, help me with my hair. Quick, a hairpin. Kitty, tidy up that corner. (*They run around doing her bidding.*) Dear me! Of all times for Lady Catherine to call! (MAID *enters.*)

MAID (*Announcing*): Lady Catherine de Bourgh. (BENNETS *spring to attention, and curtsy deeply.* MAID *exits.* LADY CATHERINE *enters, looks about haughtily.* BENNETS *make deeper curtsies. Only* ELIZABETH *appears slightly less obsequious.*)

ELIZABETH (*Going forward to greet* LADY CATHERINE): Good morning, Lady Catherine. We are pleased to see you in Hertfordshire.

LADY CATHERINE (*Distantly*): Good morning. (*Looks around disdainfully*) You have a very small park here.

MRS. BENNET: It is nothing in comparison to yours, my lady, I dare say.

LADY CATHERINE (*Looking around room scornfully*): This must be a most inconvenient sitting room for the evening, in summer; the windows are full west.

MRS. BENNET: Oh, we never sit here after dinner. Would your ladyship like some refreshment?

LADY CATHERINE: Thank you, no. Miss Bennet (*Looking at* ELIZABETH), I should like a word with you, alone.

MRS. BENNET: Oh, certainly, your ladyship. Lizzie will be charmed to entertain you. Come, girls. (*She exits with* KITTY, JANE *and* MARY.)

LADY CATHERINE: You can be at no loss, Miss Bennet, to understand the reason for my journey hither. Your own heart, your own conscience, must tell you why I come.

ELIZABETH: Indeed, you are mistaken, madam. I cannot account for the honor of seeing you here. (*They sit.*)

LADY CATHERINE (*Angrily*): Miss Bennet, a report of a most alarming nature reached me two days ago. I was told that not only was your sister Jane on the point of being advantageously married (ELIZABETH *gasps*), but that *you,* Miss Elizabeth Bennet, would, in all likelihood, be soon afterwards united to my nephew, Mr. Darcy! Though I know it must be a scandalous falsehood, I instantly resolved on setting off for this place, that I might make my sentiments known to you.

ELIZABETH (*Coyly*): If you believed it impossible to be true, I wonder you took the trouble of coming so far. What was your ladyship's purpose?

LADY CATHERINE: To insist on having the report of your engagement to Mr. Darcy universally contradicted at once!

ELIZABETH: Your coming to see me will be rather a confirmation of it, if, indeed, such a report is in existence.

LADY CATHERINE: What! Do you then pretend to be ignorant that it has been spread abroad?

ELIZABETH: I never heard that it was.

LADY CATHERINE (*Haughtily*): Miss Bennet, I insist on being satisfied. Has my nephew made you an offer of marriage?

ELIZABETH: Your ladyship has declared it to be impossible.

LADY CATHERINE: Miss Bennet, I have not been accustomed to such impudence. I am almost his nearest relation and am entitled to know all his dearest concerns.

ELIZABETH (*Tartly*): But you are *not* entitled to know mine.

LADY CATHERINE: Let me be rightly understood. This match, to which you have the presumption to aspire, can never take place. No, never. Mr. Darcy is engaged to *my daughter.* (*Rising triumphantly*) Now, what have you to say?

ELIZABETH (*Coolly, rising*): Only this: If he is so, you can have no reason to suppose he will make an offer to me. (LADY CATHERINE *is taken aback for a moment.*) But if he does, I shall certainly not be kept from accepting by knowing that his aunt wishes him to marry Miss de Bourgh. If I am his choice, why may I not accept him?

LADY CATHERINE (*Hotly*): Because honor, decorum, prudence, nay, interest, forbid it. Yes, Miss Bennet, interest. For do not expect to be noticed by his family and friends. You will be censured, slighted, despised. (*Triumphantly*) Your name will never even be mentioned by any of us!

ELIZABETH (*Sarcastically*): These are heavy misfortunes. But the wife of Mr. Darcy must have such extraordinary sources of happiness attached to her situation that she could, on the whole, have no cause to complain.

LADY CATHERINE (*Angrily*): Obstinate, head-strong girl! If you were sensible of your own good, you could not wish to quit your own sphere.

ELIZABETH: In marrying your nephew, I should not quit that sphere. He is a gentleman; I am a gentleman's daughter. So far we are equal.

LADY CATHERINE (*Leaning forward and speaking sharply*): Who was your mother? Who are your uncles and aunts?

ELIZABETH: If Mr. Darcy does not object to them, they can be of no concern to you.

LADY CATHERINE: Tell me once and for all, are you engaged to him?

ELIZABETH (*After a fractional pause*): I am not. (LADY CATHERINE *smiles, well pleased.*)

LADY CATHERINE: And will you promise me never to enter into such an engagement?

ELIZABETH: I will make no such promise!

LADY CATHERINE: You are, then, resolved to have him?

ELIZABETH: I have said no such thing. I shall act for my own happiness, without reference to you, or to any person so wholly unconnected with me.

LADY CATHERINE: Do not imagine, Miss Bennet, that your ambition will ever be gratified. (*She walks to door and turns back halfway.*) I am most seriously displeased! (*She exits.* ELIZABETH *stares after her. She sits, as* JANE *enters.*)

JANE: Lizzie, what did she want?

ELIZABETH (*Excited*): She came to tell me that Mr. Darcy wants to marry me, and she is trying to prevent it.

JANE (*Astonished*): Mr. Darcy—marry you? But is that true?

ELIZABETH: It is, oh, it is! I didn't know he still loved me, and she has been so kind as to tell me.

JANE: *Still* loves you! Lizzie, Lizzie, do explain!

ELIZABETH: Mr. Darcy offered once to marry me, and I refused him.

JANE (*Shocked*): Lizzie! But why did you refuse?

ELIZABETH: He made no secret that he despised my family. I could not accept him, knowing this. But I did not think he still cared. And now, in spite of all this disgrace with Lydia, it is obvious that he does! And Mr. Bingley loves you—intends to *marry* you!

JANE (*Overjoyed*): If only it is true!

ELIZABETH: That is the glorious, wonderful thing. It *must* be true, or she would not have come all this way to try to prevent it! (JANE *and* ELIZABETH *clasp hands ecstatically.* MRS. BENNET *enters.*)

MRS. BENNET: Upon my word, what an odd manner her ladyship has. I suppose she had nothing important to say to you, Lizzie?

ELIZABETH (*With a smile*): No—nothing important! (*Noisy sounds of excitement are heard offstage.* MARY, KITTY *and* LYDIA *enter.*)

JANE *and* ELIZABETH (*Together*): Lydia!

MRS. BENNET: Oh, my darling, darling child! I thought you were lost forever! (*She embraces* LYDIA, *who is immediately surrounded by others.*) To think of it! I have you back, and I thought you had run away with Wickham and had one of those disgraceful Gretna Green marriages with none of us there!

LYDIA: But I *am* married to Wickham, Mama! Look! (*Proudly displays her wedding ring*) But it was in a London church with Papa and Mr. Darcy there.

ALL: Mr. Darcy!

LYDIA: Oh, dear, now I've let the cat out of the bag, and Wickham said I wasn't to tell, for Darcy would be furious if Lizzie ever knew.

MRS. BENNET: Lizzie?

JANE: Knew what? Lydia, you must explain.

LYDIA: Well, we *were* going to Gretna Green, but Wickham has tons of debts and couldn't afford the coach fare. So we went to his old lodgings—to think it out—and Mr. Darcy turned up. He'd searched high and low for us, he said. He settled Wickham's debts and gave him a sum of money, to be settled on me—about a thousand pounds, I believe—and arranged the wedding and let Papa know. It was all lovely, and great fun, and only spoiled by Mr. Darcy looking so grave, the stodgy man.

ELIZABETH (*Gravely*): Lydia, do you quite realize how much you owe to Mr. Darcy?

LYDIA: Oh, don't look so serious, Lizzie! You're as bad as he is.

MRS. BENNET (*Embracing her*): My darling child! To think I've my youngest daughter married, and only sixteen, too!

LYDIA: Oh, I must show the servants my wedding ring! (*She links arms with* KITTY *and* MARY *and they exit.*)

MRS. BENNET: Heavens! I must begin a search for suitable lodgings for Lydia! (*As she exits*) So much to do! I shall go distracted! (*Exits.* JANE *and* ELIZABETH *look at each other, and laugh.*)

JANE: Mama is overjoyed. I dare say she may faint from excitement, so I'd better follow her around with smelling salts! (*They laugh.*)

ELIZABETH: Jane, before you go—tell me, why has Mr. Darcy done this for us?

JANE (*Tenderly taking* ELIZABETH's *hands*): Because he loves you, Lizzie dear. (JANE *exits.* ELIZABETH *looks wistfully out window.* MAID *enters and stands at door.*)

MAID: Miss Bennet, Mr. Darcy is here to see you. (*She exits.* DARCY *enters.*)

ELIZABETH (*Surprised; curtsying*): Why, Mr. Darcy!

DARCY: Miss Elizabeth, it is good to see you again.

ELIZABETH: It is good to see you. (*Impulsively*) Mr. Darcy, ever since I have known about your unexampled kindness to my poor sister, I have been most anxious to tell you how grateful I feel. Let me thank you again and again, in the name of my family.

DARCY: If you will thank me, let it be for yourself alone. I shall not attempt to deny that the wish of giving you happiness led me on. (*Hesitates*) Elizabeth, my—my feelings and wishes about you are unchanged. But one word from you will silence me on this subject forever.

ELIZABETH: Mr. Darcy, my feelings have undergone a change.

DARCY (*Eagerly*): Then it is true! Just as I came up the drive, I saw my aunt, Lady Catherine, and she told me what had passed between you. I knew enough of your disposition to be certain that if you had absolutely, irrevocably decided against me, you would have acknowledged it to Lady Catherine frankly and openly.

ELIZABETH (*Laughing*): Yes, you know that after abusing you so abominably to your face, I could certainly have no scruple in abusing you to all your relations.

DARCY: What did you say of me that I did not deserve? You called me proud, I believe. And so I was. But you, my dear Elizabeth, have humbled me. I hope I have proven that to you.

ELIZABETH: And I, dear Darcy, was prejudiced. But no longer. (*They gaze at each other.*)

DARCY: Then what I have hoped for all these months has come true. I shall go right in and speak to your father. The sooner I am your husband, the better! (DARCY *and* ELIZABETH *hold hands, as curtain closes.*)

THE END

Production Notes

PRIDE AND PREJUDICE

Characters: 8 female; 3 male.

Playing Time: 35 minutes.

Costumes: Early 19th century. Consult illustrated editions of *Pride and Prejudice* for costuming suggestions. Kitty, Lydia and Mrs. Bennet wear fussy, frivolous clothes. Elizabeth and Jane are more tastefully dressed. Mary's clothes are staid. In Scene 2, Jane and Elizabeth wear ball gowns, jewelry. Lydia wears wedding ring in Scene 3.

Properties: Embroidery, sketch book and pencil, books, fan.

Setting: Scenes 1 and 3: The Bennet parlor, in rural England, furnished in the style of the period. Sofa is up center, and other chairs, small tables, etc., are placed around room. Window is left, exit right. Cabinet upstage holds small bottle (smelling salts). Scene 2, Assembly Ball, may be played before curtain.

Lighting: No special effects.

Sound: Horses' hooves and dance music as indicated.

▣▣The Moonstone

by *Wilkie Collins*
Adapted by *Adele Thane*

Characters

CAPTAIN JOHN HERNCASTLE ⎫ *British*
MAJOR CHARLES HERNCASTLE ⎭ *Officers*
KUMAR, *an Indian boy*
THREE BRAHMIN PRIESTS
STATUE ⎫ *offstage voices*
SOLDIER ⎭
RACHEL VERINDER
LADY VERINDER, *her mother*
BETTEREDGE, *Lady Verinder's butler*
FRANKLIN BLAKE ⎫ *Rachel's suitors*
GODFREY ABLEWHITE ⎭
BECKY ⎫ *Godfrey's sisters*
BETH ⎭
MR. MURTHWAITE, *an explorer*
MATHEW BRUFF, *Franklin's lawyer*
GOOSEBERRY, *Bruff's office boy*
LANDLORD
SAILOR

SCENE 1

TIME: *1799.*
SETTING: *Corner of a British camp outside the walls of Serin-*

142

gapatam, India. Army tent and campfire are down right. At left there is a screen which conceals statue of Hindu Moon God. This scene is played in front of curtain.

BEFORE RISE: *Spotlight comes up on* CAPTAIN JOHN HERNCASTLE, *seated on wooden crate near campfire, deep in thought.* KUMAR, *an Indian boy, enters from right, carrying armful of wood.*

KUMAR (*As he places wood on fire*): The nights are cool, Sahib, here on the plains of Mysore.

JOHN (*Complaining*): And the days are hot enough to light their own fires. The fickle temperatures of India, Kumar, do little to endear your country to me. (MAJOR CHARLES HERNCASTLE *enters.* JOHN *rises to meet him.*) Well, Charles, what news?

CHARLES: Action at last! I've just learned from General Baird that tomorrow we attack Seringapatam. (JOHN *turns away without comment.*) Aren't you happy with my news, Cousin John?

JOHN (*Shrugging*): It's all the same to me as long as there is plenty of loot.

CHARLES (*Sharply*): Don't disgrace the family name, John. Remember, you are a soldier, not a thief.

JOHN: Soldier or thief, I'd like to get my hands on some of those Indian diamonds.

KUMAR (*Slyly*): Perhaps Sahib would like—the Moonstone?

JOHN (*Eagerly*): What is the Moonstone?

KUMAR: For thousands of years, the Hindus have worshiped the Moon God. In his forehead, there is set a priceless yellow diamond called the Moonstone.

JOHN (*Musing*): The statue holds a yellow diamond, you say? (*Excitedly*) That would be worth taking!

KUMAR: But not possible, Sahib. Three Priests guard the stone day and night. And it is prophesied that any mortal who touches the sacred stone is doomed to die a horrible death. The Moonstone bears the death curse of the great god Brahma.

CHARLES (*Laughing*): That is the most fantastic tale I've heard since I came to India.

KUMAR: My tale is true! (*Turning to* JOHN) You believe it, don't you, Sahib?

JOHN: Yes, I do.

CHARLES (*Quickly*): Kumar, we won't need your services any more tonight. (*Gives him a coin*) You may go.

KUMAR: Thank you, Sahib. (*Salaams*) Brahma protect thee. (*Exits*)

CHARLES: Come, John, we both need a good night's sleep if we are to be ready for duty tomorrow. We attack at dawn. (*Exits into tent.*)

JOHN (*With a sneer*): Charles may laugh at the story of the Moonstone, but tomorrow when we take Seringapatam, the Moonstone will be mine (*Clenching his fist*)—curse or no curse! (*Blackout. JOHN exits. Sound of temple bells is heard. Spotlight comes up left. Screen has been removed to reveal statue of Moon God, which has large sparkling yellow jewel in its forehead. THREE BRAHMAN PRIESTS are prostrate before statue.*)

PRIESTS (*Chanting*): All praise and glory to Brahma, the Creator, and the Preserver, and the Destroyer of life. Thou art Master of the Universe, the Supreme Being. (*Sound of cannon fire offstage. PRIESTS rise in alarm.*)

1ST PRIEST: The British are attacking the city! Go guard the door to the temple. I will stay here and guard the Moon God. (*2ND and 3RD PRIESTS exit. 1ST PRIEST draws dagger and stands by statue, ready for action. Shouts and sound of scuffle are heard from off. Two pistol shots ring out, then silence. JOHN enters, pistol in his hand.*) Stop! You must not defile the shrine of the great Moon God!

JOHN (*Pointing his pistol*): Get out of my way or I'll kill you! (*1ST PRIEST rushes at JOHN, who fires his pistol. PRIEST falls with groan, and lies still. JOHN snatches up dagger.*) Now— the Moonstone! (*He hurries to statue and pries jewel from its forehead. He holds it up to catch light, gloating.*) Ah, what a beauty! You're mine, all mine! (*He tosses away dagger and starts to leave, but stops at sound of voice coming from statue.*)

STATUE (*Deep and resonant*): Infidel! Listen to me! The Moon God speaks! (*JOHN trembles, backs away.*) Any disbeliever who touches the Moonstone shall be cursed. He shall live in misery and torture till the day he dies. And so shall all of his house and name who receive the Moonstone after him. Three of my Priests shall search constantly day and night, until the Moonstone is restored to me. Should they die, three others will take their place, to the end of the generations of men. Take heed! Beware! The Moon God has spoken!

JOHN (*With bravado*): Bah! It's a trick! A graven image cannot speak!

CHARLES (*Entering, suddenly*): John! What is the meaning of this? (*He goes and kneels beside dead* PRIEST.) He's dead. Did you kill him and the other two priests outside?

JOHN: What does it matter? I have the Moonstone.

CHARLES (*Angrily*): You are a murderer and a thief! You have disgraced our name and your uniform. I shall have you placed under arrest and held for court-martial.

JOHN: Nothing you can do will make me give up the Moonstone! (*In a frenzy*) I defy the vengeance of a heathen god! (*Runs out*)

CHARLES (*Calling out*): Guards! Arrest Captain John Herncastle!

SOLDIER (*Offstage*): Yes, sir!

CHARLES (*Worried*): I'm beginning to believe that there's some truth to the story that the Moonstone is cursed. John is behaving like a man possessed—he has gone mad with greed! I'm afraid if he keeps the diamond, he will live to regret it. And if he gives it away, others will live to regret possessing it. Poor John! (*He exits. Blackout. A brief musical interlude may be played to note passage of time.*)

* * * * *

SCENE 2

TIME: *June, one year later.*

SETTING: *Drawing room of Lady Verinder's elegant town house in London. Sofa and two armchairs sit downstage. Exit right is a set of French doors; next to doors is a tall cabinet. Exit in rear wall is an archway hung with draperies. Bookcases stand along wall near entry. Small writing desk and chair stand left. Door left leads to dining room.*

AT RISE: RACHEL VERINDER *stands at door left, smiling.*

RACHEL: Mother, do stop fussing with the dinner table. It's perfect.

LADY VERINDER (*Entering left and embracing* RACHEL): I want everything to be perfect for my daughter's eighteenth birthday. (*Going to desk*) I'll just check the guest list again.

RACHEL (*Laughing indulgently*): There's no need to do that, Mother. There are only five dinner guests. (*Counting them on her fingers*) Franklin—Godfrey—Becky—Beth—and Mr. Murthwaite.

LADY VERINDER (*Consulting list*): Five for dinner, Rachel. But many more are coming later to the reception.

RACHEL: I'm glad your old friend Mr. Murthwaite could come. He'll have some interesting stories to tell about his travels in the East.

LADY VERINDER (*Hesitantly*): My dear, speaking of Franklin and Godfrey—I'm sure they will both expect an answer to their proposals tonight. (*Pauses*) Have you decided yet which one you will accept?

RACHEL (*Smiling*): Yes, I have. I know now it is Franklin I love best. When he asks me to marry him, I will answer "yes" with all my heart.

LADY VERINDER (*Embracing her*): Darling, I hoped it would be Franklin. He was my choice from the very beginning. Bless you both! (BETTEREDGE *enters center.*)

BETTEREDGE: Mr. Franklin Blake has arrived, my lady. (FRANKLIN BLAKE *enters, carrying bouquet of roses.*)

FRANKLIN: Good evening, Lady Verinder. (*Handing roses to* RACHEL) Happy birthday, Rachel!

RACHEL: Oh, Franklin, they're lovely! Thank you. (*Hands roses to butler*) Betteredge, please put these in water and set them on that table. (*Indicates table up right.* BETTEREDGE *exits.*)

FRANKLIN: Lady Verinder, I have news that will surprise you. Your brother, John, has come back from India.

LADY VERINDER (*Surprised*): John—here in England! When did he return?

FRANKLIN: About a month ago, and I hear he's being snubbed

by everyone. It looks as if he'll be ostracized from English society just as he was drummed out of His Majesty's Army.

RACHEL (*Alarmed*): Why? What did he do?

LADY VERINDER (*Severely*): Your Uncle John has disgraced the family name. He is a thief and a murderer.

RACHEL (*Reviled*): Oh, how dreadful!

FRANKLIN: John may try to see you, Lady Verinder.

LADY VERINDER: I assure you he'll find no welcome here. Come, Franklin, let's sit out on the terrace until the others arrive. (LADY VERINDER, RACHEL *and* FRANKLIN *exit right through French doors.* BETTEREDGE *enters left, carrying vase of roses, which he sets on table up right. Front door bell rings, and he exits through center arch. After pause, he reenters with* JOHN HERNCASTLE.)

JOHN: Tell Lady Verinder that her brother, John Herncastle, has called to wish his niece a happy birthday.

BETTEREDGE: Very good, sir. (*He exits right to terrace.* JOHN *takes jewelry box from his pocket, opens it and holds up the Moonstone, now set as brooch.*)

JOHN: If my sister closes the door of her house against me, I will repay her with this birthday gift to Rachel. (*Laughs wickedly*) Then *she* will have to bear the curse of the Moonstone. (*He replaces jewel in box, as* BETTEREDGE *returns from terrace.*)

BETTEREDGE: My lady and Miss Rachel are engaged, sir, and beg to be excused from seeing you.

JOHN (*Bitterly*): So—my sister washes her hands of me. Well, it's no more than I expected. (*Taking envelope from his breast pocket*) Betteredge, please give this note to Miss Rachel, along with this birthday present (*Hands him box and envelope*), and tell her I wish her many happy returns of the day. (*With sardonic humor*) I'll show myself out, Betteredge, and save you the trouble of slamming the door in my face. (*He exits.*)

LADY VERINDER (*Peeking into room*): Has he gone?

BETTEREDGE: Yes, my lady—and he left this gift for Miss Rachel.

RACHEL (*Hurrying in, followed by* FRANKLIN): Oh, let me see it! (BETTEREDGE *gives her jewelry box and note, then exits.*) I wonder what it is. (*She opens box and gasps in amazement.*) Oh! How gorgeous!

FRANKLIN (*Looking at brooch*): Great guns! That *is* a diamond!

LADY VERINDER (*Frowning*): Read the note, Rachel.

RACHEL (*Drawing sheet of paper from envelope and reading*): "To my dear niece Rachel—may the Moonstone bring you the same luck it brought me. Uncle John."

LADY VERINDER (*Upset*): He means bad luck! Rachel, you must send it back at once.

RACHEL (*Pleadingly*): Oh no, Mother, please—let me keep it just for tonight. It's so lovely. Nothing bad can happen in one night.

LADY VERINDER: Very well, (*Firmly*) but tomorrow it goes back.

RACHEL (*Examining stone*): It's a brooch! I'll pin it to my dress now.

LADY VERINDER (*Fearfully*): I wish you wouldn't, Rachel.

RACHEL: But it's so beautiful! And it *is* a birthday present, you know. *Please?*

LADY VERINDER (*Relenting*): All right, dear. Here, I'll pin it on for you. (*She does so. Loud knock is heard.*) That's probably Godfrey with his sisters, and Mr. Murthwaite. (BECKY *and* BETH ABLEWHITE *rush in center, followed more sedately by their brother* GODFREY *and* MR. MURTHWAITE.)

LADY VERINDER: How very nice to see you all!

BECKY *and* BETH (*Ad lib*): Hello, how are you! Happy birthday, Rachel! (*Etc.*)

RACHEL: Hello! Thank you so much.

BECKY (*Spying brooch*): Your brooch—it's exquisite!

BETH: I've never seen anything like it.

GODFREY (*Approaching* RACHEL, *kissing her lightly on cheek; looking at brooch, dryly*): Carbon, my dears, mere carbon.

BECKY: It's so big!

BETH: Who gave it to you, Rachel?

RACHEL: My Uncle John.

GODFREY (*Whistling*): That must be the famous Moonstone Herncastle brought back from India.

MURTHWAITE (*Gravely*): Rachel, my dear, if ever you go to India, don't take your uncle's birthday gift with you. I know a certain temple where your life wouldn't be worth a farthing if you went there with that diamond.

BECKY: How exciting! (*Sound of drum is heard off right.*)

LADY VERINDER (*Turning toward terrace*): What's that? It sounds like a drum. (BETTEREDGE *enters.*)

BETTEREDGE: There are three Indian jugglers on the terrace, my lady, and they beg permission to perform for the guests.

BECKY: Oh, *do* let them entertain us, Lady Verinder!

BETH: We've never seen Indian jugglers.

LADY VERINDER: Ask them to come in, Betteredge. They can perform in the archway. (BETTEREDGE *exits. Ladies sit on sofa and chairs, and men stand left.* BETTEREDGE *reenters with the* THREE PRIESTS, *disguised as jugglers.* 1ST PRIEST *carries small hand drum; the others carry cloth bags holding their Indian clubs and balls.* PRIESTS *salaam, then start their juggling act. They handle clubs and balls clumsily, dropping them frequently.*)

GODFREY: I say, Lady Verinder, these fellows are not very skillful jugglers.

MURTHWAITE: Lady Verinder, I've seen good Indian jugglers perform, and I can tell these men are impostors. I advise you to send them away at once.

LADY VERINDER: Certainly. (*She nods to* BETTEREDGE, *and he ushers jugglers out.*) Mr. Murthwaite, have you ever met these Indians before?

MURTHWAITE: Never!

BECKY: Perhaps they came to steal Rachel's diamond!

GODFREY: Nonsense, Becky! How would they know Rachel has a diamond?

LADY VERINDER (*Nervously*): I need a breath of fresh air. Shall we go out on the terrace? (*Ladies exit.* GODFREY *and* FRANKLIN *are about to follow, when* MURTHWAITE *signals them to wait.*)

MURTHWAITE (*Lowering his voice, as he approaches them*): Unless I'm utterly mistaken, those Indians are high-caste Brahmans disguised as jugglers, and your sister, Godfrey, unwittingly hit on the truth when she said they might have come here to steal the Moonstone. I believe they are three Moon Priests who have taken a holy vow to restore the Moonstone to the Hindu Moon God. If that is true, they will do anything to regain possession of the sacred stone.

FRANKLIN: Then Rachel is in danger! Suppose they come back?

MURTHWAITE: They won't risk coming back tonight.

FRANKLIN: Tomorrow Rachel is sending the Moonstone back to her uncle. Lady Verinder insists on it.

MURTHWAITE: Good! It was Herncastle who stole the Moonstone—let him deal with the Moon Priests. (*Dinner bell rings off left, and ladies reenter through French doors.*)

BETTEREDGE (*Entering left*): Dinner is served, my lady. (*They all exit left. Blackout. There is a brief musical interlude to indicate the passage of time, then lights come up on drawing room, five hours later. Clock strikes twelve.* BECKY *and* BETH *are seated on sofa, in animated conversation with* MURTHWAITE, *who sits in armchair.* FRANKLIN *and* GODFREY *ad lib conversation, left, as* LADY VERINDER *and* RACHEL *enter left.*)

RACHEL (*Walking over to French window*): It was a lovely party, Mother! Thank you.

LADY VERINDER (*Walking left*): It *was* nice! The other guests have gone. (*Sitting wearily in armchair left center*) I'm ready for bed. How about the rest of you?

FRANKLIN: I haven't been sleeping well lately. . . .

GODFREY (*Rising*): What you need is a touch of brandy, Franklin. Then you'll sleep like a baby.

FRANKLIN: I'd be happy to join you in a brandy, Godfrey. (*Turning to smile at* RACHEL) But I'm afraid brandy won't cure what ails me. (RACHEL *looks away shyly.*)

LADY VERINDER (*To* RACHEL): Where will you put your diamond tonight, Rachel?

RACHEL (*Walking to cabinet beside French doors*): In this cabinet, Mother.

LADY VERINDER (*Rising*): But that cabinet has no lock to it. You'd better put the diamond in my safe.

RACHEL (*Laughing*) Good heavens, why, Mother? Are there thieves in the house? It will be perfectly safe here. (*She puts Moonstone into its box, then places box in cabinet and closes door.*) There! Now I'm off to bed. (*She pauses, slips her arm affectionately through* FRANKLIN'S, *smiling up at him warmly.*) Good night, Franklin. Pleasant dreams. (*She exits center,* BECKY *and* BETH *follow.*)

BECKY *and* BETH (*Ad lib*): Good night. A lovely party. Thank you and Happy Birthday! (*Etc.* LADY VERINDER *follows them off.*)

GODFREY (*Stoically*): Congratulations, Franklin! It looks as if you are to be the lucky man.

FRANKLIN (*Happily*): Perhaps so! We'll know tomorrow when Rachel gives us her answer.

GODFREY (*Grimly*): Yes, just so. (*Brightening*) Now how about that brandy? (*They exit left. Blackout. Short musical interlude, then clock strikes three. Lights up dimly as* RACHEL *reenters, wearing dressing gown and carrying lighted candle in candle holder.*)

RACHEL (*Walking over to bookcase*): If only I could fall asleep! I'll read a dull book. That should help. (*She takes book from bookcase.*) Reverend Budge's *Sermons.* That's just the thing. (*Creaking of floorboards is heard off.*) Someone's coming! (*Startled, she blows out candle and hides behind draperies.* FRANKLIN *enters, wearing bathrobe and carrying lighted candle in candlestick. He walks slowly to cabinet near French window, staring vacantly ahead as if in trance.* RACHEL *watches, as he sets down candle, opens cabinet, takes out Moonstone brooch from drawer. Then he closes cabinet, picks up candle mechanically and exits.* RACHEL *comes out from hiding and paces about the room; upset*) I can't believe it! Franklin has taken the Moonstone! Is the man I love a thief? He can't be! (*With a sob, she sinks onto sofa and covers her face with her hands. Blackout. Musical interlude. Lights come up on drawing room, next morning.* LADY VERINDER, GODFREY *and* FRANKLIN *enter left from dining room.*)

LADY VERINDER: Rachel is sleeping late this morning. (*RACHEL enters from hall.*) Ah, there you are! Rachel, I want you to send the Moonstone back to your uncle as soon as possible. I won't rest easy until it is out of this house. (*She crosses to cabinet, followed by* GODFREY.)

RACHEL (*Speaking to* FRANKLIN *earnestly*): Franklin, do you have anything to say to me about the Moonstone?

FRANKLIN: Why, no, what should I say? (LADY VERINDER *opens cabinet and stands gasping.*)

LADY VERINDER (*Shocked*): The Moonstone! It's gone!

GODFREY (*Walking to cabinet*): It may be lost amongst some clutter in there. (*They search through cabinet carefully.*)

RACHEL: *Now* do you have anything to say, Franklin?

FRANKLIN: We must call the police at once! And their first job is to catch those Indian jugglers. They have stolen the Moonstone.

RACHEL (*Coldly*): The Indians didn't steal the Moonstone, Franklin, as you well know. *You stole it! You* are the thief!

LADY VERINDER (*Shocked*): Rachel! What are you saying?

RACHEL: I saw Franklin take the Moonstone with my own eyes!

GODFREY: What!

RACHEL: After I went to bed last night, I couldn't sleep, so I came down here to get a book. I heard someone in the hall and Franklin came into the room. He didn't see me. He walked straight to the cabinet and took out the Moonstone—then he left. (*To* FRANKLIN, *angrily*) Where is it, Franklin? What have you done with it? (FRANKLIN *is silent, staring at* RACHEL *in bewilderment.*)

LADY VERINDER: Well, Franklin, have you any answer?

FRANKLIN (*Confused*): It—there must be some mistake.

RACHEL (*Miserably*): There is *no* mistake! I *saw* you take it!

FRANKLIN: But I don't understand. As far as I know, I did nothing but sleep last night. (*To* GODFREY) You believe me, don't you, Godfrey?

GODFREY (*Coldly*): Why did you do it, Franklin?

RACHEL (*In tears*): I loved and honored you, Franklin, but now I know you for what you are—a liar and a thief! (*She runs out, crying.*)

LADY VERINDER (*Stonily*): Franklin, since I deplore scandal, I shall not notify the police, at present. I will give you some time to consider your actions, and to return the Moonstone. Now leave!

FRANKLIN (*Stiffly*): I shall do my best to recover the Moonstone,

Lady Verinder—to prove my innocence! (*Bows and exits. Curtain*)

* * * * *

SCENE 3

TIME: *One week later.*

SETTING: *Office of Mathew Bruff, a solicitor. There are a desk and two chairs at left, and a coatrack at right holding Bruff's hat and coat. This scene is played in front of curtain.*

BEFORE RISE: MATHEW BRUFF *is seated at desk, reading newspaper.* FRANKLIN BLAKE *hurries in from right.*

FRANKLIN: Good day, Mr. Bruff. (*Walks to desk and shakes hands with* BRUFF) I came as soon as I received your message.

BRUFF: I'm glad you did. I have some urgent—quite unpleasant—news to tell you. Will you sit down?

FRANKLIN (*Sitting*): What is it? What has happened? Is there any trace of the Moonstone?

BRUFF: Yes, there is. (*Hesitating*) But before we go into that, I must tell you that John Herncastle was found stabbed to death in his flat this morning.

FRANKLIN (*Shocked*): What? How did it happen?

BRUFF: The police aren't sure yet, but another tenant in the house said he saw three Indians leave John's flat about the time he was murdered.

FRANKLIN: Murdered! What a horrible end! But not wholly unexpected—or even undeserved. I honestly believe, Mr. Bruff, that John Herncastle was one of the greatest blackguards that ever lived. (*Pause*) Do you think that the Moonstone is behind his murder?

BRUFF (*Nodding*): Yes, I do. (*Handing* FRANKLIN *newspaper*) Read the item on the front page of the *Daily Chronicle* about the robbery of a diamond merchant.

FRANKLIN (*Glancing briefly at paper, then reading*): "Police are still mystified by the strange attack last Thursday on Mr. Septimus Luker, diamond dealer, by three Indians. Though

Mr. Luker was carrying valuable gems, the only item stolen was a document relating to an extremely valuable diamond deposited by Mr. Luker in the National Bank."

BRUFF: I'm convinced that the valuable diamond referred to there is the Moonstone—and that the three Indians are the ones you told me came to Rachel's party, posing as jugglers.

FRANKLIN (*Thoughtfully*): And the same three men who killed John Herncastle. (*Pause*) What shall we do now?

BRUFF: Gooseberry, my office boy, has been keeping an eye on Luker, and he found out that Luker is going to the bank today to take out the diamond. So I've sent Gooseberry to the bank to wait and watch. He will see who it is that receives the diamond from Luker, and will follow that person and report back here.

FRANKLIN (*Surprised*): You trust a mere office boy with that responsibility?

BRUFF (*Dryly*): I only wish my clerks were as dependable as Gooseberry.

GOOSEBERRY (*From offstage*): Mr. Bruff! Mr. Bruff!

BRUFF (*Rising*): It's Gooseberry. (*He walks toward door, meeting* GOOSEBERRY *as he rushed in, breathless.*) What happened, lad? Tell me!

GOOSEBERRY (*Panting*): Well, sir, in the bank I noticed a sailor with a black beard who looked as if he were disguised—so I watched him. And sure enough, I saw Mr. Luker pass him a small box. When the sailor left the bank, I followed him. After a while, I became aware that I wasn't the only one following the sailor. I noticed a man dressed as a mechanic walking on the other side of the street. He looked like an Indian.

BRUFF (*To* FRANKLIN): One of the Indian jugglers, no doubt. Oh, Gooseberry, this (*Gesturing to* FRANKLIN) is Mr. Franklin Blake, who has an interest in this affair. (FRANKLIN *and* GOOSEBERRY *nod to each other.*) Do go on, now, Gooseberry.

GOOSEBERRY: In Lower Thames Street, the sailor went into a lodging house called The Wheel of Fortune and asked for a room. I heard the landlord say there was only one room available—Number 10 on the top floor, and he gave the sailor a key. As soon as the mechanic heard what the landlord said, he left, and I followed him out into the street. There I saw two men join him. They looked like Indians, too. They were talking and pointing up at the top of the house to a window where a light was shining. Then I came straight here to tell you what I had discovered.

BRUFF: Good work, Gooseberry! (*Patting his shoulder*) I am very pleased with you. (*Taking his hat from coatrack*) Come, Franklin, we must get to that lodging house without delay. A man's life is in danger! (GOOSEBERRY *dashes off right, followed by* BRUFF *and* FRANKLIN. *Curtain*)

* * * * *

SCENE 4

TIME: *Half an hour later.*

SETTING: *The Wheel of Fortune Lodging House, Room Number 10. Room is scantily furnished with iron bed set against right wall, night table with lighted candle on it, chair, and bureau against left wall. Box containing Moonstone is on bureau. Next to bureau there is door leading to hall. In rear wall there is window opening onto roof.*

AT RISE: SAILOR *is lying on bed, fully clothed, snoring loudly. Beside him is a pillow.* 1ST PRIEST, *dressed as mechanic, appears outside window, which he opens without a sound. He looks around room, then turns head and makes beckoning motion over his shoulder, then enters room noiselessly, followed immediately by other* TWO PRIESTS.

1ST PRIEST (*Whispering*): He's asleep. Work quietly, brothers. I'll look for the Moonstone. (*Searches room.* 2ND *and* 3RD PRIESTS *go over to bed.*)

2ND PRIEST (*Whispering*): You hold him down while I smother him with the pillow. (*He picks up pillow beside* SAILOR *but is interrupted by* 1ST PRIEST, *who stands at bureau and holds box with Moonstone.*)

1ST PRIEST (*Whispering excitedly*): At last, brothers, we have come to the end of our quest. Here is the sacred Moonstone! And, now (*Pointing to* SAILOR), death to him who would keep it from us! (*He starts toward bed, when excited voices are heard off left, followed by loud pounding on hall door.*)

BRUFF (*From outside door*): Open up, open up! (PRIESTS *pause over sleeping* SAILOR.) Landlord, your passkey! (SAILOR *awakens with a start, springs up, catching* PRIESTS *by surprise and tries to fight them off.* 1ST PRIEST *pulls out dagger and stabs* SAILOR, *who falls to floor.* THREE PRIESTS *climb out through window. Hall door bursts open, and* FRANKLIN, BRUFF, GOOSEBERRY, *and* LANDLORD *rush in. They look around quickly.* SAILOR *groans.*)

FRANKLIN: We're too late! They've killed him! (BRUFF *goes to* SAILOR *and examines him briefly.*)

BRUFF: No, they haven't. He's still alive. Landlord, fetch the nearest doctor and send for the police. (LANDLORD *exits. As* FRANKLIN *and* BRUFF *help* SAILOR *onto bed,* SAILOR's *beard becomes disarranged.*)

GOOSEBERRY: Look, sirs! His beard is all sideways. I *knew* it was false! He's wearing a wig, too! (BRUFF *bends over* SAILOR *and removes beard and wig, then he steps back from bed.*)

FRANKLIN (*Crying out in astonishment*): Why, it's Godfrey! Godfrey Ablewhite! (GODFREY *moans and opens his eyes.*)

GODFREY (*Weakly, gasping for breath*): Franklin—is that you?

FRANKLIN: Yes, Godfrey.

GODFREY: Come closer. (FRANKLIN *sits beside him on bed.*) Franklin—that night—the night of Rachel's birthday—I gave you a large snifter of brandy—remember?

FRANKLIN: Yes, I remember.

GODFREY: After you became drowsy, I put you in an hypnotic trance. I compelled you to steal the Moonstone—and bring it to me. The next morning—you had no recollection—of what you had done.

FRANKLIN (*Bewildered*): What made you do it, Godfrey?

GODFREY: I was deep in debt. The Moonstone—would save me from ruin. And I was jealous of you—Rachel loved you. (*His voice trails off to whisper.*) Forgive me, Franklin. (*He sinks back with sigh, and closes his eyes.*)

FRANKLIN (*Rising*): He's dead. Poor fellow! If he had only come to me—

GOOSEBERRY (*At bureau*): Look here! It's the box I saw at the bank, but it's empty.

FRANKLIN: Thank heaven the Indians have their Moonstone back again. They will restore it to the Moon God—and we will be free of its evil curse forever.

BRUFF (*Patting* FRANKLIN's *shoulder*): Franklin, I know someone who will be deliriously happy when she hears that you are innocent.

FRANKLIN: Rachel!

BRUFF: Yes. Hadn't you better go and tell her? I'll stay here and wait for the police.

FRANKLIN: Thank you, Mr. Bruff. I must go to her at once. (*Happily*) You shall be the first guest invited to the wedding. (*He walks briskly to door and turns.*) And Gooseberry shall be the second! (GOOSEBERRY *grins with pleasure,* BRUFF *and* FRANKLIN *laugh.* FRANKLIN *exits. Fast curtain*)

* * * * *

SCENE 5

TIME: *One month later.*

SETTING: *Temple of the Moon God in India. Statue of Moon God is at left side of stage.*

AT RISE: *Sound of temple bells is heard.* THREE PRIESTS *enter in front of curtain and file slowly up to statue.* 1ST PRIEST *carries Moonstone on cushion.* 2ND PRIEST *and* 3RD PRIEST *follow, bearing incense and temple bells on cords, which they ring. They salaam and kneel before Moon God statue.* 1ST PRIEST *rises and sets Moonstone in statue's forehead. Then he returns to kneel with others.*

1ST PRIEST: O Moon God, we thy servants restore to thee the mystic light of heaven, the sacred Moonstone, that it may shine forth once again from thy celestial brow and shed its light upon thy faithful worshippers to the end of time. (*Spotlight fades slowly to blackout.*)

THE END

Production Notes

THE MOONSTONE

Characters: 4 female; 13 male. Godfrey and Sailor are played by the same actor. The same actors play Priests throughout play. Offstage voices for statue and soldiers.

Playing Time: 30 minutes.

Costumes: Appropriate early nineteenth century dress and military uniforms of the period.

Properties: Firewood; coin; dagger; pistol; Moonstone; bouquet of roses; vase; jewelry box; envelope containing note; drum; cloth bags containing Indian clubs and balls; candles in candlesticks; newspaper; hat; incense; bells.

Setting: Scene 1: British camp, played before curtain. Army tent and campfire are down right. Scene 2: Drawing room in Lady Verinder's elegant town house in London. Sofa and two armchairs are downstage. There are French doors in right wall; next to doors is a cabinet. In rear wall is an arched entry, with draperies. Bookcases stand along wall near entry. Door left leads to dining room and study. Small writing desk and chair stand left. Scene 3: Lawyer's office, played before curtain. Desk and two chairs are left. Coatrack is right. Scene 4: Room 10 in the Wheel of Fortune Lodging House, London. Room is scantily furnished. Iron bed is set against right wall. Night table with lighted candle on it, chair, and bureau stand against left wall. Box containing Moonstone is on bureau. Next to bureau there is door leading to hall. In rear wall there is a window opening onto roof. In Scenes 1 and 5, statue of Moon God, which may be painted on a cardboard flat or attached to a screen, is placed at left.

Lighting: Spotlights are used in Scene 1, as indicated in text. In Scene 2, lighting should give the appearance of moonlight when Rachel reenters.

Sound: Temple bells; shots; drums; creaking floorboards; clock chimes; and musical interludes as indicated in text.

⚟The Necklace

by *Guy de Maupassant*
Adapted by *Earl J. Dias*

Characters

CECILE FORESTIER
MATHILDE LOISEL
CHARLES LOISEL, *Mathilde's husband*
MADAME GROUET, *a peddler*
RENAULT, *a peddler*
LISETTE, *15*

SCENE 1

TIME: *A January evening in the late 19th century.*
SETTING: *The Loisel apartment in Paris. The shabbily furnished room includes worn armchair. Table at center is set for two, with a large soup bowl at each place, and a loaf of French bread in center of table. Exit left leads outside.*
AT RISE: MATHILDE LOISEL *sits at table, and* CECILE FORESTIER *sits in armchair.*
CECILE: To think, Mathilde, that I have seen you only twice since our school days. That is why I took the liberty of dropping by today.
MATHILDE: I'm glad you did, Cecile. It is pleasant to see you. (*Looking around room*) But you can see why I do not invite any of my old school friends here. This is scarcely a palace, and certainly not the kind of luxury you are accustomed to.

159

CECILE: You deserve better, Mathilde—a woman as beautiful as you. (*She smiles.*) Do you remember how you used to dream?

MATHILDE (*Bitterly*): I remember. I used to hope that some day I would live in a huge mansion. I'd have vestibules hung with Oriental tapestries and lighted by tall lamps of bronze. (*Laughing wryly*) I was to have large parlors decked with old silk, and, oh, yes, little rooms, prepared and perfumed for a five o'clock chit-chat with intimate friends. (*Shrugs*) So, here I am.

CECILE: And your husband, Charles. How is he?

MATHILDE: Charles means well. He is good-hearted and does his best, but the salary of a minor clerk in the Ministry of Education is not much.

CECILE: You could have done better. Do you remember how the Marquis de Montfleury was taken with you? He used to send you flowers, and . . .

MATHILDE (*Dreamily*): Ah, the Marquis. He was so elegant, so charming. (*She sighs in resignation.*) But he was not for me— a poor girl with no dowry to offer. My parents did the best they could for me by arranging my marrige to Charles.

CECILE: And a lucky man he is to have won himself such a beauty.

MATHILDE: Beauty? (*Gestures around room*) What good is it in these surroundings? All my life I have dreamed of dining in famous restaurants—Maxim's, Fouquet's—of dancing among the rich, but you see where I am. What have I to look forward to?

CECILE (*Rising and coming to her*): My poor Mathilde.

MATHILDE: The least I can do is to offer you a cup of tea.

CECILE: No. Thank you, but I must be on my way. Marcel and I are dining tonight with the Count de Guiche.

MATHILDE: How I envy you! (*Bitterly*) Charles and I are dining here as you can see. (CHARLES LOISEL *enters, with newspaper under his arm.*)

CHARLES: Good evening, Mathilde. (*Surprised*) Why, Madame Forestier! I have not seen you in many months.

CECILE (*Shaking* CHARLES' *hand*): How nice to see you, Monsieur Loisel.

CHARLES: I am glad you paid us a visit. Mathilde is alone a good deal. Will you stay to eat with us?

MATHILDE (*Quickly*): Cecile has a dinner engagement, Charles. (*Rises*)

CHARLES: That is too bad. Perhaps another time.

CECILE (*Kindly*): Of course, another time. But now I must go. We must see each other soon, Mathilde. There is no reason for us to be strangers.

MATHILDE (*Accompanying her to door*): Yes, we will meet again soon. (MATHILDE *and* CECILE *exit.* CHARLES *sits at table, tucks napkin under his chin, unfolds newspaper and begins to read. After a moment,* MATHILDE *reenters.*)

CHARLES: Madame Forestier looks most prosperous.

MATHILDE: As well she should. Her husband has one of the great fortunes in France.

CHARLES: Lucky fellow.

MATHILDE: Lucky woman.

CHARLES: I am devilishly hungry tonight. This winter air gives a man an appetite.

MATHILDE (*Dully*): I'll get the dinner. (CHARLES *continues to read the newspaper.* MATHILDE *exits and then returns with a tureen of soup. She ladles soup into* CHARLES' *bowl.* CHARLES *puts newspaper aside.*)

CHARLES (*Breaking off piece of bread from loaf and sniffing his soup*): Ah, such good soup!

MATHILDE (*Ladling soup into her own bowl; ironically*): Ah, yes, such good soup. (*She place tureen on table and sits.* CHARLES *eats eagerly, dipping his bread into bowl.* MATHILDE, *watching him with distaste, eats more delicately.*)

CHARLES: This soup is as good as my mother used to make! (*Mops his bowl with bread*)

MATHILDE: Would you like more?

CHARLES: All in good time, but first I have a surprise for you.

MATHILDE (*Taken aback*): A surprise?

CHARLES: Something that should please you very much. (*He takes envelope from his pocket, opens it and draws out a card.*) Listen. (*Reading; importantly*) "The Minister of Education and Madame Georges Ramponeau request the honor of M. and

Mme. Loisel's presence at the Place of the Ministry on Monday, January 18." (*Proudly*) Now, what do you think of that, Mathilde?

MATHILDE (*Sharply*): What do you expect me to think of that?

CHARLES (*Bewildered*): But, my dear, I thought you would be pleased. You never go out, and here's a chance—a fine one. These invitations are greatly sought after, and not many are given to the clerks. Everyone in the official world will be at this party.

MATHILDE (*Impatiently*): What do you expect me to wear?

CHARLES: Why, the dress in which you go to the theater. That looks very pretty to me. (MATHILDE *puts her face in her hands and begins to sob.* CHARLES, *in surprise*) What is the matter, Mathilde? Why are you crying?

MATHILDE (*Controlling herself; wiping tears from her cheek*): I have no clothes to wear to this party. Give your invitation to some colleague whose wife has a more suitable gown than I. (CHARLES *looks hurt. He frowns, deep in thought.*)

CHARLES: See here, Mathilde—how much would a simple dress cost? Something that would do on other occasions, too?

MATHILDE (*Hesitating*): I—I don't know, exactly. (*Frowns*) But it seems to me that four hundred francs might do.

CHARLES (*Alarmed*): Four hundred francs! (*Shakes his head, then continues quickly*) Still, we might do it. I had been saving for a gun. I thought I might do some shooting at Nanterre next summer, but this is more important. (*Firmly*) Yes, you shall have the four hundred francs. (*Forcing a smile*) But take care to buy a pretty dress.

MATHILDE: Oh, Charles! (*She jumps up, comes to* CHARLES, *and kisses him on the cheek.*) How generous you are! And I assure you it will be a pretty dress. (*She frowns suddenly.*) But no, it is really impossible.

CHARLES: Impossible? Why?

MATHILDE: The women at the Ministry will not only be beautifully dressed but will wear handsome jewels as well. (*She returns to her place at the table.*) It annoys me not to have a jewel, not a single one. I shall look plain and homely.

CHARLES: You can wear some natural flowers. They are very

stylish this time of year. For ten francs, you can get two or
three magnificent roses.

MATHILDE (*Shaking her head*): No, there's nothing more humiliating than to look poor among a lot of rich women.

CHARLES: But, Mathilde, I'm afraid I cannot help you there. The
dress, yes, but jewelry is beyond our reach.

MATHILDE: That is just what I have been telling you. (CHARLES
stares moodily at his plate. MATHILDE *toys with a piece of
bread. Suddenly,* CHARLES *bangs the table.*)

CHARLES: I have it! Why did I not think of it before? Your friend,
Madame Forestier.

MATHILDE: What about her?

CHARLES: Ask her to lend you some jewelry. She has so much.
Why, she was wearing a ring with a diamond as big as an
onion. She likes you. I am sure she would let you borrow some
bauble or other.

MATHILDE (*Musing*): That's true. I had not thought of it. (*More
cheerfully*) What a wonderful idea, Charles! (*Rising*) I shall
go to her house at once. I'm sure I can catch her before she
leaves for dinner at the Count's.

CHARLES (*Relieved*): Good! I'll clean up here while you're gone.

MATHILDE (*Happily*): It will be a splendid party, will it not,
Charles?

CHARLES: You will be the most beautiful woman there.

MATHILDE: I hope so. But now I must get dressed and run. (*She
exits hurriedly.* CHARLES *rises, sighs, shrugs, and begins to
clear dishes from table. Curtain*)

* * * * *

SCENE 2

TIME: *A few days later; the day of the party.*

SETTING: *Same as Scene 1.*

AT RISE: CHARLES, *wearing a suit, sits at table. He draws his
watch from his pocket, looks at it, and shakes his head.*

CHARLES (*Loudly*): Mathilde! Are you ready? We should be there
by eight.

MATHILDE (*Offstage*): Coming, Charles. (*After a moment or two,* MATHILDE, *wearing a lovely gown, appears in doorway and poses for a moment. She holds a necklace.*) How do I look?

CHARLES (*Rising and gazing at her admiringly*): You are more beautiful than ever, Mathilde.

MATHILDE: Now you shall see what I borrowed from Cecile. I did not show it to you before because I wished to surprise you. (*She displays the necklace.*) Look. Is it not lovely?

CHARLES: It is magnificent!

MATHILDE: Help me clasp it around my neck. (CHARLES *does so.*)

CHARLES (*Standing off to look at her*): Perfect!

MATHILDE (*Posing happily*): You see, it is simple but expensive looking. Oh, I thought for a long time before I chose it, Charles. Cecile has such a collection of jewelry; I was tempted by all of it. Bracelets, a pearl necklace, a Venetian brooch set with precious stones. I tried on all of them and posed before the glass. And then I discovered in a box lined with satin this superb necklace of diamonds, I was in ecstasy when I put it on.

CHARLES: It was a wise choice, my dear.

MATHILDE: And now I shall get my wrap, and I will be ready. (*Happily doing a little pirouette*) Oh, Charles, it will be a wonderful evening—one of the great nights of our lives. (*They exit. Lights dim briefly to denote the passage of time.*)

* * * * *

SCENE 3

TIME: *A few hours later.*

SETTING: *Same as Scene 2*

AT RISE: CHARLES *and* MATHILDE *enter.*

MATHILDE (*Gleefully*): What a glorious party!

CHARLES (*Sinking wearily into chair*): You certainly were a success, Mathilde. (*Wryly*) After midnight, I just retired to the anteroom with three other men whose wives were also having a good time.

MATHILDE: I danced with everyone—all the most distinguished

men! The Count de Brisaille, the Marquis Saint-Challet, Monsieur Deveau—even the Minister himself.

CHARLES: So I observed. All the men were looking at you, inquiring your name, and asking to be introduced.

MATHILDE (*Dancing gracefully around the room*): I shall never be able to sleep tonight. I am on a cloud of happiness.

CHARLES (*Yawning*): As for me, I shall sleep like a log. Night life is too much for me.

MATHILDE: Charles, how can you say that? Tonight was life as it should be—glittering, romantic, joyful. (*Removes her wrap, throws it onto table, continues to dance*)

CHARLES (*Stifling another yawn*): Aren't you too tired to dance, my dear? (MATHILDE *laughs, twirls about, then stops suddenly, her hand at her neck. She utters startled cry.*)

CHARLES (*Alarmed*): What is it?

MATHILDE (*Terrified*): The necklace! It's gone!

CHARLES (*Jumping up*): It must be here somewhere. (*Picks up wrap*) Perhaps in the folds of your wrap. (*He searches frantically.*) It's not here!

MATHILDE (*Disturbed*): Look in your coat pocket, Charles. Perhaps I gave it to you.

CHARLES: No, I am sure you did not. But let us see. (*Turns his pockets inside out.*) No, not there. (*He goes toward door.*) Perhaps you dropped it on the stairs. I shall look. (*He exits hurriedly.* MATHILDE *begins to look frantically around room— under table and chairs—then looks again in folds of her wrap. In distress*) Oh, where could it be? (*After a moment,* CHARLES *reenters.*)

MATHILDE (*Hopefully*): Did you find it?

CHARLES (*Shaking head*): Not a trace. It is not on the stairs. And I was lucky because the cab we came in is still outside. The driver is feeding his horse. The necklace is not in the cab.

MATHILDE (*Miserably*): What are we to do?

CHARLES: Are you sure you had it when we left the party?

MATHILDE: Yes. I touched it in the vestibule of the Ministry.

CHARLES: Perhaps it will turn up, but I fear we are out of luck, Mathilde. The chances are you dropped it on the street. And the streets of Paris being what they are, I doubt if anyone who finds so valuable a necklace will even report it to the police.

MATHILDE (*Bitterly*): Why did this have to happen? Does fate begrudge us one night of pleasure?

CHARLES (*Sharply*): I do not know about fate, Mathilde. But I know that we must do something about this. First of all, you must write to Madame Forestier. Tell her that you have broken the clasp of her necklace and are having it repaired. That will give us more time to search for it.

MATHILDE (*Eagerly*): Yes, I will do that at once. (*She exits quickly and returns in a moment with paper, pen, and ink, which she places on table.*)

CHARLES: If the necklace does not turn up, we must, of course, replace it.

MATHILDE (*Incredulously*): Replace it? But, Charles, the necklace must be worth a fortune!

CHARLES: I *know* it is worth a fortune. There is a jeweler's shop in the Palais Royal not far from the Ministry. I pass it every day. There is a necklace in the window that is almost an exact replica of Madame Forestier's.

MATHILDE (*Eagerly*): And the cost?

CHARLES (*Grimly*): Forty thousand francs.

MATHILDE (*In dismay*): Forty thousand francs! We could not afford it in a lifetime!

CHARLES: If the other is not found, we must afford it. After all, Mathilde, I may not have much money, but I pride myself on being an honest man.

MATHILDE: But forty thousand francs!

CHARLES: I have, as you know, eighteen thousand francs which my father left me. I have never touched it. That can be a start.

MATHILDE: And the rest?

CHARLES: We must borrow it.

MATHILDE: But, Charles, we shall then be in the hands of the moneylenders. You remember what happened when Monsieur LeBreque's business failed. He borrowed, asking a thousand francs here, five hundred there, a few louis elsewhere. He gave promisory notes, dealt with usurers. When he died, he was living in poverty, and the debt was still unpaid.

CHARLES (*Miserably*): I know. But what would you have us do? Do you want to go to Madame Forestier and say, "I'm sorry, Cecile, but a little accident happened. I lost your forty-thousand-franc necklace. Ha! Ha! These things will happen, won't they?"

MATHILDE (*Tearfully*): You are being cruel, Charles.

CHARLES: Not cruel, Mathilde—honest. One has to face the troubles that come in life. (*More gently*) Come now, Mathilde. Write that note to Madame Forestier. I will post it before I go to bed. (MATHILDE *picks up her pen, thinks for a moment, and then begins to write.* CHARLES *sits staring thoughtfully into space. Suddenly,* MATHILDE *stops writing, puts her head down on table, and begins to sob.* CHARLES *rises and goes to her, putting his hand on her shoulder.*)

CHARLES: There! There! We will meet this together. (*She continues to sob. He pats her shoulder and shakes his head.*) What a little thing it takes to save you or to ruin you. (*Curtain*)

* * * * *

SCENE 4

TIME: *Ten years later.*

SETTING: *The Loisels' attic room, in the Paris slums. The only furniture is a battered old table and three or four rickety wooden chairs.*

AT RISE: MATHILDE, *mop in hand, a bucket of water by her side, is washing the floor. She looks older, and there are traces of gray in her hair. Her sleeves are rolled to her elbows, and she wears a dirty apron. Children's voices are heard shouting outside.* MATHILDE, *irritated, goes to window, and calls out.*

MATHILDE: Shut your mouths down there, you street rats! You get noisier every day! Can't one get at least a little peace and quiet in this miserable neighborhood? Go home to your mothers—if you have any! (*Children's voices die away.* MATHILDE *returns to center and resumes mopping.*) Noisy brats! (CHARLES *enters. He looks tired, seedy, and much older. He is carrying a ledger.*)

CHARLES (*Yawning*): I was up all night with these accounts. I tell you, Mathilde, to work all day at my own job and then to do accounts on the side for the little money they bring in is almost too much.

MATHILDE (*Harshly*): You should be used to it by now. We've had ten years of this miserable life.

CHARLES: At least our debts are finally paid.

MATHILDE: Oh, yes, our debts are paid. (*Bitterly*) And look at me. Is this the Mathilde you married?

CHARLES (*Wearily*): We have both changed. Time changes us all. (*Sighing*) Well, I must be off to the Ministry. I'll be lucky if I can keep my eyes open. (*He exits.*)

MADAME GROUET (*Offstage*): Vegetables! Vegetables for sale!

MATHILDE (*Going to window and speaking coarsely*): Come up! Let us see what garbage you are peddling this morning! (*After a moment,* MADAME GROUET *enters. She carries a basket of cabbages and carrots.*)

MADAME GROUET: Bonjour, Madame Loisel. I have some lovely vegetables today.

MATHILDE: You've been saying that for ten years, Madame Grouet, and your vegetables get worse each year. (*Taking a cabbage from basket and feeling it*) Ugh! This cabbage is old enough to be your grandmother.

MADAME GROUET: But, madame, I swear it was picked fresh this morning.

MATHILDE (*Fingering carrots*): And these carrots are loaded with worms.

MADAME GROUET: But no, madame—they are jewels of carrots.

MATHILDE: How much for this grandmother cabbage!

MADAME GROUET: Twenty sous.

MATHILDE (*Throwing cabbage back into basket*): Take your basket and sell your wares to the other fools in the neighborhood, you old fraud. Twenty sous! Why, you old robber, it is not worth ten.

MADAME GROUET: Please, madame at twenty sous it is an immense bargain.

MATHILDE (*Turning her back on* MADAME GROUET): Do you think I'm a lunatic?

MADAME GROUET: Madame is unkind. (*Slyly*) But I will offer you a real bargain. You may have the cabbage for fifteen sous. (MATHILDE *resumes mopping, pushing mop at* MADAME GROUET'*s feet.*)

MATHILDE: Be off with you!

MADAME GROUET (*Trying to avoid the mop*): But it is a real bargain.

MATHILDE (*Stopping her work and leaning on mop*): I'll give you twelve sous. No more.

MADAME GROUET: Ah, madame drives a hard bargain. But one must live. It is yours, madame, for twelve sous.

MATHILDE: And robbery at that. (MATHILDE *puts the cabbage on table, then takes a worn purse from her apron pocket and counts out twelve coins, one by one, into* MADAME GROUET'*s hand.*)

MADAME GROUET: Ah, thank you, madame. You will find that cabbage to be the king of all cabbages. Delicious!

MATHILDE: Save the speeches for the other poor fools you deal with. Now go. I'm busy. (MADAME GROUET *exits quickly, as* MATHILDE *resumes mopping furiously. Grumbling as she works*) Ah, what a miserable life! I work all day and eat rotten vegetables at night!

RENAULT (*Offstage*): Beef! Veal! Freshly killed chickens! (MATHILDE *stops mopping, smiles grimly, exits, and returns with a paper bag, which she places on table. Then she goes right and calls.*)

MATHILDE: Monsieur Renault! Come up!

RENAULT: Oui, madame! At once! (RENAULT *enters, wearing a stained butcher's apron and carrying a basket.*)

RENAULT: Bonjour, Madame Loisel. I have here a special piece of veal for you. Young, tender—the dew is still on it.

MATHILDE (*Taking paper bag from table and shaking it in his face*): Listen, you old goat. I have here a piece of beef you sold me yesterday.

RENAULT: Yes, I remember. A magnificent cut. Fit for a king.

MATHILDE (*Throwing the bag at him*): It's as tough as rope. I cooked it all day, and we still couldn't eat it. And for this gristle, you charged me fifty sous, you old crook!

RENAULT (*Picking up bag*): But, madame, there must be some mistake.

MATHILDE: There is—and you made it! I want my fifty sous back!

RENAULT: But that is not good business, madame. I sold you the meat in good faith.

MATHILDE (*Advancing with the mop and shaking it at him*): I want my fifty sous!

RENAULT (*Retreating and speaking coaxingly*): But, madame, that is not business. (*She again shakes the mop at him.*) Be reasonable. I will give you this piece of tender veal in exchange for the beef. This will prove I am an honest man.

MATHILDE (*Angrily*): You don't have an honest bone in your body! I want my fifty sous back.

RENAULT: Very well, madame. (*He reaches into his pocket and hands her coins, which she counts carefully.*)

MATHILDE (*Looking up*): You robber! There are only forty-eight sous here!

RENAULT: Forty-eight? (*He looks carefully at coins in* MATHILDE's *hand.*) But, of course. I made a mistake in counting. (*He gives* MATHILDE *two sous more.*) There. Again I prove I am an honest man.

MATHILDE: Ha! That's the best joke I've heard today.

RENAULT: But now about this veal, madame. You have my word for it—it is an exquisite cut. From a prize calf, no less. (*He takes bag from his basket, holds it up.*) And at the unbelievably low price of fifty-five sous. Reduced from sixty, just for you, madame.

MATHILDE: That veal would probably break whatever teeth I have left.

RENAULT: But, madame, I swear on my honor—

MATHILDE (*Advancing on him and shaking the mop at him*): Get out! I've had enough of your tricks for one day!

RENAULT (*Retreating*): But the veal—

MATHILDE: This is for the veal! (*She takes a vicious swipe at him with the mop, and he exits hurriedly.* MATHILDE *goes to table, sits, and counts the fifty sous again. She begins to laugh robustly.* LISETTE, *a girl of 15, enters.*)

LISETTE: You seem happy, Madame Loisel.

MATHILDE: When one outwits a thief, one has a right to be happy. What do you want, Lisette?

LISETTE: There is a woman out there who has been asking for you.

MATHILDE: What does she look like?

LISETTE: She is very pretty, and she is wearing the loveliest dress.

MATHILDE: Well, tell her to come up. Anyone dressed well will be a welcome change in this neighborhood of scarecrows.

LISETTE (*Meekly*): Yes, madame. (*She goes to door.*) I'll tell the lady she may come up. (*Exits.* MATHILDE *resumes mopping. After a moment,* CECILE FORESTIER *enters.*).

CECILE: Oh, I am sorry. There must be some mistake. I was looking for Madame Loisel. (MATHILDE *looks up, is surprised, and smiles.*)

MATHILDE: Good morning, Cecile.

CECILE: But, madame, I do not know you. Are you not making a mistake? (MATHILDE *goes to her, takes her hand, and leads her to center.*)

MATHILDE: There is no mistake, Cecile. I am Mathilde Loisel.

CECILE (*Gazing closely at her and uttering a startled cry*): Oh! My poor Mathilde! How you have changed!

MATHILDE: Yes, I have had hard days since I last saw you. And many troubles—all because of you.

CECILE (*Stunned*): Because of *me?* How so? It has been at least ten years since I have seen you.

MATHILDE: You remember the diamond necklace that you lent me to wear to the ball at the Ministry?

CECILE: Yes. What of it?

MATHILDE: Well, I lost it.

CECILE: But how can that be? You brought it back to me soon after the ball.

MATHILDE: I brought you back another just like it—one that cost forty thousand francs. And now for ten years Charles and I have been paying for it. You must understand that it was not easy for us who have nothing. But, at last our debt is paid, and I am very glad. (*Long pause*)

CECILE (*With difficulty*): You—you say that you bought a diamond necklace to replace mine?

MATHILDE (*Smiling proudly*): Yes. You did not even notice it, did you? They were exactly alike! (CECILE *looks desolate and sadly shakes her head. Much moved, she takes both of* MATHILDE'*s hands.* MATHILDE *looks questioningly at her.*) Cecile, what is it?

CECILE: Oh, my poor Mathilde! (*She pauses.*) The necklace that I lent you was only a paste imitation—they were not *real* diamonds! (MATHILDE *looks horrified.*) At most, it was worth five hundred francs. (MATHILDE, *stunned, sways as though about to faint as* CECILE *grasps her. Quick curtain*)

THE END

Production Notes

THE NECKLACE

Characters: 2 male; 4 female.

Playing Time: 25 minutes.

Costumes: French, late 19th century. In Scene 1, Mathilde and Charles wear simple but neat clothing; in Scenes 2 and 3 they wear elegant evening dress; Mathilde wears a wrap over her gown. In Scene 4, their clothes are threadbare and faded. Mathilde wears a dirty apron. Cecile is expensively dressed. Madame Grouet, Lisette, and Renault wear shabby clothes; Renault also wears a stained butcher's apron.

Properties: Newspaper; soup tureen and ladle; envelope with invitation inside; watch; diamond necklace; paper, pen and ink; mop and pail; ledger; two baskets, one containing cabbages and carrots, one holding paper bags; purse and coins.

Setting: Scenes 1, 2, 3: A shabby but neat apartment. The furniture is old and worn. There is a table with tablecloth on it, several chairs, an armchair, and other furniture as desired. In Scene 1, the table is set for two, with napkins, soup plates, and loaf of French bread. Scene 4: An attic room in the slums. The only furniture is a battered old table and a few rickety wooden chairs.

Lights: Dim at end of Scene 2.

Sound: Children's voices.

▣▣ The Red-Headed League

by *Sir Arthur Conan Doyle*
Adapted by *Nancy B. Thum*

Characters

SHERLOCK HOLMES
DR. WATSON
JABEZ WILSON, *a red-head*
VINCENT SPAULDING
DUNCAN ROSS, *a red-head*
PETER JONES
MR. MERRYWEATHER

SCENE 1

TIME: *June, 1890.*

SETTING: *Divided stage. Holmes's comfortably furnished study on Baker Street is left. Table and chair are down far right.*

AT RISE: SHERLOCK HOLMES *and* JABEZ WILSON *are in earnest conversation.* DR. WATSON *enters left.*

WATSON: Sorry, Holmes, I didn't know you were busy. I can wait in the next room.

HOLMES (*Motioning to* WATSON): Not at all! Come in, my dear Watson. I would like you to join us. Mr. Wilson, this is Dr. Watson, my partner and assistant in many of my most successful cases. I have no doubt he will be of great assistance in yours, too.

WILSON (*Rising; bowing slightly to* WATSON): Good day, sir. (*Sits*)

WATSON: Good day to you, Mr. Wilson. (WATSON *sits.*)

HOLMES: Mr. Jabez Wilson is telling me a very strange tale. I shall ask him to start over again—not only for your benefit, Dr. Watson, but because I wish to hear all the details again. So far, I cannot tell whether or not a crime has been committed at all.

WILSON (*Pulling newspaper from pocket*): Let me find the advertisement. (*He searches the paper.*)

HOLMES: By the way, Watson, it's quite obvious, isn't it, that Mr. Wilson has done manual labor, is a Freemason, has been to China, and has done a considerable amount of writing lately.

WILSON (*Startled*): How could you possibly know that about me?

HOLMES: Your hands tell us that you were a ship's carpenter. Your right hand is larger than your left. You've worked with it, and the muscles are more developed.

WILSON (*Looking at right hand*): That is so. But the Freemasonry?

HOLMES: Your tie tack.

WILSON (*Putting hand to tie*): Ah, yes, of course.

HOLMES (*Pointing*): And the fish you have tattooed on your right wrist could have been done only in China. The Chinese coin on your watch chain gave me another clue.

WATSON: Brilliant deduction as usual, Holmes. Tell us—how do you know that Mr. Wilson has been writing a great deal?

HOLMES: The lower edge of his right jacket sleeve is shiny for a length of about five inches. The left sleeve has but one shiny spot. (*To* WILSON) Isn't that where you rest your arm on the desk?

WILSON (*Laughing*): I must say, I'm impressed with your powers of observation, Mr. Holmes.

HOLMES: Thank you, Mr. Wilson. (*After a pause*) Can you find the advertisement?

WILSON (*Flustered*): Ah, yes, I have it now. (*To* WATSON) This is what began it all. (*Points to place in newspaper*) You just read it for yourself, sir.

WATSON (*Taking paper from* WILSON; *reading*): "To the Red-headed League: On account of the bequest of the late Ezekiah Hopkins, of Lebanon, Pennsylvania, U.S.A., there is now another vacancy open which entitles a member of the League to a salary of £4 a week for purely nominal services. All red-headed men who are sound in body and mind and above the age of twenty-one years are eligible. Apply in person on Monday, at eleven o'clock, to Duncan Ross, at the offices of the League, 7 Pope's Court, Fleet Street." (*Looks up*) What on earth could this mean?

HOLMES (*Chuckling*): It is odd, isn't it? Make note of the paper and the date, Watson.

WATSON (*Looking at front of paper*): It is *The Morning Chronicle* of April 27, 1890. Just two months ago.

HOLMES: Very good. Now, Mr. Wilson, proceed. Tell us all about yourself, and what happened after you read this advertisement.

WILSON: Well, it's just as I was telling you, Mr. Holmes. I have a pawnbroker's business here in London, in Coburg Square. It's not a large business, and it hasn't earned much the past few years. I once employed two assistants, but now I have only one.

HOLMES: And what is his name?

WILSON: Vincent Spaulding. He's very smart, eager to learn the business. He could earn twice as much as I'm able to pay him. (*Shrugs*) But since he doesn't mention it, why should I put ideas in his head?

HOLMES: Why, indeed? You seem most fortunate to have an employee who comes for half price.

WILSON: He has his faults, too. (*Pause*) I never saw a fellow so keen on photography—snaps away with his camera, then dives down into the cellar to develop his pictures. But he's a good worker.

HOLMES: How did you come to see that advertisement?

WILSON (*Rising, walking right*): It was eight weeks ago this very day. Spaulding came into the office with the paper. . . . (*Lights dim on main stage and spotlight comes up right.* WILSON *crosses right.* SPAULDING *enters, carrying newspaper.*)

SPAULDING: I certainly wish I had red hair, Mr. Wilson.

WILSON (*Puzzled*): Why, for heaven's sake?

SPAULDING: Because there's a vacancy in the League of Red-headed Men. It's worth quite a bit of money to any man who gets it. If my hair would only change color, here's a nice little job ready to step into.

WILSON: What is this League?

SPAULDING (*Amazed*): You have never heard of the Red-headed League?

WILSON (*Shaking his head*): Never.

SPAULDING (*Pointing to* WILSON): You're eligible yourself for the vacancy. The work is slight and need not interfere with your business here.

WILSON (*Showing great interest*): Tell me about it, Spaulding.

SPAULDING (*Handing him newspaper*): Well, as far as I know, the league was founded by Ezekiah Hopkins, a very peculiar—but very rich—American. He was red-headed and wanted to share his great wealth with other red-headed men. So when he died, he left instructions that the league be set up.

WILSON: I imagine there would be millions of red-headed men who would apply.

SPAULDING: Not many would qualify. They must be adults, and they must live in London. Hopkins was a Londoner before going to America. And I've heard that there's no use applying if your hair is light red or dark red, or anything but bright, blazing, fiery red.

WILSON (*Touching his hair*): Bright, blazing fiery red.

SPAULDING: You could certainly apply, but you probably wouldn't want to put yourself out for only a few hundred pounds. (*Exits. Lights dim down right,* WILSON *rejoins* WATSON *and* HOLMES. *Lights up.*)

WILSON: Well, you can see for yourself, gentlemen, that my hair is a full and rich red. I felt I had as good a chance as any other red-headed man. Spaulding seemed to know quite a bit about it. So I asked him to close the shop and come with me.

WATSON: And you went to the address given in the advertisement?

WILSON: Yes, and what a sight! The streets were choked with red-headed men! I almost gave up, but Spaulding pushed and shoved until he got us through the crowd.

HOLMES: Your story is most entertaining. Pray continue.

WILSON (*Rising, talking as he moves down right*): Inside the office there was nothing but a table and a couple of chairs. Behind the table sat a red-headed man who spoke to each applicant. (*Lights dim center. Spotlight comes up at right where* DUNCAN ROSS *sits behind table.* SPAULDING *enters, joins* WILSON.)

SPAULDING: Mr. Ross, this is Mr. Jabez Wilson, and he is willing to fill the vacancy in the League.

ROSS (*Observing* WILSON): He seems to be admirably suited for it. (*Stands, studies* WILSON *from side to side*) I cannot recall seeing hair that so perfectly fills the specifications. You will, I'm sure, excuse me for taking one precaution. (*Grabs* WILSON's *hair with both hands and pulls*)

WILSON (*In pain*): Oh—oh, stop, please!

ROSS (*Releasing hair, looking closely at* WILSON): Ah, there are tears in your eyes. That's proof enough your hair is real. (*Stepping back*) We have been twice deceived by wigs. (*Holds out hand*) My name is Duncan Ross, and I am one of the members of the League. (*They shake hands.*) When can you start your duties?

WILSON: Well, I have a business to run.

SPAULDING: You need not worry, Mr. Wilson. I'll be able to look after that for you.

WILSON (*To* ROSS): What would be the hours?

ROSS: Ten to two. You must stay in the office during these hours from Monday through Saturday. If you leave, you forfeit the job.

SPAULDING: That will work perfectly. Our pawnbroker business is mainly in the evening. (WILSON *nods*.)

WILSON: And the pay?

ROSS: It's £4 a week.

WILSON: And what will the work be?

Ross: Very easy. You simply copy out the *Encyclopaedia Britannica*. We have the supplies; you will sit here to work. (*Indicates table and chair*) Can you be ready to start tomorrow?

WILSON (*Nodding*): Yes, I can. (*Lights out down right.* WILSON *returns center, where lights come up.* SPAULDING *and* ROSS *exit right.*) I went home quite pleased. But as the night wore on I began to fear that it was a hoax. However, the next morning Spaulding encouraged me to give it a try, so I set out for Pope's Court.

WATSON: How did it go?

WILSON: Everything was fine. The supplies were ready, and Mr. Ross was there to get me started with the letter A. Then he left, but dropped in from time to time. At two o'clock he returned, complimented me on the work I had done, and locked the office as we departed.

HOLMES: And so you continued.

WILSON: Day after day, week after week. I worked faithfully, and was paid, as promised, each Saturday. Then, after eight weeks had passed and I had worked my way through Abbots and Archery and Armor, the whole thing suddenly came to an end.

HOLMES: To an end?

WILSON: Yes, sir. This very morning I went to work as usual, but the door was locked. (*Takes card from pocket*) This card was nailed to the door. (*Hands it to* HOLMES)

HOLMES (*Reading*): "The Red-headed League is dissolved."

WATSON (*Puzzled*): What did you do when you found this?

WILSON: I asked the manager of the building what had happened to the Red-headed League, but he had no knowledge of the organization. He told me the office had been rented to William Morris, a lawyer who had been waiting for his new office to be decorated. He had moved out yesterday.

HOLMES: Did he have William Morris's new address?

WILSON: Yes, he gave it to me. When I went there, I found out it was a manufacturer of artificial legs. No one there had ever heard of William Morris or Duncan Ross.

HOLMES (*Leaning forward*): What did you do then?

WILSON: I went back to my shop. Spaulding suggested that per-

haps I'd soon get an explanatory letter. But that did not sat-
isfy me, Mr. Holmes. I did not wish to lose such a job without
an explanation, and so I came to you right away.

HOLMES (*Seriously*): I think there might be something more serious than you think at stake here.

WILSON (*Angrily*): What's more serious than losing my extra £4
a week?

HOLMES (*Calmly*): Mr. Watson and I will do our best to help you,
Mr. Wilson. First, let's try to clear up a few questions.

WILSON: Very well.

HOLMES: How long had Spaulding been with you before he
pointed out the advertisement?

WILSON: About a month. He had answered an advertisement I'd
placed in the paper.

HOLMES: Was he the only applicant?

WILSON: Oh, no. There were many, but as I mentioned earlier,
he was willing to work for half wages.

HOLMES: What is he like?

WILSON: Small, stout, quick. Has a streak of blond hair upon his
forehead.

HOLMES (*Excitedly*): Ah, I thought as much. Have you ever noticed whether his ears are pierced for earrings?

WILSON: Why, yes, sir. He told me a gypsy had done it when he
was a lad.

HOLMES: Hm-m-m. Was the business well tended during your
absences?

WILSON: Yes, sir. Nothing to complain of. There's usually little
to do from ten to two.

HOLMES (*Standing*): That will do for now, Mr. Wilson. I should
be able to give you an opinion in a day or two. Today is Saturday, and I hope by Monday we shall come to a conclusion.
(WATSON *and* WILSON *rise; all shake hands.*)

WILSON: Thank you, sir. I shall look forward to hearing from
you. (WILSON *exits.*)

HOLMES: Well, Watson, what do you make of it?

WATSON (*Baffled*): I make nothing of it. It is most mysterious.

HOLMES: Do you have any patients scheduled today?

WATSON: No, I'm free, and curious to follow your thinking on the Red-headed League. Where do we start?

HOLMES: Coburg Square. At Mr. Jabez Wilson's shop. (*Quick curtain*)

* * * * *

SCENE 2

TIME: *Later that morning*

SETTING: *London street with storefronts and a sign reading* CO-BURG SQUARE. *Sign on store left reads* JABEZ WILSON. *Three gold balls hang in front. Painted on backdrop are pharmacy, restaurant, newspaper kiosk, and bank.*

AT RISE: HOLMES *and* WATSON *enter right, cross left.*

HOLMES (*Pointing*): Ah, look. There is Mr. Wilson's shop. (*They cross to storefront.* HOLMES *pounds on floor with his cane, then knocks on "door."* SPAULDING *enters left, as if answering.*

SPAULDING: Can I help you?

HOLMES: Yes, please, I need directions from here to Trafalgar Square.

SPAULDING (*Briskly*): Third right, fourth left. (*Exits quickly*)

WATSON: I gather you asked for directions in order to see Mr. Wilson's assistant.

HOLMES: Not him. The knees of his trousers.

WATSON (*Interested*): And what did you see?

HOLMES: What I expected to see.

WATSON: And why did you beat on the pavement with your cane just now?

HOLMES: My dear Watson, it is time for observation, not talk. We have seen Coburg Square. Now let us go around the block and see the buildings on the other side. (*They cross right.*) Unlike the quiet street we just left, this is quite busy. I wish to memorize the order of businesses.

WATSON (*Pointing as he enumerates*): Pharmacy, newspaper shop, restaurant, and the City Bank on the corner.

HOLMES: Good. Our explorations are now complete. There is serious business afoot at Coburg Square. I shall need your help tonight. (*They stroll center.*)

WATSON: Certainly. What time?

HOLMES: Ten o'clock, at Baker Street.

WATSON: I'll be there.

HOLMES: And I say, Watson, there may be some danger, so kindly bring along your army revolver. (*Waves his hand and exits left.* WATSON, *shaking head, exits right. Curtain*)

* * * * *

SCENE 3

TIME: *Saturday night.*

SETTING: *Street in front of Holmes's house.*

BEFORE RISE: *Stage is very dim.* HOLMES, PETER JONES, *and* MR. MERRYWEATHER *enter left with lantern. Lights come up.* WATSON *enters right and crosses stage to join others.*

HOLMES (*As* WATSON *nears group*): Ah! Our party is complete. Watson, you know Peter Jones of Scotland Yard. And this is Mr. Merryweather, manager of the City Bank. (*All ad lib greetings.*)

WATSON: I'm ready for the chase, Holmes.

MERRYWEATHER (*Sourly*): I hope it won't be a wild goose chase. This is the first Saturday night in twenty-five years that I've missed my bridge game.

HOLMES: Mr. Merryweather, I think you'll find tonight's stakes the highest you've ever played for—£30,000. And for Mr. Jones, a man he has wanted to get his hands on for years.

JONES (*Nodding*): John Clay—murderer, thief, and forger. He's young, but he's a master criminal.

HOLMES: Let's be on our way. I have a cab waiting around the corner. (*They exit left. After a pause, curtain opens.*)

* * *

TIME: *Minutes later.*

SETTING: *Bank vault, dimly lit. There are packing boxes scattered around stage, tall boxes at rear, low boxes at front.*

AT RISE: MERRYWEATHER, *with large ring of keys, leads* HOLMES,

WATSON, *and* JONES *on stage from left.* WATSON *and* JONES *carry lanterns.*

WATSON: I take it this is the vault of the City Bank?

HOLMES: That it is. (*Taking* WATSON's *lantern, peering upward*) I see that we are not vulnerable from above. The ceiling is thick enough.

JONES: Nor are we vulnerable from below. (*Stamping on floor*) Oh, dear, this sounds quite hollow.

HOLMES (*Firmly*): I really must ask you to be more quiet. I would ask all of you, please, to sit on those boxes and not interfere. (*They comply.* HOLMES *kneels and examines floor with magnifying glass, moving around behind small boxes that are arranged across front of stage.*) Ah-h-h. (*He rises, puts magnifying glass in his pocket, addresses* MERRYWEATHER.) Sir, please explain to Watson why criminals would be particularly interested in your vault right now.

MERRYWEATHER (*Indicating boxes*): These boxes contain our French gold.

WATSON: Your French gold?

MERRYWEATHER (*Nodding*): A special shipment from the Bank of France. We've had warnings that an attempt might be made to steal it, so we are arranging to transfer portions of it to other branches.

HOLMES: Very wise. However, I think the robbers will strike tonight, while the gold is all here. I'd like you all to post yourselves behind the taller boxes in the back. Watson, have your revolver ready. (WATSON *takes gun from his pocket, places it in front of him on a box.*) The thieves have only one way out through the shop in Coburg Square, and you've blocked that, haven't you, Jones?

JONES: I have two officers guarding the door.

WATSON: Then how will the thieves enter?

HOLMES: Through a hole in the floor.

WATSON: What?

HOLMES (*Sternly*): Hush! Now we must wait patiently. (*All huddle behind boxes. Suddenly a light gleams from behind low boxes, and a hand reaches up, grasping for edge of box.* SPAULDING *hoists himself up from "hole" onstage.*)

SPAULDING (*Speaking down into "hole"*): It's all clear, Archie. Hand up the bags and the chisel. (*Reaching down, he pulls up chisel and bags, then gives a hand to* ROSS, *who starts to come up from the hole.* HOLMES *steps from behind his box, and* SPAULDING *notices him.*) Great Scott! Jump, Archie, down the hole and away. (JONES *lunges out from behind box, reaching for* ROSS.)

JONES: Hold it right there! (ROSS *disappears.*)

HOLMES (*Grabbing* SPAULDING): You'll not leave. (SPAULDING *pulls out gun, but* HOLMES *knocks it from his hand with his walking stick.*) It's no use, Clay. You have no chance.

SPAULDING (*Coolly*): I see. But my friend got away.

JONES: You'll see him again presently, Clay. There are two officers waiting at the front door.

SPAULDING (*With surprise*): Oh, indeed. You seem to have planned this very completely. (*Nodding to* HOLMES) I must compliment you.

HOLMES: And I you. Your red-headed idea was quite clever and effective.

JONES (*Grabbing* SPAULDING's *arm*): Let's go see your friend, shall we, Clay? (*Puts handcuffs on* SPAULDING)

SPAULDING (*Pulling hands away*): You may not be aware that I have royal blood in my veins. (*Haughtily*) Have the kindness when you address me always to say "sir" and "please."

JONES (*Mockingly*): Well, sir, if you would please climb upstairs, we'll take Your Royal Highness to the police station.

SPAULDING (*Bowing*): Certainly. (JONES *and* SPAULDING *exit left.*)

MERRYWEATHER (*Extending hand*): Really, Mr. Holmes, I don't know how the bank can thank you or repay you.

HOLMES (*Shaking his hand*): I'm quite happy to catch John Clay, Mr. Merryweather. I had a couple of old scores to settle with him.

MERRYWEATHER: Well, you've saved us. (*Nods and exits left*)

HOLMES: Well, Watson, now we know why the Red-headed League was created.

WATSON (*Nodding*): Clay—then known as Spaulding—wanted to get poor Mr. Wilson out of his shop so that he and his accomplice could dig a tunnel from the pawn shop to the bank.

That's why you were looking at Clay's knees when you first saw him. Correct?

HOLMES: That's right. You, too, must have noticed how worn and stained they were. The man was busy burrowing his way underground. As soon as I knew he was willing to work for Wilson for half wages, I knew he had a very strong reason to be in that particular building.

WATSON: And it was well worth his paying out £4 a week to get Wilson out of his office.

HOLMES: Precisely. Then there was the business of going to the cellar to develop pictures.

WATSON: The cellar! Of course. Another opportunity for Clay to do some digging.

HOLMES: You wondered why I'd been beating on the pavement with my stick. I was finding out whether the tunnel stretched out in front of the building or behind it.

WATSON: But how could you tell Clay would make his attempt tonight?

HOLMES: I decided that when they closed the League office, Clay and his accomplice no longer worried about Mr. Wilson's presence in the shop. In other words, the tunnel was completed. But it was vital that they use it before it was discovered. Saturday would be ideal since the bank was closed, and the thieves would have two days to escape.

WATSON: Once again, Holmes, you've reasoned it masterfully.

HOLMES: But now it's over. Perhaps a new case will come our way before we have time to get bored. *(Curtain)*

THE END

Production Notes

THE RED-HEADED LEAGUE

Characters: 7 male.

Playing Time: 25 minutes.

Costumes: Victorian dress. Wilson and Ross are played by red-headed actors or may wear red wigs. Spaulding wears trousers with worn, dirty knees and has a tuft of blond hair. Holmes carries walking stick; Wilson wears tie tack, and pocket watch with coin attached.

Properties: Newspaper; card; large ring of keys; two lanterns: magnifying glass; chisel; two empty canvas bags; two guns; handcuffs.

Setting: Scene 1: Divided stage. Holmes's comfortably furnished study on Baker Street is left. Three large chairs are center around small table. Door left leads out. Bookcases, desk, small table with books and papers neatly stacked complete the furnishings. Table and chair are down right. Scene 2: London street with sign reading CO-BURG SQUARE. Down left is store with sign reading JABEZ WILSON and three gold balls hanging in front. Down right, painted on backdrop, are pharmacy, restaurant, newspaper kiosk, and bank. Scene 3, Before Rise: Baker Street in front of Holmes's house. At Rise: Bank vault. Packing boxes are scattered around stage, tall boxes are rear, low boxes at front.

Lighting: Dim lights, spotlight.

▣▣The Pickwick Papers

by *Charles Dickens*
Adapted by *Lewy Olfson*

Characters

NARRATOR
TRACY TUPMAN
SAMUEL PICKWICK ⎫
NATHANIEL WINKLE ⎬ *The Pickwick Society*
AUGUSTUS SNODGRASS ⎭
MRS. MARTHA BARDELL, *landlady*
MR. FOGG
MR. JACKSON ⎫ *law clerks*
MR. WICKS ⎭
SOLICITOR, *extra*
COURT CLERK
MRS. ELIZABETH CLUPPINS
JURY, *extras*
FOREMAN OF THE JURY
JUDGE

SCENE 1

BEFORE RISE: NARRATOR *enters and walks to center.*
NARRATOR: The Corresponding Society of the Pickwick Club was
    one of the most unusual fraternal organizations ever founded
    in London. It was comprised of four members: by name, Tracy

187

Tupman, Esquire; Augustus Snodgrass, Esquire; Nathaniel Winkle, Esquire, all members-at-large, and Samuel Pickwick, Esquire, F.A.G.C.M.P.C.—that is to say, Founder and General Chairman and Member of the Pickwick Club. The purpose of the organization was never made quite clear. However, it soon became apparent that the Club's activities were to be confined to the members getting themselves involved in all sorts of remarkable predicaments at their own expense—not the least of which was the adventure of Samuel Pickwick's encounter with his widowed landlady, Mrs. Martha Bardell. As our story begins, the members of the Pickwick Club—Mr. Tupman, Mr. Snodgrass, Mr. Winkle and Mr. Pickwick himself, are seated in the latter's apartment on Goswell Street, enjoying an afternoon cup of tea. (*Exits as curtain rises*)

* * *

TIME: *One afternoon in the early 1800s.*

SETTING: *Samuel Pickwick's apartment in London. Settee, easy chairs, and low table with tea tray are center. Exit right leads to rest of apartment. Exit left leads outside.*

AT RISE: SAMUEL PICKWICK *is pouring tea for his guests*: TRACY TUPMAN, NATHANIEL WINKLE, *and* AUGUSTUS SNODGRASS.

TUPMAN: I say, Mr. Pickwick, these are very fine quarters you have here.

PICKWICK: Thank you, Mr. Tupman, thank you. I find them quite suitable. You know, I've been here two years.

WINKLE: Two years! Has it really been that long?

PICKWICK: Yes, Mr. Winkle, two years. It's an admirable establishment. Mrs. Bardell, my housekeeper, is a remarkable woman.

TUPMAN: But I should think you'd need a manservant, Mr. Pickwick.

WINKLE: Yes, Mr. Pickwick. How do you manage without one?

PICKWICK: Why, gentlemen, you must be mind readers! That is the very subject I am going to speak to Mrs. Bardell about. (*Blackout and light musical interlude, during which* WINKLE, TUPMAN, *and* SNODGRASS *exit. Tea things are removed. Lights*

up on MRS. BARDELL *dusting furniture with feather duster,
humming to herself.*)

PICKWICK (*Tentatively*): Er . . . Mrs. Bardell.

MRS. BARDELL: Yes, sir? (*Continues dusting*)

PICKWICK: There is something I've been wanting to ask you for
quite a while now. (MRS. BARDELL *stops dusting.*)

MRS. BARDELL: Oh? What is that, sir?

PICKWICK: Do you think it a much greater expense to keep two
people than to keep one, Mrs. Bardell?

MRS. BARDELL (*Giving a start, then simpering*): Why, Mr. Pickwick, what a question!

PICKWICK: Well, but *do* you?

MRS. BARDELL (*Flirtatiously*): That depends a good deal upon the
person, you know, Mr. Pickwick, and whether it's a saving
and careful person.

PICKWICK: That's very true, but the person I have my eye on I
think possesses those qualities; and moreover, has a considerable knowledge of the world, and a great deal of sharpness,
which may be of material use to me.

MRS. BARDELL (*Coyly*): Oh, Mr. Pickwick!

PICKWICK: To tell you the truth, Mrs. Bardell, I have made up
my mind.

MRS. BARDELL: Dear me, sir!

PICKWICK: You'll think it very strange that I never consulted
you about this matter and never even mentioned it—eh? Well,
what do you think?

MRS. BARDELL (*Gushing*): Oh, Mr. Pickwick, you're very kind,
sir, to make this proposal.

PICKWICK: It'll save you a good deal of trouble, won't it?

MRS. BARDELL: Oh, I never thought of the trouble, sir. And, of
course, I should take more trouble to please you then, than
ever. But it is so kind of you, Mr. Pickwick, to have so much
consideration for my loneliness.

PICKWICK (*Thoughtfully*): Ah, to be sure, I never thought of that.
When I am in town, you'll always have somebody to sit with
you.

MRS. BARDELL: I'm sure I ought to be a very happy woman!
(*Overwhelmed*) Oh, you dear man!

PICKWICK (*Startled*): I beg your pardon?

MRS. BARDELL: Oh, you good, kind, loving dear! (*She embraces him.*)

PICKWICK (*Pulling away from her*): Really, Mrs. Bardell—my good woman—pray consider if anybody should come.

MRS. BARDELL (*Ecstatically*): Oh, let them come. I'll never leave you, dear, good, kind soul! (*She faints, falling against him.* PICKWICK *grasps her about the waist and struggles to prop her up.*)

PICKWICK: Mercy me! She's fainted! What a situation! (*Sound of approaching footsteps is heard.*) Oh, dear, who could that be? (*Desperately*) Please, Mrs. Bardell! Please! (*Door opens and* TUPMAN, WINKLE, *and* SNODGRASS *enter.*)

WINKLE (*Shocked*): Mr. Pickwick! What is going on?

PICKWICK (*Agitated*): Oh, my good friends, Mr. Winkle, Mr. Tupman, Mr. Snodgrass. (*Pulls handkerchief from pocket and fans* MRS. BARDELL'*s face with it*)

TUPMAN (*Concerned*): What *is* the matter?

PICKWICK (*Straining under* MRS. BARDELL'*s weight*): I don't know! Please, help me lead this woman downstairs.

MRS. BARDELL (*Coming to her senses*): Oh, I am better now. (*Straightens up*)

TUPMAN (*Offering his arm*): Let me take you downstairs, madam.

MRS. BARDELL (*Happily*): Oh, thank you—thank you! (TUPMAN *takes her arm and they exit right.*)

PICKWICK: Really, gentlemen, I cannot conceive what came over that woman. I had merely announced to her my intention of keeping a manservant, when she fainted and I could not bring her to her senses. Very extraordinary!

WINKLE *and* SNODGRASS (*Together*): Indeed!

PICKWICK: Well, so long as you both are here, how about a round of whist? Tupman may join us when he returns. (*He starts off right.*)

SNODGRASS: Splendid idea, Mr. Pickwick. (*He and* WINKLE *follow* PICKWICK.) A game of cards may do much to calm the nerves. (*Murmuring agreement, all exit. Curtain*)

* * * * *

SCENE 2

BEFORE RISE: NARRATOR *enters left, walks to center.*

NARRATOR: Without thinking too long on what had passed, Mr. Pickwick and the other gentlemen of the Pickwick Club became enmeshed in other adventures, and soon forgot completely what had transpired with Mrs. Bardell. A few weeks later, the friends were having supper in a comfortable inn, when news came which caused great consternation, indeed! (*Exits as curtain rises*)

* * *

SETTING: *An English country inn. Stage is bare but for a long table, surrounded by four chairs. Table is set for supper, with loaf of bread and knife on a cutting board.*

AT RISE: PICKWICK, SNODGRASS, *and* TUPMAN *are seated at table.* PICKWICK *saws at bread and dispenses slices as* WINKLE *enters right, carrying a letter.*

PICKWICK: Ah, Winkle, my good friend. What have you there?

WINKLE: I called at the post office and found this letter for you. It has been there for two days. (*Hands letter to* PICKWICK)

TUPMAN: From whom is it, Mr. Pickwick?

PICKWICK (*Examining letter*): I don't recognize the hand. Here, let me open it. (*He opens letter with bread knife and reads.*)

SNODGRASS: Well?

PICKWICK (*Agitatedly*): Mercy on us! (*Staring at letter*) This must be a joke; it—it can't be true!

SNODGRASS (*Delicately*): Nobody dead, is there?

PICKWICK: No, Mr. Snodgrass, no one is dead—yet! Mr. Tupman, will you be so good as to read the letter aloud? (*Hands letter to* TUPMAN)

TUPMAN (*Reading*): "Freeman's Court, Cornhill, August 28th. Bardell against Pickwick."

WINKLE (*Astonished*): You don't mean to say it's a lawsuit!

PICKWICK: Yes, he does, Mr. Winkle! Please read on, Tupman.

TUPMAN (*Reading*): "Mr. Samuel Pickwick. Sir: Having been instructed by Mrs. Martha Bardell to commence an action against you for a breach of promise of marriage, for which the plaintiff sets her damages at fifteen hundred pounds, we beg to inform you that a writ has been issued against you in this suit in the Court of Common Pleas; and request to know, by return post, the name of your attorney in London, who will accept service thereof. We are, Sir, your obedient servants, Dodson and Fogg."

PICKWICK (*Furiously*): It's a conspiracy! A base conspiracy between these two grasping lawyers, Dodson and Fogg. Mrs. Bardell would never do it—she hasn't the heart to do it—she hasn't the case to do it! It's ridiculous!

SNODGRASS (*Sarcastically*): Of her heart, you should certainly be the best judge, Mr. Pickwick. But I should certainly say that of her case, Dodson and Fogg are far better judges than any of us can be.

PICKWICK (*Pounding fist on table; angrily*): It's a vile attempt to extort money! No one has ever heard me address her in any way but as a lodger would address his landlady. Who has ever seen me with her? Not even you, my friends . . .

TUPMAN (*Wryly*): Except on one occasion. . . .

PICKWICK: When was that?

TUPMAN: Er . . . I don't know how it happened, mind—but she certainly was reclining in your arms when we came to call on you that one time.

PICKWICK (*Astonished*): I remember now . . . when I told her I would engage a manservant! She fainted and fell into my arms.

WINKLE: And you were soothing her anguish.

PICKWICK: I can't deny it. What a dreadful conjunction of appearances! I'll see this Dodson and Fogg. I'll go to London tomorrow and explain the situation to them.

SNODGRASS: Not tomorrow. You're too tired.

PICKWICK: Well, then, the next day.

TUPMAN: Next day is the first of September, and you're pledged to ride with us to Sir Geoffrey's.

PICKWICK (*Firmly*): Well, then, the day after Thursday! I'll get to the bottom of this nonsense. I won't go to trial! You just wait and see! (*Curtain*)

* * * * *

SCENE 3

SETTING: *Law offices of Dodson and Fogg. Table is cleared and moved down right. Brass lamp and piles of papers, notepad, and pen and inkstand sit on table. File cabinets stand on either side of table. One chair stands behind desk, another in front of it.*

AT RISE: MR. FOGG *sits behind table, poring over papers, and does not look up as* PICKWICK *enters.* PICKWICK *stands before table and clears his throat loudly.*

PICKWICK (*Imperiously*): Dodson and Fogg, I believe. Which have I the pleasure of addressing?

FOGG (*Finally looking up*): I am Fogg, sir.

PICKWICK: And I am Samuel Pickwick.

FOGG: Ah, yes. You are the defendant, sir, in Bardell against Pickwick? Do sit down.

PICKWICK (*Sitting*): I came here to express the astonishment with which I received your letter of the other day, and to inquire what grounds of action you can have against me.

FOGG: For the grounds of action, sir, you will consult your own conscience, and your own feelings. We are guided entirely by the statement of our client.

PICKWICK (*Annoyed*): Am I to understand, then, that it is really your intention to proceed with this action?

FOGG (*Coolly*): Understand, sir? That you certainly may!

PICKWICK: And that the damages are actually laid at fifteen hundred pounds?

FOGG (*Sternly*): To which understanding you may add my assurance that if we could have prevailed upon our client, they would have been laid at treble the amount, sir. I believe Mrs. Bardell specifically said, however, that she would not compromise for a farthing less.

PICKWICK (*Angrily*): Very well, sir, very well. You shall hear from my solicitor. But before I go, permit me to say, that of all the disgraceful and rascally proceedings . . .

FOGG (*Interrupting politely*): Oh, just a moment, Mr. Pickwick. (*Calling off*) Mr. Jackson! Mr. Wicks! Come up here, please. (*To* PICKWICK) I just want my clerks to hear what you were about to say. (MR. JACKSON *and* MR. WICKS *enter briskly, and stand beside desk.*) Here they are. Pray continue, Mr. Pickwick. Disgraceful and rascally proceedings, I think you said?

PICKWICK: I did! I said, sir, that of all the disgraceful and rascally proceedings that ever were attempted, this is the most so.

FOGG: You hear that, Mr. Wicks? You will remember that expression? (WICKS *nods.*) Now, Mr. Pickwick, perhaps you would like to call us swindlers? Pray do, if you feel so disposed, sir.

PICKWICK (*Taken aback; blustering*): I do. You *are* swindlers!

FOGG (*Pleased*): Oh, very good. Do go on. You had better call us thieves, sir; or perhaps you would like to assault one of us? Pray do it, sir, if you would. I will not resist! (JACKSON *and* WICKS *nod eagerly.*)

PICKWICK (*Backing away; warily*): I believe I am finished, for now. Good day, Mr. Fogg. Good day! (*Exits. Curtain*)

* * * * *

SCENE 4

BEFORE RISE: NARRATOR *enters, walks to center.*

NARRATOR: And so the day of the trial finally arrived. Mr. Tupman, Mr. Winkle, and Mr. Snodgrass, Pickwick's three most loyal friends, accompanied him to the courthouse, to help him prepare for the great ordeal. (*Exits right as* PICKWICK, WINKLE, SNODGRASS, *and* TUPMAN *enter left, and stroll to center, before curtain.*)

WINKLE (*With concern*): Are you very nervous, Mr. Pickwick?

PICKWICK (*Weakly*): Not *too* nervous, Mr. Winkle.

SNODGRASS: I wonder what the foreman of the jury, whoever he'll be, has had for breakfast.

TUPMAN: Ah, I hope he's had a good one!

PICKWICK: Why so?

TUPMAN: A good, contented, well-fed juryman is always to be hoped for. Discontented or hungry jurymen will invariably find for the plaintiff. (PICKWICK *nods thoughtfully. All exit right.*)

* * *

SETTING: *The Court of Common Pleas. Judge's bench is center, with chair for witness beside it. Row of chairs for jury is right of bench. Tables and chairs for defendant and plaintiff are left, behind which is row of chairs for spectators.*

AT RISE: COURT CLERK *stands beside judge's bench.* MRS. BARDELL *and* FOGG *sit at plaintiff's table.* MR. PICKWICK *and* SOLICITOR *sit at defendant's table.* JURY *sits in chairs to right of bench.* MRS. CLUPPINS, WINKLE, SNODGRASS, *and* TUPMAN *sit left, in spectator's chairs. All ad lib quiet conversation.*

COURT CLERK (*Calling out*): Silence! Order in the court for the case of Bardell against Pickwick! All rise. (*All stand as* JUDGE *enters and sits behind bench.* CLERK *remains standing as others sit.*)

JUDGE: Very good, sir. We will now hear the case!

FOGG (*Rising and clearing his throat; crossing to* JURY): Gentlemen of the jury: Never, in all the years of my professional experience, have I approached a case with feelings of such deep emotion, or with such a feeling of responsibility upon me—a responsibility that I could never have supported were I not buoyed up by a conviction so strong that the cause of truth and justice—or, in other words—the cause of my abused and injured client, Mrs. Bardell—must prevail with you, as high-minded, intelligent men who comprise this jury. My client will now testify as to Mr. Pickwick's breach of promise of marriage. (MRS. BARDELL *rises, crosses to judge's bench.* FOGG *helps her into witness chair.*)

MRS. BARDELL (*Takes in a deep breath, pauses dramatically; tearfully*): Yes, gentlemen, we were to be married. "Mrs. Bardell," he says to me, "do you think it a much greater expense to keep two people than one?" (*She bursts into tears, then sobs quietly throughout* FOGG's *speech.*)

FOGG: You have heard, gentlemen, a clear breach of promise of marriage, in which the damages are laid at 1500 pounds. Before I am through, I am sure you will see fit to make such an award to my client. I should like to supply as evidence two letters, written in the hand of that villain, Pickwick. They are not open declarations of love, oh, no! They are sly, underhanded, covert communications—letters that must be viewed with a cautious, suspicious eye. Let me read the first. (*Reading*) "Garaway's, twelve o'clock. Dear Mrs. B: Chops and tomato sauce! Yours, Pickwick!" (*Shocked*) Gentlemen of the jury, what does this mean? Chops! Yours, Pickwick! Gracious heavens, such skulduggery have we here! The next has no date at all—which is suspicious in itself! "Dear Mrs. B. I shall not be home till tomorrow. Don't trouble yourself about the warming pan." (*Insinuatingly*) Gentlemen, what is the meaning of this warming pan? See how artfully contrived are these letters by that perpetrator of systematic villainy, Samuel Pickwick! (*Pats* MRS. BARDELL *comfortingly*) You may go back to your seat now, Mrs. Bardell. (*She does so.* FOGG *addresses* CLERK) Call Elizabeth Cluppins.

CLERK: Elizabeth Cluppins, please step forward! (MRS. ELIZABETH CLUPPINS *rises and walks to witness chair.*)

FOGG: Now, Mrs. Cluppins. Have you ever received love letters?

MRS. CLUPPINS (*Gushing*): Oh, yes, sir. My husband sent 'em to me all the time afore we was married.

FOGG: Did he ever, in those letters, call you "Tomato Sauce"? Or, "Chops"?

MRS. CLUPPINS: No, sir, while I was keeping company he never called me them things.

FOGG: What *did* he call you?

MRS. CLUPPINS (*Smiling*): He called me "Duck." That was because he was particular fond of ducks. (*Authoritatively*) Now, perhaps if he had been as fond of chops and tomato sauce, he might have called me them things—out of affection, don't you know.

FOGG: That will be all, thank you, Mrs. Cluppins. (*She returns to her seat. To* CLERK) Nathaniel Winkle, if you please.

CLERK (*Calling out*): Nathaniel Winkle to the stand. (*Surprised,* WINKLE *rises uncertainly and goes to witness chair.*)

FOGG (*Accusingly*): Now, Mr. Winkle, you are a particular friend of Pickwick, the defendant, are you not?

WINKLE (*Nervously*): I have known Mr. Pickwick, now, (*As though thinking aloud*) as well as I recollect at this moment, nearly—

FOGG (*Sharply*): Pray, Mr. Winkle, do not evade the question. Are you, or are you not, a particular friend of the defendant's?

WINKLE: I, ah—

FOGG (*Quickly*): Will you or will you not answer my question, sir? Yes or no?

WINKLE (*Weakly*): Yes, I am.

FOGG: Now, sir, if I am not mistaken, you went to the home of the plaintiff, Mrs. Bardell, on purpose to see your friend, the defendant, Mr. Pickwick, along with two other friends, Mr. Tupman and Mr. Snodgrass, on the morning with which we are concerned. Did you not?

WINKLE: Yes, I did, sir.

FOGG: Now, sir, tell the gentlemen of the jury what you saw on entering the defendant's room on this particular morning. (*Pauses*) Come, come, sir. Speak up!

WINKLE (*Uneasily*): Well, I—I saw the defendant—Mr. Pickwick, that is—holding the plaintiff in his arms, with his hands clasping her waist, and the plaintiff appeared to have fainted away.

FOGG: What did you hear him say?

WINKLE: I heard him call Mrs. Bardell a good creature, and I heard him ask her to compose herself, for what a situation it was, if anybody should come, or words to that effect.

FOGG (*Pleased*): That will be all, Mr. Winkle. Step down. (WINKLE *returns to his seat as* MRS. BARDELL *speaks up.*)

MRS. BARDELL (*Tearfully*): That's right, sir. Them was his very words. "Mrs. Bardell," says he, "Mrs. Bardell, this extra person won't be too expensive for me. And it'll save you a deal of trouble. And when I am in town, you'll have somebody to keep you company." (*Wailing*) Oh-h-h-h-h!

FOGG: Gentlemen of the jury, this wretch, this cur, this villain known as Pickwick, is guilty, guilty, guilty!

MRS. BARDELL (*Indignantly*): And he has never since mentioned matrimony to me—

FOGG (*Interrupting her*): Gentlemen of the jury, take pity on this poor, abused, friendless widow, who was so misled by the villainous Pickwick. Whose arm, you have heard in this court, *encircled her waist!*

MRS. CLUPPINS (*Breaking in*): I should say "Tomato Sauce" and "Chops" are both very affectionate terms of endearment!

MRS. BARDELL: And I fainted right in his arms—dead away!

FOGG (*Solemnly*): Thank you, gentlemen of the jury. We rest our case. (*Blackout briefly while* FOGG *returns to his seat. Lights up as* JUDGE *stands.*)

JUDGE: Gentlemen of the jury, are you all agreed upon your verdict?

FOREMAN (*Rising*): We are, Your Honor.

JUDGE: Do you find for the plaintiff, gentlemen, or for the defendant?

FOREMAN: For the plaintiff.

JUDGE: Have you assessed the damages?

FOREMAN: Yes, Your Honor. Seven hundred and fifty pounds. (*All ad lib amazement.* MRS. BARDELL *embraces* FOGG *in gratitude.*)

JUDGE (*Pounding gavel*): You have heard the verdict. This case is closed. Jury is dismissed. (*All exit except for* PICKWICK, SNODGRASS, WINKLE, *and* TUPMAN.)

SNODGRASS: Well, Mr. Pickwick, what is to be done now?

PICKWICK (*Mustering his dignity*): There is nothing to be done, Mr. Snodgrass. The Pickwick Club will go on as usual, and I pray that you will all forget this unfortunate episode, and remove it entirely from memory.

SNODGRASS, WINKLE, *and* TUPMAN (*Ad lib*): Of course. Surely. As you wish. (*Etc.*)

PICKWICK: And if I may, Mr. Winkle, Mr. Tupman, and Mr. Snodgrass, allow me to give you a piece of advice: Never allow yourself to be alone with a single member of the opposite sex—no matter how honorable or innocuous your intentions. I can assure you, gentlemen, that such a situation can amount to nothing but trouble! (*All murmur agreement. Curtain*)

THE END

Production Notes

THE PICKWICK PAPERS

Characters: 11 male; 2 female; 1 male or female for narrator; male extras for Jury.

Playing Time: 25 minutes.

Costumes: Appropriate Victorian dress: breeches or trousers, vests and waistcoats for men; long, dark dresses and bonnets for women. Mrs. Bardell wears mob cap in Scene 1.

Properties: Tea, tray, feather duster, handkerchief, letter.

Setting: Scene 1: Samuel Pickwick's London apartment. Exit right leads to rest of apartment. Exit left leads to outside. Settee and easy chairs are center. Low table set with tea tray stands before one chair. After blackout, tea things are cleared. Scene 2: An English country inn. A long table, center, is surrounded by four chairs. Table is set for supper, with loaf of bread and knife on cutting board. Scene 3: Law offices of Dodson and Fogg. Table is cleared and moved down right. Brass lamp and piles of papers, notepad, and pen and inkstand sit on table, with file cabinets on either side. One chair sits behind table, another in front of it. Scene 4: The Court of Common Pleas. Judge's bench with gavel is center, with chair for witness beside it. Row of chairs for jury is right of bench. Tables and chairs for defendant and plaintiff are left, behind which is row of chairs for spectators.

Lighting: Blackouts as indicated.

Sound: Light musical interludes, as indicated.

The Squire's Daughter

by *Alexander Pushkin*
Adapted by *Joellen Bland*

Characters

LISA MUROMSKY, *the Squire's daughter, 18*
NASTYA, *her maid*
MISS JACKSON, *her English governess*
GRIGORY MUROMSKY, *the Squire*
IVAN BERESTOV, *his neighbor*
ALEXEI, *Berestov's son*

SCENE 1

TIME: *Early 19th century.*
SETTING: *The stately drawing room of Grigory Muromsky's house near village of Priluchino, in Russia. It is handsomely furnished, with settee center, comfortable armchairs left and right. Door left leads to rest of house; door right leads to garden. A large window is in rear wall, center. Cabinet stands next to window.*
AT RISE: *LISA enters left, followed by NASTYA, her maid.*
NASTYA: My dear mistress, what are you up to now? There is a mischievous look in your eye that I know only too well!
LISA (*Stopping by settee*): Hush, Nastya. Listen! (*Shrieks are heard off left.*)
NASTYA: Goodness! That sounded like Miss Jackson.

LISA (*Laughing*): Yes! She must have found the toad.

NASTYA: What toad?

LISA: The one I hid under her wig! (*Laughs again*)

NASTYA (*Giggling*): Oh, mistress, your old governess will box your ears!

LISA: Only if she can catch me! I shall play some other pranks on her later. What else is there to do? It is so dull here!

NASTYA: You are never dull, mistress, and neither am I when I am with you. I cannot think what I shall do when you get married and leave me forever.

LISA (*Sighing*): Why should you worry about that? How can I hope for marriage when the only bachelors in the province are fat old men? If Papa arranges a match for me with one of them, I shall run away—and take you with me, of course, for I could never get along without you.

NASTYA: You are so good to me, mistress. (*Pause*) May I ask a favor?

LISA (*Warmly*): Of course. You know I seldom refuse you anything.

NASTYA: May I go to the Berestovs' this evening? It is their cook's birthday, and I've been invited to a party.

LISA (*Surprised*): Another party! My papa and Ivan Berestov hate each other, but their servants make merry behind their backs!

NASTYA: Why should our masters' arguments concern us?

LISA: You are quite right, Nastya. It is foolish of the two richest men in the province to argue and insult each other. My dear papa, Grigory Muromsky, a man of culture and learning, and Ivan Berestov, a worthy old-fashioned farmer who cares only for land, corn, and cattle. (*Shakes her head*) Two totally different gentleman. Why can't they accept their differences and stop their silly quarrels?

NASTYA: We servants do not quarrel, and, mistress, you have no quarrel with young Alexei Berestov, do you?

LISA: Alexei Berestov? Ivan Berestov's son?

NASTYA: Yes. Surely you knew he has come home from the University.

LISA (*Feigning indifference*): Has he? I hadn't heard. But I certainly have no quarrel with a young gentleman I haven't seen since I was a very little girl.

NASTYA: Then let the old men argue, if it pleases them. The rest of us will enjoy ourselves!

LISA (*Excitedly*): Yes! Go to the party and have a good time, Nastya, and while you are there, try to get a glimpse of Alexei Berestov. I want to know what he looks like.

NASTYA: I already know that. I saw him at the party last week.

LISA: Then, tell me—is he good-looking?

NASTYA: Amazingly so! Tall, red-cheeked, bright-eyed—

LISA: And his manner? Is it pleasant?

NASTYA: Very pleasant, mistress. He joined in our games, and whenever he caught a maid, he kissed her.

LISA (*Laughing*): Nastya, you are making this up to tease me!

NASTYA: I swear I am not! He stayed at the party all day.

LISA: I once heard a rumor that he was in love with a young lady in Moscow.

NASTYA: How could he possibly be in love with anyone, when he danced so merrily with me and all the other girls? (*Giggles*)

LISA: If only I could see him for myself. . .

NASTYA (*Slyly*): He goes hunting every morning in the forest. If you should happen to be walking there, you would be sure to see him.

LISA: But I couldn't do that!

NASTYA: What other way is there?

LISA (*Suddenly*): I have an idea! I could disguise myself as a peasant girl!

NASTYA: How clever of you, mistress! I'll lend you some clothes and you can easily pretend to be a village girl.

LISA (*Clapping her hands*): Oh, Nastya, this will be such fun! Hurry, now, and bring me a coarse shirt and a smock, and something to cover my hair.

NASTYA: Right away, mistress! (*Runs off left, just as* MISS JACKSON *enters right*)

MISS JACKSON (*Scolding*): Lisa, I've been looking everywhere for you. It is time for your lessons.

LISA (*Teasingly*): Oh, Miss Jackson, good morning. How very charming you look! Your maid has curled your wig to perfection.

MISS JACKSON (*Scowling*): I've had quite enough of your pranks, young lady! Now, bring your books at once!

LISA: Very well. But I will have my lessons in the garden where the sun is shining, the bees are humming, and Papa's playful hounds run freely.

MISS JACKSON: Lisa, you know I don't like to sit in the hot sun. Bees terrify me, and your father's dogs have already torn two of my gowns by jumping on me.

LISA: Don't worry. I will protect you. (*Pushes her toward door right*) Wait for me by the fountain. I'll join you in just a moment.

MISS JACKSON: Very well, but no more of your tricks, young lady! (*Exits*)

LISA: What a fussy old prune she is! If only she would relax and have a little fun.

NASTYA (*Peeking in door at left*): Mistress?

LISA: It's all right. Come in.

NASTYA (*Entering with peasant clothes over her arm*): I've brought these for you.

LISA (*Examining garments*): Oh, they'll do perfectly! Nastya, I can't wait! I'll put these on and walk in the forest this very morning.

NASTYA: But your lessons, mistress! What will Miss Jackson say? (*Off right shrieks are heard, followed by sounds of barking dogs.*)

LISA: Oh, she won't mind. She is playing with Papa's dogs. (*Laughs*) Come, help me get ready. (*They exit. After a moment,* MISS JACKSON *hurries on shrieking and holding up her skirts. Her wig is askew.*)

MISS JACKSON (*Upset*): Go away, you nasty creatures! Lisa! Lisa! Now where has that girl gone? Leaving me to the mercy of those horrible dogs! (MUROMSKY *enters.*)

MUROMSKY (*Cheerfully*): Ah! Good morning, Miss Jackson. What is the trouble? You wear such a cloudy look on this bright, sunny morning.

MISS JACKSON: Mr. Muromsky! (*Curtsies*) Your daughter has run away from me, and your dogs have attacked me again!

MUROMSKY (*Laughing*): My dogs are the gentlest, most playful animals in the world. They like you! And my Lisa is as lively as a butterfly. You just have to be quick to keep up with her.

MISS JACKSON (*Unamused*): But I do not like dogs. I am not a butterfly, and I am not quick, sir. How can I be expected to educate your daughter properly if she will not attend to her lessons!

MUROMSKY: You mustn't worry. Lisa is a clever girl, and full of spirit, but it won't be long before I choose a husband for her and she will settle down. Come, I want to show you a fine painting I have just purchased.

MISS JACKSON (*Upset*): But what about Lisa's lessons?

MUROMSKY (*Taking her by the arm*): Let them wait until tomorrow. You won't forget them by then, will you? Come!

MISS JACKSON: Very well, sir. But where has your daughter gone?

MUROMSKY (*Leading her out left*): Don't worry. Wherever my Lisa is, she is enjoying herself! (*Curtain*)

* * * * *

SCENE 2

SETTING: *Woods, with bushes, etc. Played before the curtain.*

BEFORE RISE: LISA, *in peasant dress and carrying small basket, enters. She looks around eagerly.*

LISA: This is the main path through the wood. If Alexei Berestov comes this way, I'll be sure to see him. (*Looks off, suddenly*) What's that? Something is moving behind those bushes! (*Loud gunshot is heard off. LISA screams, drops basket, and ducks down with her hands over her ears. ALEXEI rushes in from right, with gun, and sees LISA.*)

ALEXEI (*Horrified*): Oh, what have I done? (*Rushes to her*) My poor girl, are you hurt? I thought you were a pheasant!

LISA (*Smiling bashfully*): Surely, sir, you must know the difference between a pheasant and a peasant.

ALEXEI (*Helping her up*): I assure you I'll not make such a mistake again. (*Smiling*) I haven't seen you in this wood before. Where do you come from?

LISA (*With an awkward curtsy*): I am the daughter of the blacksmith at Priluchino. Do you come from Tugilovo, sir?

ALEXEI: Yes. I am . . . ah . . . the young master's valet.

LISA (*Laughing*): Come, sir, do you think I am a fool? It is plain to see that you are a gentleman, possibly the young master himself.

ALEXEI: Oh? And what makes you say that?

LISA: Everything about you. Your rich dress, your gallant manner. You could never be mistaken for a servant.

ALEXEI (*Laughing*): But you, clever little one, are very much a saucy maid, and I may put my arm around you.

LISA (*Moving quickly away*): If you wish to remain friends with me, sir, you will let me go on picking mushrooms, as I was.

ALEXEI: Wait! (*Seizes her hand*) Won't you tell me your name?

LISA (*Trying to pull away*): Akulina. Now, please let me go.

ALEXEI: Very well, Akulina. (*Releases her hand*) I shall soon pay a visit to your father, the blacksmith, and tell him how very pretty his daughter is.

LISA (*Quickly*): Oh, you mustn't! If he found out I had been speaking so freely with a gentleman, he would beat me.

ALEXEI: Then I won't see him. But I want to see you again.

LISA: What good would it do? You are the young master Berestov, and I am only a peasant girl.

ALEXEI: Surely we can be friends.

LISA: Just friends? Are you in earnest, sir?

ALEXEI (*Bowing*): On my honor as a gentleman.

LISA: Well, then, I may walk this way again. Now I must go. (*Runs quickly off left*)

ALEXEI (*Calling after her*): I come here every morning! (*To himself*) What a charming girl! So unlike all the other maids. (*Exits right*)

LISA (*Entering cautiously*): Oh, he is handsome! And how he looked at me! I shouldn't come again . . . but I will! (*Laughs and runs off*)

* * *

TIME: *One morning, a month later.*

SETTING: *Same as Scene 1.*

AT RISE: MISS JACKSON *sits on settee with embroidery.* MUROMSKY *enters.*

MUROMSKY: Have you seen Lisa, Miss Jackson? She didn't come to breakfast this morning. I hope she isn't ill.

MISS JACKSON: No, sir, she is not ill. For the past month she has been rising at dawn to go for a walk in the fields. It's disgraceful!

MUROMSKY: Oh, not at all! There is nothing quite so good for the health as early rising and walking.

MISS JACKSON: But, sir, she could catch her death of cold. Can't you forbid her to take these early walks?

MUROMSKY: Why should I? If she is happy, then I can forbid nothing that makes her so.

MISS JACKSON: Oh, she is quite happy, sir, always cheerful and laughing, but her lessons do not go well. It is all I can do to make her sit still for ten minutes.

MUROMSKY (*With a hearty laugh*): If you have managed that, Miss Jackson, you have worked a small miracle! (*Glancing out window*) Ah! Here is the groom with my horse. I am off for a ride. (*Exits*)

MISS JACKSON: Humph! The master goes off for a ride, and my pupil goes off for a walk. I may as well go to my room and take a nap! (*Exits left.* LISA, *wearing her own clothes, and* NASTYA *enter right.*)

NASTYA: You look very thoughtful this morning, mistress.

LISA: Nastya, I believe Alexei Berestov is falling hopelessly in love with his Akulina.

NASTYA: Are you sure?

LISA: Yes! The handsome young heir to the Tugilovo estates is now at the feet of a mere peasant girl. (*Laughs*) Can you imagine!

NASTYA (*Worried*): Perhaps you have carried your prank too far, mistress.

LISA: Oh, it is harmless, Nastya, as long as Papa doesn't know.

NASTYA: But, what do you think of Alexei Berestov?

LISA (*Trying to sound casual*): Oh, I am fond of him. We have very pleasant walks together, and he says lovely things to me

... and I believe he means them. He is very handsome and gentle, and ... and ...

NASTYA: And I believe you are falling in love with him! Oh, mistress, I think it would be wise to stop your little masquerade before it goes any farther.

LISA: But it's been such fun! I don't know when I've been happier. And how should I ever see him if I took no more walks in disguise?

NASTYA: I hear a carriage outside. (*Goes to window*) It is your father.

LISA (*Running to window*): Good heavens! He is limping. What could have happened? (MUROMSKY *enters left, limping, his clothes disheveled.*) Papa! (*Runs to him*) What has happened? Whose carriage was that?

MUROMSKY: You will never guess, my dear. (*He limps to chair and sits.*)

NASTYA (*Looking out window*): I see the Berestov crest on the carriage door.

MUROMSKY: Yes. Ivan Berestov drove me home.

LISA (*Surprised*): Ivan Berestov? Your enemy?

MUROMSKY: We are no longer enemies, Lisa. While I was out riding this morning, my foolish mare threw me into a ditch. Berestov was passing by and came to my aid. We talked, and discovered that we do not dislike each after all. We have come to good terms, and he and his son Alexei are coming to dine with us this evening.

LISA (*Alarmed*): What? Ivan Berestov... and *his son,* did you say?

MUROMSKY: Yes. You must look your loveliest, Lisa, my dear.

LISA (*Frantically*): Oh, no, Papa! I cannot attend the dinner. It must be for you gentlemen only.

MUROMSKY: Oh, no, my girl! Ivan Berestov clearly stated that he wished to meet you. His son is a handsome, eligible young man, just graduated from the University! (*Winks at her*)

LISA: But, Papa—

MUROMSKY: I am relieved to be rid of this quarrel with Berestov.

And who knows what may happen if his son should take an interest in you, eh?

LISA: Papa!

MUROMSKY: You must make the most of this opportunity. Alexei Berestov is an excellent match. No more protesting! They are expected here at seven o'clock.

LISA (*Reluctantly*): Very well Papa. (*Suddenly*) But you must promise me one thing!

MUROMSKY: And what is that?

LISA: No matter how I look or what I do, you must not scold me or give any sign of surprise or displeasure.

MUROMSKY: Up to some trick, are you, Lisa? (*Laughs*) All right, my girl, I'll do as you ask. But mind you—someday one of your pranks will get the better of you.

LISA: Yes, Papa. (*Kisses him on forehead and helps him up*)

MUROMSKY: Remember, now, seven o'clock. (*Limps out left*)

LISA: Yes, Papa.

NASTYA: Oh, my poor mistress! What will you do when Alexei Berestov sees you?

LISA: I won't let him see me, Nastya. I can't!

NASTYA: But you promised your father you would be at the dinner.

LISA: And I shall be. Come, you must help me. I'll tell you my plan as we go upstairs. (*They exit, as curtain falls.*)

* * * * *

SCENE 3

TIME: *Seven o'clock that evening.*

SETTING: *The same.*

AT RISE: MUROMSKY, BERESTOV, *and* ALEXEI *enter left.*

MUROMSKY: Tell me, now, Berestov, what do you think of my English-style garden?

BERESTOV (*Bowing stiffly*): Very interesting, Muromsky. However, if all that land were mind, I should plant it in corn and see a rich profit from it at harvest time. But let us not dispute, sir. My son is anxious to meet your daughter.

ALEXEI (*Aside*): It is my father who is anxious, not I! I will be polite to the young lady, of course, but my heart belongs to Akulina!

MUROMSKY: Ah, yes, my lovely Lisa! You will be charmed with her, Alexei.

ALEXEI (*Bowing*): I have heard her well spoken of, sir.

MUROMSKY: She has studied music, art, and French, and now she enjoys the personal attention of an English governess I've brought here at great expense.

BERESTOV: I'm told she is a most beautiful young lady.

MUROMSKY: Flashing eyes! A smile that would melt a stone! (*In* BERESTOV's *ear*) And her dowry is a generous one!

BERESTOV: Ah! (MISS JACKSON, *overdressed and heavily made-up, enters stiffly.*)

MUROMSKY: Ah, here is Miss Jackson, Lisa's governess. Miss Jackson, may I present Ivan Petrovitch Berestov, and his son, Alexei.

BERESTOV (*Bowing*): Madam!

MISS JACKSON (*Curtsying*): Gentlemen. (ALEXEI *bows and nods, trying to hide a smile.*)

MUROMSKY (*In a loud whisper, to* MISS JACKSON): Where is Lisa?

MISS JACKSON (*Whispering*): I haven't see her all afternoon.

NASTYA (*Entering left and curtsying*): Miss Lisa Muromsky! (*She hides a giggle behind her hand as* LISA *sweeps in, dressed in a bright, billowy dress with a hoop skirt, wearing too much jewelry and a frizzled wig. Her face is made-up heavily, and she carries a fan, which she waves clumsily. She assumes a wide-eyed, silly expression, and speaks in a high, squeaky voice throughout the scene.* MUROMSKY *stares at her in amazement.* MISS JACKSON *looks on in horror.* NASTYA *exits.*)

LISA (*Tripping across stage*): Dear Papa, I hope I haven't kept everyone waiting.

MUROMSKY (*Coughing, trying to hide a smile, then loudly clearing his throat*): No, no, come here, my dear, and meet Ivan Berestov and his son, Alexei. As you can see, gentlemen, my daughter imitates the fashions of her English governess.

BERESTOV: Very charming, my dear. (*Bows and kisses her hand*)

ALEXEI (*Reluctantly kissing her hand*): Miss Muromsky.

MUROMSKY: Come, sit down. (*He leads her to settee, where she struggles with hoop skirt.*)

BERESTOV (*Pushing* ALEXEI *toward settee*): Why don't you sit over there, Alexei? (ALEXEI *falls into seat beside* LISA, *who giggles and wildly flutters her fan.*)

MISS JACKSON (*In a loud whisper; to* LISA): You little vixen! That is my dress! Those are my jewels, my wig! Just wait until I get my hands on you! I'll box your ears!

BERESTOV: Ahem! You know, Muromsky, it has been foolish for us to remain aloof all these years. Our children have missed the opportunity of knowing each other.

MUROMSKY: You are quite right, Berestov. We must see that they become better acquainted. (LISA *giggles and fans herself.*)

BERESTOV: Yes, yes. (*Pause*) I believe, Muromsky, that you are a close relative of Count Pronsky—is that not so?

MUROMSKY (*Proudly*): Yes! The Count is my first cousin. A man of great distinction and power, you know, and well acquainted with members of the nobility. Ah, *your* estate is, I believe, the largest in the province, isn't it?

BERESTOV (*Pompously*): Yes, the largest and the richest!

MUROMSKY: And is Alexei your only child?

BERESTOV: Yes. Someday all I have shall be his.

MUROMSKY (*Approvingly*): Ah!

NASTYA (*Entering left*): Dinner is served.

MUROMSKY: Good! Come, everyone. This way. (*He offers* MISS JACKSON *his arm.* LISA *manages to get up with help from* BERESTOV, *who then shoves* ALEXEI *to her side, and they all exit. There is a blackout to indicate passage of time. When lights come up full,* BERESTOV *and* ALEXEI *reenter.*)

ALEXEI: Now that you have had your talk with Grigory Muromsky, and I have been released from the stifling company of Miss Muromsky and her ridiculous governess, may we go home? I have a headache!

BERESTOV: Alexei, my boy, you have always been an obedient and dutiful son. In time you will enter the government service as I wish you to do, but now, I think it would be wise for you to marry Lisa Muromsky. Grigory has already agreed to it.

ALEXEI: But Father! She is a clumsy, foolish, ridiculous girl!

BERESTOV: She is only young and shy. She brings a handsome dowry, and by marrying her, you can make use of her father's connection with Count Pronsky to gain a high position in the government service. You could not find a more suitable match anywhere!

ALEXEI: Father, with all respect, you are thinking only of yourself. I do not want a career in the government, and I will not marry Lisa Muromsky. I love another girl.

BERESTOV (*Astonished*): Another girl? Who?

ALEXEI: I cannot tell you.

BERESTOV: Nonsense! You will marry Lisa Muromsky, or I shall disinherit you!

ALEXEI: Father, surely you don't mean that!

BERESTOV: I do! I'll give you twenty-four hours to think over my wishes. If you do not agree to marry Lisa Muromsky, then you must leave my house forever!

ALEXEI (*Stiffly*): Very well, Father. Excuse me. I will walk home. I need the fresh air. (*Bows and hurries off*)

BERESTOV: What a fool that boy is! But, of course, he will not give up the Tugilovo estates! He will see it my way.

MUROMSKY (*Entering left*): Your carriage is ready, Berestov. Did you speak to your son?

BERESTOV: Yes, yes! Don't worry. We shall have the wedding before the summer is over! (*Claps* MUROMSKY *on the shoulder*)

MUROMSKY: Lisa will be so happy! Come, I'll walk out with you. (*Curtain*)

* * * * *

SCENE 4

TIME: *Next morning.*

SETTING: *The woods.*

BEFORE RISE: ALEXEI *paces restlessly.* LISA, *in her peasant disguise, enters.*

ALEXEI (*Embracing her*): Akulina! I thought you would never come! Oh, let me look at you, and I shall smile forever!

LISA: And why should you wish to look at me? I hear you were at Grigory Muromsky's house last night. Surely you prefer to look at his lovely daughter.

ALEXEI: Never! She is a monster!

LISA (*Pretending to be shocked*): What? Lisa Muromsky a monster?

ALEXEI: Yes! For all her high birth and education, she dresses like a circus clown and giggles like a kitchen maid!

LISA: Still, she is the squire's daughter, and I am only a poor peasant. We must not see each other again.

ALEXEI: Don't say that, Akulina! My day is not complete until I have seen you and held your hand. (*On his knees*) Dear Akulina, I must never lose you. I love you! I want to marry you!

LISA (*Turning away; flustered*): You mustn't talk like that! You could never marry me!

ALEXEI: And why not?

LISA: Your father would never allow it.

ALEXEI: It's true that last night my father threatened to disinherit me if I refuse to marry Lisa Muromsky, but I never will! It is you I love, dear Akulina!

LISA (*Startled*): What? Oh, but Alexei, you cannot disobey your father!

ALEXEI: I will explain it to him. I love you enough to give up my inheritance and adopt the life of a peasant and earn my living by my own labor. Tell your father the blacksmith that I shall come and speak to him tomorrow.

LISA: Oh, no, Alexei, please . . .

ALEXEI: Don't be afraid. (*Turns aside; excitedly*) I am the happiest man alive! We will build our own small house and work together in the fields.

LISA (*Backing away*): No, Alexei, it can't be. No! (*Panic-stricken, she runs off.*)

ALEXEI (*Unaware she is gone*): We'll take long walks in the mornings just as we have been doing, and there will be no other couple in the province as happy as we! (*Looks around*) Akulina! Akulina? (*Smiling*) She has run home to tell her family the happy news. And I must go to Grigory Muromsky and explain to him why I cannot marry his daughter. The sooner, the better. (*Exits*)

* * *

TIME: *An hour later.*

SETTING: *Muromsky's drawing room.*

AT RISE: LISA, *in her own dress, enters followed by* NASTYA.

LISA (*Anxiously*): Nastya, what am I to do? If Alexei goes to Vasily the blacksmith, he will see the real Akulina. And if my father has determined that I shall marry Alexei, I will have to face him and then he will never want to see me again.

NASTYA: Dear mistress, I'm afraid your trick has turned against you. (ALEXEI *enters left, unseen by them, and waits in door-way.* LISA *has her back to him.*)

LISA: If only I hadn't fallen in love with him! At first it was just a pleasant game, a joke, but now, I love Alexei more than I can say! And I must lose him forever! (*She turns, sobbing, and* ALEXEI *recognizes her. He drops his hat in surprise.*)

NASTYA: No, mistress, you mustn't lose him! He loves you!

LISA: But what can I do?

NASTYA: Tell him the truth!

LISA: What! Tell him his poor Akulina is really Lisa Muromsky, who disguised herself so she could meet him? What would he think?

ALEXEI (*Stepping into the room*): He would think Lisa Muromsky is the cleverest, dearest girl in the world!

LISA: Alexei! Oh! (*Tries to run past him, but he catches her*) Let me go!

ALEXEI: Never! My Akulina . . . my Lisa!

LISA (*Sobbing*): Please, let me go.

ALEXEI: That is impossible. A moment ago I was happy, but now I am ecstatic!

LISA: Do you mean you still wish to marry me?

ALEXEI: Of course! More than ever!

LISA: But what about my foolish prank?

ALEXEI: Without your foolish prank, we might never have met and fallen in love! (*He kisses her, as* MISS JACKSON, BERESTOV *and* MUROMSKY *enter.*)

MISS JACKSON: Lisa! What is the meaning of this?

ALEXEI: It means, madam, that you may soon help Lisa plan her wedding.

MISS JACKSON: Wedding!

BERESTOV: Alexei! Who is this young lady?

ALEXEI: The girl I love and the girl I am going to marry. Lisa Muromsky!

BERESTOV (*Staring at* LISA): I don't understand.

MUROMSKY (*Laughing*): Never mind. We should have left it to them in the first place. Come, this calls for a toast! (NASTYA *hurries to cabinet, brings wine glasses and decanter. Fills glasses and serves them.*)

BERESTOV (*Raising his glass*): To the squire's daughter!

MUROMSKY (*Raising his glass*): And her husband-to-be!

ALEXEI: And to all the little pranks my Lisa may play in the future! (*All drink; curtain*)

THE END

Production Notes

THE SQUIRE'S DAUGHTER

Characters: 3 female; 3 male.

Playing Time: 30 minutes.

Costumes: Early 19th-century Russian dress. Muromsky, Berestov, and Alexei wear tailed coats, knee breeches, tall boots, and hats. Miss Jackson is heavily made-up and wears long, full dress and powdered wig; in Scene 3 she wears brightly colored dress, jewelry. Lisa wears long, full dress. When disguised as peasant, she wears blue smock, coarse shirt, and kerchief. In Scene 3 she has on heavy makeup, brightly colored, billowy dress with hoop skirt and full sleeves, jewelry, and powdered wig. Nastya has plain dress, apron, and cap.

Properties: Small basket; a toy hunting rifle; embroidery; fan; tray with five wine glasses and decanter of apple cider.

Setting: Stately drawing room of Muromsky's house. Settee is center, armchairs are left and right. Window center rear has rich, heavy draperies. Cabinet is next to window. Bookcases, small tables, etc., complete the setting. Door at right leads to garden. Door at left leads to rest of house. The wood is played before curtain. Bushes or trees may be painted on flats if desired, but they must be easy to move on and off stage.

Lighting: No special effects.

Sound: Dogs barking; loud gunshot, as indicated in text.

▣▣ Alice in Wonderland

by *Lewis Carroll*
Adapted by *R. Rochelle*

Characters

ALICE
WHITE RABBIT
CATERPILLAR
DUCHESS
CHESHIRE CAT
MAD HATTER
MARCH HARE
DORMOUSE
QUEEN OF HEARTS
MOCK TURTLE
ALICE'S MOTHER, *Offstage voice*

BEFORE RISE: *Soft music is heard, as* ALICE *enters left, wearing dress with white pinafore and shiny black shoes, book in hand. She crosses right, sits on floor.*

ALICE: I think I'll just sit here awhile and read. (*Starts reading, begins to yawn*). Dear me, I'm getting so sleepy. (*Continues reading, but then drops book, lies down, and falls asleep.* WHITE RABBIT *hops in right, wearing vest with very large pocket watch. Music stops.*)

RABBIT (*Looking at his watch*): I'm late, I'm late! (ALICE *wakes with a start, sits up.*) Oh, dear! I'm very late!

217

ALICE (*Rubbing her eyes in amazement*): A rabbit!

RABBIT (*Pushing past* ALICE): Out of my way, girl. I'm very late.

ALICE (*Confused*): Late for *what*, Mr. Rabbit?

RABBIT: No time to visit, my dear—she'll behead me for sure if I'm late.

ALICE (*Alarmed*): Who'll behead you?

RABBIT (*Excitedly*): The Queen of Hearts, the jury, *everyone!* Oh, my ears and whiskers! What a terrible fate—a rabbit without his head!

ALICE: Mr. Rabbit, do tell me what is wrong! (*He ignores her and exits through curtain. She calls after him.*) Mr. Rabbit, Mr. Rabbit! Come back! (*Peering off*) I suppose he's gone down that rabbit hole. (*She gets up, follows him through curtain, then cries out, her voice getting fainter, as if she were falling.*) Oh-h-h-h! (*Curtain rises*)

* * *

SETTING: *A strange garden filled with huge, brightly colored flowers. There are large rocks right, which hide an exit.*

AT RISE: ALICE *is sitting on ground.* CATERPILLAR *is lying on rocks, right, unnoticed by* ALICE.

ALICE (*Looking around, bewildered*): Where am I? I must have fallen down the rabbit hole! It felt as if I were falling right *through* the earth! (*Puzzled*) But I've hit the bottom, and it didn't hurt a bit! (*Pointing to flowers*) I'm not on the other side of the earth at all—I'm in someone's garden! (RABBIT *rushes in right.*)

RABBIT: I'm late.

ALICE: Why, what are *you* doing here?

RABBIT: I live here. And what, may I ask, are *you* doing in my garden?

ALICE: I seem to have fallen down your rabbit hole.

RABBIT (*Annoyed*): Yes, and through my house, and now you're trampling on my garden. Such a clumsy girl. You'd best fix yourself up and hurry along or you'll be late, too. (*He starts off left.*) Oh dear, now I'm later than ever! (*He exits quickly.*)

ALICE (*Shouting after him*): Late for *what?* I just arrived! Mr.

Rabbit, please come back! (*She gets up, starts after him, then stops. Angrily*) How rude of him! I asked him a civil question, and he deliberately ran off without giving me an answer!

CATERPILLAR (*From rocks; calmly*): Who are *you*?

ALICE (*Startled, turning around*): I—I hardly know, sir, at the moment. (*Pause*) I knew who I was when I got up this morning, but I think things must have changed a great deal since then. (*Walks over to* CATERPILLAR)

CATERPILLAR: What do you mean by that? Explain yourself.

ALICE: I can't explain *myself*, sir, because I'm not myself.

CATERPILLAR: I don't understand.

ALICE: This morning, I was just a girl reading by the river bank, and now I'm lost in this strange place.

CATERPILLAR (*Looking about*): I don't find this place a bit strange.

ALICE: Well, all I know is, it seems very strange to *me*!

CATERPILLAR: But who *are* you?

ALICE (*Irritably*): I think you ought to tell me who *you* are first.

CATERPILLAR: Why?

ALICE (*Frustratedly*): Oh! (*She stamps her foot and starts off.*)

CATERPILLAR: Come back! I've something important to say! (ALICE *pauses, as if to reconsider, and approaches* CATERPILLAR.)

ALICE: Yes?

CATERPILLAR (*Moving closer, nose-to-nose*): Keep your temper.

ALICE (*Annoyed*): Is that all?

CATERPILLAR: No. You have no business standing in the Duchess's kitchen. (ALICE *looks around her.*)

ALICE (*Angrily*): I'm *not* in the Duchess's kitchen! (*During the rest of* ALICE's *speech*, DUCHESS *and grinning* CHESHIRE CAT *enter left. They carry in table, large soup pot, spoon, large pepper shaker, and baby wrapped in blanket.* DUCHESS *sits on ground beside table, holds baby in her lap, and begins stirring soup, shaking pepper into it from time to time.*) I am standing in the White Rabbit's garden—wherever *that* is! There is no house here, and you can't have a kitchen without a house around it. And I don't know any Duchess, anyway!

CATERPILLAR: You certainly are standing in her kitchen, and I must say you are very rude to barge in without knocking.

ALICE: Who is the Duchess?!

CATERPILLAR: *Who are you? (He disappears behind rocks and exits.)*

ALICE *(Upset)*: Well, really! *(She begins sneezing.)* I certainly don't *(Sneezes)* understand him at all! *(Sneezes, then turns around to find herself facing* DUCHESS.) Oh! My goodness! You must be the Duchess!

DUCHESS *(Imperiously)*: Yes, and what do *you* have to say for yourself?

ALICE: Uh . . . there's certainly too much pepper in that soup! *(Sneezes loudly)*

DUCHESS: Nonsense. There's not nearly enough pepper in that soup. *(Shakes more into soup, then sneezes herself)* Ach-oo! Not—achoo!—nearly enough.

ALICE *(Noticing* CHESHIRE CAT): Why does your cat grin like that?

DUCHESS: It's a Cheshire cat, that's why.

ALICE: I didn't know Cheshire cats always grinned. In fact, I didn't know that cats *could* grin.

DUCHESS: They all can, and most of them do.

ALICE: I don't know of *any* that do.

DUCHESS: You don't know much! *(She begins hitting baby with spoon.* CAT *hides behind rocks.)*

ALICE *(Upset)*: You're hurting the baby!

DUCHESS *(Matter-of-factly)*: It doesn't matter. He's a pig, anyway.

ALICE *(Indignantly)*: He's not a pig. And I don't think you're a bit kind to him.

DUCHESS: Oh, go away and don't bother me. *(She picks up baby and begins to sing offkey lullaby while tossing baby about.)*
Speak roughly to your little boy,
And beat him when he sneezes;
He only does it to annoy,
Because he knows it teases.
(To ALICE) Here! You take care of him. I have to go play croquet with the Queen. *(She roughly hands baby to* ALICE, *then exits left, taking pepper shaker and spoon.)*

ALICE (*To baby*): What a strange-looking little baby. (*Pause*) Why, the baby's grunting! Don't grunt. That's not at all a proper way of expressing yourself. My, your face is turning awfully pink. And your hands are turning into feet! If you're going to turn into a pig, I'll have nothing more to do with you! (DUCHESS *reenters*.) Mind now! I'll have nothing to do with a pig! (ALICE *sets baby on table.* DUCHESS *grabs him, stuffs him into soup kettle, and exits calmly with kettle.* ALICE *looks after her, shocked.* CAT *climbs onto rock, as* ALICE *starts right, then notices him and stops.*) Cheshire Cat, would you tell me, please, which way I ought to walk from here?

CAT: That depends a good deal on where you want to get to.

ALICE: I don't much care where.

CAT: Then it doesn't matter which way you walk.

ALICE: So long as I get *somewhere*.

CAT: Oh, you're sure to do that, if you only walk long enough!

ALICE: What sort of people live here?

CAT: In that direction (*Waving to right*), lives a Hatter; and in *that* direction (*Waving to left*), lives a March Hare. Visit either you like. They're both mad.

ALICE: But I don't want to visit anyone who's mad!

CAT: Oh, you can't help that. We're all mad here. I'm mad. You're mad.

ALICE (*Angrily*): How do you know I'm mad?

CAT: You must be, or you wouldn't have come here.

ALICE: And how do you know that you're mad?

CAT: Well, a dog growls when it's angry, and wags its tail when it's pleased. Now, *I* growl when I'm pleased, and wag my tail when I'm angry. Therefore, I'm mad.

ALICE: *I* call it purring, not growling.

CAT: Call it what you like. (*Pause*) Do you plan to play croquet with the Queen today?

ALICE: I haven't been invited.

CAT: You'll see me there. (*After a pause,* ALICE *starts off left.*) By the by, what became of the baby?

ALICE (*Turning*): It turned into a pig.

CAT: I rather thought it would. Well, goodbye.

ALICE: Goodbye. (CAT *disappears behind rocks and exits.* ALICE

continues left. Singing and laughter are heard off right, then
MAD HATTER, MARCH HARE, *and* DORMOUSE *enter right. They
are carrying tea cups, teapot, etc., with which they set table.*
ALICE *turns to watch them, then speaks to herself.*) I certainly
didn't have to go far at all. It's just as well. I'm not sure the
cat's directions were very precise anyway. (MAD HATTER *and*
MARCH HARE *sit on ground beside table.* DORMOUSE *sits between them and quickly dozes off.* HATTER *and* HARE *spy* ALICE
and give a start.)

HATTER *and* HARE (*Shouting*): No room! No room!

ALICE (*Indignantly*): There's plenty of room! (*She sits beside
table.*)

HARE: It wasn't very civil of you to sit down at our table without
being invited.

ALICE: I didn't know it was *your* table—it's set for a great many
more than three.

HATTER: Why is a raven like a writing desk?

ALICE (*Gleefully*): Oh, a riddle! I believe I can guess that.

HARE: Do you mean you think you can find the answer to it?

ALICE: Exactly!

HARE: Then you should say what you mean.

ALICE: I do. At least—at least I mean what I say—that's the
same thing, you know.

HATTER: Not the same thing a bit! Why, you might just as well
say that "I see what I eat" is the same thing as "I eat what
I see."

HARE: You might just as well say that "I like what I get" is the
same thing as "I get what I like."

DORMOUSE (*Sleepily*): You might just as well say that "I breathe
when I sleep" is the same thing as "I sleep when I breathe."

HATTER (*To* DORMOUSE): It *is* the same thing with you, Dormouse! (HATTER *and* HARE *drink their tea.* HATTER *takes his
watch out of his pocket, shakes it several times, and holds it to
his ear.*) What day of the month is it?

ALICE: The fourth.

HATTER: Two days off! (*To* HARE) I told you the butter wouldn't
be good for fixing my watch.

HARE: It was the *best* butter.

HATTER: Yes, but some crumbs must have fallen into it as well. You shouldn't have used the bread knife to spread it. (HARE *takes watch, shakes it, dips it into his tea, then puts it down.*)

HARE: It was the *best* butter, you know.

ALICE (*Looking at watch*): What a funny watch! It tells the day of the month but doesn't tell which o'clock it is!

HATTER: Why should it? Does *your* watch tell you what year it is?

ALICE: Of course not, but that's because it stays the same year for such a long time.

HATTER: Which is just the case with *mine*.

ALICE (*Puzzled*): I don't quite understand you.

HATTER (*To* ALICE): Have you guessed the riddle yet?

ALICE: No, I give up. What's the answer?

HATTER: I haven't the slightest idea.

ALICE (*Exasperated*): I think you might do something better with the time than wasting it in asking riddles that have no answers.

HATTER: If you knew Time as well as I do, you wouldn't talk about wasting *it*. It's *him*!

ALICE: I don't know what you mean.

HATTER: Of course not! I dare say you've never even spoken to Time!

ALICE (*Hesitantly*): Perhaps not.

HATTER: If you only keep on good terms with him, he'll do almost anything you like with the clock. For instance, suppose it were nine o'clock in the morning, just in time to begin lessons; you'd only have to whisper a hint to Time, and round goes the clock in a twinkling! Half past one, time for dinner!

HARE (*To himself*): I only wish it were.

ALICE: That would be grand, certainly, but then—I shouldn't be hungry for it, you know.

HATTER: Not at first, perhaps, but you could keep it to half past one as long as you liked.

ALICE: Is that the way *you* manage?

HATTER (*Sadly*): Not I. We quarreled with Time last March— just before *he* (*Pointing to* HARE) went mad, you know. It was at the great concert given by the Queen of Hearts, and I had

to sing. (*Singing*)
Twinkle, twinkle, little bat!
How I wonder what you're at!
(*Speaks*) You know the song, perhaps?

ALICE: I've heard something like it.

HATTER: It goes on, you know, in this way. (*Singing*)
Up above the world you fly,
Like a teatray in the sky,
Twinkle, twinkle—

DORMOUSE (*Singing sleepily*): Twinkle, twinkle, twinkle, twinkle—(*He stops when* HATTER *and* HARE *poke him.*)

HATTER: Well, I'd hardly finished the first verse when the Queen bawled out, "He's murdering the time! Off with his head!"

ALICE: How dreadful of her!

HATTER: And ever since then, Time won't do a thing I ask! It's always six o'clock now.

ALICE: Is *that* the reason so many tea things are put out here?

HATTER (*Sighing*): Yes, that's it. It's always teatime, and we've no time to wash the dishes in between.

ALICE: Then you keep moving round the table, I suppose?

HATTER: Exactly so, as the cups get used up.

ALICE: But when do you come to the beginning again?

HARE: There is no beginning.

ALICE: Of course there is! Everything must have a beginning!

HARE: Exactly so. The beginning already began, so the beginning is used up and now there is no beginning.

ALICE (*Confused and irritated*): Then what do you do when you come to the end?

HATTER: There is no end until it finishes, and it's always six o'clock, so we haven't gotten there yet.

ALICE: Then what do you do when you're in the *middle*?

HARE: Drink tea. Will you have some more?

ALICE: I've had nothing yet, so I can't take more.

HATTER: You mean you can't take less. It's very easy to take *more* than *nothing*.

DORMOUSE: Twinkle, twinkle, twinkle, twinkle—

ALICE (*Stamping her foot*): Oh! (*She walks left in disgust, then turns*) That's the stupidest tea party I ever saw! (*Walks down left and sulks*)

HARE: My cup is dirty. Everyone move left to the next place. (*He shoves* DORMOUSE, *who falls onto ground.*)

HATTER (*Picking up* DORMOUSE): Move to the right. We've moved left three times already. (*He shoves* DORMOUSE *right, and he again falls onto ground.* RABBIT, CATERPILLAR, DUCHESS, CAT, *and* QUEEN OF HEARTS *enter left, carrying croquet mallets and hitting croquet balls.* RABBIT *hits ball, which rolls to* HATTER, *who picks it up.*)

QUEEN OF HEARTS (*Loudly*): Off with your head.

RABBIT: Who has my ball? Oh, my ears and whiskers, I shall never be able to play without my ball!

HATTER (*Holding up ball*): I believe I have it. Would you care to join us for tea?

CATERPILLAR (*To* HATTER): Who are *you*?

QUEEN (*Seeing* HATTER *with ball*): Off with his head! (*At this,* HATTER *and* HARE *run out right, taking their table and tea things.* DORMOUSE *is left behind, asleep. Croquet game continues.*) Whose turn is it?

DUCHESS (*Imperiously*): Mine, of course.

QUEEN: Off with your head! (HARE *and* HATTER *run back in, unnoticed by players, and drag* DORMOUSE *off.* QUEEN *notices* ALICE, *who has been dodging balls and people all this time.*) Who are you?

ALICE (*Startled; curtsying*): My name is Alice, Your Majesty.

QUEEN (*Shouting*): Can you play croquet?

ALICE (*Shouting back*): Yes!

QUEEN: Then play! Or off with your head!

ALICE: If you please, Your Majesty, I don't have a mallet or a ball. If you would be so kind as to— (*As she speaks, they all exit right, hitting their balls offstage as they go.* ALICE *is left alone on stage.*) Oh, well, at least I still have my head, and that's something to be grateful for! They're dreadfully fond of beheading people here. It's a great wonder that there's anyone left alive! (*Sobbing is heard from behind rock.*)

MOCK TURTLE (*Coming out from behind rock; sadly singing*): Beautiful Soup, so rich and green,

Waiting in a hot tureen!
Beautiful Soup, beautiful Soup,
Beautiful, beautiful, beautiful Soup.

ALICE: I beg your pardon, but who are you?

TURTLE (*Still sobbing*): I'm the Mock Turtle.

ALICE: What is a Mock Turtle?

TURTLE: The thing they make Mock Turtle soup from. Once I was a real turtle.

ALICE: What happened?

TURTLE: Sit down and I'll tell you, and don't speak a word until I've finished. (ALICE *sits.* TURTLE *stops sobbing, but still speaks in melancholy tone.*) When I was little, I went to school in the sea. The Master was an old turtle. We used to call him Tortoise.

ALICE: Why did you call him Tortoise if he wasn't one?

TURTLE (*Angrily*): We called him *Tor-toise* because he *taught us.* Really, you are very dull!

ALICE: Please, go on with your story!

TURTLE: Very well. I went to school in the sea, though you may not believe it.

ALICE (*Interrupting*): I never said I didn't!

TURTLE: You did. We had the best of educations. In fact, we went to school every day.

ALICE: You needn't be so proud as all that. I've been to school, too. What subjects did *you* learn?

TURTLE: Reeling and Writhing, of course, to begin with, and then the different branches of Arithmetic—Ambition, Distraction, Uglification, and Derision.

ALICE: I never heard of Uglification. What is it?

TURTLE: Never heard of Uglification! Do you know what beautification is?

ALICE (*Doubtfully*): Yes, it means to make anything prettier.

TURTLE: Well, then, if you don't what to uglify is, you *are* a simpleton.

ALICE: And how many hours a day did you do lessons?

TURTLE: Ten hours the first day, nine the next, and so on.

ALICE: What a curious plan!

TURTLE: That's the reason they're called lessons—because they *lessen* from day to day.

ALICE: Then the eleventh day must have been a holiday.

TURTLE: Of course, it was.

ALICE: Then how did you manage the twelfth day?

TURTLE (*Ignoring her*): That's enough about lessons. You may not have lived under the sea, and perhaps you were never even introduced to a lobster, so you can have no idea what a delightful dance a Lobster Quadrille is!

ALICE: No, indeed. What sort of dance is it?

TURTLE (*Gesturing as he explains*): First you form two lines along the seashore—seals, turtles, salmon, and so on. Then, when you've cleared all the jellyfish out of the way—which generally takes a long time—you advance twice, set to partners.

ALICE (*Puzzled*): Advance twice, set to partners?

TURTLE: Of course. Would you like me to show you a little of it?

ALICE: Very much indeed. (TURTLE *grabs her, swings her about rapidly, making her almost lose her balance.*)

TURTLE (*Reciting as they dance*):

Will you walk a little faster? said a whiting to a snail,

There's a porpoise close behind us, and he's treading on my tail.

See how eagerly the lobsters and the turtles all advance!

They are waiting on the shingle, will you come and join the dance?

(*He ends dance by giving* ALICE *one last twirl, which lands her on the ground.*)

ALICE (*Breathlessly*): Thank you. It's a very interesting dance. And I like that curious song about the whiting. (*She stands up.*)

TURTLE: Do you know why it's called a whiting?

ALICE: I never thought about it.

TURTLE: It does the boots and shoes!

ALICE (*Puzzled*): Does the boots and shoes?

TURTLE: What are *your* shoes done with? What makes them so shiny?

ALICE (*Looking down at her shoes*): That's done with *blacking*.

TURTLE: Boots and shoes under the sea are done with whiting. Now you know.

ALICE: And what are the shoes made of?

TURTLE: Soles and eels, of course. Any shrimp could have told you that.

ALICE (*Apologetically*): Oh.

TURTLE: Would you like to dance the Lobster Quadrille again, or would you rather I sing a song?

ALICE (*Much relieved*): Oh, a song would be lovely.

TURTLE (*Singing*):

Beautiful Soup, so rich and green,
Waiting in a hot tureen!
Who for such dainties would not stoop?
Soup of the evening, beautiful Soup!
Soup of the evening, beautiful Soup!
  Beautiful Soooooop!
  Beautiful Soooooop!
Sooooop of the evening,
  Beautiful, beautiful Soup!

(*As he sings,* ALICE *starts to leave, unnoticed by* TURTLE. *Before song ends,* RABBIT *enters, scroll in hand.*)

RABBIT: The trial's beginning! Hear ye! The trial's beginning! (*Pointing left*) The jury sits here. (RABBIT *is followed by* CATERPILLAR, DUCHESS, *who carries pepper shaker,* CAT, HATTER, *who carries teacup,* HARE *and* DORMOUSE. *All carry slate and chalk, with an extra slate for* TURTLE, *who joins them as a jury member. Jury sits on floor.* RABBIT *rushes off and returns with large chair, which he places center.*)

ALICE (*To* RABBIT, *who is running around nervously*): What trial is this? (*He ignores her. All look on attentively as* QUEEN *enters right. She takes her place in large chair.* ALICE *points to jury members writing on their slates.*) What are they doing? There's nothing to write down before the trial begins.

RABBIT: They're putting down their names for fear they will forget them before the end of the trial.

ALICE (*Quite loudly*): Stupid things!

QUEEN: Silence in the court! Herald, read the accusation.

RABBIT (*Unrolling his scroll*):

The Queen of Hearts, she made some tarts,
All on a summer day;
The Knave of Hearts, he stole those tarts,
And took them quite away!

QUEEN: Consider the verdict.

RABBIT: Not yet, not yet! There's a great deal to come before that.

QUEEN: Call the first witness.

RABBIT: Mad Hatter!

HATTER (*Stepping forward, teacup in hand*): I beg your pardon, Your Majesty, for bringing my tea in, but I hadn't quite finished it when I was sent for.

QUEEN: You ought to have finished. When did you begin?

HATTER: Fourteenth of March, I *think* it was.

HARE: Fifteenth.

DORMOUSE: Sixteenth.

QUEEN (*To jury*): Write that down. (*To* HATTER) Take off your hat.

HATTER: It isn't mine.

QUEEN: Stolen!

HATTER (*Nervously*): I keep them to sell. I've none of my own. I'm a hatter.

QUEEN: Give your evidence, and don't be nervous, or I'll have you executed.

HATTER: I'm a poor man, Your Majesty, and I had just begun my tea, when the March Hare said—

HARE: I deny it!

QUEEN: He denies it—leave that part out!

HATTER: Well, at any rate, the Dormouse said . . . (*Frowns in concentration*) . . . and then I cut some more bread and butter—

CATERPILLAR: What did the Dormouse say?

HATTER (*Helplessly*): I can't remember.

QUEEN: You *must* remember, or I'll have you executed.

ALICE: That's not fair!

QUEEN: *Silence!* Or off with *your* head. (ALICE *steps back*. QUEEN *turns to* HATTER.) If that's all you know about it, you may sit down.

HATTER: I'd rather finish my tea. (QUEEN *glares at him, and he sits.*)

QUEEN: Call the next witness!

RABBIT: Duchess! (*She steps forward with pepper shaker in her hand.*)

QUEEN: Give your evidence.

DUCHESS (*Defiantly*): Shan't.

QUEEN (*Shouting in anger*): What are tarts made of?

DUCHESS: Pepper, mostly.

DORMOUSE (*Sleepily*): Tea!

QUEEN: Arrest that Dormouse! Behead him! Pinch him! Off with his whiskers! (*He promptly falls asleep.*) Never mind. Call the next witness.

RABBIT: Alice!

ALICE (*Stepping forward*): Yes?

QUEEN: What do you know of this business?

ALICE: Nothing.

QUEEN: Nothing *whatever*?

ALICE: Nothing whatever.

QUEEN (*To jury*): Members of the jury, consider your verdict.

ALICE: You can't consider the verdict yet. You haven't proper evidence.

RABBIT: Of course, we have. The jury has it all written down.

ALICE: If any one of them can explain the evidence, I'll give him a sixpence. *I* don't believe there's an atom of meaning in it.

QUEEN: If there's no meaning in it, that saves a world of trouble. We needn't try to find any.

CAT: Consider the verdict!

QUEEN: No, no! Sentence first—verdict afterward.

ALICE: Stuff and nonsense! The idea of having the sentence first!

QUEEN: *Off with her head!*

ALICE: Who cares about you? You're nothing but a pack of cards!

ALL (*Ad lib; standing and pointing at* ALICE): Guilty! *You* stole the tarts! Off with her head! (*Etc. Their voices grow louder and louder.* ALICE, *as if dazed, backs away from them to edge of stage, sits and falls asleep, as curtain closes behind her. Voices stop abruptly. After a moment of silence,* ALICE'S MOTHER *is heard calling from off left.*)

MOTHER (*Calling*): Alice, where are you?

ALICE (*Awakening*): Oh, what a curious dream I've just had.

MOTHER (*Calling louder*): Alice!

ALICE (*Calling back to her*): Coming, Mother! (*To herself, sleepily and puzzled*) It all began when the White Rabbit ran across the bank ... and I followed him. (*She looks around, as if trying to remember.*) I followed him over here. (*She goes to center of curtain, but cannot find opening.*) At least I *thought* there was a rabbit hole here—and somehow I fell down it ever so far and found myself among curious creatures in a strange land—a *wonder*land. (*She runs off left, as soft music is played.*)

THE END

Production Notes

ALICE IN WONDERLAND

Characters: 7 male or female; 3 female; 1 offstage voice for Mother.

Playing Time: 25 minutes.

Costumes: Alice wears dress, white pinafore, and shiny black shoes. Duchess wears a long dress and an apron. The Queen's robe has red hearts on it, and she wears a crown. Others wear appropriate costumes, suggesting the traditional *Alice in Wonderland* characters.

Properties: Book, very large pocket watch, standard size pocket watch, low table, spoon, soup kettle, pepper shaker, doll wrapped in blanket, teacups and teapot, five croquet mallets and balls, eight slates with chalk, scroll.

Setting: A strange garden, filled with flowers of extraordinary size and color. Rocks up right, large enough for Mock Turtle to hide behind. Exits are at right, left and behind rocks, right.

Sound: Soft music, as indicated.

ᵽᵽ The School for Wives

by *Molière*
Adapted by *Paul T. Nolan*

Characters

ARNOLPHE, *rich old man, using the alias M. de la Souche*
LUCINDE, *his somewhat deaf neighbor*
ALAIN, *his male servant*
GEORGETTE, *his female servant*
AGNES, *his ward and intended wife*
CHRYSALDE, *his friend*
HORACE, *a young man in love with Agnes*
ORONTE, *Horace's father*
ENRIQUE, *Chrysalde's brother-in-law*

SCENE 1

TIME: *Seventeenth century.*
SETTING: *The garden outside a country home. At center are white wrought-iron chairs and table. Backdrop of trees and shrubs.*
AT RISE: ARNOLPHE, *sitting at table, is speaking to* LUCINDE, *who is knitting. Throughout scene,* LUCINDE *appears to be so deaf that she does not understand a word he says.*
ARNOLPHE: All men are fools with women. But not I, not Arnolphe. (*Turns and gestures toward* LUCINDE) Do you follow me, old neighbor?
LUCINDE (*Nodding in agreement*): True, this is not the season for rain.

233

ARNOLPHE (*Smiling*): Your deafness, dear Lucinde, may be a trial for you, but I consider it your greatest virtue. At times a man needs to confide in a woman. If he's wise, he'll pick one who is deaf. Don't you agree?

LUCINDE: In the first year of the reign of our good King Louis, it rained almost every day.

ARNOLPHE (*Smiling*): I love your understanding. Now, I'll tell you my secret. I am going to be married. But I am not going to be a fool. The girl I mean to marry has every virtue, for she was trained in my special school for wives.

LUCINDE: Sometimes I like rain.

ARNOLPHE (*Half to himself*): Some friends will say my Agnes is nothing but a young, silly girl. True, she is a trifle younger than I am.

LUCINDE: I remember the rain depressed you that summer.

ARNOLPHE (*Reasoning to himself*): I am not silly to marry a young, naive girl. It's the man who marries a clever wife who is silly.

LUCINDE: I wondered at the time if it was the rain that depressed you. I thought perhaps it was love.

ARNOLPHE (*Caught off-guard; to* LUCINDE): What's that? (*To himself*) Once I was a young fool in love with a woman of great wit. But she married another. That's how I learned about women.

LUCINDE: Of course, the years have proved that you have never been in love. But I did wonder.

ARNOLPHE: I love Agnes, in my own way. She will be an excellent wife, as I have had her well trained all these years. When Agnes was four, I saw her in an orphanage. I made her my ward and took her to a little, isolated convent to be reared. I told the nun there to keep her as ignorant as possible. Now Agnes is old enough to marry, and she is everything I desire in a woman—sweet, kind, and naive.

LUCINDE: The weather is like women. One never knows what tomorrow will bring.

ARNOLPHE (*Looking at her questioningly*): If I didn't know better, Lucinde, sometimes I would think you understood every word I say.

LUCINDE: But rain has its good side, too.

ARNOLPHE (*Musing*): There is one dark cloud on my horizon—that young fool, Horace, the son of my friend, Oronte. He is in love with my Agnes. He knows her as the ward of M. de la Souche. But fortunately he does *not* know that in the country *I* use the name of M. de la Souche. Thus, he has told me all about his plot to steal Agnes, little suspecting that I am the de la Souche he mocks. I'll trip him up, but first I must know how far this romance has gone. I'll pretend to be his friend. But I first must question Agnes, to find out what happened between them during my absence.

LUCINDE (*Putting aside knitting and rising*): I have enjoyed our talk about the weather, but now I must go.

ARNOLPHE (*Going to her*): I'll walk to the carriage with you, good Lucinde. (*Aside to audience*) Perhaps I am a fool to talk so freely to her. She could destroy me if she knew my plans. (*Shrugs*) But she is deaf, and I must confide in someone. (LUCINDE *and* ARNOLPHE *exit right, as* ALAIN *and* GEORGETTE *enter left.*)

ALAIN: Our master has gone with Mme. Lucinde.

GEORGETTE: Good. He scares me. He looked so fierce when he found out that Agnes has a young admirer.

ALAIN: That visit did make him angry. I told you it would.

GEORGETTE: Why does he keep Agnes in the house all the time?

ALAIN: Because he is jealous. He is afraid that some young man will try to steal her from him.

GEORGETTE (*Looking off right*): Here he comes, and he still looks angry. Play dumb.

ARNOLPHE (*Entering and going over to them*): Where is Miss Agnes?

GEORGETTE: In her room, sir, as you ordered.

ARNOLPHE: Go quickly and fetch her here.

GEORGETTE: Yes, sir. Right away, sir. (*Runs off left*)

ARNOLPHE (*To* ALAIN): I'm still angry with you, Alain, for letting that young fool visit Miss Agnes in my absence.

ALAIN: He bribed me, sir, or I never would have betrayed you.

ARNOLPHE: Now you must help me, or I'll discharge you.

ALAIN (*Aside*): Threats are stronger than bribes. (*To* ARNOLPHE)
  You can count on me.
ARNOLPHE: Good. First, don't say a word to Miss Agnes about
  my discovery of her adventure.
ALAIN: She knows you're angry.
ARNOLPHE: But she doesn't know why. She's a good, simple child,
  and I can convince her of anything. When she gets here, I'll
  trick her and find out what happened. I must know how seri-
  ously she takes that young man's attentions. (AGNES *enters*.)
  She's here. Leave us alone.
ALAIN: Yes, sir. (*Exits down left*)
ARNOLPHE (*Turning to* AGNES *and pretending to be pleased*): Ah,
  Agnes, is this not a fine day?
AGNES (*Sweetly*): Very fine, now that I'm out of my room.
ARNOLPHE: Did anything happen in my absence?
AGNES: The kitten died.
ARNOLPHE: That's a pity, but we are all mortal. (*Pauses and
  asks casually*) Were you bored in my absence?
AGNES: I am never bored.
ARNOLPHE: I've been gone nine days. How did you spend the
  time?
AGNES: I made six shirts and six nightcaps.
ARNOLPHE: Agnes, the world is filled with gossip. Do you know
  that some of our neighbors are so ridiculous that they are
  saying a young man visited you in my absence? (*False laugh*)
AGNES: That isn't gossip, sir.
ARNOLPHE: What! Is it true, then, that a man visited you?
AGNES: Every day.
ARNOLPHE (*Angrily*): Didn't I forbid you to see anyone in my
  absence?
AGNES: Yes, but you would have done the same in my place.
ARNOLPHE (*Aside*): She is so simple she always speaks the truth.
  (*To* AGNES) Tell me about it.
AGNES (*Sighing*): It was wonderful. I was on the balcony when
  this young man passed below. When he saw me, he bowed
  very respectfully. You told me never to be rude; so I made him
  a curtsy. He bowed again. So I made another curtsy. He made
  a third bow, and I a third curtsy. And on and on he went,

bowing. And on and on I went, curtsying. I became so dizzy that I would have fainted, but I thought that might be rude.

ARNOLPHE (*Aside*): I did tell her never to be rude.

AGNES: I was afraid that with my curtsying I might, by accident, have knocked a flower pot from the balcony and hit him.

ARNOLPHE (*Aside*): I wish the whole balcony had landed on his head.

AGNES (*Pleased*): But Georgette told me that it was my eyes that had given him a blow. She said that the young man was sick with pining for me, that he would die if he could not see me again. I didn't want to be a murderess, so I sent Georgette to bring him to me immediately.

ARNOLPHE (*Aside*): That cursed Georgette.

AGNES: And that is how Horace came to see me. Could any kind woman leave such a handsome young man in pain?

ARNOLPHE (*Aside*): This is the danger of innocence.

AGNES (*Innocently*): Did I do something wrong?

ARNOLPHE: No, no. What happened next?

AGNES (*Smiling*): That's the best part. He was wonderful, and as soon as we were together, he recovered completely.

ARNOLPHE (*Struggling to control his anger*): What did he say to you when you were alone?

AGNES: He swore he loved me, and with the prettiest words.

ARNOLPHE (*Aside*): The villain! (*To her*) With all these sweet words, did he also . . . steal a few kisses?

AGNES: He wouldn't steal anything from me, sir.

ARNOLPHE (*Relieved*): That's some comfort.

AGNES: I gave them to him willingly.

ARNOLPHE (*Exploding*): Thunderation! (*Pauses*) But it's not your fault, Agnes, so I'll say no more about it. But that young rogue took advantage of you.

AGNES: Oh, no, sir. He was very sincere.

ARNOLPHE: It's a sin to let a strange man kiss you.

AGNES: He wasn't strange, and his kisses were wonderful.

ARNOLPHE (*Sharply*): A woman shouldn't know about such things until she is married.

AGNES: After she is married, is it all right?

ARNOLPHE: Of course.

AGNES: Good. Then I want to be married.

ARNOLPHE: I have returned for just that purpose.

AGNES (*Gleefully*): I am so happy! When can my marriage take place?

ARNOLPHE: This very evening, if you like.

AGNES: I would like even sooner. I saw him just yesterday, (*Sighs*) but it seems like a year. But soon he'll be my husband.

ARNOLPHE: Who is *he?*

AGNES: Horace, of course.

ARNOLPHE: Him! No, no, no! I don't mean him. I've someone else in mind for you. (*Angrily*) Now, listen to me. When Horace comes, you tell him to go away. If he calls outside your window, throw a stone at him.

AGNES: I couldn't do that. He's too beautiful.

ARNOLPHE: You'll do as I say.

AGNES (*Almost weeping*): I couldn't be so cruel.

ARNOLPHE: I'll teach you what cruel means if you disobey me. Now, go to your room. (*Points upstage;* AGNES *exits.*) What good is a school for wives if this is the result? (*With resolve*) But I'll end this romance. I'll tell Horace's father that the young fool is chasing a poor, country girl, and I'll *make* Agnes send him away. (*Reflects*) She has a will of her own. I thought my training would have rid her of that fault. (*Stamps his foot*) Let poetic fools talk about women's rights. Women were born to serve men. And that's all there is to it. (CHRYSALDE, *reading papers, enters left, sees* ARNOLPHE.)

CHRYSALDE (*Going to him*): Ah, my good friend, Arnolphe.

ARNOLPHE: Sh-h! Please. Here in the country I am known as M. de la Souche.

CHRYSALDE: Is this part of your program to marry a perfect wife? (*Waves papers*) I've been reading your rules for wives. I'd like to meet any woman who would agree to these.

ARNOLPHE: You will—right after the wedding.

CHRYSALDE (*In disbelief*): Have you really found a woman to agree to these?

ARNOLPHE: Certainly.

CHRYSALDE: This one, for example? (*Reads*) "A woman should

dress only to suit her husband, even if her friends think her costumes plain."

ARNOLPHE: That's what a wife should do.

CHRYSALDE: And this one? (*Reads*) "A woman should neither read nor write. Her husband should be her only source of information." (*Laughs*) That one's pretty outrageous.

ARNOLPHE: I don't want a modern woman, all tongue and temper.

CHRYSALDE (*Laughing*): Well, preach on, Arnolphe, but you'll surely stay single. Now, you said you had some bad news about Horace. Is the boy in trouble?

ARNOLPHE: The worst kind, I fear. The young fool has fallen in love with a simple country girl without a sou to her name. He means to marry her. Because Oronte is my good friend, I'd do anything to save his son.

CHRYSALDE: This news is not going to please Oronte.

ARNOLPHE: The girl is dirt poor and not very attractive.

CHRYSALDE: Then why does Horace want to marry her?

ARNOLPHE: Because he's a young fool. Any man who wants to marry before he's fifty is a fool.

CHRYSALDE: His father has other plans for Horace. It has been arranged for him to marry my niece.

ARNOLPHE (*Surprised*): Why, Chrysalde! I didn't know you had a niece.

CHRYSALDE: Nor did I, until a short time ago. She's my late sister's child. You may remember that my sister died seventeen years ago. It was supposed the child had died with the mother, but recently, Enrique returned from America, and he discovered his daughter is still alive.

ARNOLPHE: And he found her?

CHRYSALDE: I think so. Oronte and Enrique asked me to come here to find Horace. They'll join us here—with my lost niece, I presume. The wedding is set for this week. You must be present, Arnolphe.

ARNOLPHE (*Pleased*): I'll be there. (*Reflects*) Suppose Horace already has another wife picked out?

CHRYSALDE: Oronte will expect his son to obey him, but we'll see. As you know, he dotes upon the boy. It shouldn't be difficult to make Horace forget this country girl you mention. If my niece looks like her mother, she is the loveliest woman in all France.

ARNOLPHE (*Aside*): Not as lovely as my Agnes. (*To* CHRYSALDE) Oronte should be stern. A soft father makes a spoiled son.

CHRYSALDE: I must find Horace now. I'd think over those rules of yours if I were you. Hard laws make tough rebels. Good day. (*Exits right*)

ARNOLPHE (*To himself*): My Agnes will never be a rebel. She'll be proof to the world that women were made to serve. She's not my problem anyway. It's that rascal, Horace. (*Looks off left*) Here comes the villain now. I'll handle him.

HORACE (*Entering left*): Ah, my good friend, Arnolphe. I didn't expect to find you here so close to the house of M. de la Souche.

ARNOLPHE: But I expected you. As you are the son of my good friend, I have decided to help you.

HORACE: I need help. M. de la Souche has returned.

ARNOLPHE: That's bad luck.

HORACE: He knows I love Agnes, though how he found out I don't know. I told no one but you.

ARNOLPHE: Perhaps the servants told him.

HORACE: Perhaps. When I called on Agnes just now, her maid, Georgette, told me to leave and slammed the door in my face.

ARNOLPHE: Maybe she doesn't speak for her mistress.

HORACE: I know she doesn't. Just now I called beneath Agnes's window, and she threw a stone at me.

ARNOLPHE: Georgette did?

HORACE: No. Agnes did.

ARNOLPHE: Do women in love now throw stones at their lovers?

HORACE: She was just doing what her cruel jailer, M. de la Souche, made her do.

ARNOLPHE (*Nervously*): Perhaps he is really a good fellow who is doing what he thinks best for Agnes.

HORACE: He's a cruel man, but in spite of his attempts to drive me away, Agnes and I will trick him. (*Whispers*) I have sent a message to her.

ARNOLPHE (*Aside*): Chrysalde may laugh at my rule against a woman learning to read and write, but this proves the wisdom of that rule. (*To* HORACE) Are you sure she loves you?

HORACE: Listen to what she writes. (*Reads from letter*) "I have not had much practice in writing, for my guardian has tried to keep me in ignorance. I may be ignorant, but I know enough to be angry at what M. de la Souche is trying to force me to do to you. He told me not to believe you, but I trust you more than I do him and all his rules."

ARNOLPHE (*Aside*): The vixen!

HORACE: What's that?

ARNOLPHE: Nothing. I just sneezed.

HORACE: But tonight, if you will help, Agnes and I are going to run away together to be married. I'm going to climb up her balcony and get her. I'll need a ladder, however. Can you get one for me?

ARNOLPHE: You should speak to your father first.

HORACE: There isn't time. My father wants me to be happy.

ARNOLPHE: Speak to him first. Don't be a fool.

HORACE (*Looking at him suspiciously*): Should I get help elsewhere?

ARNOLPHE: No, no, dear boy. I'll help you.

HORACE: Then you'll get the ladder for me. Now I must leave before de la Souche sees me. (*Exits right*)

ARNOLPHE: Am I to be tricked, at my age, by a young girl and a scatter-brained young man? (*Almost shouting*) Is there no virtue in women at all? (ALAIN *and* GEORGETTE *enter.*) You two, come here.

ALAIN: Yes, master. (ALAIN *and* GEORGETTE *go to* ARNOLPHE.)

ARNOLPHE: Listen to me. I have learned that Horace means to elope with Miss Agnes tonight. We must lay a trap for him. He is going to climb a ladder to her balcony, but when he reaches there, I want you to fall upon him and give him such a beating that he'll never come back.

ALAIN: If you want a man beaten, I am your servant.

ARNOLPHE: Good. Get inside now and don't say a word of this. (ALAIN *and* GEORGETTE *exit right.* ARNOLPHE *starts off down left, as* LUCINDE *enters.*)

LUCINDE: Arnolphe, I've been thinking about the rain.

ARNOLPHE: Not now, not now, Lucinde. I'm busy. (*He runs off right.*)

LUCINDE (*Shrugging*): I was just going to tell him to expect a storm. (*Curtain*)

* * * * *

SCENE 2

TIME: *That night.*

SETTING: *Same as Scene 1. Stage is dimly lit.*

AT RISE: ALAIN *and* GEORGETTE *run on, followed by* ARNOLPHE, *who carries a lantern.*

ARNOLPHE: Villains! What have you done by your violence?

ALAIN: We were just following orders, Sir.

ARNOLPHE: I said beat Horace, not murder him. What am I to do with a dead man on my hands? Go back to the house. I must think. (ALAIN *and* GEORGETTE *exit.*) What will Horace's father say when he hears of this?

HORACE (*Groaning, staggering on right*): Is that you, M. Arnolphe?

ARNOLPHE (*Trembling*): Yes. Who are you?

HORACE: Horace. I need help.

ARNOLPHE (*Almost in panic*): A ghost. Risen from the dead.

HORACE: Almost. (*Goes to him*) Our plan failed. Just as I was reaching Agnes's balcony, some rogues fell upon me with clubs. I fell to earth, and they thought I was dead. That frightened them and they ran away.

ARNOLPHE: Did you see who it was?

HORACE: No, but it doesn't matter. Agnes came after they left. She really loves me. No matter the cost, she will be my bride.

ARNOLPHE: But your father?

HORACE: At first he may be angry, but Agnes and I will find a way to show him how important our marriage is. But I need help. Will you hide Agnes in your house so M. de la Souche won't find her while I make arrangements for our marriage?

ARNOLPHE (*Quietly*): I am delighted at the opportunity to serve you. I thank my stars for such a chance.

HORACE: M. Arnolphe, I am deeply touched. Agnes is waiting for me by the tree at the pond.

ARNOLPHE: I know the place. I'll get Agnes now. (*Puts cloak around his head*)

HORACE: But sir, why do you need a disguise?

ARNOLPHE: I am willing to help, but I wouldn't want your father to know. My disloyalty to him much disturbs me.

HORACE: You are a man of tender conscience, M. Arnolphe. (AGNES *enters right.*)

AGNES (*Whispering*): Horace? Where are you?

HORACE: I am here, my love. (*Starts to go to her*)

ARNOLPHE (*To* HORACE): Do not tell her who I am.

HORACE: I won't. (*Goes to* AGNES *and brings her to* ARNOLPHE) Agnes, my love. We have a trusted friend who will hide you for a few days.

ARNOLPHE (*In a disguised voice*): Yes, dear, you must come with me. I'll keep you safe. (*Takes* AGNES'*s hand*)

AGNES: Horace, don't leave me.

HORACE: I have to go. M. de la Souche will be searching for us, and I must lead him astray.

ARNOLPHE (*Trying to pull* AGNES *away*): Come, my dear.

AGNES (*Resisting* ARNOLPHE): Horace, your friend is pulling me too hard.

HORACE: He knows it's dangerous here and is trying to save us.

AGNES: I don't want to go with a stranger.

HORACE: He is no stranger. He is a friend.

AGNES: Take me with you, Horace. (*To* ARNOLPHE) Please, sir, don't pull me so hard.

HORACE: I must leave. It is getting light.

AGNES: When shall I see you again?

HORACE: Soon. Goodbye, my love, for now. (*Exits left*)

ARNOLPHE: Come, young lady. I'll take you where you'll be safe.

AGNES: Your voice! I know it.

ARNOLPHE: Do you, hussy? (*Throwing back cloak*) And my face, is it familiar, too? Don't bother to cry out. Your lover is gone. You young serpent!

AGNES: Why are you speaking so harshly to me?

ARNOLPHE: I caught you running after a young man.

AGNES: But Horace is to be my husband. Didn't you say I should never disobey my husband?

ARNOLPHE: Yes, but I meant for you to be *my* wife. I thought you understood that.

AGNES: I did. But to be frank with you, Horace is more to my taste than you are. Besides, I love him.

ARNOLPHE: How dare you tell me so!

AGNES: You told me always to speak the truth to you.

ARNOLPHE: Well, it shouldn't be the truth.

AGNES: Alas, I can't help whom I love.

ARNOLPHE (*Almost screaming*): Why don't you love me?

AGNES: In all the time I have known you, you have never been lovable.

ARNOLPHE: I tried.

AGNES: Then you must not be very skillful. Horace taught me to love him, and he didn't even have to try.

ARNOLPHE: Listen, little wretch, I'll forgive you if you love me.

AGNES: I would if it were in my power.

ARNOLPHE: You can if you will. Just listen to this sigh of love. (*Sighs loudly*) See this dying look. (*Stares at her with mouth open*) See what a handsome fellow I am. (*Strikes a pose*) This young villain must have thrown a spell over you, but you'll be much happier with me. What would you have me do? Beat myself? Tear out half my hair? Kill myself? Just say the word and I will do what you ask.

AGNES: Say no more. All of this does not touch my heart. Horace can do more with one wink of an eye.

ARNOLPHE: You've gone too far. I'll put you in a safe place and you will stay there the rest of your life. (ALAIN *comes running in.*)

ALAIN: Master, master! Sound the alarm! We have been robbed.

ARNOLPHE: What are you talking about?

ALAIN: Someone has stolen our corpse and Miss Agnes, too.

ARNOLPHE: Listen, you idiot. Here is Miss Agnes. Take her to her room and keep her locked up until I give further orders. (*To* AGNES) Perhaps in solitude, you will learn to love me. Go. (ALAIN *leads* AGNES *off right.* LUCINDE *enters left.*)

LUCINDE: M. Arnolphe, I want to talk to you.

ARNOLPHE (*Shouting angrily*): Go away. I have troubles enough of my own. (*Runs off right*)

LUCINDE: He is a most peculiar man, and somewhat rude. (*Curtain*)

* * * * *

SCENE 3

TIME: *Morning.*

SETTING: *Same as Scene 2.*

AT RISE: HORACE *and* ARNOLPHE *enter left.*

HORACE: I am plunged in grief, M. Arnolphe. I just saw my father. He has made a match for me. Without a word of warning, he is here to attend my wedding—to a woman I don't even know. Please help me.

ARNOLPHE: What can I do, my friend?

HORACE: Don't tell him about Agnes. Perhaps, if he doesn't learn of my true love, I can convince him—with your help, good friend—that this proposed match is not a good one.

ARNOLPHE: With my help? Ah, to be sure.

HORACE: I look upon you almost as more of a real father than my own. (*Looks off left*) Here he comes now, with this unknown girl's father. (ENRIQUE, ORONTE, *and* CHRYSALDE *enter.*)

ARNOLPHE: And my friend, Chrysalde. (*Aside*) I hope he doesn't reveal that I am M. de la Souche. (*Goes to* ORONTE *and embraces him*) Ah, good friend, your son just told me you were coming. Welcome.

ORONTE: Thank you, Arnolphe. Do you remember Enrique?

ARNOLPHE: It has been many years. Welcome.

ENRIQUE: Many thanks, M. Arnolphe.

CHRYSALDE: Am I welcome, too? And by what name shall I call you?

ARNOLPHE: By *my* name, of course—Arnolphe! I know no other. (*Laughs*) You are always joking, Chrysalde.

CHRYSALDE: And you are sometimes otherwise.

ARNOLPHE (*Turning to* ORONTE; *seriously*): I know what brings you here.

ORONTE: You have heard already?

ARNOLPHE: I must tell you that your son is opposed to the match.

He asked me to urge you to delay his marriage. But instead I urge you to be firm.

HORACE (*Aside*): Oh, the traitor!

CHRYSALDE (*Startled*): The young woman is my niece, but I don't think we should force Horace into marriage.

ENRIQUE: I agree. I've yet to see my daughter, and I'm not anxious for her to marry a man who is unwilling.

ARNOLPHE: Will three grown men be ruled by a mere boy?

LUCINDE (*Entering left*): Arnolphe! I have been looking for you.

ARNOLPHE: Not now, you old fool. Go away.

ENRIQUE: Sir, is that any way to speak to a lady?

ARNOLPHE: It doesn't make any difference how I speak. She is deaf.

LUCINDE (*Smiling*): Or would you rather I call you M. de la Souche?

HORACE: What's that? *You* are M. de la Souche? *You* are my rival?

ARNOLPHE: That is so. My Agnes has nothing to do with you. You are pledged to another.

ENRIQUE: I don't understand what this is all about.

ARNOLPHE: It doesn't concern your daughter, sir, but someone near and dear to me. Where is your daughter?

ENRIQUE: There is a problem, sir.

ORONTE: Just a temporary one, I'm sure. We found the convent in which the child was reared. But the old nun there has forgotten the name of the family that adopted her.

CHRYSALDE: But she did say it was in this province. So we have come to you, Arnolphe. We knew you could tell us who in this area adopted a seventeen-year-old beauty.

ARNOLPHE (*Shocked*): What? There is no such person in the province. Go away now. I want to be alone.

LUCINDE: I know who it is.

ARNOLPHE: You? You cannot even hear.

LUCINDE: I hear what I wish to hear, and I know what I know.

ARNOLPHE (*Aside*): I am undone.

LUCINDE (*To* ENRIQUE): I not only know where your daughter is, sir, but I have arranged to bring her here.

ARNOLPHE: Don't bring her here. Take them to her, and let me take care of my own affairs.

LUCINDE: This affair concerns you. (*Calling*) All right, Georgette, bring forth the mysterious woman. Her husband-to-be awaits her.

HORACE: But I don't want anyone but Agnes. (GEORGETTE *enters right, leading* AGNES.)

ARNOLPHE: My Agnes, what is she doing here?

HORACE: *My* Agnes, what is she doing here?

AGNES: What *am* I doing here?

ENRIQUE (*Embracing* AGNES): My daughter, my daughter!

ARNOLPHE: That's not your daughter. That is my Agnes.

LUCINDE: She is Enrique's daughter. When you told me your plans, I investigated and discovered all.

ARNOLPHE (*Angrily*): This is too much. I . . . I . . . (*He stalks up right.*)

ORONTE: What *is* all this?

HORACE: Father, in time I shall tell you the whole story. But now, just let me say that I intend to be a dutiful son and marry the woman you've chosen for me at once. (*Going to* AGNES) This is the only woman I ever loved.

ENRIQUE: Then everyone is happy, after all.

LUCINDE: I suppose Arnolphe will never marry now.

CHRYSALDE (*Going to* ARNOLPHE *and clapping him on the back*): Don't despair. You still have your health and the use of all your senses.

LUCINDE (*Cupping ear and speaking loudly*): The use of his what? (*All laugh as curtain falls.*)

THE END

Production Notes

THE SCHOOL FOR WIVES

Characters: 6 male; 3 female.

Playing Time: 35 minutes.

Costumes: Seventeenth-century French dress. In Scene 2, Arnolphe wears cloak.

Properties: Knitting, papers, letter, lantern.

Setting: Yard outside a country home.

Stylized back drop of house and gardens may be used. At center are white wrought-iron chairs and table. Screens depicting trees and shrubs enclose the scene.

Lighting: Stage may be slightly darkened for Scene 2.

🔁 Tom Sawyer, Whitewasher

by *Mark Twain*
Adapted by *Walter Hackett*

Characters

TOM SAWYER
AUNT POLLY
JIM
BEN ROGERS
BILLY FISHER
JOE HARPER
JOHNNY MILLER

TIME: *One Saturday afternoon in the 1800s.*
SETTING: *Sidewalk in front of Aunt Polly's house. At rear is a shoulder-high fence.*
AT RISE: *Street is deserted.*
AUNT POLLY (*From off right*): No more argument from you, young man. (AUNT POLLY *and* TOM SAWYER *enter. He carries large brush and pail full of whitewash.*) The job has to be done, and that's all there is to it.
TOM: Couldn't it wait until tomorrow, Aunt Polly?
AUNT POLLY: Tomorrow is Sunday.
TOM: It's so hot.
AUNT POLLY: It wasn't too hot for you to skip off last night and go fishing.

TOM: That was different.

AUNT POLLY (*Sternly*): You're to whitewash this fence.

TOM (*Looking at fence*): All of it?

AUNT POLLY: Every single inch.

TOM: Can I go swimming after I'm done?

AUNT POLLY: By the time you finish this job, it will be too late.

TOM: Maybe I can work fast.

AUNT POLLY: I doubt that. When you're finished, call me. (AUNT POLLY *exits right.* TOM *surveys fence and sighs deeply. He dips his brush and paints one plank. Unenthusiastically he repeats this, then stops.* JIM *enters right, carrying pail.*)

TOM: Hello, Jim.

JIM (*Pausing*): Hello, Tom.

TOM: You going after water? (JIM *nods.*) Say, Jim, I'll fetch the water if you'll whitewash some of this fence.

JIM: Can't! Missus Polly told me to go and get this water. She said she expected you would ask me to whitewash, but told me to go along and tend to my own business.

TOM: That's the way she always talks. Give me the bucket—I won't be gone a minute. She'll never know.

JIM: I don't dare, Tom. She'd tar the head off me.

TOM: Aw, she talks awful, but talk doesn't hurt. Come on, Jim, I'll give you a white alley. (TOM *reaches in pocket and takes out white marble.*) Look!

JIM: My! That's a beauty. But, Tom, I'm powerful afraid of your aunt.

TOM (*Quickly*): If you will, I'll show you my sore toe. (TOM *sits on barrel and starts taking bandage off his toe.* JIM, *setting down pail, bends over to watch* TOM. AUNT POLLY *enters right, holding up a slipper. She swiftly descends upon boys and gives* JIM *a whack.* JIM *yelps, quickly picks up his pail, and runs off.*)

AUNT POLLY (*Threateningly, to* TOM): And as for you, Tom . . . (TOM *quickly adjusts his bandage, picks up his brush and starts painting rigorously.* AUNT POLLY *exits right. As* TOM *paints,* BEN ROGERS *enters left, eating apple. Waving his arm like a paddle wheel, he shuffles along slowly.*)

BEN: Ting-a-ling, ting-a-ling! (*Imitating a whistle*) Whew-whew-

whew! I'm the side-wheeler *Big Missouri,* and I'm ready to dock. Whew-whew! Come out with your spring line. Lively, now! Stand by that stage. Now let her go. (TOM *glances quickly at* BEN, *who stops and watches* TOM.) You're up a stump, aren't you? (TOM *ignores him, stands back and surveys his work. He makes another stroke.*) You have to work, hey?

TOM (*Turning around, casually*): Why, hello, Ben. I didn't notice you.

BEN: I'm going swimming. Don't you wish you could? But of course you'd rather work—

TOM: What do you call work?

BEN: Why, isn't whitewashing work?

TOM (*Resuming his work*): Maybe it is, and maybe it's not. All I know is, it suits Tom Sawyer.

BEN (*Doubtfully*): You don't mean to let on you like it?

TOM: I don't see why I shouldn't like it. It's not every day a boy gets a chance to whitewash a fence. (TOM *continues to work, whistling cheerfully.*)

BEN: Say, let me whitewash a little.

TOM (*Shaking his head*): It wouldn't do, Ben. Aunt Polly's awful particular 'bout this fence. I reckon there's not one boy in a thousand, maybe two thousand, that can do it the way it's got to be done.

BEN (*Pleading*): Let me try, please!

TOM: If you were to tackle this fence and anything was to happen to it, why—

BEN: Aw, let me try it. Say—I'll give you the core of my apple.

TOM: N-no, Ben, I'm scared to.

BEN: I'll give you all the rest of my apple. (TOM *reluctantly gives up the brush to* BEN, *who hands him the apple.* BEN *starts working, while* TOM, *seated on barrel, munches on apple.*)

TOM: Be sure you do as good a job, as I'd do.

BEN (*Dipping brush*): I promise. (*Paints*) Say, this is fun.

TOM: It's serious work—it takes just the right touch to do it. (TOM *finishes apple, while* BEN *works. He makes motion to throw the core away, reconsiders, and puts it in his pocket. Then he settles back to watch and nods off. Seconds pass, and sound of whistling is heard off left.* TOM *wakes up. He looks up as* BILLY FISHER *enters, and pauses to fix the tail of a kite he is carrying.* TOM *stares at kite, then at* BEN. *He screws up his face as if thinking hard.* BEN *has whitewashed a good portion of the fence.*) That's enough, Ben.

BEN: Lemme finish.

TOM: No, Ben. If you do any more, you may get sloppy, and Aunt Polly'll be mad as can be at me.

BEN: But I like doing it.

TOM: That may be. But you can't expect me to let you do the whole fence just 'cause you gave me an apple. Give me the brush. (BEN *reluctantly hands the brush to* TOM.) Maybe some other time I'll let you do some more.

BEN: Golly! Thanks, Tom.

TOM: Of course I don't promise. (BEN *exits left, waving to* BILLY. TOM *surveys fence, ignoring* BILLY, *who crosses over and watches.*)

BILLY: Bet you wish you were me. (*No answer*) I said, I'll bet you wish you were me.

TOM: Don't bother me. Can't you see I'm busy.

BILLY: Seems to me all you're doing is whitewashing that ol' fence.

TOM (*Turning to him*): And just what do you know about whitewashing?

BILLY: I've whitewashed before.

TOM: Hah! You mean you slapped on whitewash without even thinkin' what you were doin'.

BILLY: Well, isn't that the way to whitewash—slap it on?

TOM: 'Course not. Why, whitewashing a fence is—is an art. You have to know what you're doing every second. Now, my Aunt Polly could hire a man to do it, but she won't. You know why? (BILLY *shakes his head.*) Because she knows that I'm the only person 'round that can do it the way it should be done.

BILLY: My ma says I'm pretty good at it. (TOM *looks doubtful.*) Here, lemme show you.

TOM: Oh, no—not on my fence.

BILLY: Why not?

TOM: Go whitewash your own fence. Besides, I don't think you'd know how to use this kind of whitewash.

BILLY (*Looking into pail*): What kind is it?

TOM: A very special mixture.

BILLY: Looks like just any old whitewash to me.

TOM: That proves you don't know anything 'bout whitewash.

BILLY: Maybe I don't, but I can whitewash just as good as you can.

TOM: Huh!

BILLY: Just to prove I'm right, let me do some, and I'll give you this kite.

TOM: What do I want with an old kite?

BILLY: It's a humdinger of a kite. I'll even throw in the cord. (*Reaches into pocket, pulls out ball of twine*)

TOM: Mm-m! Don't know if I should. If I do, you have to promise not to tell a soul that I let you do it.

BILLY (*Eagerly*): I promise. Lemme have that brush.

TOM (*Handing him the brush, and taking kite and twine*): I think I may be making a mistake.

BILLY: I'll show you. (TOM *sits on barrel, examining kite.* BILLY *starts whitewashing.*)

TOM: Mind you do a good job. Use plenty of wash. (JOE HARPER *and* JOHNNY MILLER *enter left, the latter tossing a ball into the air. They stop to watch* BILLY.)

JOE: Well, did you ever? (*He and* JOHNNY *start laughing.*)

TOM: Look, you two, if you want to watch, it's all right, but keep quiet.

JOHNNY: What's Billy doin' whitewashing?

TOM: A special kind of job, Joe. Isn't that right, Billy?

BILLY: Sure! Don't bother to explain to them. They wouldn't understand. (*He continues whitewashing.*)

JOE: We thought you'd like to go swimming with us, Tom.

TOM: Can't. I've got to stay and look after this job. Swimming is just what you and Johnny ought to do. It doesn't take any brains to swim.

JOHNNY (*Pointing at fence*): And I suppose that does?

TOM: You're right, it does.

JOE: Why?

TOM: Look at that fence real close. (*They stare at it.*) Did you ever see wood just like it? (*Quickly*) Of course you never did. Know what kind of wood it is?

JOE: Pine?

TOM (*Scoffing*): Pine! That's Norwegian balsam—a very special kind of wood. And in order to whitewash it right, you have to have just the right kind of whitewash. And your brush has to be just right, too. On top of that, the person usin' the brush has to stroke just right.

BILLY: Like me, huh?

TOM: At first I didn't want to let Billy do it, but I must say he's doin' a good job—better'n I expected.

BILLY (*Proudly*): Thanks, Tom.

JOE: I'll bet I could whitewash that fence better'n Billy. (BILLY *and* TOM *exchange looks, and then both shrug in disbelief.*)

TOM: It's easy for you to say that, Joe, but you're just talkin' big.

JOE: You give me a brush and I'll show you.

TOM: Not on this fence.

JOE (*Turning to* JOHNNY): Come on home with me for a minute, Johnny. (*They start to exit left. To* TOM) We'll be right back. (*They exit.*)

TOM (*Calling after them*): Don't come 'round here, botherin' us when we're workin'.

BILLY (*Working away*): To hear Joe talk, you'd think he could do everything.

TOM: Better stop talkin' so much, Billy, or you'll spoil the fence. You have to concentrate. (BILLY *works faster.*)

BILLY: Tom.

TOM: Keep workin'.

BILLY: But, I—

TOM (*Warningly*): You heard me.

BILLY: But I'm going to sneeze.

TOM (*Grudgingly*): All right. (BILLY *sneezes. After a pause,* JOE *and* JOHNNY *rush in left, each carrying paint brush. They cross to* TOM.)

JOE (*Waving brush in front of* TOM): How about this brush? Is it all right?

TOM (*Blandly*): For what?

JOHNNY (*Holding up his brush*): What about mine?

JOE: I took them from my father's work shed. They're good ones, aren't they?

TOM (*Examining each*): Yes, they're pretty good brushes. But why show them to me?

JOE: We want to help.

TOM: You mean with—? (*Points to fence.* JOE *and* JOHNNY *both nod.*) No.

JOE: Please! (BILLY *stops working and turns.*)

BILLY: I wouldn't if I were you, Tom. I'm doing such a good job, they might spoil what I've done.

TOM: I think you're right, Billy.

JOHNNY: We'll be real careful.

TOM: I'd like to, but—

JOE (*Pleading*): Be a good fellow.

TOM: I'm not sure my Aunt Polly would like it.

JOE (*Making a motion*): Want me to go ask her?

TOM (*Hastily*): No! She might get real mad.

JOHNNY (*Taking ball out of his pocket*): If you let me, I'll give you this ball. (*He reaches into pocket again, takes out piece of chalk.*) And this piece of chalk, too. (TOM *accepts ball and chalk grudgingly.*)

JOE (*Taking several articles from his pocket*): If you let me help, I'll give you this piece of blue bottle-glass. (*He holds it up.*) See—you can look through it. And you can have these two aggies and twelve marbles and this brass doorknob. (*He presses them upon* TOM.) Is it a bargain?

TOM (*Motioning to* BILLY): Move over, Billy. (JOE *and* JOHNNY *start to paint.*) Be sure you'd do the kind of a job I'd do.

JOE: Did you say this was special whitewash?

TOM: I did.

JOE (*Doubtfully*): Seems like any old whitewash to me.

TOM: That's because you don't know any better. This whitewash is a secret mixture, and no one knows what's in it but Aunt Polly'n me. By the way, do you fellows have enough left?

BOYS: Yes!

JOE: You think maybe you might give me the secret formula?

TOM: I couldn't do that; it's a real secret. Tell you what, though.

When you get ready to whitewash your own fence, let me know, and I'll mix up a batch for you.

JOE: Golly! That'll be great.

TOM: That's if you'll give me that set of tin soldiers of yours.

JOE (*Dubiously*): Well—

BILLY: Better take him up on it, Joe.

JOHNNY: It's a good swap.

JOE: All right. I'll do it.

JOHNNY (*Hopefully*): You think you might do the same for me?

TOM: Well—

JOHNNY: My cat's havin' kittens. I'll give you one, if you say yes.

TOM: All right, I'll swap.

BILLY: Maybe you'd like like that brass whistle of mine?

TOM: I might. I'll think it over. (*The three paint in silence.*)

AUNT POLLY (*Calling off right*): Tom?

TOM (*Jumping to his feet*): Everything's goin' fine, Aunt Polly. (*Fence is completely whitewashed.* BILLY *drops his brush into pail. Boys stand back, as though asking* TOM's *approval. He nods.*) Must say as how you did a pretty fair job—almost as good as I could. Yup, not bad at all.

JOE: Thanks for lettin' us do it.

TOM: That's all right.

JOHNNY: Maybe we can do it again some time, hey?

TOM: I'll have to think it over. Don't want to make a habit of it. Where you fellows goin' now?

JOE: Swimmin'.

BILLY: You comin'?

TOM: Maybe after I inspect your work again. (*The three boys exit left.* TOM *goes to barrel and, tipping it up, puts his newly acquired presents into it. He barely finishes this before* AUNT POLLY *enters right.*)

AUNT POLLY: How much have you done? (TOM *points to fence.*) Well, I never! There's no getting around it, you can work when you've a mind to. But it's powerful seldom you've a mind to. Well, go along and play; but be sure to get back some time in a week, or I'll tan you. (TOM *exits left, as curtain falls.*)

THE END

Production Notes

TOM SAWYER, WHITEWASHER

Characters: 6 male; 1 female.

Playing Time: 20 minutes.

Costumes: Boys wear overalls. Tom is barefoot; he has a bandaged toe. Aunt Polly wears long house dress.

Properties: Pail of whitewash; three large brushes; marbles; pail; slipper; apple; kite; ball of twine; ball; chalk; piece of glass; brass doorknob.

Setting: Sidewalk outside Aunt Polly's house. At rear is shoulder-high fence made of boards badly in need of whitewashing. Downstage is a large empty barrel.

Lighting: No special effects.

🔲🔲Monsieur Beaucaire

by *Booth Tarkington*
Adapted by *Lewy Olfson*

Characters

TWO GENTLEMEN
MONSIEUR BEAUCAIRE
DUKE OF WINTERSET
FRANCOIS, *Beaucaire's bodyguard*
TWO LADIES
LADY MALBOURNE
LADY MARY CARLISLE
OTHER GUESTS, *extras*
FOOTMAN
LE COMTE DE BEAUJOLAIS

SCENE 1

BEFORE RISE: TWO GENTLEMEN, *dressed as English aristocrats of late eighteenth century, enter left. They stroll across stage.*

1ST GENTLEMAN: Are you going to play cards this evening, my friend?

2ND GENTLEMAN (*Airily*): Cards! There is no one worth playing with.

1ST GENTLEMAN: Yes, that's true. In all of Bath there's only one man who can be counted on to play fairly, at any time of the day or night, and for whatever stakes one wishes.

2ND GENTLEMAN: You mean—?

1ST GENTLEMAN: Yes, Monsieur Beaucaire, the French barber.

2ND GENTLEMAN: Pity he's of such low class. One feels a fool—
slinking up to his poor apartment to play cards.

1ST GENTLEMAN: But what can one do? Surely we cannot invite
such a person to our own clubs, or introduce him to society.

2ND GENTLEMAN (*Shocked*): No, no, of course not. After all, he
is just a commoner—no better than our own servants. (*Sighs*)
Still, he does gamble so magnificently.

1ST GENTLEMAN: I wonder which of our noble friends has gone
off to visit him for a hand this evening?

2ND GENTLEMAN: The Duke of Winterset, I'd wager. (*Laughs*)
He has to play with the French barber if he wishes to play at
all.

1ST GENTLEMAN: True. The Duke may be noble, but no gentleman enjoys the way he plays. He probably will be at the barber's tonight.

2ND GENTLEMAN (*Laughing*): I can tell you one thing. I shan't
be there.

1ST GENTLEMAN: Oh?

2ND GENTLEMAN: No, I played with the barber last night, and
he gave me quite a shaving! (*Laughing, they exit right, as
curtains rise.*)

* * *

TIME: *That evening.*

SETTING: *Monsieur Beaucaire's apartment.*

AT RISE: MONSIEUR BEAUCAIRE *and* DUKE OF WINTERSET *are
playing cards.* BEAUCAIRE *is dressed as barber.* WINTERSET
wears fashionable clothes of an elegant Englishman. FRANCOIS
*has pistol stuck into his belt and sits idly in chair tipped back
against side wall behind* WINTERSET. *There is a large pile of
chips on table in front of* WINTERSET; *a smaller pile in front of*
BEAUCAIRE.

BEAUCAIRE: You play extremely well, Lord Winterset. The time
has come for me to play very cautiously—very cautiously
indeed.

WINTERSET (*Gruffly*): Come, come. Less talk. Play your cards.

BEAUCAIRE: But this is the time for careful strategy. I think I can anticipate what you will do. And so I play—this. (*Plays card. Triumphantly, WINTERSET plays his on top.*)

WINTERSET: And there, my fine young Frenchman. A heart. Take the next if you can.

BEAUCAIRE (*Suavely*): Yes, yes, Monsieur le Duc, I think the next trick will be mine.

WINTERSET: I wouldn't count on that, if I were you. (*He leans across table toward BEAUCAIRE. Immediately, BEAUCAIRE grabs WINTERSET's wrist and pins his arm to table. He pulls an ace of spades from WINTERSET's cuff.*)

BEAUCAIRE (*Smiling*): Merci, Monsieur le Duc. I told you I would anticipate you. A card up your sleeve! (*FRANCOIS jumps up, pulling his gun from his belt. He stands menacingly looking for a sign from BEAUCAIRE.*) So now at last I have caught you cheating.

WINTERSET (*Sputtering*): Why, you devil, Beaucaire! (*BEAUCAIRE releases him, and WINTERSET immediately rises and leans both hands on table.*) But now that you have found me out, I shall have to silence you with my bare hands.

BEAUCAIRE (*Sharply*): Do not move. Observe behind you—my bodyguard, Francois. (*WINTERSET half turns his head.*) Behind that door are five others, all waiting for a sign from Francois. (*Slowly WINTERSET returns to his seat.*) Is it not a compliment to you that I procure six large men to subdue you? For, you see, I knew what others only suspect—that you cheat at cards. And so I made ready for you. It is a pity that you came alone. But then, could it be that you did not want the society of Bath to know that you play with a lowly barber?

WINTERSET: You plan to murder me, you carrion?

BEAUCAIRE (*Shaking his head; mildly*): No, no, no. No killing, not murder, only—disgrace.

WINTERSET: You devil! Do you dream that a soul in Bath will take your word that I—that I—

BEAUCAIRE (*Flipping card*): That Monsieur le Duc had a card up his sleeve?

WINTERSET: You pitiful creature, born in a stable—

BEAUCAIRE: Is it not an honor to be born where you must have been bred?

WINTERSET: You miserable footboy, you lowly barber, you cut-throat—

BEAUCAIRE (*Rising, laughing lightly*): I am overwhelmed.

WINTERSET: There are not five people in Bath who will talk to you.

BEAUCAIRE: They will not talk to me in public, but all of your high society gentlemen come to gamble, because I will always play fairly.

WINTERSET: You outrageous varlet! Everyone knows you came to England as the French ambassador's barber. Who would believe you?

BEAUCAIRE: *Everyone* will listen to me. Do you think I have made plans to trap you at cheating for nothing? No, no. With your help, everyone will listen to me.

WINTERSET: With *my* help? How dare you . . .

BEAUCAIRE: Francois, you may go out into the hall now, and wait for me there—with your five friends. Monsieur le Duc and I will talk alone.

FRANCOIS: Very good, Monsieur. (*Raises pistol slightly, then exits.*)

WINTERSET (*Impatiently*): Well? What do you want of me?

BEAUCAIRE: Here is my plan. Everyone knows that I am a fair and honest man, so they will believe what I say. Everyone also knows—or at least suspects—that you cheat at cards, and are a liar as well. You would not want them to know what happened here tonight, would you?

WINTERSET (*Furiously*): How much money do you want, you devil?

BEAUCAIRE (*Airily*): Money, poof! What care I for money? Every-one comes here to gamble, and I have won much. It is this that I demand of you, Monsieur: In spite of your reputation, you are a member of society, and are welcome in all the ball-rooms and salons of Bath. I wish to be admitted to those ball-rooms and salons as well.

WINTERSET (*Sneeringly*): You dare attempt to force me—

BEAUCAIRE (*Smiling*): You and I, Monsieur, are going to Lady Malbourne's ball tonight—you and I together.

WINTERSET: Curse your impudence!

BEAUCAIRE: Yes, yes. You are going to present me to the lovely Lady Mary Carlisle.

WINTERSET (*Scornfully*): Lady Mary Carlisle would prefer the devil to a man of low birth, barber.

BEAUCAIRE: That would concern me, *if* I were a barber. But, you see, I have renounced that profession. I am now a man of honor, a man of substance, is it not so?

WINTERSET: You will be recognized at once as the barber of the Marquis de Mirepoix and will be thrust from Lady Malbourne's door five minutes after you have entered.

BEAUCAIRE: No, Monsieur. I think not. Observe: I'm going to remove this horrible wig. (*He pulls off wig, hurls it across room.*) You see? My hair is blond and long. I shall shave off my mustache. Wearing a fine suit of white satin and my own hair, I shall be a new man. No one shall recognize Monsieur Beaucaire. You have nothing to fear.

WINTERSET: Curse you! Do you think I am going to be saddled with you wherever I go for as long as you choose?

BEAUCAIRE: No. All I require is this one evening. That is all that shall be necessary. After that I shall not need you.

WINTERSET (*Threatening*): Take heed, then, after tonight.

BEAUCAIRE: Indeed, Monsieur, indeed. (*Pauses*) Do you want to know why I insist on accompanying you to Lady Malbourne's ball?

WINTERSET (*Coldly*): 'Tis ever the wish of the vulgar to be seen with people of fashion.

BEAUCAIRE (*Good-naturedly*): No, no, no. It is not that simple, for you see, after tonight, I am a man of fashion myself. By shaving off his mustache, the barber, Monsieur Beaucaire, will be done to death by his own razor. Henceforth I shall be le Duc—le Duc de what? (*Laughs*) I know: le Duc de Chateaurien!

WINTERSET (*Contemptuously*): Chateaurien! Castle Nowhere!

BEAUCAIRE: And tonight, Chateaurien will be presented to the beautiful Lady Mary Carlisle. Ah, but beautiful is not a strong enough word for Lady Mary—*bellissima*, divine, *glorieuse!* It has been sad for me to see her surrounded by you and your kind. Yet I have been content to stand aside and gaze at her in admiration.

WINTERSET (*With a sneer*): But now you are no longer content to stand aside and look on.

BEAUCAIRE (*Ignoring* WINTERSET'S *remark*): I well recall, Monsieur, one day when I—who worship her so—had to look on as she threw a rose to you. But tonight, ah, tonight you and I, Winterset and Chateaurien, will go arm in arm to Lady Malbourne's ball. And I shall have a rose from Lady Mary Carlisle! (*Quick curtain*)

* * * * *

SCENE 2

TIME: *A week later.*

SETTING: *A room in Lady Malbourne's home.*

AT RISE: *Dance music of the period is heard briefly.* TWO GENTLEMEN *and* TWO LADIES *are seated about room.*

1ST LADY: I say, Lady Malbourne's party this evening is even a greater success than the last.

1ST GENTLEMAN: Lady Malbourne is always the perfect hostess.

2ND GENTLEMAN (*Gallantly*): The ladies here this evening are certainly at their loveliest.

2ND LADY: And the gentlemen never looked more handsome. Especially the Duke of Chateaurien.

1ST LADY (*Dreamily*): Chateaurien. Such a lovely name; so—so French.

2ND LADY: So handsome with his impeccable suit of white satin.

1ST LADY: Well, my dear, don't get your hopes too high. He has been paying court to Lady Mary Carlisle.

2ND LADY (*Glumly*): How well I know. Ever since the Duke of Winterset introduced him into society a week ago, he seems to have eyes only for Lady Mary.

1ST GENTLEMAN: They have been dancing together all evening. (LADY MALBOURNE *enters with* WINTERSET.)

LADY MALBOURNE (*To guests*): Come, come, dear friends, you must dance. It is for the older folks like the Duke and me to be resting. But not youngsters like you.

2ND LADY: *Dear* Lady Malbourne, your party is a grand success.

1ST GENTLEMAN (*Bowing*): As always, Lady Malbourne.

LADY MALBOURNE: Thank you. But the real credit, I think, must go to the Duke of Winterset.

WINTERSET (*Surprised*): I, Madam? Why so?

LADY MALBOURNE: Because it was you who introduced le Duc de Chateaurien to us. Clearly he is the success of my party. What a shame you didn't introduce him sooner. (*Teasingly, she prods him with her fan.*) Imagine, keeping a delightful man like your French friend a secret from us all this time. Really, the ladies should be quite cross with you! (*All laugh good-naturedly.* BEAUCAIRE *enters with* LADY MARY, *who carries roses.*) Ah, Lady Mary, I see you have finally agreed to share your charming friend with us.

LADY MARY (*Embarrassed*): I—I did not mean to keep him from you, Lady Malbourne.

LADY MALBOURNE: Don't mind my teasing you, my dear. But all the ladies *have* been jealous, you know. (*To* BEAUCAIRE) Dear Chateaurien, are you enjoying my party?

BEAUCAIRE (*Kissing her hand*): It has been charming, Madame, charming.

LADY MALBOURNE: I am so glad. Tomorrow evening you must come again.

BEAUCAIRE: You are too kind, Lady Malbourne.

LADY MALBOURNE (*To others*): All of you must come. And for now, I bid you good night. (*All murmur "good nights," as* LADY MALBOURNE *exits.* BEAUCAIRE *goes to* LADY MARY.)

BEAUCAIRE: I cannot thank you enough, Lady Mary, for the extreme honor you have given me. But am I to be left in such unhappiness?

LADY MARY: Unhappiness?

BEAUCAIRE: That rose that I have begged for so long . . .

LADY MARY (*Coquettishly*): Never!

BEAUCAIRE: Ah, I do not deserve it, but—

LADY MARY: Never!

BEAUCAIRE (*Pleading*): Let your kind heart give one little red rose to this poor beggar.

LADY MARY: Never! And now I must go. (*She goes to door, turns, pulls rose from bouquet, and tosses it to* BEAUCAIRE, *who catches it and smiles happily. She exits.*)

WINTERSET (*Dryly, after a moment*): A rose lasts only till morning.

BEAUCAIRE (*Happily*): But it is almost dawn already.

WINTERSET: Yet, the rose is of an unlucky color, I think.

BEAUCAIRE: The color of a blush, my friend. Good night. (*He bows to* WINTERSET *and exits. Curtain*)

* * * * *

SCENE 3

SETTING: *The same, a day later.*

AT RISE: LADY MARY *and* BEAUCAIRE *are seated on a small sofa.*

LADY MARY: Ah, Monsieur, such a charming tale. Why, I could cry out of pity for the poor wandering hero.

BEAUCAIRE: Mademoiselle, I, too, have been a wanderer, but my dreams were not of France, but of the blue sky of a lady's eyes.

LADY MARY (*Coyly*): I thought the ladies of France were dark-eyed, sir.

BEAUCAIRE: Do I speak of the ladies of France? No, no. I speak of the ladies of—heaven.

LADY MARY: A very pretty compliment, Monsieur; but does it not hint at a notable experience in making such speeches?

BEAUCAIRE: You torment me! No, it proves only the inspiration that it is to know you. (*Kisses her hand. There is commotioon offstage.* LADY MALBOURNE *enters hurriedly.* BEAUCAIRE *rises*). Lady Malbourne, what is the matter?

LADY MARY: Is something wrong?

LADY MALBOURNE (*Flustered*): Monsieur le Duc, I do not want to upset you, but—

BEAUCAIRE: What is it? What's troubling you, kind lady?

LADY MALBOURNE: It's the Duke of Winterset. He's saying the most dreadful things about you. (BEAUCAIRE *shakes his head.*)

LADY MARY (*Shocked*): About le Duc de Chateaurien?

LADY MALBOURNE: Yes. And, dear Monsieur, I think it would be best if you would avoid him for a while.

BEAUCAIRE (*Gently but firmly*): Madame, I know you have my interests at heart; but a Frenchman does not run away from an enemy. (*Angry commotion is heard.*)

WINTERSET (*Offstage; loudly*): Where is the lying villain? I'll curse his face. (WINTERSET *bursts into room, followed by* GENTLEMEN, LADIES, *and* OTHER GUESTS.) So here you are—(*With sarcasm*) le Duc de Chateaurien. Hiding behind a woman's skirts.

LADY MARY (*With spirit*): Hiding! Le Duc de Chateaurien is the bravest man in the world.

BEAUCAIRE (*Gently*): You do me too much honor, Lady Mary. I am just a poor Frenchman.

WINTERSET: That you are indeed!

LADY MARY (*Defiantly*): I would, Lord Winterset, that an Englishman might show himself as poor.

WINTERSET: Madam . . .

LADY MARY (*Coldly*): Address me no more, sir. I had not thought that you, Lord Winterset, would turn to slander. (*To* BEAUCAIRE) Will you see me home, Monsieur le Duc?

BEAUCAIRE: It would be a pleasure, Lady Mary, but I think Lord Winterset has something to say. Maybe it is best you hear it now.

WINTERSET (*Wildly*): When I have done my tale, Madam, you will agree that this scoundrel deserves a lashing.

LADY MARY (*Moving toward door*): I'll hear no more.

LADY MALBOURNE: You must stop this ugly scene at once, Winterset.

WINTERSET: You will bitterly repent it, Madam, if I do. For your own sake, I beg—

BEAUCAIRE: And I, also. Please, ladies and gentlemen, let him speak.

LADY MARY (*Impatiently*): Then let him be brief, for I am eager to be quit of him.

WINTERSET: Madam, the man you see before you is not the Duke of Chateaurien. (*Some guests gasp; others shake their heads.*)

There is no such person. Instead, he is Victor Beaucaire, a lowly barber to his Grace, the Marquis of Mirepoix. Disguising himself as a nobleman, he has taken us all in. Yes, I'll admit I was the first to be fooled, and so I introduced him to society. But (*Scornfully*) this Duke of Chateaurien is nothing but a fake, a fraud, and an imposter. He is nothing but a lowly servant—a barber!

OTHERS (*Ad lib*): A barber! Impossible! (*Etc.* LADY MARY *weaves slightly, as though about to faint.* GENTLEMEN *hurry to her side.*)

LADY MALBOURNE: This is infamous!

WINTERSET: And now, Madam, I will not detain you one moment longer. I beg you to believe that the desire to avenge a hateful outrage, next to the wish to serve you, forms the dearest motive in my heart.

BEAUCAIRE (*Ironically*): Bravo!

LADY MARY (*Slowly turning to face him*): Monsieur. Were you ever called Monsieur Beaucaire and a barber?

BEAUCAIRE (*Quietly*): Yes, Mademoiselle.

LADY MARY: But—but you behaved like a gentleman.

BEAUCAIRE (*Bowing*): I thank you.

LADY MARY (*Moving to door*): Will you join me in my carriage, Lord Winterset?

WINTERSET: Gladly. And as for you, Beaucaire, if you have not left Bath tomorrow noon, you will be clapped into jail, and get the lashing your deserve.

BEAUCAIRE (*Calmly, but firmly*): I shall be at the Assembly Room at nine o'clock, one week from tonight. I promise it. I swear it.

LADY MARY: Lord Winterset, I await you. (WINTERSET *joins her at the door.*)

BEAUCAIRE (*With a bow*): Mademoiselle, farewell. (*She stares at him coldly, then sweeps out on* WINTERSET's *arm.* BEAUCAIRE *bows to company and exits.* LADY MALBOURNE *sinks down on sofa.*)

LADY MALBOURNE (*Stunned*): Nothing but a common barber!

2ND LADY: To think we should all have been taken in by that worthless scoundrel.

1ST LADY (*Haughtily*): Well, *you* might have been taken in, but not I. I knew he was a charlatan.

1ST GENTLEMAN: Did you hear him defy Winterset's order to leave Bath?

2ND LADY: He said he'd be in the Assembly Room a week from tonight. He swore it!

2ND GENTLEMAN (*Blandly*): Don't believe a word of it. This town has seen the last of Monsieur Beaucaire. (*Curtain*)

* * * * *

SCENE 4

TIME: *One week later.*

SETTING: *The Assembly Room.*

AT RISE: WINTERSET *and* 2ND GENTLEMAN *are seated talking.*

2ND GENTLEMAN: Are you not afraid of the barber's threat to be here tonight? It would be embarrassing if he were to arrive while we were entertaining the Comte de Beaujolais.

WINTERSET (*Laughing*): It isn't possible. Fourteen baliffs are on guard outside. If they see him, they will hustle him directly to jail. (*With a laugh*) The impertinent rogue swore he'd be here by nine, eh?

2ND GENTLEMAN: He did. (LADY MARY, LADY MALBOURNE, TWO LADIES, 1ST GENTLEMAN, OTHER GUESTS *enter.*)

WINTERSET (*Rising*): Lady Malbourne. Lady Mary.

LADY MALBOURNE: Good evening, Lord Winterset. I see you have taken the proper precautions against a return visit of the French barber.

LADY MARY: There seem to be more guards here than guests this evening. But you did well. Nothing could be worse than the scandal if that man were here tonight.

WINTERSET: I am always glad to oblige you, Lady Mary.

LADY MARY: It's humiliating to think how we were taken in.

1ST GENTLEMAN: He would not dare attempt another such outrage.

LADY MALBOURNE: It is precisely nine. (*Laughing*) But where is the French barber? (BEAUCAIRE *steps from behind window drapery and bows. Everyone gasps, draws back.*)

BEAUCAIRE (*Lightly*): I am here, Lady Malbourne. A Frenchman never goes back on his word.

WINTERSET (*Angrily*): How did you get in here? The Assembly is surrounded!

BEAUCAIRE: I am a French gentleman, Monsieur. I do what I set out to do.

LADY MARY (*Haughtily*): A French *what*?

LADY MALBOURNE: Do you dare to keep up the pretense?

WINTERSET: I shall have him thrown in jail this instant.

LADY MARY (*Holding up hand*): Wait. Let him stay.

1ST LADY: What are you thinking of, Lady Mary? This man is a scoundrel.

LADY MARY (*Coldly*): No one knows that better than I. But let us call his bluff. Let us see if he will be as brazen when he meets one of the *true* French nobility.

1ST GENTLEMAN (*Aghast*): You mean—?

LADY MARY: Yes. Let this impudent barber be presented to le Comte de Beaujolais. He will soon learn that his masquerade has gone too far.

LADY MALBOURNE (*Smiling*): You are an admirable strategist, Lady Mary. It is a clever plan.

LADY MARY (*Scornfully*): Are you prepared for what will occur when you are face to face with a true French nobleman?

BEAUCAIRE (*Ironically*): I am sure we will all be surprised at the outcome.

LADY MALBOURNE: Impudent to the last!

WINTERSET (*To* BEAUCAIRE; *furiously*): I'll stuff your lying mouth with your false ribbons, scoundrel!

BEAUCAIRE (*Coolly*): Of what are you afraid, Monsieur? That I will reveal the secret that we both share?

LADY MARY: What secret does he speak of, Lord Winterset?

WINTERSET (*Angrily*): Tell what you like, barber. Tell all the wild lies you wish.

BEAUCAIRE: Very well. I shall tell you everything. (*To all*) I learned something about Monsieur de Winterset that he did not wish to be revealed. He was so eager for me to keep his secret that he agreed to join me in a masquerade. I was nothing; but with his help, I became le Duc de Chateaurien.

WINTERSET (*With a dismissive wave of his hand; with irritation*): Need I deny these accusations?

LADY MARY: Of course not, Lord Winterset. (*Eyes* BEAUCAIRE *with disdain*) No one believes this man.

BEAUCAIRE: Shall I tell you why I must be "Monsieur Beaucaire" and "Chateaurien" and not myself? Not the man I really am?

1ST GENTLEMAN: To escape the bailiffs, no doubt.

BEAUCAIRE: No, Monsieur. In France I have a cousin who is a man of great power, with a very bad temper, and he was angry with me. He wished me to marry a beautiful and honorable lady, but I objected because this marriage was arranged for me. So I decided to escape from my powerful cousin for a while and to play this masquerade. (FOOTMAN *enters, followed by* LE COMTE DE BEAUJOLAIS, *a French nobleman wearing many medals.*)

FOOTMAN (*Announcing*): Le Comte de Beaujolais. (FOOTMAN *exits.* LADIES *curtsy.* BEAUJOLAIS *goes directly to* BEAUCAIRE *and throws arms around him, ignoring others.*)

BEAUJOLAIS: Philippe! My dear brother! How glad I am to see you.

BEAUCAIRE (*Happily*): Welcome to England, Henri. It is good to see you. I have missed you. (*Others look on mystified, some horrified.*)

LADY MALBOURNE (*With a forced smile*): What is the meaning of this cordiality between you?

BEAUCAIRE: Dear brother, I forget my manners. I must introduce you to my English friends—le Comte de Beaujolais, Lady Malbourne, the Duke of Winterset, and the fairest of the fair, Lady Mary Carlisle. (BEAUJOLAIS *nods politely to others, who ad lib greetings.*)

BEAUJOLAIS: But tell me, Philippe, why the masquerade? Good Mirepoix told me you were pretending to be his barber. I cannot understand.

BEAUCAIRE: Ah, that. That was to escape the wrath of the King.

BEAUJOLAIS (*Smiling*): The King has forgiven you, brother. He says he should have known better than to try to select a bride for you.

BEAUCAIRE: Ah, Henri, it is I who know better now. I see that our royal cousin was wise indeed in selecting the Princess Henriette to be my bride. I regret that my foolishness has cost me the love and hand of so worthy a lady.

BEAUJOLAIS: But, Philippe, the Princess Henriette is wise, too. She loves you still. And if you are willing, your marriage may take place.

LADY MARY (*Upset*): Marriage!

BEAUJOLAIS (*Continuing*): Will you come home again to France?

BEAUCAIRE (*Facing others; ironically*): Yes, I shall, Henri. But I wish you could have shared my masquerade. It has been such fun. And I am a good actor; these people are not yet convinced that I am not a barber. They believe my name to be Monsieur Beaucaire.

BEAUJOLAIS (*Laughing*): Monsieur Beaucaire! That's a good one.

LADY MALBOURNE (*To* BEAUCAIRE): Who *are* you, sir?

BEAUJOLAIS: Permit me to present to you all his Highness, Prince Louis-Philippe de Valois, Duke of Orleans, Duke of Chartres, Duke of Nemours, First Prince of the Blood Royal, Lieutenant-General of the French Infantry, and cousin to his Majesty, Louis the Fifteenth, King of France.

BEAUCAIRE (*Lightly*): Now you see that I did not lie in calling myself a French gentleman.

LADY MALBOURNE (*Meekly*): Oh, Monsieur, what you must think of us.

BEAUCAIRE: I think only that I do not belong in this English society of yours which rejects a good man because he is lowly born, but willingly accepts an aristocrat who is a scoundrel. The man who introduced me to you at the price of his honor and then betrayed me to redeem it is Winterset—a coward and a card cheat. (*All stare at* WINTERSET *in horror.*)

WINTERSET (*Exploding*): The French Ambassador will hear from me within the hour.

BEAUCAIRE: I promise you, sir, no gentleman will soil his hands with you.

LADY MARY (*Distraught; to* BEAUCAIRE): It is a bitter mistake I have made. Can you forgive me, Monsieur?

BEAUCAIRE: There is nothing to forgive, Lady Mary. I am going home to France where people accept one another for who they are, not for their titles. (*He bows low, kisses her hand.*) Au revoir, Lady Mary. (*All make way, as he exits. Curtain*)

THE END

Production Notes

MONSIEUR BEAUCAIRE

Characters: 7 male; 4 female; extras.

Playing time: 30 minutes.

Costumes: Courtly dress of the late 18th century. In Scene 1, Beaucaire is dressed as a barber, with black wig and mustache; later he has blond hair, no mustache, and wears elegant clothes.

Properties: Cards, gambling chips, pistol, fans, bouquet of roses.

Setting: Scene 1, Monsieur Beaucaire's modestly decorated apartment. Card table is at one side. Scenes 2 and 3, an elegant room in Lady Malbourne's home. Scene 4, Assembly Room, decorated in lavish style.

Lighting: No special effects.

Sound: Scene 2, dance music.

▨▨Romance for Jo March

from Louisa May Alcott's *Little Women*
Adapted by *Olive J. Morley*

Characters

JO MARCH
MRS. KIRKE, *owner of a boarding house*
MINNIE KIRKE, *8*
KITTY KIRKE, *7*
PROFESSOR BHAER
TINA, *6*
MR. MARCH
MRS. MARCH
AMY LAURENCE ⎱ *Jo's sisters*
MEG BROOKE ⎰
JOHN BROOKE, *Meg's husband*
DEMI ⎱ *their twin children, age 5*
DAISY ⎰
HANNAH, *the March family servant*
MR. LAURENCE
LAURIE, *his grandson*
SHOPPERS ⎱ *extras*
SHOPKEEPER ⎰

SCENE 1

TIME: *1871.*
SETTING: *Mrs. Kirke's private sitting room in her New York City*

274

boarding house. There is a fireplace at left, with sofa at an angle, half facing fire, and an easy chair beside fire. Table and chairs are at center. Door leading to hall is up center, and curtained glass door in right wall leads to another room.

AT RISE: MRS. KIRKE *enters followed by* JO.

MRS. KIRKE (*Walking to sofa*): Come sit here, Jo, my dear, and collect yourself before the children come in. (Jo *sits.*) You must be tired and cold after that long journey. (*Sits beside her*) How is your dear mother?

JO: Very well, thank you—but a little anxious about Beth.

MRS. KIRKE (*Sighing*): Beth has been delicate since she had scarlet fever. But you mustn't worry. (*Pats Jo's hand*) It was good of your mother to let you come to work for me. You may give the children their lessons in this room, quite undisturbed.

PROFESSOR BHAER (*From off right; with heavy German accent*): *Nein, nein!* It goes not like that! (Jo *looks up, startled.*)

MRS. KIRKE: Oh, that's only Professor Bhaer, a German teacher who lives here. I let him use that room for his lessons. His own is such a muddle! Books, toys for his nephews, shoes, a ragged bird without a tail, always chirping beside a bust of Plato—hopeless confusion! (Jo *laughs.*) But he's a dear man. (*Slight pause*) I'm sorry your own room is so high up, but it's the only one I had vacant.

JO: But it's a lovely room—and you've given me a writing desk!

MRS. KIRKE: A little bird told me you were fond of scribbling, so when the children are in bed you can always go up there and indulge in your hobby. Now I must find those little imps of mine, so you can get acquainted. (*She exits, center. Jo takes off her bonnet.*)

PROFESSOR (*From off right*): It is not so! You have not attended to what I say! (Jo *gets up, crosses to glass door, raises curtain, peeks in.*)

MRS. KIRKE (*From offstage*): Now, Kitty, behave yourself! (Jo *hurries back to sofa, as* MRS. KIRKE *reenters with* MINNIE *and* KITTY.)

KITTY: But we don't have to do lessons today, Mamma! You promised us!

MRS. KIRKE: No, dear. I just want you to meet your new governess. Miss March, this is Minnie.

MINNIE (*Curtsying*): Good afternoon, Miss March.

JO: Good afternoon, Minnie.

MRS. KIRKE: And this is Kitty.

KITTY (*Boisterously*): Hello!

JO: I'm happy to meet you, Kitty.

MRS. KIRKE (*A bit sharply*): Kitty! Remember your manners. (*To* JO) I'm afraid you'll have to teach them more than you thought, Miss March! Now, I'll leave you to get acquainted. (*Exits*)

KITTY: Did you come a long way to get here?

JO: Yes, a very long way, on the train.

KITTY: Oh, what fun!

MINNIE: Mamma told us you write stories, Miss March. Will you tell us some of them?

JO: Perhaps, if you're good at your lessons. But there are lots of interesting stories in your schoolbooks, too—Hannibal crossing the Alps, with twenty-four elephants.

KITTY: Twenty-four elephants! (MINNIE *and* JO *laugh.*) We play elephants sometimes—on Sundays, when Franz and Emil come.

JO: Who are they?

MINNIE: They're Professor Bhaer's nephews.

KITTY: Franz and Emil play lions, and Professor Bhaer is an elephant, and we ride on his back! (*Glass door opens suddenly, and* PROFESSOR BHAER *enters. He has rumpled hair, a beard, and wears a shabby coat.*)

PROFESSOR: Oh, I beg your pardon! I thought Mrs. Kirke was here.

MINNIE: Professor Bhaer, this is our new governess, Miss March.

KITTY: Yes, and she's jolly, and we like her lots already. (PROFESSOR *smiles and bows to* JO, *who nods to him, laughing at* KITTY.)

PROFESSOR: Ah, I hope these naughty ones will not vex you. (*With mock sternness*) If so, call me, and I will attend to them. (MINNIE *and* KITTY *giggle.*) And you are to teach these sprites of mischief, Miss March?

Jo (*Good-naturedly*): I'm going to try to!

PROFESSOR: It is uphill work at first, with the young. Sometimes one sees nothing for the work one puts in—then suddenly, a spark! That is joy indeed! (*He sits in chair by fire.* KITTY, MINNIE, *and* Jo *sit on sofa.* Jo *watches* PROFESSOR *intently.*) It will be easier for you, Miss March, for you teach in your own language.

Jo: Do you come from Germany, Professor?

PROFESSOR: Yes, from Berlin. I came to help my sister, Minna, who was widowed and had two sons to raise. Then she died, and I felt I must stay to look after the boys. So you see I am tied. And you, Miss March, do you plan to teach in a school one day?

Jo: No. I came here only to help Mrs. Kirke, and to see fresh scenes and meet new people. I write, you see.

PROFESSOR: Ah, that is interesting!

Jo: I have written only a few little stories.

PROFESSOR: It is the first steps that count. No ladder can reach the rooftops without them. (*Pauses then rises*) But I must go. I have a lesson to teach. (*Bows and exits right*)

Jo (*Looking after him*): What an interesting man!

KITTY (*Coaxingly*): Tell us about the elephants! (*Curtain closes, as* Jo *begins to tell story.*)

* * * * *

SCENE 2

TIME: *A few weeks later.*

SETTING: *Same.*

AT RISE: Jo *and* MRS. KIRKE *enter.* MRS. KIRKE *carries several men's shirts and socks;* Jo *carries sewing basket.*

MRS. KIRKE (*Putting clothes on table*): Now you see, my dear, the Professor's things are in such a hopeless mess! Socks with heels all lumps—he does his own darning, you know. I wish I had time to spare to darn these properly for him, but with all the household duties. . . .

Jo (*Eagerly*): I can darn his socks. But won't he guess that someone's been doing it for him?

MRS. KIRKE (*Laughing*): He's so absent-minded, he didn't notice when you sewed the buttons on his coat—he probably forgot he'd lost them. But if you can do these socks and some of the mending, it would be a lifesaver for him—and for me. The Professor simply can't afford to buy new socks.

Jo (*Putting socks into her basket*): I'll be happy to help. (TINA *enters carring two books, which she puts on table. She sits at table, opens books and pretends to study.* Jo *smiles.*) And who is this? Another pupil?

MRS. KIRKE: Another of the Professor's protégés! This is Tina. Her mother does the laundering here. Well, I'll leave you to it. (*Exits*)

Jo (*Sitting and starting to darn sock*): And what are you doing, Tina?

TINA (*Importantly*): I must study my lesson.

Jo: Does the Professor teach you German?

TINA (*Gravely*): Yes.

Jo: Is it very difficult?

TINA: Yes. (*Solemnly*) I must study this page (*Turning page*), and that, and that. . . .

Jo (*Laughing*): I couldn't do all that at one sitting—not even if I *knew* German! (PROFESSOR *enters quietly, unnoticed by* Jo *or* TINA.)

TINA: Don't you know German?

Jo: No. (*Wistfully*) I wish I did. (PROFESSOR *crosses to them.* TINA *sees him, jumps up, and runs to him.*)

TINA: My Bhaer!

PROFESSOR: And how is my Tina! (*Gives her a hug and tousles her hair; then turns to* Jo) Miss March, you have a wish to know German? I will be happy to teach you.

Jo: But you are too busy.

PROFESSOR: *Nein!* We will make the time. I shall give little lessons with much gladness, for I have this debt to pay. (*Points to sock she holds*) These ladies say, "He is a stupid fellow. He will never see that his socks no longer have holes. He will think his buttons grow out new when they fall off!" (Jo *smiles.*) Ah, but I have an eye and I see. I have a heart and I feel the thanks for this. A little lesson then and now, or no more good works for me and mine!

Jo: If you really have the time. . . .

Professor: *Gut!* It is a bargain! You mend, I teach. Now I will find some books for you. (*Exits.* Tina *runs off after him.* Jo *puts sock in basket.*)

Mrs. Kirke (*From offstage, calling*): Tina! (*Sound of door closing.* Professor *reenters, carrying books and wearing a hat made of newspaper.* Jo *puts her hand over her mouth, to hide laugh.*)

Professor (*Putting books on table*): This book is the grammar— come, sit down, Miss March. (Jo *sits in* Tina's *chair, and he sits at head of table.*) Here are some pleasant little stories, what we call *Märchen.* (Jo *laughs out loud.*) Miss March, are you laughing in your professor's face?

Jo: Sir, you have forgotten to take off your hat. (Professor *puts his hand on his head and touches hat.*)

Professor: Ah! That imp, Tina! (*Unfolds paper, looks at it and frowns*) Pah! (Jo *looks curiously at paper, then quickly looks away, embarrassed.*) This is a terrible paper. (*Hotly*) I do not like to think that good young girls should see such things! (*He crumples paper into ball, rises and throws it into fireplace. Then he sits and leans toward* Jo.) Miss March, I have no right to speak of this, but in the last few weeks I have felt that we were friends.

Jo (*Looking up; softly*): Oh, yes!

Professor: I have seen you often down near the newspaper offices—the papers that print such trash as this. I hope you are not writing rubbish for these papers.

Jo: But "moral" stories don't sell!

Professor: I do not say, write the tales with a neat ending and a little moral added—for life is not like that. Write of what you see and know, (*With a sweeping motion*) here, perhaps, or in your own home. And one day, who knows? The whole world may read your books.

Jo: You are right. I've been writing nonsense, just to get published.

Professor: Do not despair. The opportunity for you to publish wonderful stories will come. Tell me, how long do you stay here?

Jo: Until June. (*Impetuously*) Oh, I do hope you can come to see us then!

PROFESSOR (*Eagerly*): Do you? Shall I come?

Jo: Yes! Come in July. Laurie graduates then.

PROFESSOR: Who is Laurie?

Jo: He is my best friend! I am so proud of him! (PROFESSOR *stares at her, and she suddenly looks down, turning the pages of book, confused.*)

PROFESSOR (*Suddenly very formal*): I fear I shall not make the time for that—but I wish the friend much success, and you all happiness.

MINNIE (*Offstage*): Stop, Kitty, stop! Oh, Miss March, Miss March!

Jo (*Jumping up*): Oh, dear! Those naughty children. I must see what the girls are up to. Excuse me. (*Exits hastily. He rises, looks after her, then sits down again, with a sigh.*)

PROFESSOR (*Sadly*): Ah, no, it is not to be. The handsome young friend. . . . I have no hope to win her affections now. (*Sits with his head in his hands as curtain closes*)

* * * * *

SCENE 3

TIME: *A year later.*

SETTING: *The March family parlor. Same set as for Scene 1, but sofa is draped with bright cover, and pillows of various sizes. Table stands right, covered with fringed cloth. Coatrack is up left, and a desk with books stands nearby. Sideboard and mirror are down right; piano is down left. Other chairs, pictures, and ornaments complete furnishings.*

AT RISE: MRS. MARCH *and* Jo *are sitting on sofa, each reading a page of a letter.*

Jo (*Looking up*): Well! So Laurie and Amy are engaged! Do you approve, Marmee?

MRS. MARCH (*Smiling*): Yes—I hoped it would be so.

Jo: And you never said a word to me!

Mrs. March: Since Beth died, I couldn't help seeing that you were very lonely, dear. And I was afraid it might pain you to know that your Laurie loved someone else.

Jo: I *am* lonely, Mother, but it's better as it is. Amy is *right* for Laurie. I wasn't. What a mercy Mr. Laurence took him abroad, and he found Amy at the right moment!

Mrs. March (*Smiling*): You're growing up fast, Jo.

Jo: Growing up! (*Sighs*) I feel ancient!

Mrs. March (*Laughing*): Oh, Jo! (*Stands*) I must go and talk to your father. We have a wedding to arrange! (*Exits. Jo rises and stands looking into mirror, smoothing her hair.*)

Jo: An old maid, that's what you'll be, Jo March! (*Goes to desk and takes out book, flips through it, finding a slip of paper, which she reads.*) "Wait for me, my friend. I may be late, but I shall surely come." Oh, if only he would come! My dear Professor. I never valued his friendship then. (*Puts paper into drawer of desk, locks it, then crosses to sofa and sits, gazing into fire. Door up center opens slightly.* Laurie *peers in, sees* Jo, *tiptoes up to her, taps her shoulder. She springs up, surprised.*)

Jo (*Stunned*): Oh, Laurie! Why, you've come back already!

Laurie (*Taking her hands*): Dear Jo! You *are* glad to see me?

Jo: Glad! Words can't express my gladness! Where's Amy?

Laurie: Down at Meg's. We stopped on the way, and there was no getting my wife away.

Jo: Your *what*?

Laurie: Oh, now I've done it!

Jo (*Pointing at him accusingly*): You've gone and married Amy!

Laurie: I plead guilty.

Jo (*Laughing*): You ridiculous boy! Tell me all about it.

Laurie: Only if you will let me sit in my old place again.

Jo (*Sitting and patting sofa invitingly*): Of course.

Laurie (*Sitting beside her*): Now, don't I look like a married man?

Jo: Not a bit! You're the same rascal you always were.

Laurie: Really, Jo! (*Pretending to be serious*) You ought to treat me with more respect.

Jo: How can I, when the idea of Amy and you—just children—getting married is so funny that I can't keep from laughing?

Laurie: As one of the "children" is older than you are, you needn't talk like a grandma.

Jo (*Seriously*): You may be older, Laurie. But this last year has been so hard on us that I feel like a grandma.

Laurie (*Compassionately*): Poor Jo! You had to bear the sadness all alone. (*Rising*) But it will be different now that Amy and I are home.

Jo (*Brightening*): You were always such a comfort. Now, tell me—the wedding—where, when and how?

Laurie (*Proudly*): Six weeks ago, at the American Consul's, in Paris. You see, I did it to please Amy—

Jo (*Interrupting*): Fib number one. Amy did it to please you! Now tell the truth, if you can, sir.

Laurie: Well, Grandpa wanted to come home. They wouldn't let Amy come with us—some foolish notion about chaperones—so I said, "Let's be married, then!"

Jo: Of course you did! You always manage things to suit you.

Laurie: Not always. . . . (*Crossing to stand near fireplace*) Jo, dear, I see now that you were right to turn down my proposal. What I felt for you was the affection I would have for a sister. You do understand. . .

Jo (*Gently*): Of course I do, Laurie. (*Sound of doors closing and voices*)

Amy (*From offstage*): Where is she? Where's my dear old Jo? (Jo *turns as* Amy *rushes in, runs to* Jo *and hugs her.* Mr. *and* Mrs. March, Meg *and* John Brooke, Mr. Laurence, Daisy, *and* Demi *enter, talking and laughing happily.*)

Jo: Amy, let me look at you. (*As* Amy *twirls to show her clothes*) You look wonderful! And talk about Paris style!

Mrs. March: Do you realize you've come just in time for Jo's birthday tomorrow?

Jo: Oh, Marmee, couldn't we have the birthday tea tonight?

Mrs. March: That's a lovely idea. (*Goes to door right, calls*) Hannah!

Hannah (*Entering*): Yes, ma'am? (*Seeing* Amy *and* Laurie) Why, Miss Amy! Master Laurie!

AMY: Hannah! (*Runs to her and hugs her*) But I'm not *Miss* Amy any longer! (*Shows* HANNAH *her wedding ring*)

HANNAH: Well, I never! (*Looks at* LAURIE, *who's beaming*) You young jackanapes! You've done us out of a home wedding!

MR. MARCH: Never mind, Hannah. We'll have a celebration tonight.

MRS. MARCH: Bring out the birthday cake and all those special dishes you were preparing.

HANNAH: Right away! (*Hurries out*)

JOHN: Come, Laurie, help me with the table. (JOHN *and* LAURIE *carry table and put it in front of sofa.* MR. MARCH *turns up a lamp.* HANNAH *reenters with tray of dishes, cups, food, etc.*)

DEMI: Are there raisin buns?

DAISY: And chocolate cake?

HANNAH (*Putting tray on table*): Get along with you! (*Exits*)

MEG: Come, Daisy! Demi! Come tidy up for tea. (*Exits with* DAISY *and* DEMI)

MRS. MARCH (*To* AMY): Come take off your hat and cloak, Amy. (AMY *and* MRS. MARCH *exit.* HANNAH *reenters with birthday cake.*)

HANNAH (*To* MR. LAURENCE): Excuse me, Mr. Laurence, sir.

MR. LAURENCE: I beg your pardon, Hannah. (*To* MR. MARCH) I'm afraid we're getting in Hannah's way.

MR. MARCH: We'll go into my study until tea is ready. Come, John—Laurie. (MR. MARCH *and* MR. LAURENCE *exit left, followed by* JOHN *and* LAURIE.)

HANNAH (*To* JO, *as they set table*): Will Miss Amy ride in a fine carriage now, and use all those silver dishes stored away in Mr. Laurence's big house?

JO (*Cheerfully*): Shouldn't wonder if she drove six white horses and wore diamonds every day. Laurie thinks nothing is too good for her.

HANNAH: And I agree. Will you have the muffins or the apple roll first?

JO (*Suddenly gloomy*): Oh, I don't care, Hannah. Whatever you think is best. (HANNAH *exits.* JO *counts candles on cake.*) Twenty-five! Oh! (*Loud knock is heard off.*) Who can that be?

(*Exits; offstage*) Professor Bhaer! (*She reenters with* PROFES-
SOR, *who carries hat and coat.*) I am so glad to see you!

PROFESSOR: And I to see you, Miss March. (*Sees tea table*) But,
no, you have a party—

JO: No, we haven't, it's only the family. My sister and friends
have just come home from abroad, and we are very happy.
You must join us. (*Takes his hat and coat and hangs them
on coatrack*)

PROFESSOR: I will gladly do so. (*Looks at* Jo *sharply*) You have
been ill, my friend?

JO: Not ill—but we have had a lot of trouble since I saw you
last.

PROFESSOR: Ah, yes, your little sister Beth. . . My heart was sore
for you when I heard that. (*Takes her hand.* MR. *and* MRS.
MARCH *enter right.*)

JO: Father, Mother, this is my friend, Professor Bhaer!

MR. MARCH (*Coming forward and shaking* PROFESSOR's *hand*):
We are glad to meet you at last, Professor. (AMY, LAURIE,
JOHN, MEG, MR. LAURENCE, DAISY *and* DEMI *enter.*)

MRS. MARCH: Jo has told us what a good friend you were to her
in New York.

MR. MARCH: You come from Berlin, I understand, Professor.

PROFESSOR: Yes, but family ties brought me to America.

JO: Now come and meet *my* family. (*Leads* PROFESSOR *to* AMY
and LAURIE) This is Amy, my sister who's just come from
abroad. And this is Laurie, the great friend I told you about.
(PROFESSOR *nods stiffly to* LAURIE.) Now that he and Amy are
married, he's part of the family, too. (PROFESSOR *brightens
visibly and ad libs greetings.*) This is Mr. Laurence, Laurie's
grandfather, my sister Meg and her husband John—

PROFESSOR (*As* DAISY *and* DEMI *stare at him*): And these must
be the twins? (*To* DEMI) What is your name?

DEMI: Demi. (*Pointing to* PROFESSOR's *watch chain*) May I see
your watch? (PROFESSOR *takes out pocket watch and holds it to*
DEMI's *ear.*) It has a lovely loud tick!

PROFESSOR (*To* DAISY): And what is your name? (Jo *goes to table
and begins to pour tea.*)

DAISY (*Importantly*): I'm Daisy. I look after Demi.

PROFESSOR (*Laughing*): That must be quite a job!

JO: Come and have tea, everyone! (*All move toward tea table as lights dim to blackout, indicating passage of time. When lights come up, all are standing around piano, at which* AMY *is seated, singing last line of an old song.*)

MEG: Now we shall really have to take the children home.

JOHN: Yes, come along, Daisy and Demi. (*All ad lib good-byes, as* JOHN, MEG, DAISY, *and* DEMI *exit.*)

AMY: We must be going, too. Come, Laurie.

LAURIE (*To* PROFESSOR): We are very glad to have met you, sir.

PROFESSOR: You have no idea how pleased I am to have met you and your wife.

LAURIE: Do remember that there is always a welcome waiting for you at our house. (PROFESSOR *shakes* LAURIE's *hand warmly.*)

PROFESSOR: Thank you, thank you so very much! (*To* MRS. MARCH) I, too must go, but I shall gladly come again if you will give me leave, dear madam. (*Looking at* JO) I have a little business in the city which will keep me here some days.

MRS. MARCH: We shall be delighted to see you again, Professor.

MR. MARCH: Most definitely. (*As* LAURIE, AMY *and* MR. LAURENCE *go to door, shaking hands with* MR. *and* MRS. MARCH, PROFESSOR *goes to* JO, *who is standing downstage.*)

PROFESSOR: And will *you* be glad to see me again, Miss March?

JO (*Softly*): Yes. Do please come again. (*Curtain*)

* * * * *

SCENE 4

TIME: *A few weeks later.*

SETTING: *Busy street. Scene may be played in front of the curtain. Fruit and flower store is at left, and shop windows of a large store, displaying children's clothing, is painted on backdrop.*

AT RISE: SHOPPERS *pass back and forth carrying open umbrellas. Jo enters, without umbrella, looking up at sky.*

JO: Serves me right for wandering about, looking for him. (*Turns up her collar and strides on.* PROFESSOR *enters, carrying shabby umbrella. He sees* Jo, *quickly follows her and holds umbrella over her. She does not notice at first, then, puzzled, turns and sees* PROFESSOR.)

PROFESSOR: I feel I know the strong-minded lady who goes so bravely through much mud. What are you doing here, my friend?

Jo: I—I'm shopping. (*After a pause*) We thought you had left.

PROFESSOR (*As they walk slowly*): Did you believe that I should go with no farewell to those who have been so kind to me?

Jo: No, but we missed you—Father and Mother especially.

PROFESSOR (*Intently*): And you?

Jo (*Embarrassed*): I'm always glad to see you, Professor.

PROFESSOR: I thank you, and will come one more time before I go.

Jo: You *are* going, then?

PROFESSOR (*Disappointed*): I no longer have any business here.

Jo: You have been successful, I hope?

PROFESSOR: I ought to think so, for I have a way opened to me by which I can make my living and help my nephews.

Jo (*Eagerly*): Tell me, please. I'd like to know all about it.

PROFESSOR: That is so kind. I will gladly tell you. My friends found me a place in a college, where I shall teach! I should be grateful, should I not?

Jo: Indeed you should! How splendid it will be for you to be doing what you like and for us to be able to see you often (*Quickly*)—and the boys, of course.

PROFESSOR: Ah! But we shall not meet often. This place is in the West.

Jo (*In despair*): So far away! (*He smiles broadly.*)

PROFESSOR: May I join you in your shopping?

Jo: Of course. (*Trying to sound enthusiastic*) We should shop for a farewell feast. You must come for dinner tonight and we'll celebrate your good fortune.

PROFESSOR: Splendid idea. (*He leads her to fruit store.*) Does your family like oranges and figs?

Jo (*Laughing*): When we can get them.

PROFESSOR: Do *you* care for nuts?

Jo: I love them!

PROFESSOR: And grapes?

Jo: Oh—delicious! But you mustn't be extravagant.

PROFESSOR (*Smiling*): For this once, I must. But first, Miss March, I have a great favor to ask of you.

Jo (*Eagerly*): Yes, sir?

PROFESSOR: I am bold to say it, but so short a time remains to me.

Jo (*Nervously; excited*): Yes, sir?

PROFESSOR: I wish to get a little dress for Tina, and I am too stupid to choose it alone. Will you kindly help me? (Jo *turns away, disappointed, then quickly looks back.*)

Jo: Of course! (*Leads him to shop window and points*) I see a very pretty frock. That would suit Tina perfectly. Shall I go in and see if they have her size?

PROFESSOR: Ah, yes, if you would be so good. (*He gives her some money.*) And meanwhile, I will buy the fruit. (Jo *exits.* PROFESSOR *crosses to fruit shop, where he selects fruit.* SHOPKEEPER *enters from shop and they mime transaction.* PROFESSOR *puts fruit into his pocket, as* SHOPKEEPER *exits into shop and* JO *reenters with parcel.*)

Jo: Here is the dress.

PROFESSOR: Thank you! Now may I accompany you home?

Jo: Oh, yes! I'm *so* tired. (*Pointing off left*) Look, there's the bus. (*She starts to hurry off, but* PROFESSOR *draws her back.*)

PROFESSOR: That is not the right one.

Jo: Oh, I didn't see the name distinctly. (*Tearfully*) Never mind. I can walk. (*Brushes her hand across her eyes*)

PROFESSOR (*Tenderly*): Heart's dearest, why do you cry?

Jo (*Sniffing; breaking down*): Because—you are—going away!

PROFESSOR (*Joyfully*): *Ach,* that is so good! Jo, I came to see if you could care for me. Can you make a place for me in your heart?

Jo: Oh, yes! (*Taking hold of his arm with both hands*) Friedrich, why didn't you tell me all this sooner?

PROFESSOR: My Jo, I had a wish to tell you in New York, but I thought the Laurie, your "best friend," was betrothed to you. (*Sadly*) Ah, the first love is the best, but that I cannot expect.

Jo: Yes, the first love *is* the best, and I never had another.

PROFESSOR: *Wunderbar!* That is so good to hear!

JO: But tell me, what brought you here, just when I wanted you?

PROFESSOR (*Taking clipping out of his pocket*): This. I read it in a paper. I knew it was yours by the names. One little verse seemed to call me. . . .

JO (*Taking clipping and reading*):
"Four little chests, all in a row. . .
'Meg' on the first lid, smooth and fair. . .
'Jo' on the next lid, scratched and worn,
A woman in a lonely home, hearing, like a sad refrain,
'Be worthy, love, and love will come,'
In the falling summer rain."

PROFESSOR: Yes. I read this, and I thought, "She has a sorrow. I have a heart full for her—I will go to her." And then, "How can I ask her to give up everything for a poor old fellow like me?"

JO: You're not poor. And you're certainly not old. But I would love you even if you were!

PROFESSOR: Oh my Jo! I have nothing to give back but a full heart and (*Holding out his hands*) these empty hands!

JO (*Taking his hands*): Not empty now! (*She reaches up to kiss him as curtains close, or they exit arm in arm.*)

THE END

Production Notes

ROMANCE FOR JO MARCH

Characters: 6 male; 10 female. Male or female for shopkeeper. As many extras as desired.

Playing time: 30 minutes.

Costumes: Victorian period dress. Jo's clothes are plain. She enters wearing bonnet. In Scene 4 she wears long cloak, bonnet with red ribbon. Professor wears neat but shabby suit, pocket watch on chain. In Scene 4 he wears overcoat with large pockets, carries money and news clipping in suit pockets. Mrs. March, Mrs. Kirke, and Hannah wear dark dresses, small caps. Amy wears elegant gown, hat, and cloak.

Properties: Books, work basket, darning materials, men's socks and shirts, hat made of newspaper, two sheets of a letter, slip of paper in a book, tea tray with cups, plates, etc., and birthday cake, fruits, nuts, parcel, umbrellas.

Setting: Same parlor set is used for Scenes 1, 2, and 3, with changes in furniture and accessories to alter appearance of room for Scene 3. Scenes 1 and 2, Mrs. Kirke's sitting room, with a fireplace left, and sofa at an angle before it. Easy chair beside fire. Work table and chairs are center. Exit up center leads to hall. Curtained glass door in right wall leads to another room. Scene 3, March family parlor; sofa is covered with bright drape and pillows of various sizes. Table now stands up right and is covered with fringed cloth. Coatrack is up left; desk near it holds books. Sideboard and mirror are down right. Piano is down left (optional).

Lighting: Lights fade in and out.

Sound: Doors opening and closing. Loud knock.

▣▣ An Enemy of the People

by *Henrik Ibsen*
Adapted by *Paul T. Nolan*

Characters

PETER STOCKMANN, *mayor*
ASLAKSEN, *chairman of the majority party*
HOVSTAD, *editor of* People's Messenger
CAPTAIN HORSTER
DR. THOMAS STOCKMANN
KATHERINE, *his wife*
PETRA, *their daughter*
MORTEN ⎫
EILIF ⎭ *their sons*
MORTEN KIIL, *Katherine's father*
TOWNSPEOPLE

TIME: *Late nineteenth century.*
SETTING: *Town meeting hall in southern Norway. Podium is up center.*
BEFORE RISE: *Scene is played before curtain.* PETER STOCKMANN *stands at podium.* ASLAKSEN *and* HOVSTAD *sit at his right;* DR. THOMAS STOCKMANN *and* CAPTAIN HORSTER *sit at left.* TOWNSPEOPLE *stand and sit downstage.* MORTEN KIIL *and* PETRA *stand down right, almost offstage.*

TOWNSPEOPLE (*Chanting*): Enemy of the people! Enemy of the people!

1ST MAN: He'll ruin us with his talk of contamination.

2ND MAN: What will happen to town property values?

1ST WOMAN: We need the tourist trade to survive.

TOWNSPEOPLE: Enemy of the people!

PETER: Ladies and gentlemen! Fellow citizens, please come to order! (TOWNSPEOPLE *become quiet.*) Now, let us review the situation. As you all know, your town has just completed a fine set of baths.

THOMAS: Contaminated baths, you mean.

PETER (*Ignoring* THOMAS): As I was saying, the public baths are ready for the summer tourist trade. I don't need to tell you what this will mean for our town—more business, increased property values, more income for the town to build better schools, better streets.

THOMAS (*Rising; heatedly*): And more disease, too. Don't forget more disease, for that's exactly what you'll have if you allow the public to use those baths.

PETER (*Angrily*): Dr. Stockmann, will you be quiet and wait your turn? (*To* TOWNSPEOPLE) You know what the baths will mean to your prosperity. What you have heard may be only rumor. My own brother, our town medical officer, Dr. Stockmann, wants these same baths torn down. If he succeeds—but I know you people will not let him—there will be unemployment, business failures, decrease in property values. Ah, but I will let Dr. Stockmann speak for himself. (*Turning to* THOMAS) You may speak now, Thomas.

THOMAS (*Rising and going to podium*): Fellow townspeople, you are my last hope. I have spoken to the council, the press, and the trade unions. For their own reasons, they have not listened. You, I think, will listen.

1ST MAN: Not if you tear down the baths.

2ND MAN: You're an enemy of the people.

PETER (*Rising*): Let him speak! He has asked for this meeting; let him learn, once and for all, that he is really alone here. (*Crowd becomes quiet.*)

THOMAS: The idea of the baths is a good one. I have long believed that our waters could prove a valuable tourist attraction because they contain health-giving minerals. Indeed, I was the one who first brought the idea to the council.

PETER: You just had the idea. We had to raise the money and get the work done.

THOMAS: What the mayor says is true. The council did get the work done, and that's the source of the trouble. Against my advice, the baths were built in the marsh land where the spoilage from a tannery drains. The cheapest possible pipe was used. As a result, what is being piped into the baths is not our clear, health-giving water, but the sewage from the tannery, filled with germs. I have taken samples and sent them to the university at Oslo. I have the reports.

1ST WOMAN (*Viciously*): Traitor!

1ST MAN: You will ruin our reputation.

THOMAS: What will happen to your reputation if the baths become the source of disease? Editor Hovstad (*Pointing to* HOVSTAD) was going to publish the reports.

HOVSTAD (*Defensively*): Don't try to make me a party to this, Thomas. When I agreed, I didn't know what your report would do to the town.

THOMAS (*To* ASLAKSEN; *imploringly*): Mr. Aslaksen, won't you speak? You are chairman of the majority party. It is your people who will suffer if these baths are allowed to operate.

ASLAKSEN: It is my people who will be ruined if the baths are not opened.

2ND WOMAN: Drive him out of town.

1ST MAN: Tar and feather him.

CAPTAIN HORSTER (*Rising and going to* THOMAS): Come on, Thomas. It is foolish to try to speak here.

2ND MAN: We'll remember you, too, Captain Horster.

THOMAS (*Defeated*): It is useless, Captain. Let's go home. (THOMAS *and* HORSTER *exit.*)

PETER: The meeting is adjourned.

1ST MAN: Drive the doctor out of town!

TOWNSPEOPLE (*Picking up chairs and exiting as they chant*): Enemy of the people! Enemy of the people!

ASLAKSEN (*To* PETER): Your brother may be hurt. They'll follow him home.

PETER (*Harshly*): It's his own affair. He brought all this on himself.

HOVSTAD: True. There's nothing we can do. If a man won't listen to reason, he's a fool for all his learning. One can't flout the will of the majority, no matter how right he thinks he is. (*They exit, taking chairs and podium.* PETRA *and* KIIL *move downstage. She tries to follow crowd, but* KIIL *holds her back.*)

PETRA: Don't stop me, Grandfather. The mob will kill my father!

KIIL: Don't worry. Mobs just yell and scream. They like that better than thinking. They will follow your father home, throw some rocks, scream, and then go to sleep.

PETRA: Poor Papa.

KIIL: Your father may have the last laugh yet. I have a plan. (*Laughs*) Oh, what a wonderful plan!

PETRA: What plan?

KIIL: I'll tell you when the time comes. (*Blackout.* PETRA *and* KIIL *exit as curtain opens.*)

* * *

TIME: *The next morning.*

SETTING: *Victorian living room of Thomas Stockmann's home. A broken window is up center, large stones are on floor nearby.*

AT RISE: THOMAS *enters, sees stones and picks one up.* KATHERINE *enters and surveys room.*

KATHERINE (*Shaking her head; sadly*): The whole house is a shambles. Windows broken. The vase Mother gave me, shattered.

THOMAS (*Picking up another stone*): I've found another stone.

KATHERINE: You'll find a lot more, I'm sure.

THOMAS (*Bending to pick up another stone, then drawing back as though he has been cut, licking finger*): Broken glass—I've cut my finger. Where's the glazier? I sent for him hours ago!

KATHERINE: He said he didn't know if he could come today.

THOMAS (*Disgustedly*): He's afraid to come.

KATHERINE: It's understandable. (*Hands him letter*) This letter came for you a few minutes ago. It's from the landlord.

THOMAS (*Opening letter and reading it*): He's given us notice. He wants us to move.

KATHERINE (*Surprised*): To move?

THOMAS (*Still reading letter*): He says he doesn't have any choice. Public opinion would ruin him. (*Throws letter on table*) They are all cowards. The whole lot of them. I'll be glad to be rid of them when we leave for the New World.

KATHERINE: Thomas, have you given this business of leaving serious thought?

THOMAS: I can't stay here, not after the way people have been talking, calling me the enemy of the people, breaking our windows. After last night, I know I don't belong here.

KATHERINE: I know you've been hurt, Thomas. But do we have to leave the country?

THOMAS: Every town in Norway is the same. They are ruled by the establishment, the press, the vested interests.

KATHERINE: But, Thomas, what about the children?

THOMAS: Do you want them to grow up in a society like this? Half the people in town are insane, and the other half are stupid.

KATHERINE (*Scolding*): Thomas, you shouldn't talk like that.

THOMAS: I speak the truth. For men to say they believe in truth and then to act the opposite, that's insanity. (PETRA *enters, carrying a load of books, which she puts on table.*)

KATHERINE: You're home early, Petra. Did you let your students have a holiday?

PETRA (*Upset*): No, Mother. Mrs. Busk gave me my notice. I thought it best to leave at once.

KATHERINE: Oh, Petra, no! I didn't think Mrs. Busk was that kind of woman.

PETRA: I could see that she didn't like firing me, but she was afraid to do anything else.

THOMAS (*Bitterly*): Afraid to do anything else! They are all afraid, merely because one man wants to speak the truth.

KATHERINE: I guess after the riot last night, Mrs. Busk *was* afraid. Thomas, perhaps you shouldn't have tried to hold a public meeting when you knew all the influential people were against it.

PETRA: It wasn't just the meeting, Mother. Mrs. Busk has been getting letters.

THOMAS: Anonymous, of course.

PETRA: Yes. Two of them made accusations against me. Said I had some advanced ideas for a woman.

THOMAS: I hope you didn't deny it. Advanced ideas, indeed! Is there any other kind of idea?

PETRA: I didn't deny it. Mrs. Busk has some pretty advanced ideas of her own, when she talks to me privately.

THOMAS (*Sneeringly*): Yes, of course, privately. I'm telling you, the sooner we get out of this place the better we will be. You'd better go pack, Petra.

PETRA (*Starting out*): Yes, Father. (*Exits*)

THOMAS (*Sighing*): It's a sorry state when even the educators are afraid to think, except privately. (PETRA *reenters with* HORSTER.)

PETRA: Father, we have a visitor.

THOMAS (*Going to* HORSTER *and shaking his hand warmly*): Oh, yes, our good friend. Welcome to our home, Captain Horster— such as it is and for as long as it is.

HORSTER: Good morning, Doctor. I thought I'd just see how things are going.

THOMAS: I thank you for that.

KATHERINE: And thank you for helping Thomas home last night. That mob might have killed him, if you had not helped.

PETRA: How did *you* get home, Captain?

HORSTER: I managed. Mostly, they were just yelling.

THOMAS: Yes, for all their numbers, mobs are cowards. (*Picks up stones*) Look at these stones they threw at the house last night. It was fair that they called me an enemy of the people. I am an enemy—of the kind of people in this town.

KATHERINE: You're not really, Thomas. You shouldn't talk like that.

PETRA: Just laugh at them, Papa.

HORSTER: Give them time, Doctor. People come around to the truth in time.

THOMAS: Only when it's too late—after disease has broken out.

But I shall be gone. When do you sail, Captain? I am anxious to leave this country.

HORSTER (*Gravely*): That's one of the reasons I came by. I can't take you.

THOMAS: Why not? Is something wrong with the ship?

HORSTER: The owner has relieved me of my command.

PETRA (*Upset*): Oh, dear. They took my school, now your ship!

THOMAS: I'm truly sorry, Captain.

HORSTER (*Brightening*): It's all right, Doctor. I can get another berth with some company away from here.

PETRA: If you hadn't helped Papa last night, maybe—

HORSTER: I'm not sorry. If I had it to do over again, I'd do the same thing. But don't take this too hard. If you still want to leave Norway, I have another idea.

THOMAS: Every minute I want to leave more. (*Knock on door is heard.*)

PETRA: I'll see who that is. (*Exits*)

KATHERINE: Thomas, whoever it is, promise me you won't lose your temper. (PETER *enters, followed by* PETRA.)

PETER (*Seeing* HORSTER): Oh, Thomas, I didn't realize you were busy. I wanted to see you alone.

KATHERINE: The Captain and I can wait in the other room. Come, Captain. (HORSTER, KATHERINE, *and* PETRA *exit.* PETER *looks at broken window.*)

THOMAS (*Sarcastically*): Maybe you'd better put a hat on, Peter. You'll catch a cold from the draft in here.

PETER: I'm sorry that I couldn't stop the mob. But you brought it on yourself, Thomas.

THOMAS (*Coolly*): Have you something to tell me?

PETER (*Reaching into his coat pocket for letter*): I have a letter for you from the Director of the Baths.

THOMAS (*Taking letter*): My dismissal, I assume.

PETER (*Matter-of-factly*): It's dated today. We are very sorry, but public opinion being what it is, we can't keep you on any longer.

THOMAS (*Coldly*): Whenever a man wants to do something he cannot justify, he blames it on public opinion.

PETER: I don't think you will have much of a medical practice in this town anymore, Thomas. The Homeowners Association is sending a notice to all its members to avoid you. It might be a good idea for you to move somewhere else.

THOMAS: That's one opinion of yours I share.

PETER: Good. Maybe in six months or so—when things calm down—you could write a letter of apology and maybe—

THOMAS (*Ironically*): Maybe I could be reinstated?

PETER: It's possible.

THOMAS: And what about public opinion?

PETER: Opinions change. Especially if you would be cooperative.

THOMAS: Ah, yes, if I would be cooperative.

PETER: Frankly, Thomas, it's very important to us that we have a statement from you now—about your charges that the baths are contaminated.

THOMAS (*Firmly*): I have given you a report on the condition of the baths. It is available for publication. (*Pauses*) Ah, but I see the truth is not what you want. I told you from the beginning, Peter. I cannot change the facts.

PETER: Things have changed, Thomas.

THOMAS (*Sadly*): For me, they have. I have lost my position. My home has been stoned. My daughter and my one remaining friend have been discharged from their positions.

PETER: Your stubbornness is costing you a great deal.

THOMAS (*Sternly*): But things have not changed with your baths. They are corrupt—a breeder of disease. It would be criminal to bring people here for their health and send them away sicker than they came.

PETER: You're a father, a husband, Thomas. I won't even mention what you are doing to my position as mayor, since you are my brother. You have no right to hurt your family like this!

THOMAS (*Hotly*): I am a free man, and free men have no right to live by lies.

PETER (*Accusingly*): You'd like people to see this whole business as just a matter of your virtue, wouldn't you? But you had private reasons for trying to ruin the reputation of the baths.

THOMAS (*Puzzled*): What are you talking about?

PETER: I know the terms of Morten Kiil's will.

THOMAS (*Matter-of-factly*): As I understand it, my father-in-law's money—whatever little there is—will go to an old folks' home. What's that got to do with me?

PETER: Are you telling me that you don't know your children are his only heirs? You and Katherine will have use of the money during your lifetime.

THOMAS (*Unconvinced*): I've never heard such a thing. All I've heard from my father-in-law are complaints about taxes.

PETER: Well, I know the facts. He's rich, and your family will get his money.

THOMAS: Well, well. (*Pauses*) So Katherine is a rich heiress. Why, this means that the family is secure!

PETER: Wait a minute, Thomas. *Maybe* you're secure. Your father-in-law can change the will any time he pleases.

THOMAS: He won't. He's very pleased that I've made things uncomfortable for you and your friends. He told me so.

PETER: That's what I suspected. You've been attacking us just to please the old man. That's your plot.

THOMAS (*Angrily*): Peter, you are the most thorough scoundrel I've ever met.

PETER (*Hotly*): Don't think you're fooling me. When I expose your plot, no one will take your lies seriously again. (*Exits*)

THOMAS (*Shouting after him*): Scoundrel! (*He picks up stone as if to throw it, then puts it on table.*)

PETRA (*Entering*): Papa, Grandfather is here. Can you see him now?

THOMAS: I certainly can. (*She exits. After a moment* KIIL *enters.*) Come in, Father-in-law.

KIIL: You must have a good conscience today.

THOMAS: I suppose I have.

KIIL (*Tapping his head*): Do you know what I have here?

THOMAS: I hope a good conscience, too.

KIIL: Something better than that. A plan. (*Reaches into inside pocket, and draws out large envelope*) Look at these. (THOMAS *takes envelope, opens it, and looks at certificates.*)

THOMAS: These . . . these are shares in the baths. Did you buy these?

KIIL: They were easy to buy. And cheap. Throw what stones they may, many of the townspeople fear you speak the truth.

THOMAS: Of course I speak the truth! I fear, Father-in-law, that you have bought worthless stock. (*Hands envelope back to him*)

KIIL: Not if you'll be reasonable.

THOMAS: What can I do?

KIIL: First things first. Do you know what money I have used to buy this stock? It's the money that Katherine and your children are to inherit. You didn't know about that, did you?

THOMAS (*Incredulously*): You bought those stocks with the money for Katherine?

KIIL: Every penny of it.

THOMAS (*Aghast*): Why didn't you speak to me before you bought the stock?

KIIL: It's too late for that now.

THOMAS: If only there were some doubt. But the baths are contaminated, and there's no way of cleaning them up without rebuilding the whole sewer system. That would take a couple of years.

KIIL: If you continue with your accusations against the baths—blaming my tannery for polluting the waters—these stocks will be worth nothing. You will make your wife and children poor. Any father who would do that would be insane.

THOMAS: Well, then, I'm insane.

KIIL: Thomas, you're joking. Think about this carefully.

THOMAS (*Considering*): Maybe some chemical could be developed. . . . something that would kill the germs. But it would take too long.

KIIL: So what are you going to do?

THOMAS (*Coldly*): Why should I do anything? If the people want to wallow in baths filled with disease, that's their business. I owe them nothing more.

KIIL (*Enthusiastically*): Now you're making sense, Thomas. And don't forget last night. They tried to kill you.

THOMAS (*Musing aloud*): Perhaps I haven't thought enough of my family.

KIIL: That's right, Thomas. Talk to Katherine. She's a good sensible girl.

THOMAS (*Upset*): But why did you do a thing like this? Risking Katherine's money and now tempting me. When I look at you, Father-in-law, I seem to think I am seeing the devil himself.

KIIL: If that's your attitude, I'd better leave. I'll give you some time to think this over. Be sensible, Thomas. Think of your family. (*He exits, as* PETRA *enters.*)

PETRA: Father, more visitors. Editor Hovstad and Mr. Aslaksen.

THOMAS: What can they want? After last night, I thought they would be ashamed to show their faces in my house. (HOVSTAD *and* ASLAKSEN *enter.* PETRA *exits, closing door.*) What could you two possibly want with me?

HOVSTAD: Now, Doctor, I can understand why you may resent my attitude.

THOMAS (*Angrily*): Your attitude! Your cowardice, you mean. Promising me your support and then turning on me at the meeting.

HOVSTAD: I had no choice. The editor of the paper is not his own master, you know.

THOMAS: No one, it seems, is his own master in this town.

ASLAKSEN (*Pleasantly*): We'd have supported you if you had told us *all* your plans.

THOMAS: What are you talking about?

ASLAKSEN: Your father-in-law's going around town buying up all the stock in the baths.

THOMAS: What does that have to do with me?

ASLAKSEN (*Conspiratorially*): It would have been smarter to have used someone not in the family to buy the stock.

HOVSTAD: If you had shared the plan with us, we could have used a man who wasn't tied to you.

THOMAS (*Bluntly*): What do you want?

HOVSTAD: Perhaps it would be better for you to explain, Mr. Aslaksen, since you represent the majority.

ASLAKSEN: Briefly, Doctor, now that we know how matters stand, you can count on our support.

HOVSTAD: As soon as your attack on the baths has done its work—

THOMAS (*Sharply*): As soon as the price of the stocks drops further so that my father-in-law can buy the stocks cheap, you mean.

HOVSTAD: We can say that you took over the baths because they needed the direction of a man of science.

ASLAKSEN: You'll be a hero.

THOMAS: I see. Then we can do a few little things—nothing very expensive—and announce that the baths are pure. Right?

HOVSTAD: Exactly! Everyone will believe you if my paper backs you.

ASLAKSEN: In a free society, the newspaper is strong, Doctor. And don't forget that I have the Homeowners Association as support, too. Public opinion will be no problem.

THOMAS: I see. (*Pauses*) What do you two want for your—your cooperation?

HOVSTAD: We would like to cooperate just because it's a good thing for the community. But it does take money to run a newspaper.

THOMAS (*Exploding*): And they call *me* the enemy of the people. Let me tell you something. You'll never get a cent from me.

HOVSTAD (*Coldly*): My paper will expose you, then.

THOMAS: Get out. Get out before I throw you out!

HOVSTAD: You're not serious, Doctor.

THOMAS (*Unrelenting*): I'm going to count to three. If you are not out by then, I'm going to throw you right through that window that your mob broke last night.

HOVSTAD: Now, Doctor, think what you're doing.

THOMAS (*Advancing toward them*): One. Two.

ASLAKSEN: He's crazy!

THOMAS (*Grabbing* HOVSTAD *by collar*): Three! (HOVSTAD *yells as* THOMAS *drags him toward window.* KATHERINE, HORSTER, *and* PETRA *rush in.*)

KATHERINE: Thomas! Let him go!

HOVSTAD (*Escaping from* THOMAS): You all saw it. An unprovoked attack. I'll have the law on him. (*Rushes out*)

ASLAKSEN: He's crazy! (*Rushes after* HOVSTAD)

KATHERINE (*Grabbing* THOMAS's *arm as he starts after them*): Thomas, please! Just let them go. What was that all about?

THOMAS: I'll tell you later. But first, Petra, I want you to take a message to your grandfather. (*Pauses*) Tell him the answer is "no, no, no."

PETRA: That's simple enough. I shouldn't forget it. (*Exits*)

THOMAS: I'm through with the whole lot of them.

KATHERINE: Since we are leaving, Thomas, we'll leave it all behind us.

THOMAS: No, Katherine, we are staying here.

KATHERINE (*In disbelief*): Staying here?

THOMAS (*Emphatically*): Yes, here is where the fight is, and here I will win. Soon I shall go into the town and look for another house.

HORSTER: Doctor, you can have my house. I have too much room. Besides, I'll be shipping out soon. While I'm here I'll be glad for the company.

KATHERINE: How kind of you, Captain. You are indeed our friend.

THOMAS (*Gratefully*): Thank you, Captain. That's a load off my mind. (PETRA *enters breathless.*)

PETRA: I met Grandfather at the corner, Papa, and gave him your message. I'm not sure what it meant, but I think it displeased him.

THOMAS: Good. Did he have any message for me?

PETRA: Not as short as yours, but just as simple. He told me to tell you that you are a fool.

THOMAS: No doubt I am, in his view. Petra, we are staying here.

KATHERINE: But you won't be able to practice medicine here.

THOMAS: Yes, I shall. The poor will keep coming to me. They can't pay me, but they are the ones who need a doctor most, anyway. And the poor will listen to me. I'll doctor their minds as well as their bodies.

PETRA: What will you teach them, Papa?

THOMAS: A simple lesson, Petra. People owe their first loyalty to the truth and to giving the best that's in them, not to the establishment, or the majority, which can be a cruel tyrant.

KATHERINE (*Worriedly*): How shall we live, Thomas?

THOMAS: We'll get on, so long as I can find honest men who will work for truth—now and in the future. (EILIF *and* MORTEN *enter.*)

PETRA: Here's your answer to the future—your sons, Eilif and Morten. They will continue your work.

EILIF: We will help you, Papa.

MORTEN: Even if it's weeding in the garden.

THOMAS (*Laughing*): That's just what it is boys—weeding the garden. Petra, you are right. It's always the young who give us the right to hope for the future. I am a lucky man, Katherine.

KATHERINE: Lucky, Thomas? You?

THOMAS: Yes. I am lucky because I have stumbled onto an important truth: I am the strongest man in town.

KATHERINE: You are a sweet man, Thomas, but sometimes absurd. You have no position, no friends, no money.

THOMAS: But the truth is, Katherine, the strongest man in the world is he who stands alone.

KATHERINE (*Smiling; putting her arm around him*): Ah, dear Thomas.

PETRA: Yes, Papa, you are. (*She and boys hug* THOMAS. *Curtain*)

THE END

Production Notes

AN ENEMY OF THE PEOPLE

Characters: 8 male; 2 female; male and female extras for townspeople.
Playing Time: 30 minutes.
Costumes: Appropriate late nineteenth-century costumes.
Properties: Stones, books, two letters, envelopes containing certificates.

Setting: Before Rise: Town meeting hall. Chairs and podium are placed before curtain. At Rise: Victorian living room, with broken window up center. Chairs, tables, bookcases, etc., stand about room.
Sound: Knock on door.

▨▨The House of the Seven Gables

by *Nathaniel Hawthorne*
Adapted by *Adele Thane*

Characters

MATTHEW MAULE
COLONEL PYNCHEON
CLERGYMAN
TWO MEN
MAID
HEPZIBAH PYNCHEON
TWO WOMEN
THOMAS HOLGRAVE, *an artist*
NED, *a schoolboy*
HOUSEWIFE
UNCLE VENNER, *a handyman*
PHOEBE PYNCHEON
CLIFFORD PYNCHEON
JUDGE JAFFREY PYNCHEON
VOICES OF MOB, *four or more*
GHOST OF ALICE PYNCHEON

SCENE 1

TIME: *1692.*
SETTING: *Gallows Hill, in Salem Village, Massachusetts. This*

305

scene may be played in front of curtain. Flight of wooden steps left leads to scaffold, with gallows, from which hangman's noose dangles.

AT RISE: *Stage is dark.* VOICES OF MOB *are heard offstage.*

1ST VOICE (*Harshly*): Here come the witches!

2ND VOICE: Die, witch, die! You sickened my cow!

3RD VOICE: You curdled the milk!

4TH VOICE: My hens wouldn't lay! My butter wouldn't churn!

VOICES (*Ad lib*): Hang the witches! String them up! (*Etc. Spotlight comes up on gallows.* MATTHEW MAULE *and* CLERGYMAN *stand at foot of steps.* COLONEL PYNCHEON *stands center, his back to* MAULE.)

CLERGYMAN: Matthew Maule, will you confess your sin of witchcraft and save your immortal soul?

MAULE (*Firmly*): I am no more a witch than you are, Reverend.

CLERGYMAN (*Shouting*): Confess, confess! Did you not have dealings with the Evil One? Is he not here with you now?

MAULE: Yes! He is standing over there! (*Pointing to* COLONEL PYNCHEON) *He* is the real Evil One—Colonel Pyncheon! (PYNCHEON *looks scornfully at* MAULE.) He has robbed me of my land so that he could build his great house upon it. He has falsely accused me of witchcraft and sent me here to the gallows to die. (*Fiercely, to* PYNCHEON) But you will be punished, Colonel Pyncheon, you will be punished! If you take my life, I will take yours. I, Matthew Maule, put a curse on you and your descendants from this day forth: *God will give you blood to drink!* (*Blackout. They exit as dramatic music is heard offstage, fading out. Spotlight comes up on* TWO MEN, *right.*)

1ST MAN (*Pointing off right*): See there! Colonel Pyncheon's house with the seven gables is all lit up.

2ND MAN: He's holding open house tonight. All the bigwigs in town are invited.

1ST MAN: It's a grand family mansion, to be sure, but the Colonel never should have built it where Matthew Maule's home had once been. (*With foreboding*) That land is cursed.

2ND MAN (*Pointing off; suddenly*): The Colonel's maid is running out the front door. (*Wailing in fear,* MAID *runs in.*)

1ST MAN (*Taking her by the shoulders*): Here, here, what's the matter?

MAID (*Excitedly*): Colonel Pyncheon is dead! There's blood on his beard!

1ST MAN (*To* 2ND MAN): What did I tell you? It's Maule's curse! God *has* given him blood to drink! (*Curtain*)

* * * * *

SCENE 2

TIME: *June, 1850.*

SETTING: *Hepzibah Pyncheon's shop in the House of the Seven Gables. Door to street is in rear wall. Over door is a bell that rings when door is opened. Left of door is a wide window, in which are displayed toys, jars of hard candy and marbles, and gingerbread men. Table with sewing materials stands right. Counter left holds weigh scales, cash box, plate of biscuits, and stack of paper bags. A chair stands behind counter. In front of counter are chair and stool. Several shelves on right wall are stocked with household goods and other items for sale. Barrels marked* FLOUR, APPLES, CORNMEAL, *etc., are set about shop. Door down left leads to main part of house.*

AT RISE: HEPZIBAH *enters left, carrying box of lace and ribbons. She goes to table, and starts to arrange articles on it. Door at rear opens, concealing* HEPZIBAH, *as* TWO WOMEN *peek into shop, then enter timidly.*

1ST WOMAN: Well, will you look at this! Old maid Pyncheon is setting up a shop! (*They look about.*)

2ND WOMAN: She'll never make a go of it. Her face would frighten the devil himself.

1ST WOMAN (*Spitefully*): She's a real vixen. Have you ever noticed the mischief in her eye?

2ND WOMAN: Indeed I have! If you ask me, it has something to do with that curse Matthew Maule put on the family over a hundred and fifty years ago. (HEPZIBAH *steps from behind door, startling* WOMEN.)

HEPZIBAH (*Sharply*): What can I do for you, ladies?

1st WOMAN (*Flustered*): Nothing—nothing, Miss Pyncheon. We were just looking. (WOMEN *edge away and back out of door, bumping into* THOMAS HOLGRAVE *as he enters. He tips his hat to them as they exit.*)

HOLGRAVE (*Kindly*): My dear Miss Pyncheon, I'd like to offer my best wishes on the opening of this store. Can I assist you in any way?

HEPZIBAH (*Nervously*): Oh, Mr. Holgrave, I never can go through with it—never! I am too old, too feeble. To think that I, a born lady, should be reduced to running a shop!

HOLGRAVE (*Reassuringly*): I don't think any lady of your family has ever done a more heroic thing in this house than you are doing in it today. If the Pyncheons had always acted so nobly, I doubt if Maule's curse would have had much effect.

HEPZIBAH (*Sighing*): If Maule's ghost could see me now, he would be well pleased at the success of his curse. But I thank you for your kindness, Mr. Holgrave. I will strive to be a good shopkeeper.

HOLGRAVE (*Gallantly*): Well, then, may I have the pleasure of being your first customer? (*Points to jar*) A few of those biscuits are just what I need for breakfast. What is the price of six?

HEPZIBAH (*Crossing behind couner*): Let me be a lady a moment longer and give you the biscuits. A Pyncheon shouldn't take money for a morsel of bread from her only friend. (*Puts biscuits into paper bag and hands it to* HOLGRAVE)

HOLGRAVE: Thank you, Miss Hepzibah. (*He bows.*) I'll look in again later. (*He exits, closing door. A moment later,* NED *enters shop, carrying school books.*)

HEPZIBAH: Well, good day, Ned. What would you like?

NED (*Pointing to window*): A gingerbread man. (*Holds out penny*)

HEPZIBAH (*Getting gingerbread man*): Never mind the penny. You're welcome to the gingerbread.

NED (*Surprised*): Golly, thanks, Miss Pyncheon. (*Takes cookie and runs out, leaving door open.* HEPZIBAH *shuts it, then goes to apple barrel, takes cloth from apron, and polishes apples.* HOUSEWIFE, *flour on hands and wearing apron, bursts in.*)

HOUSEWIFE (*Breathlessly*): Oh, Miss Pyncheon, I'm in the middle of making bread, and I'm out of yeast. May I have a penny's worth? Hurry!

HEPZIBAH: I'm sorry. I don't have any yeast.

HOUSEWIFE (*Indignantly*): What? A shop without yeast? Whoever heard of such a thing! (*Tartly*) *Your* loaf won't rise any more than mine will today, Hepzibah Pyncheon. You might as well close shop at once! (*She stalks out, nearly knocking down* NED *as he reenters.*)

NED: Golly, she sure is mad, isn't she!

HEPZIBAH (*Wearily*): What is it now, Ned?

NED: I want another gingerbread man.

HEPZIBAH (*Getting cookie*): Here it is, but this time I will take your penny. (NED *hands her penny reluctantly.*) And please close the door when you go out. (*He exits, closing door quietly.* HEPZIBAH *drops penny into cash box.*) There, it's done! I'm no lady now, but simply a forlorn old shopkeeper. (UNCLE VENNER *enters.*)

UNCLE VENNER: Ah, Miss Hepzibah, I see you've begun trade already.

HEPZIBAH: Yes, Uncle Venner. I must earn my own living or starve.

UNCLE: I met your cousin, Judge Pyncheon, just now. It's to your credit, Miss Hepzibah, to be working like this, but it's not to the Judge's credit to let you.

HEPZIBAH (*Proudly*): I'd rather die than accept charity from Jaffrey Pyncheon.

UNCLE (*In a low voice*): They're saying all over town that your brother Clifford is being released from prison. When do you expect him home?

HEPZIBAH (*Nervously*): Almost any day now, and I'm so worried! He left this house a young, handsome man, and he will return to it old and broken. It's been thirty years, you know.

UNCLE (*Soothingly*): There, there, you must welcome him as best you can. I'll never believe he murdered his uncle—in spite of Jaffrey Pyncheon's testimony.

HEPZIBAH (*Bitterly*): It was Jaffrey's testimony that sent Clifford to jail. I'll never forgive Jaffrey for that. (UNCLE *looks out window.*)

UNCLE (*Pointing out window*): See there, a coach has stopped in front of the house. A young woman with a carpetbag is getting out. (HEPZIBAH *crosses to window.*)

HEPZIBAH: Phoebe Pyncheon! How like a country cousin to come without so much as a day's notice! (*Grumbling*) Well, she can stay one night, but no longer. If Clifford were to find her here, it might disturb him.

UNCLE (*Smiling as he looks out window*): Bless my eyes, what a brisk little soul she is! I'll take her luggage up to the guest room. (*Exits left, as* PHOEBE *enters, rear*)

PHOEBE (*Brightly*): Cousin Hepzibah?

HEPZIBAH (*Coolly*): How do you do, Phoebe? You might have let me know you were coming.

PHOEBE (*Cheerfully*): Oh, but I did! I wrote you a letter.

HEPZIBAH: I did not receive it, but no matter, do sit down. (PHOEBE *sits on stool.* HEPZIBAH *sits in chair before counter.*) What brings you here?

PHOEBE: Well, my father died a year ago and my mother has married again. It seemed best to leave home for a while, so I thought I'd pay you a visit.

HEPZIBAH (*Uneasily*): Phoebe, I really can't see my way clear to let you stay with me. I'm so poor I barely have food enough for myself.

PHOEBE (*Jumping up eagerly*): Oh, I mean to earn my keep. I will run this shop for you. You shall see what a good saleslady I am! Please let me stay and help you, cousin.

HEPZIBAH (*Rising, clasping* PHOEBE's *hand gratefully*): You are a dear girl, Phoebe, and it would brighten my lonely days to have a sunny person like you here with me. You are welcome to such a home as I can offer you.

PHOEBE (*Gratefully*): Thank you, Cousin Hepzibah!

HEPZIBAH (*Smiling*): Come. I will show you to your room. (*They exit down left. Curtain*)

* * * * *

SCENE 3

TIME: *Afternoon of the next day.*

SETTING: *Garden behind the House of the Seven Gables. Backdrop includes gnarled old tree and several bushes, with arched trellis, right, which leads to house. An old stone well stands left center and down left is a white rose bush, next to which is exit to street. Scene may be played before curtain.*

AT RISE: HOLGRAVE *is kneeling by rose bush, pruning it. Beside him is a pail for clippings.* PHOEBE *enters right, carrying basket of gardening tools.*

PHOEBE (*Crossing to center*): Good afternoon! (HOLGRAVE *turns.*) You must be Mr. Holgrave, the artist who lives in the east gable. I'm Phoebe Pyncheon, Miss Hepzibah's cousin. (*He stands and tips his hat.*)

HOLGRAVE: It's a pleasure to meet you, Miss Pyncheon. I didn't know Miss Hepzibah had a young cousin.

PHOEBE: I arrived yesterday from the country. I thought I'd do a little gardening, but I see you are ahead of me. (*Sets basket on chair*)

HOLGRAVE: Oh, I dig and hoe and weed to refresh myself. My real occupation is making daguerreotypes. (*Impulsively*) Would you like to see a sample of my work? (*Takes small leather case from pocket, opens it, and hands it to* PHOEBE)

PHOEBE (*Looking at picture inside case*): Why, this is a picture of my Puritan ancestor, Colonel Pyncheon! But here he is wearing modern clothes.

HOLGRAVE (*Smiling*): Because it is a modern face. It belongs to our most prominent citizen, Judge Pyncheon.

PHOEBE (*Fascinated*): Cousin Jaffrey?

HOLGRAVE: It's a sly, hard face, don't you agree? (*Points to picture*) Look at that eye! Would you like to be at its mercy? And yet you should see how kindly the Judge can smile in public.

PHOEBE: His face is far different from the miniature of my Cousin Clifford that Cousin Hepzibah has.

HOLGRAVE: Ah, you have seen that picture. Tell me, did you see anything sinister in Clifford's face? Could you imagine the man to be guilty of a great crime?

PHOEBE (*Emphatically*): Certainly not! There never was a sweeter face. (*Turns toward well*) What an old well this is.

HOLGRAVE: Yes, it's Maule's Well. (*With mock seriousness*) But be careful not to drink the water—it's bewitched!

PHOEBE (*Laughing*): What nonsense!

HOLGRAVE: Don't you know the story of Matthew Maule and the curse he put on Colonel Pyncheon, long ago?

PHOEBE (*Sighing*): Yes, indeed. Cousin Hepzibah believes that all the calamities that befell the Pyncheons began with that curse.

HOLGRAVE (*Earnestly*): I think so, too—not as a superstition, but as something proved by unquestionable fact.

PHOEBE (*Puzzled*): Why do you say that?

HOLGRAVE (*Pointing off right*): Since the Colonel's time, there has been nothing but misery, death, and disgrace under those seven gables. On this very ground a tragic drama has been acted out for over a hundred and fifty years. (*Sighs*) Let us hope the end of that drama is near. And now, Miss Pyncheon, will you please excuse me? I have some work that must be finished by evening. (*Picks up pail; cheerfully*) Any bright day, if you will put one of those roses in your hair, and come to my studio in Central Street, I will make a picture of the flower and its wearer.

PHOEBE (*Smiling*): That would be lovely. Thank you. (HOLGRAVE *tips hat and exits.* PHOEBE *carries basket to rose bush, takes out shears, and snips off a few roses and places them in basket.* HEPZIBAH *enters, greatly agitated.*)

HEPZIBAH (*Clutching* PHOEBE'S *arm*): Bear with me, Phoebe, for my heart is filled with woe.

PHOEBE (*Alarmed*): Dear cousin, what has happened?

HEPZIBAH: Clifford has come home! I can barely recognize him, he's so old and feeble. He wants to sit out here in the sunlight—he has been so long in the dark. (*Pulling* PHOEBE *center*) Stand where he can see you, Phoebe. (*Urgently*) And be cheerful! Whatever happens, be nothing but cheerful! (CLIFFORD PYNCHEON *enters haltingly, his shoulders stooped. His hair is white. He stares vaguely about garden, and* HEPZIBAH *hurries to him.*) Dear Clifford, this is our Cousin Phoebe, Arthur's only child. She has come from the country to stay with us a while.

CLIFFORD (*In a monotone*): Phoebe? Arthur's child? Ah, I forget, but no matter—she is very welcome.

HEPZIBAH (*Leading him to chair*): Come, take this chair. (CLIFFORD *sits.*)

CLIFFORD (*Leaning back in chair, gazing about*): How pleasant! How delightful! Those roses—that young girl. (*Puts hands to eyes*) It's all a dream. I shall awake to four stone walls.

HEPZIBAH (*Gently*): Never again, Clifford. You are at home now—home to stay. (PHOEBE *takes a rose from basket and gives it to* CLIFFORD.)

PHOEBE: This is the most perfect rose of them all, dear Clifford—and it is for you.

CLIFFORD (*Smelling rose*): Ah, this rose makes me feel young again. Hepzibah, I've just remembered something! Didn't we blow soap bubbles in this garden when we were children? (*She nods, smiling.*) Bring me a pipe—I want to blow bubbles now.

HEPZIBAH: I'll be right back. (*Exits right*)

CLIFFORD (*Rising*): Phoebe, take my hand and pinch it hard. Prove to me that I am awake. (*She takes his outstretched hand in both of hers and holds it tightly. He looks about.*) Once there was a well in this garden.

PHOEBE: It's over here. (*Guides him to well. He bends over it, staring down into water.*)

CLIFFORD: There are faces down there—beautiful smiling faces, fair and rosy. (*Agitated*) And one dark face, scowling up at me—the dreadful dark face of my fate. (*Suddenly crying out*) I want my happiness! Give me my happiness! It is so late, so late! (*Sits on edge of well and weeps.* PHOEBE *smooths his hair.* HEPZIBAH *reenters, carrying two toy pipes and bowl of soapy water. When she sees* CLIFFORD, *she stops and stares.*)

PHOEBE (*Nodding to* HEPZIBAH): It is all right. (*Soothingly, to* CLIFFORD) Come, dear cousin, let us blow soap bubbles together. (HEPZIBAH *puts pipes and bowl on table.* PHOEBE *helps* CLIFFORD *up and leads him to table. He dips pipe into water, and begins to blow bubbles.*)

CLIFFORD (*Laughing*): I feel like a child again! (PHOEBE *takes pipe and blows bubbles, too.* CLIFFORD *laughs happily. Suddenly* JUDGE PYNCHEON *enters.*)

JUDGE (*Sternly*): So, Cousin Clifford! Still blowing soap bubbles? (CLIFFORD *drops pipe, trembling.*)

CLIFFORD (*Pointing to* JUDGE): Hepzibah, why do you keep that odious picture on the wall? Take it down at once! It is the evil genius of this house! I cannot bear it. (*Covers face with arm and rushes out, followed by* HEPZIBAH)

JUDGE (*Approaching* PHOEBE *with unctuous smile, hat in hand*): Unless I am mistaken, you are Phoebe Pyncheon. I am Judge Pyncheon. Surely you have heard of me.

PHOEBE (*Curtsying*): Yes, sir, my father often spoke of you.

JUDGE: Then you will allow an old relative to bestow a kiss of natural affection on his young cousin. (*He bends forward to kiss her, but* PHOEBE *quickly steps back, leaving* JUDGE *kissing the air. Furious, he gives her an angry look.*)

PHOEBE (*Nervously*): I don't mean to be unkind, but . . .

JUDGE (*Quickly forcing a false smile*): You are quite right, Cousin Phoebe. A pretty girl can never be too careful. (*Abruptly*) Tell me, aren't you afraid to be in the same house with that frightful old man, Clifford?

PHOEBE (*Firmly*): I do not find Cousin Clifford frightful. He may not be quite in his sound senses, but he is a gentle, childlike man.

JUDGE (*With false heartiness*): I rejoice to hear that. Many years ago, I was greatly attached to him—we were like brothers. (*Piously*) Heaven grant that he has repented of his past sins.

PHOEBE (*Coolly*): Nobody I know could have fewer to repent of.

JUDGE: Is it possible, my dear, that you know nothing of Clifford Pyncheon's history? (*Pause*) I will just step into the house and see how he is. (*As he starts toward exit,* HEPZIBAH *reenters and blocks his way.*) Hepzibah, my dearest cousin, I came to offer any assistance in my power to make Clifford comfortable. Let him come stay with me. My house shall be his home.

HEPZIBAH (*Coldly*): Clifford has a home here.

JUDGE: Do not allow any ancient animosity to sway you in this matter. I want only to help Clifford.

HEPZIBAH: He doesn't need your help. Please take your leave.

JUDGE (*In an aggrieved tone*): You do me great wrong, Hepzibah, but I forgive it, and I shall watch over Clifford's welfare as if he were my own beloved brother. Good day, Cousin Phoebe. (*Exits*)

HEPZIBAH (*Shuddering*): Oh, Phoebe, that man has been the horror of my life! Shall I never have the courage to tell him what I think of him? (*Pauses, more calmly*) Will you go talk to Clifford? Amuse him and keep him calm. I will look after the shop. (*They exit. Blackout*)

* * * * *

SCENE 4

TIME: *One month later.*

SETTING: *Parlor in the House of the Seven Gables. A large portrait of Colonel Pyncheon hangs center in back wall over fireplace. To right of fireplace stands a low bookcase, over which hangs an old map of Maine. Left of fireplace is a settle. A harpsichord and chair stand left of door to hall. Lattice windows and window seat are in right wall. Table stands center, with a straight-backed chair and armchair on either side.*

AT RISE: CLIFFORD, HEPZIBAH, *and* HOLGRAVE *are seated, listening to* PHOEBE *playing harpsichord.* NOTE: *Recorded music may be used.*

CLIFFORD (*As* PHOEBE *finishes*): Thank you, Phoebe. That is my favorite piece.

PHOEBE: It gives me great pleasure to play it for you, Cousin Clifford.

CLIFFORD: I wish you weren't returning to the country today. I shall miss your music.

HEPZIBAH: I don't know how the shop will fare without you, Phoebe. Since you took it over, it has become the most popular penny-shop in Salem.

PHOEBE (*Going to them*): But I'll be gone only a few days. You know that I've come to look upon Seven Gables as my home.

CLIFFORD (*Rising*): That is good, dear Phoebe, because we could never do without you, never! (*Weakly*) Hepzibah, help me to my room. I suddenly feel very tired—and lonely. (HEPZIBAH *rises, takes his arm, and they exit.*)

HOLGRAVE (*Crossing to* PHOEBE): Whatever joy and comfort exist in this house are embodied in your person, Phoebe. (*Taking her hand*) I shall miss you, Phoebe. I have grown very fond of you, and I look forward to your return eagerly.

PHOEBE (*Shyly withdrawing her hand*): Why—why, thank you, Thomas. (*Turning to harpsichord, embarrassed*) Would you like me to play something for you? (*Sits at keyboard*)

HOLGRAVE: You know, that harpsichord is over a hundred years old. (*Pointing to portrait*) Colonel Pyncheon gave it to his great-granddaughter, Alice. She was exceedingly beautiful and accomplished, but she met with some mysterious calamity and died young. She's supposed to haunt this house, and before one of the Pyncheons is about to die, she has been heard playing a sad tune on the harpsichord. (*Sadly*) I have a feeling that Alice's ghostly music will soon be heard again—and for the last time.

PHOEBE (*Rising in alarm*): What do you mean? Do you know of any new trouble hanging over us?

HOLGRAVE: Nothing I can put my finger on, but I've noticed that Judge Pyncheon still keeps an eye on Clifford. The Judge is a ruthless, determined man, but I can't imagine what so rich and eminent a man can want or fear from poor, broken Clifford. (HEPZIBAH *enters, carrying* PHOEBE's *straw bonnet, shawl, and carpetbag, followed by* UNCLE VENNER.)

HEPZIBAH (*Helping* PHOEBE *put on bonnet and shawl*): Uncle Venner has come to drive you to the train.

UNCLE (*Earnestly*): I shall miss you, Miss Phoebe.

PHOEBE (*Smiling*): And I shall miss all of you. (*To* HOLGRAVE) Goodbye, Thomas—take good care of our garden. (HOLGRAVE *smiles and nods.*)

HEPZIBAH: I'll see you to the carriage. (HEPZIBAH, PHOEBE *and* UNCLE VENNER *exit.* HOLGRAVE *strikes a few notes on harpsichord, then turns to portrait.*)

HOLGRAVE: Well, old tyrant, who will be the next victim of Maule's curse? Is Destiny plotting the final act of the Pyncheon tragedy—at last? (*Lights dim to blackout, to indicate passage of time.* HOLGRAVE *exits. Recorded harpsichord music is heard, then fades. Sounds of rain and thunder are heard. Lightning flashes outside parlor windows. Lights come up to dim. Sound of loud knocking is heard offstage.*)

HEPZIBAH (*From off*): I'm coming! I'm coming! (*Knocking stops.* HEPZIBAH *enters, carrying lighted lamp, which she sets on table.* JUDGE PYNCHEON *follows her in, carrying wet umbrella, which he places in fireplace corner. Thunder and lightning continue throughout scene.* HEPZIBAH *faces* JUDGE, *scowling.*) What black-hearted errand has brought you here on a night like this, Cousin Jaffrey?

JUDGE (*Unctuously*): I couldn't rest without calling to find out how this terrible weather affects our poor Clifford. I would like to see him.

HEPZIBAH (*Firmly*): You shall not see him. Clifford has kept to his bed since yesterday.

JUDGE (*With real concern*): Is he ill? Then I *must* see him! Suppose he should die?

HEPZIBAH: He won't die—unless he is hounded to death by you who attempted it long ago.

JUDGE: You are unjust, Hepzibah. When Clifford was on trial for the murder of our uncle, I did nothing but give testimony required by law. (*With mock sorrow*) No one has shed more tears over Clifford's misfortune than I.

HEPZIBAH (*Angrily pounding table*): In heaven's name, stop this loathsome pretense of affection! Admit it—you hate Clifford!

JUDGE (*Harshly*): Has it never occurred to you, Hepzibah, that it was my influence that set Clifford free from prison?

HEPZIBAH (*Startled*): You? I'll never believe that! He owed his imprisonment to you—his release was God's will.

JUDGE (*Loudly*): I had Clifford set free for a purpose of my own, and for this purpose I must see him—*now!* (*Starts toward door*)

HEPZIBAH (*Barring his way*): No! It would drive him mad. Why can't you leave him in peace?

JUDGE: I'll tell you why. Our uncle died thirty years ago and left all his property to me. Yet after his death I discovered that the value of his estate fell far below any estimate made of it. There should have been more—much more—and I am convinced that Clifford can tell me where it is.

HEPZIBAH (*Defiantly*): And what if he refuses? What if he has no such knowledge?

JUDGE: The whole town knows of his odd behavior. I, myself, can testify to his childish pastimes (*Sarcastically*)—blowing soap bubbles, for instance. If Clifford refuses me, I shall recommend he be confined to a mental asylum for the rest of his life.

HEPZIBAH (*Shocked*): You cannot mean it! *You* are diseased in mind, not Clifford!

JUDGE (*Angrily*): Talk sense, Hepzibah! I have told you my determination. (*They stare at one another in stoney silence.*)

HEPZIBAH (*Yielding*): You are stronger than I, Jaffrey Pyncheon. I will call Clifford, but for heaven's sake, be merciful to him.

JUDGE (*Triumphantly*): Bid Clifford come quickly, then. (HEPZIBAH *exits.* JUDGE *turns armchair to half face portrait, takes watch from vest pocket, checks the time, then sits, holding watch open in hand. Lights dim to spotlights on armchair and harpsichord.* GHOST OF ALICE PYNCHEON *enters, sits at harpsichord and begins to play.* JUDGE *slowly rises and speaks in a hoarse whisper.*) Who's there? Who is playing? (*Sees* GHOST *and terrified, steps back, dropping watch.*) It's Alice—Alice Pyncheon's ghost! Are you—are you playing for my death? (GHOST *nods.*) No, no! (MATTHEW MAULE *steps through doorway into spotlight.*) Who—who are you?

MAULE (*Pointing finger at* JUDGE, *ominously*): God will give you blood to drink!

JUDGE: Matthew Maule! Maule's curse! (*Starts to choke, clutching throat*) Help! Help! (*Falls back into chair, coughing and gasping for breath.* MAULE *jeers and laughs, pointing finger at* JUDGE, *whose head sinks onto his chest. There is a loud clap of thunder.* GHOST *and* MAULE *exit. Spotlights fade, and stage lights come up.* CLIFFORD *enters, goes to armchair and looks down at* JUDGE *with a triumphant smile. He picks up* JUDGE's *watch from floor, shuts case, then crosses to window seat and sits.*)

HEPZIBAH (*From off, calling*): Clifford! Clifford, where are you? (*Enters*) Jaffrey, Clifford is gone! You must help me find him.

CLIFFORD (*Rising from window seat, finger on lips*): Shh-h-h! Jaffrey is asleep. (*Bursts into hysterical laughter*)

HEPZIBAH (*Bending over* JUDGE): He's dead! There's blood on his shirt!

CLIFFORD: Yes, Hepzibah, God has given him blood to drink! Now we can laugh, sing, dance! The weight is gone—from us and from the world!

HEPZIBAH (*Moaning*): What's to become of us?

CLIFFORD: Come, Hepzibah, let us leave the house to Cousin Jaffrey. He will take good care of it. (*Sinister laugh*) Put on your cloak and hood. Get your purse, and come along. (*Puts arm protectively around her shoulder*)

HEPZIBAH (*Weeping*): Lord, have mercy on us! (*Exits with* CLIFFORD. *Curtain*)

* * * * *

SCENE 5

TIME: *Two days later.*

SETTING: *Same as Scene 4. The armchair has been turned to face front.*

AT RISE: *Sunlight is streaming in through windows. Room is empty.* PHOEBE *and* HOLGRAVE *enter.* PHOEBE *wears shawl and bonnet.* HOLGRAVE *carries her carpetbag.*

PHOEBE: Thomas, why is the house so deserted? Where are Hepzibah and Clifford?

HOLGRAVE: They are gone—I don't know where. A terrible thing has happened.

PHOEBE: Tell me, tell me!

HOLGRAVE: Judge Pyncheon is dead. He died in that very chair (*Pointing*) two nights ago. And Clifford and Hepzibah have disappeared.

PHOEBE (*Anxiously*): Disappeared? Where could they have gone? Do you think they had anything to do with the Judge's death?

HOLGRAVE: No, indeed. The Judge did not come unfairly to his end—though I have wished him dead many a time.

PHOEBE (*Surprised*): You?

HOLGRAVE (*Frowning*): Yes. There are hereditary reasons that connect me strangely with that man's fate, Phoebe, and some day I will tell you about them. He threw a great dark shadow over my life that took away my youth. (*Takes her hands*) Then you came into my life, Phoebe, and joy came with you and drove away that dark shadow. (*Overwhelmed*) I cannot let this moment pass without telling you that I love you.

PHOEBE (*Shyly*): How can you love a simple girl like me?

HOLGRAVE (*Insistently*): You are my only possibility of happiness. (*Pause*) Do you love me, Phoebe?

PHOEBE: (*Happily*): You know I love you, Thomas. (*They embrace. Suddenly* PHOEBE *breaks away.*) Listen! Somebody is at the door.

HOLGRAVE (*Hopefully*): Can it be—? (CLIFFORD *and* HEPZIBAH *enter.* PHOEBE *runs to them and embraces them.*)

PHOEBE (*Joyfully*): Oh, Hepzibah! Clifford! Thank heaven you are back!

CLIFFORD: Hepzibah brought me back. (*Gravely*) She said it was the right thing to do.

HOLGRAVE (*Helping* HEPZIBAH *to chair at harpsichord*): Indeed, it was.

CLIFFORD: I thought of you both as we came down the street and saw the flowers blooming in the garden. And now I see that the flower of love has likewise bloomed in this old house today. (PHOEBE *and* HOLGRAVE *smile at each other and clasp hands.*)

HEPZIBAH (*Fearfully*): What has been done about—Jaffrey? Are they going to arrest Clifford? (CLIFFORD *goes to her, pats her shoulder comfortingly.*)

HOLGRAVE: Neither you nor Clifford has anything to fear. The medical examiner reports that Judge Pyncheon died of apoplexy, not by Clifford's hand.

HEPZIBAH (*With a gasp of relief*): Thank heaven!

HOLGRAVE: And there's more good news. Clifford has been proven innocent of his uncle's death. The lawyers found Judge Pyncheon's secret diary with an account of what really happened that night thirty years ago. It seems that your uncle caught young Jaffrey destroying the will he had made in favor of Clifford. The shock of the discovery brought on an attack of apoplexy, and the old man fell dead. Jaffrey found an earlier will that named him as his uncle's beneficiary, and left it in place of the will favoring Clifford. Then he manufactured evidence to make it look as if Clifford had murdered his uncle.

HEPZIBAH (*Thinking aloud*): I wonder if old Matthew Maule knew that the Pyncheons were predisposed to die of apoplexy? For that would explain how he has frightened generation after generation with his prophecy—God will give you blood to drink!

PHOEBE (*Indicating portrait*): And old Colonel Pyncheon has witnessed the evil destiny of his family ever since.

CLIFFORD (*Studying portrait*): That picture! I seem to recall that many years ago I knew a secret about it, but I don't remember what it was.

HOLGRAVE: Perhaps I can help you remember. (*Steps over to portrait and puts finger on frame*) See, here is a secret spring.

CLIFFORD: That's it! The secret spring! I discovered it when I was a child. (HOLGRAVE *presses on frame and portrait swings open, revealing a recess in the wall.*)

HOLGRAVE: The hinges were eaten through with rust. But behind the portrait is a hiding place for valuables. (*Reaches into recess and takes out folded sheet of parchment*)

PHOEBE (*Excitedly*): What is it, Thomas? (HOLGRAVE *opens parchment and studies it.*)

HOLGRAVE: I believe it is the deed to the vast tracts of land in Maine shown on that map. (*Points to map, right*) So this is what the heirs of Colonel Pyncheon have sought in vain! The land, of course, has long since been sold. The deed is worthless.

HEPZIBAH: So that is the secret wealth Jaffrey said Clifford knew of. Perhaps Clifford babbled something about hidden treasure while in prison, and Jaffrey believed it was true.

PHOEBE: But, Thomas, how did you come to know the secret of the portrait?

HOLGRAVE: My dearest Phoebe, when you marry me, will you mind if your name is changed not to Holgrave but to—Maule? I am the last descendant of Matthew Maule. The secret of the portrait is the only inheritance that has come down to me from my ancestors. (*Turns to* CLIFFORD *and* HEPZIBAH) Thomas Maule, the son of Matthew, was hired by Colonel Pyncheon to build this house. He constructed that secret place behind the portrait to hide this deed so that the Colonel could never find it. It was his means of retribution.

HEPZIBAH: So Colonel Pyncheon lost his great tracts of land, because he wanted Matthew Maule's tiny lot for his House of the Seven Gables! The irony of it all!

PHOEBE (*Happily*): That's all in the past, Cousin Hepzibah. Think of the future. Now that Judge Pyncheon is dead, Clifford will come into his rightful inheritance.

HOLGRAVE (*Taking* PHOEBE'*s hand*): Let us all go out into the sunshine and the Pyncheon ghosts can leave this place forever. Matthew Maule has withdrawn his curse at last and cast a spell of love over the House of the Seven Gables. (HOLGRAVE *and* PHOEBE *lead the way out, followed by* HEPZIBAH *and* CLIFFORD. *Curtain*)

THE END

Production Notes

THE HOUSE OF THE SEVEN GABLES

Characters: 10 male; 7 female; 4 or more male or female for Mob Voices. Colonel Pyncheon is a nonspeaking part.

Playing Time: 35 minutes.

Costumes: All characters wear costumes typical of 1850, except for Matthew Maule, Clergyman, Colonel Pyncheon and Ghost of Alice Pyncheon, who are in seventeenth-century dress. Phoebe wears shawl and bonnet in Scenes 2, 4, and 5. Hepzibah, an apron in Scene 2, with cloth in pocket. Judge Pyncheon, top hat in Scene 3, and overcoat in Scene 4. Holgrave, straw hat in Scene 3. Clifford has white hair.

Properties: Schoolbooks, penny, wooden pail, basket of garden tools including shears, leather case containing photo, carpetbag, shawl, bonnet, umbrella, sheet of folded parchment.

Setting: Scene 1: Gallows Hill in Salem Village, Massachusetts. Flight of wooden steps left leads to scaffold, with gallows, from which hangman's noose dangles. Scene 2: Hepzibah Pyncheon's shop in the House of Seven Gables. Door to street is in rear wall. Over door is a bell that rings when door opens. Left of door is wide window, in which are displayed toys, jars of hard candy, gingerbread men, etc. Table with sewing materials stands right. Counter, left, holds weigh scales, cash box, plate of biscuits, and stack of paper bags. Behind counter is a chair; in front of counter are chair and stool. Stocked shelves on right wall and barrels labeled FLOUR, APPLES, CORNMEAL, etc., complete setting. Door left leads to rest of house. Scene 3: Garden behind the House of the Seven Gables. Backdrop includes large, old tree and several bushes, with an arched trellis, right, leading to house. An old stone well stands left of center, and down left is a white rose bush. Exit to street is left. Scenes 1 and 3 may be played before curtain. Scenes 4 and 5: Parlor in the House of the Seven Gables. Large portrait of Colonel Pyncheon, in 17th century dress, hangs on back wall, center, over fireplace. Built into wall behind portrait is a cubbyhole. Portrait may be hinged to wall, so that it swings open when frame is pressed. Low bookcase and old map of Maine are right of fireplace. Left of fireplace is a settle. A harpsichord and chair stand left of door to hall. Lattice windows and window seat are in right wall. Table stands center, with a straight-backed chair and armchair on either side.

Lighting: Lightning; dimming of lights; spotlight.

Sound: Thunder, music, knocking.

▣▣Great Expectations

by *Charles Dickens*
Adapted for round-the-table reading
by *Edward Golden*

Characters

PIP
MAGWITCH
MR. JOE
MRS. JOE
SOLDIER
ESTELLA
MISS HAVISHAM
JAGGERS
WOMAN

PIP: My family name being Pirrip and my given name being Philip, all that my childish tongue could make out was "Pip," and so I was called "Pip." My parents were dead, and I lived with my married sister and her husband, Joe Gargery, the village blacksmith. One bitter cold day, while visiting my parents' graves in the churchyard bordering the marshes just outside of the town, the wind came up and I heard the sound of approaching footsteps on dried leaves as I read the names on the gravestone. (*After a pause*) Philip Pirrip and his wife Georgianna. (*Praying*) Oh, Lord, be good to those who were good to me. Amen. Now, I must pull out the weeds, and—(*He suddenly screams and gasps, as if hand has been clapped over his mouth.*)

MAGWITCH (*Viciously*): Make a move, and I'll split you from ear to ear!

PIP (*In quavering voice*): I won't, sir. Please don't cut my throat, sir!

MAGWITCH: Be quiet, and tell me your name.

PIP: Pip, sir.

MAGWITCH: You young dog! What fat cheeks you've got! Who do you live with? That is, supposin' I let you live.

PIP: With my sister, sir—Mrs. Joe Gargery, wife of the blacksmith.

MAGWITCH: Blacksmith, eh? (*Pause*) Look here—the question is whether you're to be allowed to live. Do you know what a file is?

PIP: Yes, sir.

MAGWITCH: Do you know what vittles is?

PIP: Yes, sir.

MAGWITCH: You get me a file and vittles. Bring 'em both to me here tomorrow morning early, and you'll be allowed to live. If not, I'll have your 'eart and liver out!

PIP: I will, sir.

MAGWITCH: Never dare to make a sign or say a word about seein' such a one as me. Otherwise, there's a young man with me, and, compared to 'im, I'm an angel! He 'as a secret way of gettin' at a boy all snug in 'is bed and tearin' 'is guts out! Now, what do you say?

PIP: I'll get the file and food, sir.

MAGWITCH: Get yourself home, and mind what I told you.

PIP: Yes, sir. I promise. Good day, sir. (*Pause*) I ran all the way home, not stopping once to look back, afraid that I would see that demon following me. I reached the Gargerys' door, opened it quickly, and slammed it shut.

JOE: There you are, Pip! Mrs. Joe's been out a dozen times and what's more, she's got the switch! You'd better make up tidy and—quick! She's comin', Pip, old chap! Hide behind the door!

MRS. JOE: I heard Pip come in, so don't tell me he's not here!

(*Pause*) There you are, you wretched boy! (*In threatening tone*) Kindly tell me where you've been afore I beat it out of you!

PIP (*Frightened*): I've only been to the churchyard!

MRS. JOE: You'd have been buried in that churchyard long ago, and stayed there if it hadn't been for me! Who brought you up by hand?

PIP: You did.

MRS. JOE (*Sighing deeply*): I'd never do it again, let me tell you. Oh, a precious pair you'd be without me. At least the boy knows who to be grateful to, even if he's not grateful. Now, sit down, both of you, and eat what we have, and be glad and grateful that you have it.

PIP: Suddenly, we heard gun shots off in the distance. (*Pause*) Joe? Did you hear those shots? Who's firing?

JOE: There was a convict escaped last night. They're firin' warnin' of him from the hulks.

PIP: Mrs. Joe, could you tell me what hulks are?

MRS. JOE: Drat you, Pip! What a questioner you are! Hulks is prison ships. Now, keep still and eat.

PIP: I wonder who's put in prison ships.

MRS. JOE: People are put in the hulks because they rob and murder.

JOE: Like as not that prisoner's out on the marshes. I shouldn't be surprised if he was in the very churchyard itself.

PIP: Just the very mention of the churchyard made me tremble, and I was so nervous that I dropped the cup I was holding.

MRS. JOE: Oh, Pip! What's with you, boy? You broke a good cup.

PIP (*Tremulously*): If you don't mind, I should like to go to bed now.

MRS. JOE: Get along quickly, afore I haul off and take the switch to you. And you'd better wear your clothes to bed, unless you want to freeze to death!

PIP: All that night I lay awake tossing and turning, unable to get the convict's face out of my mind. Very early in the morning, I stole downstairs and took a pork pie from the pantry and a file from Joe's shop. I ran feverishly to the churchyard, terrified by the consequences promised me if I failed to obey the convict's orders. The poor wretch snatched the food and file, and backed away into the fog, saying—

MAGWITCH: If you ever breathe a word of this, I'll know about it, and some night when you're lyin' warm in bed, no matter if the door's bolted and the window's shut, that certain young man I spoke of will tear your bloomin' 'eart out, 'e will! Remember that!

PIP (*After a pause*): I scurried home without looking back. Later that day, we received a visitor. (*After a pause*) There's a soldier at the door, Mrs. Joe.

SOLDIER: Is this the 'ome of the blacksmith?

MRS. JOE: And what might you want with him?

SOLDIER: Business, mum. We've a pair of 'andcuffs what need forgin'. We've a convict 'ere who escaped last night from the 'ulks, 'e's on 'is way back right now—(*Laughing*) They can't beat me at this game!

MRS. JOE (*Interrupting*): Pip, take these handcuffs out to Joe.

PIP: Yes, mum. (*After a pause*) The soldier waited with Mrs. Joe and me while Joe fixed the handcuffs.

JOE: There they are, captain, good as new.

SOLDIER: Thank you kindly. (*Calling*) Bring the prisoner forward!

PIP: I heard the clanking of chains, and before I knew it, the convict from the churchyard was at our door.

SOLDIER: Let's try these on for size. Hold out them hands.

MAGWITCH: I want to say one thing regardin' this escape. I stole into this very house last night, and took some vittles and a file.

MRS. JOE (*Shocked*): This house!

JOE: You're welcome to them, poor wretched devil. Isn't he, Pip, old top?

PIP: Y-yes, Joe.

SOLDIER: All right, you. Step lively. We've quite a way to go.

PIP: It was with decided relief that I saw that convict go out of my life forever—or so I thought. However, my mind was soon occupied by other things, for my sister came home from town the following day in a flurry of excitement!

MRS. JOE (*Calling*): Pip! Pip! Come here this instant!

PIP: Yes'm?

MRS. JOE: Oh, if you're not grateful this day, boy, you never will
be. Through the kindness of my dear Uncle Pumblechook,
you've been asked to go to Miss Havisham's house on the hill
to *play* this afternoon. Do you know who Miss Havisham is?

PIP: She's the strange old lady who lives on the hill in the big
house.

MRS. JOE: She may be strange, but she's rich as the queen herself, and who knows, if she takes a likin' to you, your fortune's
made. And (*Threateningly*) she'd better take a likin' to you,
or I'll know the reason why! Do you understand?

PIP: Yes'm.

MRS. JOE: Look at you! You're black from head to foot. Now, get
along to the pump. Will I ever civilize you? Hurry!

PIP: We reached Miss Havisham's house, and Mrs. Joe quickly
brushed down a lock of my hair, before saying—

MRS. JOE: Well, there's the gate. Ring the bell. And remember,
Pip, you'd better play for the old lady, or I'll teach you how to
play with the switch.

PIP: I rang the bell, and after a few moments, the front door
opened.

ESTELLA (*In a cold, haughty manner*): What name, please?

MRS. JOE: Gargery, miss.

ESTELLA: Quite right. And who is this young man?

PIP: I'm Pip, miss, come to play.

ESTELLA: So this is Pip, is it? Follow me. I am Estella. Do you
wish to see Miss Havisham too, madam?

MRS. JOE: If Miss Havisham wishes to see me.

ESTELLA (*Coolly*): Ah, but you see, she doesn't. Good day.

PIP: Estella led me through the door, and slammed it behind
me, leaving Mrs. Joe alone on the doorstep.

ESTELLA (*Haughtily*): Follow me, boy.

PIP: I say, miss, your clock in the tower has stopped. It says
twenty minutes to nine, and it's rightly fifteen minutes to
three.

ESTELLA: Mind your own affairs, boy, and don't ask questions.
Take off your hat. You're among gentlefolks now, so use your
manners, if you have any. Just knock on that door, boy.

PIP: I knocked, and after a few moments, I heard a woman's voice call out—

MISS HAVISHAM: Come in, Pip.

PIP: I opened the door and stared in amazement. There in a large carved chair sat the strangest old woman I had ever seen. Her face was a knot of bone and wrinkle. She was dressed in flowing wedding clothes, yellow with age. The dusty curtains were drawn, and the whole room was littered with faded gowns of every color, and festooned with cobwebs of immense size. On a table near her chair lay a bouquet of artificial flowers, such as a bride would carry. A large candelabra coated thickly with old wax shed the only light, and in the midst of this chaos sat Miss Havisham!

MISS HAVISHAM: Come closer, Pip—closer! You're not afraid of a woman who has never seen the sun since you were born?

PIP (*Frightened*): N-no, mum.

MISS HAVISHAM: Look at me! Do you know what I touch here?

PIP: Your heart, mum.

MISS HAVISHAM: Broken—broken! (*She sobs but quickly regains her composure.*) I sometimes have sick fancies that I want to see someone play. There, Pip—play! Play! Play! Well, why don't you play?

PIP: I—I can't play just now. It's so new here!

MISS HAVISHAM: So new to you, so old to me! (*Calling*) Estella!

ESTELLA (*After a pause*): Yes, Miss Havisham?

MISS HAVISHAM: Come here, Estella. I want you to play cards with this boy.

ESTELLA (*Scornfully*): With this boy? Why, he's a common laboring boy.

MISS HAVISHAM: Well, you can break his heart.

ESTELLA: What do you play, boy?

PIP: "Beggar My Neighbor," miss.

MISS HAVISHAM: Beggar him! Yes, beggar him! Ha! Ha! Beggar him! (*She breaks into hysterical laughter.*)

ESTELLA: Well, boy, pass the cards about. (*Pause*) Why, you horrid little monster! You've dropped the cards. What coarse hands you have! What thick boots!

MISS HAVISHAM: She says many hard things of you, Pip. What do you think of her?

PIP: I don't like to say.

MISS HAVISHAM: Well, you can tell me in my ear.

PIP (*Whispering*): I think she's very proud.

MISS HAVISHAM: Anything else?

PIP: I think she's very pretty.

MISS HAVISHAM: Oh, is that all?

PIP: I think she's very insulting.

MISS HAVISHAM: Anything else?

PIP: I think I should like to go home now.

MISS HAVISHAM: Even though she is so very pretty? You may go home—after the next game. (*Pause*)

ESTELLA: Don't loiter, boy. You're to return in a week. Don't you ever brush your coat? Here's your hat. Poor thing to have to cover such a dull little head. (*Pause*) You're crying, aren't you?

PIP (*In tears*): No, I'm not!

ESTELLA: Yes, you are! You know you are! I made you cry, didn't I?

PIP: No! No!

ESTELLA: Yes, I did! I hope you cry your eyes out! I hate you. Now, get home! (PIP *sobs*.)

PIP: In spite of Estella's insulting way, I was enchanted by her. It seemed as though the time would never come for me to return, but it did.

ESTELLA: You're several minutes late today, boy.

PIP: I'm sorry, miss.

ESTELLA: Come on. Miss Havisham is waiting for you. Am I insulting today?

PIP: Not so much as last time.

ESTELLA: Why don't you cry again?

PIP (*Defiantly*): I shall never cry for you again. (*After a pause*) Taken by surprise, Estella had nothing more to say to me. Just then Miss Havisham called out from a room I'd never been in before.

MISS HAVISHAM: Pip, please come in here.

PIP: Good day, mum.

MISS HAVISHAM: You are surprised at this room? Do you know what that great heap of decay is on the table? It's a bride's cake—my cake. On this day of the year before you were born, it was brought here. I was to marry, but I was left alone by him on our wedding day. My heart was snapped in two. This cake and I have worn away together. The mice have gnawed on it, but sharper teeth than teeth of mice have gnawed at me. (*Long pause*)

ESTELLA: Come quickly, boy. I have a great deal to do. . . . Oh, bother! I've dropped the key!

PIP: Here it is, miss.

ESTELLA: For that you may kiss me if you like.

PIP (*Embarrassed*): I would like that, miss. (*He kisses her on cheek.*)

ESTELLA (*After a pause*): That will be all, boy.

PIP: Weeks became months, and months years. Each time I went to Miss Havisham's I became more entranced with Estella, but she never returned my favors. I was greatly unhappy. When my fourteenth birthday arrived, I determined to end my visits to Miss Havisham.

MISS HAVISHAM: Come in, Pip.

PIP (*Nervously*): I'm afraid I can't come next time, Miss Havisham. I'll be fourteen next week, and I begin my apprenticeship with the blacksmith.

MISS HAVISHAM: Oh! Are you glad?

PIP: I used to think I would be, mum, but not any more.

MISS HAVISHAM: We shall miss your visits, shan't we, Estella? But you will be back. Here is a present from me, Pip. Some golden sovereigns. They are all yours.

PIP: Why, thank you ever so much!

MISS HAVISHAM: Goodbye, Pip. Show him out, Estella.

ESTELLA (*After a pause*): I'm going away, too, Pip. To France. I shall go to a fashionable school there and shall someday be a fine lady. (*In sneering tone*) I won't be a—blacksmith. Are you sorry I'm leaving?

PIP: Yes, Estella. I think I should like to know when you are coming back.

ESTELLA (*Loftily*): I don't know. Probably in several years. Do you wish anything else?

PIP: If I might, Estella, I should like to kiss you again. (*He kisses her on cheek.*)

ESTELLA: That will do. You may go home now.

PIP: Thus my childhood came to a close with my parting kiss from Estella, whom I have loved from that moment with all my heart. Two years later, we laid my sister to rest in the churchyard. I had learned the blacksmith trade, and the years passed slowly and uneventfully. Then one day, about a week after celebrating my twentieth birthday, I received a caller who was destined to change my whole life.

JAGGERS: Mr. Pip, I presume. You don't remember me, of course.

PIP: No, sir, I'm afraid I don't.

JAGGERS: I'm Mr. Jaggers, Miss Havisham's lawyer in London. We met once when I visited Miss Havisham, long ago.

PIP: Oh, yes, of course. I was just a boy.

JAGGERS: Exactly. I have taken this opportunity to convey to you some happy and most fortunate news. You have been selected by one of my clients, who must, by his own wish, go anonymous, to take on an enormous sum of money.

PIP: I? But why—?

JAGGERS: You are to be removed from your present surroundings, provided with proper clothing and lodgings in London, and there you are to be educated as befits a gentleman of the better class. It is also the desire of my client that you retain the name of Pip. Have you any objections?

PIP: It seems incredible. It's too fantastic to believe. Why should anyone do this for me?

JAGGERS (*With distaste*): I haven't the remotest idea. Here is sufficient money for your passage to London—and my card. Call on me when you reach the city. Good day, Mr. Pip.

PIP: Good day, sir, and thank you kindly, sir.

JAGGERS: Don't thank me. I'm paid to do it. But allow me to say, that I feel that you have "great expectations."

PIP: I drew the conclusion at once that Miss Havisham was responsible for my good fortune, and I called on her the afternoon before I left for London.

MISS HAVISHAM: Welcome, Pip. You have grown into quite the young man. Mr. Jaggers has told me about your inheritance. I shall *try* to be happy for you, Pip.

PIP: Thank you, Miss Havisham. (*Intensely*) I'm grateful—very grateful. (*Pause*) In London I saw Mr. Jaggers again and obtained an even larger sum of money. He directed me to my lodgings, but gave me no more information about my benefactor's identity. Months passed, and my education as a gentleman progressed. What with fencing lessons, dancing lessons, music lessons, and lessons of every sort, I was soon accepted into society. I had arrived, and I was deliriously happy. Perhaps now, Estella might consider me as a suitor. Still believing Miss Havisham to be responsible for my good luck, I went to see her again and met with an agreeable surprise.

MISS HAVISHAM: Pip, you came at a most opportune moment. I have a surprise for you. Look there behind you, in the shadows. (*Pause*)

ESTELLA: Hello, Pip.

PIP: Estella! I didn't—I mean—I'm so surprised I can't speak!

ESTELLA: Well, Pip. I didn't expect such an effusive welcome. Come, come, we're just old friends.

PIP: Yes, but—

MISS HAVISHAM: Is he changed, Estella? Less coarse and common?

ESTELLA: Very much.

MISS HAVISHAM: You two must have a great deal to say to each other. Go out into the garden and talk.

PIP: Estella and I went to the garden, and I was flooded with memories. (*After a pause*) Here, look! This is the very spot where you made me cry. Do you remember?

ESTELLA (*Coldly*): I don't recall.

PIP: You must. It's all so clear to me.

ESTELLA: You must know that I have no heart, if that has anything to do with my memory. Oh, I have a heart to be stabbed in, or shot in, but you know what I mean. I have no softness there—no sympathy, no sentiment. Now that I have told you, let us go back to see Miss Havisham.

MISS HAVISHAM (*Eagerly*): Well, Pip, is she beautiful, graceful, well-grown? Do you admire her?

PIP: Everyone must who sees her, Miss Havisham.

MISS HAVISHAM: Love her! If she tears your heart to pieces, love her. As it gets older and stronger, it will tear deeper! Only love her!

PIP: I knew that Miss Havisham was right. I was as deeply in love with Estella as I had ever been. A week later I received a letter, and I knew before opening it whom it was from.

ESTELLA: I am coming to London by the midday coach in two days. It has been settled that you should meet me. Miss Havisham sends her good wishes. Estella.

PIP: I met Estella, and we took tea in a nearby inn.

ESTELLA: How do you fare in London, Pip?

PIP: As pleasantly as I could anywhere away from you, Estella.

ESTELLA: How can you talk such nonsense? I am going to Richmond. Will you take me?

PIP: Of course, Estella. (*Pause*) A few days later, Miss Havisham wrote me to bring Estella to her for a day.

MISS HAVISHAM: Estella, come close that I may see you better. Tell me, are you tired of me?

ESTELLA (*Wearily*): Only a little tired of myself.

MISS HAVISHAM: Speak the truth, you ingrate! You stick and stone! You cold, cold heart!

ESTELLA: I am what you have made me. Take all the credit, or take all the blame.

MISS HAVISHAM: Look at you, so hard and thankless on the hearth where you were reared!

ESTELLA: You have been very good to me, and I owe everything to you. What would you have?

MISS HAVISHAM: Love!

ESTELLA: All that you have ever given me is yours to command, but I can never give you what you never gave me.

MISS HAVISHAM (*Bitterly*): Did I never give you love? Better that you should call me mad!

ESTELLA: Why should I call you mad? Does anyone live who knows as well as I do what set purposes you have? Who taught me to be proud and hard? Who praised me when I learned my lesson?

MISS HAVISHAM (*Angrily*): Enough! Would it be weakness to return my love?

ESTELLA: I must be taken as I have been made. (*Pause*)

PIP: The next time I saw Estella was at a ball in Richmond.

ESTELLA: Pip, I'm tiring of Richmond.

PIP: These balls would be nothing without you. I would be nothing without you near me.

ESTELLA: Pip, will you never take warning?

PIP: Do you mean warning not to be attracted by you?

ESTELLA: If you don't know what I mean, you're blind. You recall our conversation in the garden when I first came back to Miss Havisham's.

PIP: Do you speak this way to Bentley Drummle?

ESTELLA: Whatever can you mean?

PIP: I mean that you seem to favor and encourage him, yet you hardly ever glance in my direction.

ESTELLA: Do you wish me to deceive and entrap *you?*

PIP: Do you entrap Drummle?

ESTELLA: Yes, him and many others. I'll say no more. (*Pause*)

PIP: On the night of my twenty-second birthday, I was sitting at home alone, when the clock struck twelve. All of a sudden, I heard the downstairs door squeak open. (*Calling out, after a brief pause*) Is anyone down there? What floor do you want?

MAGWITCH: The top—Mr. Pip.

PIP: I am Mr. Pip. What is your business with me?

MAGWITCH: I will explain if I may come in.

PIP: Why, I—yes, do come in.

MAGWITCH (*Nervously*): There's no one else?

PIP: Why do you, a stranger, come to my rooms and ask such a question?

MAGWITCH: I'm glad you've growed up such a game one. Look at me closely. Think, Pip, think.

PIP: I don't understand, I—wait—yes, yes, you're the convict I met in the churchyard. You had me bring you food and a file!

MAGWITCH: Magwitch, lad, that's my name. You acted nobly, Pip, and I never forgot it.

PIP: I had forgotten the incident. It is unnecessary to thank me. I cannot renew our acquaintance. You must realize we are far apart in station. I have been chosen to inherit some money, and I—

MAGWITCH: You're a cocky one! Well, might I guess to the first number of your income? Might it be five? Would the first letter of your lawyer's name be "J"?

PIP (*Pause*): You! But I never—

MAGWITCH: Yes, me, Pip! Me, who swore when I got rich, my boy would get it all. I'm your second father, Pip. I escaped again—went into sheep farming in Australia. I made thousands, but it's all for you, dear boy, all! Didn't you ever think it might be me?

PIP: Never! I don't know what to say.

MAGWITCH: Dear lad, it's been a long time, but at last I've seen my boy. At last I've seen him! (*Long pause*)

PIP: Soon after Magwitch came to see me, Mr. Jaggers paid me a visit, as well.

JAGGERS: So at last you know your true patron?

PIP: Yes, Mr. Jaggers.

JAGGERS: However, you must be aware that he is in great danger, being an escaped convict.

PIP: He has told me.

JAGGERS: Therefore, I suggest you get him out of London immediately.

PIP: But how?

JAGGERS: I've already figured that out. Now, listen—

PIP: Before getting Magwitch out of London, I went back to Miss Havisham's to try once again to convince Estella of my love for her.

MISS HAVISHAM: What wind blows you here, Pip?

PIP: I came to see Estella. What I have to say to her I shall say in your presence, Miss Havisham. (*After a pause*) Estella, you know that I love you. I simply ask you to marry me now, although I've asked that question many times with each look I've ever given you.

ESTELLA: I've tried to warn you, Pip. I shan't deceive you. I'm to marry Bentley Drummle within the month. I'm sorry, Pip.

You'll excuse me now? He's waiting to take me riding. Good-bye, Pip.

PIP (*Bitterly; after a pause*): As you must know, Miss Havisham, I am as miserable as you ever meant me to be. You led me into believing you were my benefactor, and now you have arranged this marriage to break my heart. Was that kind?

MISS HAVISHAM (*Bitterly*): Who am I to be kind?

PIP: She might have been soft and gentle, but you turned her heart to stone! If you can undo any part of the wrong you have done, it will be far greater than one hundred years of repentance. Good day, Miss Havisham.

MISS HAVISHAM: No, wait, Pip! (*Wailing*) Oh, what have I done? Forgive me—forgive me! (*Sobbing*) Don't hate me, Pip. Don't hate me!

PIP: With tears of despair in my eyes, I had closed the door on Miss Havisham and all her sick fancies. She had taken my heart and through the years had prepared it to be crushed in this moment of her vengeful triumph. I could hear her sobs as I descended the staircase, nevermore to return. But suddenly her sobs had become unearthly screams. I rushed back up the stairs and threw open the door, to find Miss Havisham moaning in agony. The candelabra had toppled over and ignited her tattered rag of a wedding dress. I snatched up a small rug and wrapped her in it, beating out the flames. But it was too late. The last words she ever spoke were—

MISS HAVISHAM (*Weakly*): Forgive me, Pip—I was wrong. (*Straining*) For-give me. . . .

PIP: In that brief moment, I learned to forgive in forgiving Miss Havisham, who had taken the light from my life. Back in London I resolved to get Magwitch away that evening. There was no moon as we rowed down the river where he might board the packet boat for France. We sat in the boat, quietly waiting, Magwitch puffing on his pipe as the minutes slipped by. I was just dozing off when the packet boat loomed into sight in the distance. Just as we started for the ship, someone cried out:

SOLDIER: You have an escaped convict there. I call on him to surrender and you to assist.

PIP: It was a police boat heading our way with the tide. They had followed us from the city. I urged Magwitch to swim for it, while I stalled for time, but he refused.

MAGWITCH: No, I don't want to get my dear boy into no trouble. He's not riskin' his life for such as me. (*Calling*) I surrender! (*Quietly*) I'm content—I've seen my boy!

PIP: Justice demanded that Abel Magwitch be taken to a place of execution and hanged by the neck until dead. I hurried to Mr. Jaggers, but he could do nothing, except reveal to me a startling, almost unbelievable fact.

JAGGERS: Estella, the late Miss Havisham's ward, is of a certainty the only child of Abel Magwitch, convict.

PIP (*Shocked*): Can it be true? Are you quite sure?

JAGGERS: There is no doubt. I transacted the adoption papers myself.

PIP: Poor old Magwitch cheated the hangman after all. They sent for me near the end.

WOMAN: 'e's in 'ere. You'd better 'urry. 'e won't last long. (*Pause*)

PIP: Dear old fellow, can you hear me? I'm heartily grateful for all you've done for me. I can't appreciate your kindness half enough.

MAGWITCH: Stop, my boy. I vowed you'd get rich if it took my whole life. I—I had a child once, a little girl. I don't know what became of her. She died, for aught I know.

PIP: She did not die.

MAGWITCH (*Getting weaker*): What do you mean?

PIP: I mean that she was adopted and has grown to be a beautiful woman, and what's more I love her.

MAGWITCH: Pip. (*Weaker*) Do you mean it, Pip? Hold my hand, my boy. (*Trailing off*) You can say I died—happier than I—I—lived. (*Gasps*)

PIP: Oh, Lord, be merciful to him—a sinner. (*Pause*) The State confiscated all of dear Magwitch's fortune. I went into business and soon became successful on my own account with a new life and new expectations. It was eleven years before I returned to the village and Miss Havisham's house, but I returned home at last. It seemed as I walked into the old house that I relived all my experiences there. But as I pushed open the door to Miss Havisham's, a familiar voice spoke to me.

ESTELLA: Pip!

PIP: Estella! What are you doing here?

ESTELLA: I live here alone. This is my home now, Pip.

PIP: But your husband—

ESTELLA: Bentley Drummle's dead, and all I have to remember of my years with him is misery. I'm sick of the world. I shall stay here in seclusion and peace, away from it all, as Miss Havisham did.

PIP: Don't sit there, Estella! That was her chair. It pains me to see you in it.

ESTELLA: I shall take her place, Pip. It's where I belong. It's what I was reared for.

PIP: Listen to me, Estella. I still love you—I've always loved you. Come away from this hateful place with me. Nothing can live here. It's a tomb of hate and bitterness. You can't stay here alone. I won't let you!

ESTELLA: I'm not alone. Miss Havisham is here.

PIP: She's not here! She's dead and gone—forever! Come out, come out, Estella.

ESTELLA: I'm so frightened, Pip!

PIP: Take my hand, and don't be afraid of what's dead and past.

ESTELLA: Oh, Pip, my life's been so miserable. I have always been afraid to admit that I have a heart. I'm not afraid any longer. I give it to you.

PIP: Estella—

ESTELLA: But I do think it will be rather difficult getting used to being called Mrs. Pip!

THE END

▣▣The Count of Monte Cristo

by *Alexandre Dumas*
Adapted for round-the-table reading
by *Maurine V. Eleder*

Characters

NARRATOR
MONSIEUR MORREL, *owner of the* Pharaon
EDMOND DANTES, *captain's mate of the* Pharaon
DANGLARS, *a sailor*
FERNAND, *suitor of Mercedes*
MERCEDES, *Edmond's fiancée*
CADEROUSSE, *a neighbor*
MAGISTRATE
MONSIEUR DE VILLEFORT, *prosecutor*
GENDARME
ABBE FARIA, *Prisoner No. 27*
TWO TURNKEYS

NARRATOR: February 18, 1815. The *Pharaon* has just arrived in Marseilles. Monsieur Morrel, eager to know about his cargo, boards the ship.

MORREL: Ah, is it you in charge, Dantes? Is something wrong?

DANTES: A great misfortune, sir. We lost our brave Captain Leclere.

MORREL (*Shocked*): Oh! What a tragedy! (*Worried*) And the cargo?

DANTES: It is all safe. Rest assured on that. But the poor Captain—to survive war and then die of the fever. Such. . . (*Abruptly; calling as if to crew*) Let go, and brail all!

MORREL: We are all mortal, Edmond, and as you have assured me that the cargo. . .

DANTES: Yes, all safe. But I must see to the ship. Here comes Danglars. He can furnish you with details of the cargo.

DANGLARS: Ah, Monsieur Morrel, you have heard of our misfortune, and of our young Dantes taking command without consulting anyone. He caused us to lose a day at the Isle of Elba.

MORREL: I'm sure he was only doing his duty as captain's mate in taking command of the vessel. But as to losing time on the Isle Elba, that was wrong—unless the ship wanted repair.

DANGLARS (*Angrily*): The ship needed no repair. Stopping at Elba was pure whim.

MORREL: I see. (*After a pause; calling*) Dantes, come this way.

DANTES: A moment, sir, and I'm with you. (*Calls as if to crew*) Let go anchor!

DANGLARS: You see, Monsieur Morrel, already he fancies himself captain.

MORREL: And so, in fact, he is, Danglars.

DANGLARS (*Objecting*): But he does not have your signature, nor your partner's.

MORREL (*Firmly*): I shall remedy that at once. After all, though he is young, he is an excellent seaman.

NARRATOR: Danglars, vexed by the ship owner's words, moved away as Dantes approached Morrel.

MORREL: Edmond, why did you stop at the Isle of Elba?

DANTES: To fulfill a last instruction of Captain Leclere. Before he died, he gave me a packet to deliver. While I was on the island, the exiled emperor approached me and questioned me about the ship.

MORREL: You did right to follow the Captain's instructions, but if it were known that you conveyed a packet and conversed with Napoleon, it could bring you trouble. Take care, Edmond, with whom you share that information.

DANTES: Yes, of course, Monsieur Morrel.

NARRATOR: Danglars had been watching Dantes and Morrel as they talked and when Dantes left, he again approached Morrel.

DANGLARS: Monsieur Morrel, I assume Dantes had no explanation for his landing at the Isle of Elba.

MORREL: On the contrary, Danglars. His reasons were most satisfactory. It was Captain Leclere himself who gave orders for the delay.

DANGLARS: Speaking of the Captain, has Dantes given you a letter from him?

MORREL (*Surprised*): No. Was there one?

DANGLARS: I believe in addition to the packet, Captain Leclere confided a letter to his care.

MORREL (*Suspiciously*): How do you know he had a packet to deliver?

DANGLARS (*Embarrassed*): I was passing the Captain's cabin and as the door was half open, I saw him give the packet *and* a letter to Dantes.

MORREL (*Disturbed*): He did not mention it.

DANGLARS: Then, I beg you, do not say a word to Dantes on the subject. I may have been mistaken. I will leave you now.

NARRATOR: Danglars left a puzzled Morrel. After a few moments Dantes returned.

DANTES: The paperwork has been completed, Monsieur Morrel, and the ship is secure. If there is nothing else, I should like to go ashore and see my father—and my beloved Mercedes.

MORREL: Of course, Dantes, of course. By the way, did Captain Leclere give you a letter for me?

DANTES: No, sir. He was too ill to write, sir.

MORREL: I see. Well, Dantes, go see your father. Take what time you require. We will need six weeks to unload the cargo and several more to reload. Just be back again in three months—for the *Pharaon* cannot sail without her captain.

DANTES (*Surprised and excited*): Captain? You intend to nominate me as captain? (*Gratefully*) I thank you, Monsieur, in the name of my father—and of Mercedes.

NARRATOR: Dantes, elated, collected his belongings, and hurried to visit his father and then to see Mercedes. Mercedes, at that very moment, was seated outside her little house with Fernand, Edmond's rival suitor.

FERNAND (*Pleading*): Mercedes, why do you refuse to marry me? Your mother has approved of me.

MERCEDES: Fernand, you know very well that I love another. (*Kindly*) I have always said I look upon you as a brother.

FERNAND: Edmond Dantes has been gone three months. The sea has been treacherous, and there have been some terrible storms. What if—

MERCEDES (*Quickly*): If he is dead, I shall die, too.

FERNAND (*Hopefully*): Perhaps he has forgotten you.

DANTES (*Calling*): Mercedes! Mercedes!

MERCEDES (*Excitedly*): Edmond! He is here! He's safe! You see, Fernand, he has not forgotten me.

FERNAND (*Crestfallen*): I see he has not, Mercedes.

NARRATOR: As Mercedes raced into Edmond's arms, happily welcoming him home, Fernand withdrew to an outdoor café down the street. He was hailed by Danglars and Caderousse.

CADEROUSSE: Come join us, Fernand. Why, your scowl is deeper than Danglars'. What's wrong?

FERNAND: It is Dantes. He has returned and I fear he will wed Mercedes. Would that he had never returned from the voyage!

DANGLARS (*Angrily*): He will have your beloved and my job. I suspect Dantes will be made the new captain of the *Pharaon*.

CADEROUSSE (*Sighing deeply*): Well, there is nothing you can do about it.

DANGLARS (*Slyly*): Maybe there is.

FERNAND: What do you mean?

DANGLARS: On our last voyage, Dantes went ashore on the Isle of Elba. What if someone denounced him as a supporter of the exiled Napoleon—a Bonapartist agent?

FERNAND (*Rashly*): I will denounce him!

DANGLARS: It is not so simple, my friend. You will have to sign your declaration, and confront Dantes. Mercedes will not look kindly on that. (*Slyly*) It would be much better to take pen and ink as I shall now, and write with the left hand something like this. (*After a pause*) "Monsieur—The *procureur du roi* is informed by a friend of the King that one Edmond Dantes, mate of the ship *Pharaon,* arrived this morning with a letter for the Bonapartists committee in Paris. Proof of this crime will be found on arresting him, for the letter is still in his possession."

CADEROUSSE (*Disturbed*): Danglars, that is cruel and unjust.

DANGLARS: Yes, you're right. It would be cruel. (*With a laugh*) I speak and write in jest. I do not want to destroy Dantes.

NARRATOR: Danglars crumpled the letter and threw it in the corner. He and Caderousse rose and left the table. Fernand remained, lost in thought. When Danglars looked back, he saw Fernand stoop to pick up the crumpled paper and put it in his pocket. Danglars smiled slyly. Several days later the three friends met again to join friends and family at the marriage feast for Edmond and Mercedes. But before the vows were made, the party was disrupted by an unexpected arrival of the Magistrate.

MAGISTRATE: Edmond Dantes, I arrest you in the name of the law.

DANTES (*Stunned*): Arrest me? What crime have I committed?

MAGISTRATE: I cannot inform you, but you will be duly acquainted with the reasons at your first examination.

NARRATOR: Neither the protests of Dantes' father nor the interventions of Monsieur Morrel had any effect. Dantes was taken into custody until the day of his interrogation by de Villefort, the prosecutor.

DE VILLEFORT: What a shame your wedding was interrupted, Monsieur Dantes. Let us hope this can be cleared up. You say you have no enemies, no political views, and you do not recognize the writing of your accuser.

DANTES: That is correct, sir. As I have explained to you, I am guilty only of following my Captain's orders. I delivered a packet on the Isle of Elba and carried away with me a letter to be delivered to a person in Paris.

DE VILLEFORT (*Pleasantly*): That seems harmless enough. Hand over this letter you have brought from Elba, and you may rejoin your friends.

DANTES (*Happily*): I will be free then?

DE VILLEFORT: Yes, but first give me the letter.

DANTES: You have it already, sir, for it was taken from me with some others which I see there in the packet on your table.

DE VILLEFORT: To whom is it addressed?

DANTES: To Monsieur Noirtier, Rue Coq-Heron, Paris.

NARRATOR: Had a thunderbolt fallen into the room, de Villefort could not have been more stupefied. He sank into his seat, and hastily drew forth the letter, and read it with an expression of horror.

DE VILLEFORT (*Greatly agitated*): Have you shown this letter to anyone?

DANTES: To no one, on my honor.

DE VILLEFORT: I'm afraid I must detain you a bit longer, but I will strive to make it as short as possible. The principal charge against you is possession of this letter, so I will toss it into this fire and destroy it. Should anyone else interrogate you, (*Forcefully*) *do not breathe a word of this letter.*

NARRATOR: Dantes spent the night in a small cell. In the morning two gendarmes escorted him first in a barred carriage and then in a small boat.

DANTES: I beseech you, tell me where we are going. I am Captain Dantes, a loyal Frenchman.

GENDARME (*Incredulously*): You say you are a sailor, and yet you do not recognize where you are?

NARRATOR: Dantes stared across the waters and saw the rocky black cliffs on which stood the gloomy fortress of Chateau d'If.

DANTES (*Bewildered*): But the Chateau d'If is for political prisoners. I have committed no crime. What of Monsieur de Villefort's promises? What of the formalities?

GENDARME: The formalities have been gone through. Our orders are to take you to Chateau d'If.

NARRATOR: Dantes was thrown into a dark, damp cell. When he refused to eat, demanded to see the governor, and attempted to throw his bench at his jailer—he was taken below ground and thrown into a dungeon. He saw no one. He spoke to no one. He did not know of the "Hundred Days" when the exiled Napoleon was back in power or of the restoration of King Louis XVIII. He did not know of his father's death in Mercedes' arms. He barely existed for weeks, months, years. One night Edmond heard a hollow scratching sound in the wall. When it was repeated for several nights, Dantes was sure it was a prisoner trying to escape. Using his fingernails and a broken water jug, Dantes loosened the mortar around the stones behind his bed. He worked every night for weeks—until he struck a smooth hard surface. It was a beam.

DANTES: Oh, do not let me despair now! There must be a way out.

ABBE (*Muffled*): Who is that who speaks of escape?

DANTES (*Frightened*): Is that a human voice? . . . Oh, speak again, though your voice terrifies me.

ABBE: Do not dig any more. How high up is your excavation?

DANTES: It is on a level with the floor. Please tell me who you are!

ABBE (*Hesitantly*): I am—I am Number 27.

DANTES (*Fearfully*): Oh, do not desert me. Do not leave me. If you are young, I will be your friend. If you are old, I'll be your son.

ABBE: I must calculate the distance. Expect me tomorrow.

NARRATOR: Dantes paced his cell. He feared Number 27 would desert him. But in the morning, he heard three knocks. A portion of the floor gave way, and there appeared, first the head, then the shoulders, and lastly the body of an old man, who sprang lightly into Dantes' cell.

ABBE: Let us remove the traces of my entrance here, for our future safety depends upon our jailers being entirely ignorant of it.

NARRATOR: The old man stooped and raised the stone back into its place.

ABBE: You removed this stone very carelessly, but I suppose you had no tools to help you?

DANTES (*Astonished*): Do you possess tools?

ABBE: Here is my chisel, made with one of the clamps of my bedstead—the very tool I used to hollow out a passageway fifty feet long.

DANTES (*Amazed*): Fifty feet!

ABBE: Do you wish to see the other fruits of my labors?

DANTES (*Eagerly*): Yes, I do.

ABBE: Follow me, then.

NARRATOR: The two men crawled through the narrow passage to the Abbe's cell. Dantes looked eagerly around for the expected marvels, but saw nothing.

ABBE: Of course, I have hidden everything. Here, behind this unused fireplace, is my treatise on the monarchy of Italy. And here is my pen for writing.

DANTES: But how did you—

ABBE (*Interrupting*): Make them? The linen scrolls came from two of my shirts and the pen from a fish bone. The ink I made from the soot of this ancient fireplace and a little wine, which my jailer brought on Sundays to his "mad old Abbe."

DANTES: How remarkable! You've made all this? A needle, lamp, matches, a rope ladder. . . ? Amazing!

NARRATOR: Dantes listened intently as the Abbe related the story of his life—how he had studied the great writers and learned to speak five languages.

DANTES: How wonderful to possess such knowledge. I am but a poor sailor and very ignorant. (*Miserably*) I cannot even understand why I am imprisoned here!

NARRATOR: By his skillful questioning, the Abbe made Dantes understand who had conspired against him: Danglars, the jealous sailor, who saw him receive the packet and return with the letter, and Fernand, the jealous suitor, who wanted to marry Mercedes. Dantes now remembered seeing them together at an outdoor café when he and Mercedes strolled past.

DANTES: But what of the prosecutor? He seemed to believe I was innocent. He even burned the sole proof against me.

ABBE: He burned the accuser's letter?

DANTES: Oh, no! The letter I was entrusted to convey to Paris.

ABBE: Ah, indeed! That alters matters. To whom was the letter addressed?

DANTES: To Monsieur Noirtier, Rue Coq-Heron, Paris.

ABBE: Noirtier! I know that name. (*Pauses*) Yes, of course. Noirtier, a radical during the Revolution. Surely a supporter of Napoleon now. What was your prosecutor's name?

DANTES: De Villefort.

ABBE (*Laughing*): No wonder he destroyed that letter! It was addressed to his own father—Noirtier de Villefort. Your prosecutor would have lost his job—perhaps even gone to prison—if that letter had become public!

DANTES (*Stunned*): Why, I can hardly believe this, but it all makes sense now. That would explain why de Villefort's manner changed when he heard the name Noirtier.

NARRATOR: When Dantes next met with the Abbe, he had a plan.

DANTES: Since you have convinced me it is impossible for us to dig our way out of this prison, we must bide our time. While we wait, you must teach me a small part of what you know.

NARRATOR: For the next twelve months, Dantes learned about mathematics, science, history, and philosophy. He learned to speak Spanish, English, and German. One night Dantes heard the Abbe call out in pain. Dantes hurried to him.

ABBE (*Weakly*): Listen carefully, Dantes. The attacks of a terrible illness are beginning again. Hidden in the leg of my bed is a small vial of fluid. When the attack is over, give me eight to ten drops. I shall be unable to do it myself.

NARRATOR: Dantes watched in terror until the attack was over, then he did as the Abbe has instructed. After an hour, the Abbe regained consciousness.

ABBE: My good Edmond, I know now I will never leave this prison alive. But you are still young—there is hope for you. Go to my hiding place, and bring me the parchment paper with a treasure map on it.

DANTES (*To himself*): Oh, the illness has made him mad! (*To* ABBE) Please, my friend, you must rest. Let us talk of this later.

ABBE: Hear me! You know that I was the secretary and close friend of Cardinal Spada, the last of the princes of that name. When he died, I was his beneficiary. There had been talk of a family treasure, but none had ever been found. By mere chance, I discovered that an old parchment, used for years as a bookmark in the family breviary, contained writing which appeared only when exposed to fire. It was the long lost will, detailing the whereabouts of the family treasure. The treasure is worth countless millions, and it shall be yours.

DANTES: The treasure belongs to you, my dear friend. I have no right to it.

ABBE: You are the child of my captivity. Take it, my dear Edmond.

NARRATOR: Dantes took the parchment from the Abbe, who rallied for a few days, then suffered more attacks. He was very weak. Dantes paced the cell helplessly. The vial of medicine was empty.

ABBE (*Weakly*): Edmond, the end is very near. Listen to me. The treasure of the Spadas exists. If you do escape, hasten to the isle of Monte Cristo, and claim the fortune. (*Sighing*) Adieu, my dear friend. Adieu.

DANTES (*Bereft*): Goodbye, my friend!

NARRATOR: Dantes stayed with the Abbe, wishing he would awake again. Realizing it was time for the jailer to make his rounds, he carefully concealed the Abbe's possessions and waited in the secret passage. Soon the turnkey arrived.

1ST TURNKEY (*Surprised*): Ho! It seems the old priest is dead. (*Calling*) I need someone to help in here.

NARRATOR: Soldiers and the governor appeared. Then came the doctor and other attendants. Dantes could see nothing and caught only fragments of their conversation. When the sounds of voices died away, Dantes reentered the Abbe's cell and looked down at his friend, now wrapped tightly in a winding sack of sheets.

DANTES (*Despairingly*): Oh, my dear friend, you have left me all alone. There is no hope for me now. I shall die in this dungeon, too. Only the dead leave here. (*Suddenly*) But wait! There is an idea. Since none but the dead pass freely from this place, I shall assume the place of the dead Abbe!

NARRATOR: Without giving himself time to reconsider, Dantes bent over the sack and opened it with the knife the Abbe had made. He removed the body and carried it to his own dungeon. There he arranged the Abbe on his own bed, kissed the ice-cold brow, and hurried back to the Abbe's cell. Taking the Abbe's knife, needle, and thread, he crawled inside the sack, and sewed it shut from the inside. Dantes assumed the jailers would not bother to bury a prisoner very deep, and he planned to cut himself out of the sack and work his way through the soft soil. He tried to control the terrible pounding of his heart when the jailers came.

1ST TURNKEY: He's heavy for an old and thin man.

2ND TURNKEY: Let's get this over with. It's a bad night. Not a pleasant night for a dip in the sea.

1ST TURNKEY: Set him here, and give me the light so I can find what I need.

NARRATOR: Dantes felt the sharp night air through the sack. What were they looking for? The spade? He felt a heavy thud next to him, and at the same moment a cord was fastened round his feet with sudden painful violence.

2ND TURNKEY: Well, if the knot is tied, let's move on.

1ST TURNKEY: A little farther—a little farther. We need to clear the rocks. Ready, then!

TURNKEYS: One, two, three, away!

NARRATOR: Dantes felt himself flung into space and then felt the sensation of falling, falling. His terrified scream disappeared when he hit the ice-cold water. Suddenly Dantes understood— the sea was the cemetery of Chateau d'If! He held his breath and cut open the sack, extricating his arm and then his body. But the weight around his feet was still pulling him down. By a desperate effort, he bent his body and severed the cord that bound his legs. Summoning all his strength, he fought his way to the surface.

DANTES (*To himself*): Swim, Edmond. The guards may have heard that scream. Swim—or die in prison.

NARRATOR: He swam for an hour. The winds increased, the waves grew stronger. Finally, he had reached the strangely formed rocks of the Isle of Tiboulen. Dragging himself onto the granite, he sought rest and shelter under an overhanging rock as the storm broke. At dawn when he woke, the sea was calm. Nearby floated broken beams and a sailor's cap—all that remained of a wrecked fishing vessel. In the distance a ship approached.

DANTES: There is hope!

NARRATOR: Dantes swam to the cap, placed it on his head, seized one of the beams, and paddled toward the ship.

DANTES (*Excitedly*): They see me. I am saved! Now for a new life! Farewell, Edmond Dantes—the Count of Monte Cristo will soon take your place. Beware, Fernand! Beware, Danglars and de Villefort, for the Count of Monte Cristo comes to avenge the unjust imprisonment of Edmond Dantes!

THE END

🔲The Admirable Crichton

by *Sir James Barrie*
Adapted for round-the-table reading
by *Lewy Olfson*

Characters

NARRATOR
LORD LOAM
LADY CATHERINE
LADY AGATHA   }   *his daughters*
LADY MARY
CRICHTON, *butler*
TWEENY, *kitchen maid*
ERNEST WOOLEY
LORD BROCKLEHURST

NARRATOR: The scene is Loam House, perhaps the stateliest of all the stately halls of England. Its master is Lord Loam, an earl typical of the turn-of-the-century British peerage.

LORD LOAM (*Pompously*): All class distinctions are, of course, completely unnatural, completely artificial! If we were all to return to Nature, which is the aspiration of my life, all would be equal. Unfortunately, it is not *practical* to do away with class distinctions, but it is helpful to remember that they are *artificial*.

NARRATOR: The ladies of Loam House are the Earl's daughters, Lady Catherine, Lady Agatha, and Lady Mary. They are typical of the daughters of the peerage.

LADY CATHERINE (*Bored*): Move your feet, Agatha. I want to sit down.

LADY AGATHA (*Sleepily*): Don't talk, Catherine, you foolish thing. I was almost asleep.

LADY MARY (*Snapping*): Be quiet, both of you. The servants will hear!

NARRATOR: The butler at Loam House is Crichton, who is perhaps *not* typical of the British butler. For Crichton is not a *gentleman's* ideal of a butler; he is a *butler's* ideal of a butler!

CRICHTON (*Stiffly*): Tea is served, my lord.

NARRATOR: Today is a very special day, and all Loam House is buzzing with whispers about the ceremony, shortly to be held, that has become a yearly tradition at Loam House.

CATHERINE (*Angrily*): Of all the days of the year that I hate, this is the day that I hate most!

AGATHA: I couldn't agree with you more wholeheartedly, Catherine. (*Incensed*) Imagine having to meet the *servants* as *equals!*

MARY: I do think Papa goes too far with his ideas of liberality and equality!

CATHERINE (*Disgusted*): To think I shall have to serve tea to my own maid.

AGATHA: To pass the crumpets to my own cook!

MARY: To engage in conversation with my own footman!

AGATHA: It's too humiliating!

CATHERINE: Preposterous!

MARY: Odious!

AGATHA: Tea with the servants! (*Dramatically*) How shall we bear it?

NARRATOR: But if the ladies of the house are upset by the prospect of socializing with the staff, the staff is even more upset by the prospect of having to socialize with their employers.

TWEENY (*Meekly*): Oh, Crichton, how shall I ever manage it? I've never been so nervous in my life!

CRICHTON: You must do your best, Tweeny, even if you *are* only a kitchen maid. You must rise to the occasion.

TWEENY: But what will I say? What will I do?

CRICHTON: You must pretend you are a lady. It is the master's wish.

TWEENY: It's humiliating, that's what it is!

CRICHTON: Yes, Tweeny, that is what it is.

NARRATOR: Only Lord Loam himself, whose idea the annual tea is, delights in the prospect. At the moment he is in the drawing room, explaining his idea to the Honorable Ernest Wooley, a brilliant but useless young man, who has long been a friend of the family.

LOAM: You see, Ernest, though society forces some men to be masters and other men to be servants, I assure you the distinction is quite artificial. I am, basically, no better than my butler, and so one day a year, I invite all of the servants up to tea, and treat them as equals.

ERNEST WOOLEY (*Uncomfortably*): I see. And today is the day, Lord Loam?

LOAM: Yes, Ernest, today is the day. You *will* stay for tea, won't you?

ERNEST (*Brightly*): Certainly. Life is like a cup of tea, is it not? The more heartily we drink, the sooner we reach the dregs.

LOAM (*Confused*): Oh, Ernest, was that an epigram? I'm sure you're being funny, but somehow I never understand you.

ERNEST (*Disappointed*): It's very simple, sir. Don't you see? Life? Teacups? Dregs? (*Pause*) You see, I call life a teacup, as—

LOAM (*Interrupting; impatiently*): Oh, never mind explaining it to me. I've too much on my mind already. Ah! Here come the girls!

ERNEST (*Eagerly*): Hello, Lady Agatha. How are you?

AGATHA: Don't be silly, Ernest. If you want to know how we are, we are dead. Even the *thought* of entertaining the servants kills us.

CATHERINE: Besides which, we had to decide which frocks to take with us on the yacht, and that is always a mental strain.

ERNEST: Ah, yes, the yachting trip! Your father has invited me to join you. There is nothing I should enjoy more than a yachting trip. Indeed, all life is like a yachting trip: It—

LOAM (*Quickly*): Oh, not another epigram! Ring for Crichton, Mary.

MARY (*Reluctantly*): Must I, Papa?

LOAM: Indeed you must. And remember, girls, no condescension.

NARRATOR: The imperturbable Crichton appeared on the scene.

CRICHTON: You rang, sir?

LOAM: We are quite ready to serve tea, Crichton.

CRICHTON: Very good, my lord. (*Announcing*) Mrs. Perkins, the cook.

NARRATOR: And so the tea party begins. Everyone, with the possible exception of Lord Loam himself, finds it a tremendous strain, and when the last cup of tea has been drunk, the last bit of conversation wrung dry, and the last crumpet crumb swept away, the whole household heaves a sigh of relief. The peace is not to last long, however. Plans for the yachting trip are under way, and much to the consternation of his daughters, Lord Loam makes a firm and surprising announcement.

LOAM: Daughters, this afternoon we witnessed at the tea that the servants are as good as ladies and gentlemen. On our yachting trip, we shall see that ladies and gentlemen are as good as servants! I have decided that my daughters, instead of having one maid each, shall on this voyage have but one maid among them.

DAUGHTERS (*Ad lib outrage*): Father! You can't be serious! It's unbearable! (*Etc.*)

NARRATOR: Such anguish as met with Lord Loam's announcement, such sighs, cries, moans, groans, weepings, and wailings had never before been heard in England.

MARY: One maid among the three of us! What's to be done?

CRICHTON: I believe, madam, that you are to do for yourselves.

MARY: Impossible, Crichton! However, I suppose it must be as Father wishes. (*Firmly*) As oldest daughter, I shall take my maid, Fisher. My sisters may use her services whenever I don't need her.

CRICHTON: If you please, my lady, Fisher has given notice.

MARY (*Horrified*): What?

CRICHTON: As eldest maid of the household, she feels it would be beneath her to wait on your sisters.

CATHERINE: Then it will be my maid, Simmons, who comes with us.

CRICHTON: I happen to know, your ladyship, that Simmons desires to give notice for the same reason as Fisher.

AGATHA: Then, sisters, we will take my maid: Jeanne.

CRICHTON: And Jeanne also, my lady.

MARY (*Wailing*): Oh, Crichton, what's to be done?

CRICHTON: I believe there is a young person in the kitchen, my lady, who will accept the position. Her name is Tweeny.

MARY (*Shocked*): A kitchen-maid for a lady-in-waiting? Never!

CRICHTON: I am afraid, my lady, that it is Tweeny or no one. Even servants have their dignity.

MARY: Very well, then. Let it be Tweeny. (*With disgust*) Oh, Father and his ideas of equality! I only hope that some day he gets a taste of his own medicine!

NARRATOR: As it happens, within the hour Lord Loam *does* get a taste of his own medicine.

LOAM (*Distracted*): I don't understand it, Crichton. My valet, Rolleston, refuses to accompany me on the yachting trip, because I have allowed my daughters one maid.

CRICHTON: My lord, even we servants respect our stations in society and regard them with dignity.

LOAM: But who will serve as my valet on this trip? Who?

CRICHTON (*Clearing his throat*): Might I suggest . . . *myself,* Lord Loam?

NARRATOR: When the daughters of the household learn that Crichton, their impeccable butler, has agreed to serve as their father's valet on the trip, they are aghast.

MARY: Crichton, I am curious. Why did you agree to do it?

CRICHTON (*Formally*): My lady, I am the son of a butler and a lady's maid, and to me the most beautiful thing in the world is a haughty, aristocratic English household, with everyone in his place and a place for everyone. If I did not agree to be your father's valet, your father would have none, and that would destroy the harmony of the social hierarchy. Do I make myself clear?

MARY: But Father says that if we were to return to Nature—

CRICHTON: If we did, my lady, the first thing we should do would be to elect a head. Circumstances might alter cases; the same person might not be the master, nor the same persons servants. Nature would decide.

MARY: I see. Thank you, Crichton. You may go.

CRICHTON (*Crisply*): Very good, my lady.

AGATHA: Oh dear, what a tiring day this has been.

CATHERINE: I feel absolutely exhausted.

MARY: I wonder what Crichton meant by circumstances might alter things.

AGATHA: Oh, do be quiet, Mary.

MARY: I wonder what he meant by the same person might not be master.

CATHERINE: Oh, Mary, Mary, leave us in peace. He said Nature would decide.

MARY (*Thoughtfully*): I wonder . . .

NARRATOR: And so it was finally arranged that Crichton and Tweeny should accompany Lord Loam, his three daughters, and the Honorable Ernest Wooley on their yachting trip. After much hustling and bustling, storing and fetching, packing, carrying, worrying, and scurrying, the little group embarks on its voyage. For the first few weeks at sea, all is serene. But suddenly, disaster strikes!

LOAM (*Frantically*): Crichton! Crichton! There's a storm coming! A storm!

CRICHTON (*Calmly*): Yes, my lord.

LOAM: Well, don't just stand there! Help me! I don't know what to do! I—I'm all at sea, as it were!

CRICHTON: Allow me take over, my lord . . . Thank you, sir.

NARRATOR: In spite of Crichton's expert maneuvering, the yacht has more and more difficulty as the storm grows more and more intense.

CATHERINE (*Crying*): Help! Help! I'm getting thoroughly drenched!

AGATHA (*Impatiently*): Oh, be quiet, Catherine. We're all just as wet as you are!

MARY: I'm not worrying about being wet; it's the waves that worry me. Look how big they are!

LOAM (*Flustered*): Oh, girls, I don't know what to do! Crichton is having the most horrid time trying to keep us afloat.

MARY (*Fearfully*): Oh, Father, you mean it's as bad as that?

CRICHTON (*Coolly*): My lord, it is of the utmost urgency that we launch the small safety dory. The yacht has struck a reef, and we are shortly to be shipwrecked.

LOAM *and* DAUGHTERS (*Ad lib panic*): Shipwrecked! Oh, dear lord! What are we to do? (*Etc.*)

ERNEST (*Lightly*): I say, everybody, isn't this a lark?

NARRATOR: Hastily, the passengers set a small dory upon the waters and clamber aboard. For days their little boat drifts aimlessly, tossed and buffeted by the storm. At last, the boat is carried to a small, uninhabited island, and there they all disembark. From the moment they set foot on the island, however, an odd—though at first imperceptible—change takes place. Everyone begins turning to Crichton, not Loam, for direction.

MARY: Crichton?

CRICHTON: Yes, my lady?

MARY: Is there any hope of a ship coming by and finding us?

CRICHTON (*Consolingly*): Of course there is, my lady.

MARY (*Firmly*): Don't treat me as a child. I have got to know the worst and face it. Crichton, the truth.

CRICHTON: We were driven off course, my lady; I fear far from the track of commerce.

AGATHA (*Cheerfully*): I say, Crichton, is that dinner we smell?

ERNEST: Look at the fire, Agatha. Crichton is cooking food for us all.

AGATHA: Oh, how wonderful! I'm nearly starved.

CRICHTON (*Politely*): I beg your pardon, Lady Agatha. For those who have done no work on this island, there will be no food.

AGATHA (*Appalled*): No work, no dinner? When did you invent that rule, Crichton?

CRICHTON: I didn't invent it, Lady Agatha. Nature did.

NARRATOR: There were other rules that Nature necessitated, too.

CRICHTON: Mr. Ernest, since we landed on this island, it seems to me that your epigrams have been particularly brilliant.

ERNEST (*Pleased*): Thank you, Crichton.

CRICHTON: But I find that epigrams are not much use on an island. Therefore, each time you speak an epigram in the future, I shall convey you to an isolated place on the island and there immerse your head in a bucket of cold water.

ERNEST (*Chuckling*): From what you say, Crichton, there is little difference between a threatening and a wetting!

CRICHTON: I said I would cure you, sir, and I shall.

NARRATOR: Crichton was, of course, as good as his word. In time the others began to notice the change that had settled over them.

MARY: Sisters, I have come to a terrible conclusion.

CATHERINE: What is it, Mary?

MARY: Crichton, who in London was our butler, is now our master!

AGATHA: *What?*

MARY: Nature has made Crichton our master. Everything that was salvaged from the wreck has been salvaged by Crichton. Everything that has been accomplished on the island has been accomplished by Crichton. He built us a house; he catches our food; he teaches us how to negotiate our lives in this wilderness. Everything we have, even our lives, we owe to this butler, the admirable Crichton.

NARRATOR: Life on the desert island, however, does have its bright spots and under the excellent guidance of Crichton, the days fly by. Lord Loam—now nicknamed Daddy—becomes sort of a kitchen boy and errand runner, which is a position in keeping with his native intelligence. Tweeny has been elevated to the post of cook of the island. The three girls have become servants, doing whatever needs to be done: hunting, sewing, cleaning, and fishing, even waiting on table. And Ernest, poor boy, is still fit for nothing, but at least he no longer annoys anyone with his epigrams. Crichton's cold-water cure has been effective! But the most important changes that have occurred on this island in the past two years are these: First, everyone has reconciled himself to the idea that there is never to be any hope of rescue, and is now happy and busy. Second, Crichton has become the master, and the former masters have become servants. And third, all of the women are secretly in love with this paragon, this idol, this admirable Crichton.

AGATHA (*Eagerly*): Has Crichton decided who is to wait on him today?

CATHERINE: It's my turn, Aggie!

AGATHA: No, it isn't! It's my turn!

TWEENY: Oh, don't argue, girls. It doesn't matter whose turn it is.

CATHERINE: Tweeny! What do you mean? Has he picked you?

TWEENY (*Bitterly*): It's to be Polly again. He wants *her* to wait on him.

MARY (*Happily*): He wants *me*! He wants *me*!

AGATHA: It isn't fair, Tweeny.

TWEENY: Fair or not, that's who he wants. Look at her— bounding like a girl out of school. To think I should ever see Lady Mary nickname herself Polly and be overjoyed at the chance to serve her own butler.

MARY: Why shouldn't I call myself Polly? It suits me better than "Lady Mary" out here on the island. And as for being happy to wait on the Gov, why shouldn't I be? You're all green with envy!

NARRATOR: And so Lady Mary dons her apron and begins to serve Crichton his dinner in the island dining room. Lady Agatha, Lady Catherine, and Tweeny the kitchen maid watch from behind the kitchen door, and every time Crichton speaks to Lady Mary, the others sigh with adoration and envy.

CRICHTON (*Formally*): Thank you. You may clear. Ah, you certainly do everything to please me, Polly.

MARY: I try to, sir. But still I'm afraid I don't try half enough.

CRICHTON: There is only one thing about you that I don't quite like.

MARY: And what is that, sir?

CRICHTON: That action of the hands—so like washing them. I have noticed that the others tend to do it also. It seems odd.

MARY: Have you forgotten?

CRICHTON: Forgotten? What?

MARY: That once upon a time a certain other person did that.

CRICHTON (*Horrified*): You mean me? Horrible!

MARY: You haven't done it for a very long time now. Perhaps it is natural to servants. . . . Why are you so quiet?

CRICHTON (*Sighing*): I was thinking of two people neither of us has seen for a long, long time—Lady Mary Lasenby and one Crichton, butler.

MARY: They are dead! Forget them!

CRICHTON: I almost had forgotten them. The butler has had a chance to become a man. He seems so far away now, but if I thought it best for you, I'd haul him back in a minute—though in my soul he is abhorrent to me—and I would let you see the man you call your master melt into him who was your servant.

MARY (*Hurt*): Don't talk like that! To me it is the past that was not real.

CRICHTON: Dare I speak what I would? It is so hard to say, and yet there is another voice in me, crying.

MARY: If it be the voice of Nature, then say whatever you want to Polly Lasenby.

CRICHTON: Dear Polly, I have grown to love you. Are you afraid to become my wife?

MARY: You are the most wonderful man I have ever known. I am not afraid, but I am so unworthy of you. It was sufficient to me that I should be allowed to wait on you at table.

CRICHTON: You shall wait on me no longer. At whatever table I sit, Polly, you shall sit there also.

MARY: As your servant at your feet.

CRICHTON: No, as my consort by my side. (*Emphatically*) I love you, Polly, and nothing will ever come between us!

NARRATOR: Suddenly there was the sound of a cannon shot.

MARY (*Startled*): What was that?

CRICHTON: It sounded like a ship's gun.

MARY: Yes, yes—a gun. I have often heard it. It is only a dream.

CRICHTON: Look! All the others are rushing to the beach!

ERNEST (*Excitedly*): Look, everyone! A ship! But they can't hear our cries! We must do something! We must signal them! Oh,

Gov, think of something. Already they're moving away from the harbor.

MARY (*Dreamily*): The ship is going away, you say? I think I'm glad.

CRICHTON (*Taking charge*): Have no fear. I'll bring them back.

MARY: What are you going to do?

CRICHTON: Ernest, go and set fire to the beacons I've placed about the island. Quickly!

ERNEST: No sooner said than done!

MARY (*Urgently*): Don't do this, Gov! Don't you see what it means?

CRICHTON (*Matter of factly*): It means that our life on the island has come to an end.

MARY (*Imploringly*): Let the ship go without us!

CRICHTON: I have a duty to fulfill.

TWEENY (*Excitedly*): It's an English ship! It's turned back! Polly! Gov! Come to the beach! We are rescued!

MARY (*Pleading*): Gov, this won't make a difference to us, will it?

CRICHTON (*Firmly*): It makes all the difference in the world.

MARY: It mustn't matter between us! It mustn't make a difference!

CRICHTON (*Weakly*): My lady . . .

MARY (*Horrified*): Crichton! You addressed me as your lady! And your hands! Oh, Crichton, that horrible gesture a servant makes! Crichton, you're washing your hands!

NARRATOR: And so the shipwrecked party, which for two years has lived a carefree and natural life, is rescued and returned to England. Once again their social order is reversed. Crichton becomes a butler, and Lord Loam becomes a master. Life continues at Loam House much the same as it had before the shipwreck.

AGATHA: Listen to this review of Ernest's book, girls. It's even better than the last!

CATHERINE: Let me see. "We heartily congratulate the Hon. Ernest Wooley. His book, regarding the adventures of himself and his brave companions on a desert isle, stirs the heart like a trumpet."

AGATHA: It continues in the same vein. "From the first to the last of Mr. Wooley's engrossing pages, it is evident that he was an ideal man to be wrecked with, and a true hero."

MARY: Here's another: "There are many kind references to the two servants who were wrecked with the family, and Mr. Wooley pays the butler a glowing tribute in a footnote."

ERNEST (*Lightly*): How the press exaggerates! It was nothing, really!

NARRATOR: Of course, now that the family is back at Loam House, no one ever speaks of the connection between Lady Mary and Crichton, and one day, soon after their return, Mary's engagement to Lord Brocklehurst is publicly announced. But there is one person to whom she fears to present her fiancé, and that person is her butler.

MARY (*Gingerly*): Brocky, darling, this is our butler, Crichton. He was with us on the island, you know.

BROCKLEHURST (*Priggishly*): Ah, yes, Crichton.

CRICHTON (*Formally*): Lord Brocklehurst.

BROCKLEHURST: While I think of it, Crichton, there's something I should like to know about the—er, how shall I put it—arrangements on the island.

MARY (*Worried*): Brocky, dear . . . that's all ancient history.

CRICHTON: Yes, my lord? What is it you wish to know?

BROCKLEHURST: Well, were the social distinctions preserved, Crichton?

CRICHTON: Just as at home, sir.

BROCKLEHURST: The servants?

CRICHTON: They had to keep their place, my lord.

BROCKLEHURST: You mean you didn't even take your meals with the family?

CRICHTON: No, my lord. I dined apart.

BROCKLEHURST: Admirable! And the servants' teas that used to take place here . . .

CRICHTON: They did not seem natural on the island, my lord, and were discontinued by the master's orders.

BROCKLEHURST: A clear proof that they were a mistake here. You are an excellent fellow, Crichton. If, after Lady Mary and

I are married, you ever wish to change your place, come to us.

MARY (*Bursting out*): Oh, no! That's impossible!

BROCKLEHURST: Why impossible?

MARY (*Nervously*): I—I—that is—

BROCKLEHURST: Do *you* see why it should be impossible, my man?

CRICHTON: Yes, my lord. I have not told Lord Loam, but as soon as he is suited, I wish to leave his service. I believe dinner is served, Madam.

MARY (*Recovering*): Oh! Dinner, yes, yes, quite so. Dinner! Do go into the dining room, Brocky darling. I shall join you in a minute.

BROCKLEHURST: Right-o, my love! Don't be long.

MARY (*Softly, after a pause*): What will you do, Crichton, now that you are leaving the domestic service?

CRICHTON: God only knows, my lady.

MARY (*Hesitantly*): I—I know it isn't quite proper, but will you take my hand? To wish you every happiness, Crichton.

CRICHTON (*Coldly*): The same to you, my lady.

MARY: Do you despise me, Crichton? (*Pause*) Ah, the man who could never tell a lie makes no answer. (*With emotion*) Crichton, you are the best man among us.

CRICHTON: On an island, my lady, perhaps; but in England, no.

MARY: Then there's something wrong with England!

CRICHTON (*Firmly*): My lady, not even from you can I listen to a word against England.

MARY: Tell me one thing. You have not lost your courage?

CRICHTON: No, my lady.

MARY: Good. (*Stiffly*) That will be all, Crichton. You may serve dinner.

THE END

▣▣The Man Without a Country

by *Edward Everett Hale*
Adapted for round-the-table reading
by *Walter Hackett*

Characters

NARRATOR
COLONEL
AARON BURR
LT. PHILIP NOLAN
PROSECUTOR
DEFENSE COUNSEL
JUDGE
PRESIDENT JEFFERSON
CAPT. SHAW
LT. MITCHELL
FIVE OFFICERS
VOICES, *at least seven*
CAPT. LANE
CAPT. RANKIN
NAVY SECRETARY
DOCTOR

NARRATOR: Fort Massac is a small yet strategic United States Army outpost that stands on the muddy banks of the lower

Mississippi River. In this year of 1805, its officers and men are lonely and none too happy about it. But on this particular day the outpost is buzzing with excitement. A famous guest has come to visit—Aaron Burr! Aaron Burr, former Vice-President of the United States, rabid Federalist, master politician, smooth-tongued orator; Aaron Burr, the man who had killed Alexander Hamilton in a duel. The Colonel, disappointed that Mr. Burr's visit will be a brief one, attempts to prolong his stay. . . .

COLONEL (*Graciously*): Are you sure I can't get you to change your mind, Mr. Burr? You're welcome to remain here as long as you wish.

AARON BURR: Thank you, Colonel, but I'm afraid I must be leaving within the next day or so.

COLONEL: Pressing business?

BURR (*Mysteriously*): Yes, of a sort.

COLONEL (*Surprised*): We thought this was a pleasure trip, Mr. Burr.

BURR (*Dryly*): My career has never allowed me to relax long enough to seek pleasure. Suppose we call this a journey of observation. By the way, I hope to talk more with some of your gentlemen before I leave.

COLONEL: All of us will look forward to that, sir. And now, I'll leave you to your quarters. You must be tired after your journey.

BURR: Thank you, Colonel. Good day. (*Knock on door is heard.*) Yes?

PHILIP NOLAN: It's Lieutenant Nolan, sir. I have the tobacco you asked for this morning.

BURR: Thank you, Nolan. Please, sit down.

NOLAN (*Surprised*): Thank you, Mr. Burr.

BURR: You haven't been in service too long, I take it.

NOLAN: No, sir. Going on four years.

BURR: Do you like the Army?

NOLAN (*Slowly*): Why, yes, sir.

BURR: The pay of a junior officer isn't very much, eh?

NOLAN: No, sir.

BURR: Ever get tired of this duty? (*Pause*) Don't be afraid to speak up, Nolan. Remember, I once was in the Army, too, so I have an idea how you younger officers think.

NOLAN (*Hesitantly*): To be frank, Mr. Burr, life on a frontier post like this is just about the most boring existence in the world. (*Hastily*) Of course, I wouldn't want the Colonel to hear me say that.

BURR (*Laughing*): Of course you wouldn't.

NOLAN: There's another thing—

BURR (*Encouragingly*): Go on.

NOLAN: I happen to be in debt.

BURR: I'm sorry to hear that.

NOLAN: I've been thinking of applying for a transfer. (*Pause*)

BURR: Perhaps I could help you on that, Nolan. (*Slyly*) But it wouldn't mean you would be transferred to another post.

NOLAN (*Puzzled*): No?

BURR (*Carefully*): No, it would mean a great chance for you. A chance for fame and position and money—a great deal of money.

NOLAN (*Intrigued*): Where is this place, sir?

BURR (*Excitedly*): In a new country. A new, glorious empire. Nolan, there is a place for you in that empire. But before I tell you more, you must swear to say nothing to anyone. Not a word! Do you agree?

NOLAN (*Enthusiastically*): Yes. I swear it! (*Pause*)

1ST VOICE (*Reading rapidly*): "Washington, D.C., July 3, 1807. To all commanding officers of United States Army posts in the Mississippi River sector: You are hereby commanded to apprehend and secure the persons of Aaron Burr, General James Wilkinson, and any other such conspirators guilty of attempting treason and plotting to seize a portion of these United States, on which to fashion a new country of their own . . . Signed, John Clarke, Secretary of War."

PROSECUTOR: To sum up my case as prosecution on this board of court martial: Gentlemen, I accuse the defendant, Lieutenant Philip Nolan, of the crime of treason against the United States of America. He is guilty of actively abetting the most odious political plot in the entire history of our beloved country. (*Loudly*) I tell you we have not seen his kind since the days of the infamous Benedict Arnold.

DEFENSE COUNSEL: Objection!

JUDGE: Objection overruled.

DEFENSE: But, sir, I can present conclusive evidence that will prove that Philip Nolan—

PROSECUTOR (*Interrupting*): There is not a bit of doubt that Philip Nolan knowingly entered into a clandestine agreement with Aaron Burr to undermine the safety of his own native land. You have heard me question him concerning his dealings with Burr. And what has been his reply? That he is under oath to say nothing of what transpired between them.

DEFENSE: Objection!

JUDGE: Objection overruled.

PROSECUTOR: And why did Philip Nolan sell his soul? For the empty promises of an egotistical dreamer who promised him money and fame. That is why Philip Nolan broke the solemn oath of fidelity to our country that he took at the time of his enlistment.

NOLAN (*Shouting*): You're a liar! (*Sound of gavel is heard.*)

JUDGE: I might warn the prisoner that any such further remarks might result in adversely swaying the members of this board of court martial. The prosecution may proceed.

PROSECUTOR: I simply repeat what is obvious: Lieutenant Nolan should be adjudged guilty.

JUDGE: Has the defense anything to say?

DEFENSE: Sir, Lieutenant Nolan wishes to speak for himself.

JUDGE: Proceed.

NOLAN (*Quietly*): For two days I have sat here and listened as the charges have piled up against me. I have heard the prosecution deliberately distort every statement, every answer I gave.

PROSECUTOR: I object.

JUDGE: Sustained.

NOLAN: I readily admit that I listened to Burr's offer to join him.

PROSECUTOR: Then why didn't you come forward and unmask him?

NOLAN (*Insistently*): Because I was under oath to him to say nothing.

DEFENSE: I object. Lieutenant Nolan is not now being cross-examined. I request the court that he be allowed to finish uninterrupted.

JUDGE: Continue, Mr. Nolan.

NOLAN: I swear that I rejected Burr's offer, but I realize that in any court of justice it is possible for an innocent man to be falsely accused of the wrongs done by others. (*In a rising voice*) For the past two weeks I have seen other officers—men guilty of the same crime I allegedly committed—go free. Free because this board wishes to find them free.

VOICES (*Ad lib*): Liar! That isn't true! Traitor! (*Etc.*)

JUDGE: Silence! This court will come to order! (*After a pause*) Are you finished, Mr. Nolan?

NOLAN (*Passionately*): No! I know well what the verdict will be. I know I will be made an example of the fate in store for others.

JUDGE: Mr. Nolan, I believe it has been easily established that you have been unfaithful to your country, that you have committed treason against the United States—

NOLAN (*Angrily*): Damn the United States! I wish I may never hear of the United States again!

NARRATOR: Lieutenant Nolan's heated statement caused a stir in the courtroom. When the judge and the board of court martial conferred to make their decision regarding Lieutenant Nolan, there was no question in anyone's mind what the verdict would be.

JUDGE: The prisoner will rise and face the board. (*After a pause*) Philip Nolan, the board of court martial, subject to the approval of the President, decrees that you shall never again hear the name of the United States! You will be taken to New Orleans and delivered to Lieutenant Mitchell, Acting Naval Commander, and be confined there until further notice from the President.

JEFFERSON: "Washington, D.C., October 28, 1807. To Secretary of the Navy Crowninshield. Your deposition relative to the case of Philip Nolan received and noted. You are hereby empowered to turn the prisoner over to Captain Ethan Shaw, commander of the *Nautilus,* now in New Orleans. Sincerely yours, Your obedient servant, Thomas Jefferson, President of the United States."

CAPT. SHAW: Lieutenant Mitchell, I can't say I like this duty.

LT. MITCHELL: Sorry, Captain Shaw, but I'm just carrying out my orders.

SHAW: I understand. Go on and read the rest of the order.

MITCHELL: "You will provide him with such quarters, rations, and clothing as would be proper for an officer of his late rank. The officers on board your ship will make arrangements agreeable to themselves regarding his society."

SHAW (*Gloomily*): That is going to be a pleasant situation. Go on.

MITCHELL: "He is to be exposed to no indignity of any kind, nor is he ever unnecessarily to be reminded that he is a prisoner . . ."

SHAW: And I suppose that is going to be an easy order to obey.

MITCHELL: "But under no circumstances is Philip Nolan ever to hear of his country again, nor to see any information regarding it; and you will caution all your officers that these rules are not to be broken. It is the unswerving intention of the government that he shall never again see the country which he has disowned. Before the end of your cruise you will receive orders with regard to transferring the prisoner. Respectfully yours, W. Southard, Assistant to the Secretary of the Navy." (*Pause*)

SHAW: Well! How is Nolan taking this news?

MITCHELL: I don't think he realizes just what his sentence entails.

SHAW (*Grimly*): He'll soon learn. (*Abruptly*) Where is he now?

MITCHELL: Waiting outside, sir. Shall I send him in?

SHAW: Yes. I'd like to see him now. (*After a pause*) Well, Mr. Nolan, I suppose you're wondering what is to happen to you.

NOLAN (*Nervously*): I am.

SHAW: You're to be given fairly comfortable quarters. The ship's commissary will supply anything you lack. Your meals will be served to you in your cabin.

NOLAN: About my uniforms—the insignia has been removed.

SHAW: You are to be allowed to wear your uniforms minus all insignia. Those are my orders.

NOLAN: I see. (*Pause*) Captain Shaw, exactly what is my position aboard your ship?

SHAW (*Fumbling*): Why—why, ah—(*Quickly recovering*) You may consider your position as that of a guest—a slightly underprivileged guest.

NOLAN: Am I to sail with you?

SHAW: Naturally.

NOLAN: Where?

SHAW: Around the Horn, into the Pacific, and across to Tahiti.

NOLAN (*Surprised*): Tahiti? That's a long way from the United States.

SHAW: A very long way.

NOLAN: How long are we to be gone?

SHAW: Two years.

NARRATOR: The *Nautilus* sailed to Tahiti, with Philip Nolan aboard. The officers and crew never mentioned or discussed the United States with him.

1ST OFFICER: It's been almost two years since I last saw my parents. In fact, it's been nine months since we sailed from New Orleans. A couple of nomads, you and I, men without a home.

2ND OFFICER: Much better than being a man without a country.

1ST OFFICER: Oh, yes. Poor Nolan! I feel sorry for him.

2ND OFFICER: I wonder if the government will ever rescind his sentence?

1ST OFFICER: It would have been more merciful to have hanged him. Anything in place of being a floating derelict.

2ND OFFICER (*Lowering his voice*): Quiet! Here he comes now. Watch what you say.

NOLAN (*Pleasantly*): Good afternoon, gentlemen. (OFFICERS *ad lib greetings.*) Mind if I join you?

2ND OFFICER: Not at all.

NOLAN (*Sighing deeply*): Ah-h! That sun feels good. Thought I would do a bit of reading. The doctor passed on this old English newspaper to me.

2ND OFFICER: You're a great reader, Mr. Nolan.

NOLAN: Oh, yes. Helps pass the time. Keeps me in touch with what is taking place in the world. (*Pause; lightly*) Would you gentlemen tell me something?

1ST OFFICER: What's that?

NOLAN: The newspapers passed on to me have certain paragraphs cut out. For example, here is a story dealing with Napoleon's campaign, and just as it apparently starts to relate the policy of the United States toward Napoleon, the rest of the account has been cut out. Could you tell me why?

1ST OFFICER (*Nervously*): No. I can't say.

NOLAN: Well, I guess it doesn't matter. (*Casually*) By the way, what is the latest news from the States?

2ND OFFICER: We have no news.

NOLAN: But last night in the wardroom you were talking over the dispatches received from the States. As soon as I came in, you stopped. Why?

2ND OFFICER (*Uncomfortably*): I wish you wouldn't ask, Mr. Nolan.

NOLAN (*Deflated*): Very well. I realize you're not supposed to talk about the United States with me. I thought I could worm some information from you.

1ST OFFICER (*Sympathetically*): What about your parents, Mr. Nolan, or your relatives? Couldn't they—

NOLAN: My parents are dead. As for my relatives, they don't know about my situation, and I doubt if they'd help. (*Sighs*) Well, if you'll excuse me, I'll go to my quarters.

1ST OFFICER: Nolan.

NOLAN: Yes?

1ST OFFICER (*Impulsively*): If I were in your position, I doubt if I could show the courage you're displaying. (*Pause*)

2ND VOICE: "Belfast, Ireland, June 14, 1810. To Captain James Wyatt, U.S.S. *General Greene*. You will receive the person of Philip Nolan, who will accompany you on your voyage to the Straits of Gibraltar and through the Mediterranean."

3RD VOICE: "From the log of the U.S.S. *Enterprise*. November 11, 1814. Havana, Cuba. Today we took on fresh supplies for our cruise to the Far East. Also received as passenger Mr. Philip Nolan."

NOLAN: Captain Lane, sir—I have heard scuttlebutt that we may engage the enemy at any moment.

LANE: That's no great secret, Nolan. What about it?

NOLAN: Well, Captain, I have heard you're a bit shorthanded. I'm wondering if you can use me. I know the ship's routine well. (*Eagerly*) Any detail would be welcome, sir, even that of a powder monkey.

LANE (*Surprised*): You mean you desire combat duty?

NOLAN: Exactly, sir.

LANE (*Kindly*): That's generous of you, Nolan, but I'm afraid it's impossible. My orders concerning you are very strict.

NOLAN (*Pleading*): Couldn't you forget them, just this once?

LANE (*Firmly*): I don't wink an eye at orders, Mr. Nolan. In fact, when and if we do engage the enemy, I must ask that you go below and remain there until the action has ceased.

NARRATOR: Four more years passed, and Nolan's requests for news of his native land continued to be denied. His newspapers were scissored, his books censored. One evening he went up on deck of the ship he then called "home," where there was a small gathering of officers.

NOLAN: Please, don't let me disturb your conversation.

3RD OFFICER: We were just reading aloud, Mr. Nolan. We like to do that, to help pass the time.

NOLAN: What an excellent idea! What are you reading?

4TH OFFICER: It's a poem by Sir Walter Scott. "The Lay of the Last Minstrel."

NOLAN: Hmm. I don't believe I know that one.

5TH OFFICER: Why don't you read it to us, Mr. Nolan? You're a much better reader than any of the rest of us.

NOLAN: Very well. I'll give it a try.
(*Clears his throat, then reads*)
"Breathes there a man, with soul so dead,
Who never to himself hath said,
This is my own, my native land!
(*Coughs slightly, then continues*)
Whose heart hath ne'er within him burn'd,

As home his footsteps he hath turn'd,
From wandering on a foreign strand!
(*Pauses*)
For him . . . (*Pauses*) for him no minstrel raptures swell;
High though his titles, proud his name,
Boundless his wealth as wish can claim,
Despite those titles, power, and pelf,
The—the wretch—the wretch concentered all in self. . . ."

NARRATOR: Nolan's eyes filled with tears, and he suddenly stopped reading. Giving a distraught look to the seated officers, he pitched the book into the sea. (*After a pause*) The years passed by . . . 1820, 1830, 1840. . . .

4TH VOICE (*Calling out*): Ho, there, *Levant*. Stand by to receive our longboat.

5TH VOICE: What have you for us? Any mail?

4TH VOICE: No mail. We are transferring Philip Nolan.

NARRATOR: During the time that Mr. Nolan was aboard the *Levant,* Captain Rankin developed not only pity for the man, but genuine fondness. Rankin became very much interested in freeing Mr. Nolan from his life of exile.

NAVY SECRETARY: I don't know what to think, Rankin. I know your word is good, but the Navy Department's records show absolutely no trace of this man you speak of—this Philip Nolan.

RANKIN: Of course not, Mr. Secretary. Those records were destroyed by fire when the British seized Washington during the War of 1812.

SECRETARY: It all sounds like a fairy tale, a nightmare.

RANKIN: Whether you want to believe it or not, Philip Nolan was sentenced back in 1807, and this is 1859. Mind you, Mr. Secretary, for 52 years Philip Nolan has been shifted from one ship to another. For 52 years he has never set foot on American soil. For 52 years he has not even heard the name of the United States mentioned. For over a half-century this unfortunate derelict has experienced a living death.

SECRETARY (*Impatiently*): Captain, why do you concern yourself with this matter?

RANKIN: Because I like Nolan. He has been committed to my

care on two occasions, and each time I found him to be a kind, mild gentleman. (*Pleading*) Mr. Secretary, won't you investigate his case? The man has only a few years of life ahead of him. Why not let him enjoy them?

SECRETARY (*Firmly*): With the possibility of war with the South, this department hasn't time for such an investigation.

RANKIN (*Angrily*): Aren't you trying to tell me that you don't care to unearth any skeletons?

SECRETARY: An unfortunate choice of words, Captain. (*Coldly*) Taking for granted there is such a man as Philip Nolan, he will have to remain an unknown; a legend, if you like.

RANKIN (*Casually*): Suppose the newspapers got hold of this story? The national election is only a year off.

SECRETARY (*Significantly*): You understand, Captain, that it is entirely within my power to depose you from your command. Then there is the Far East. That is a long voyage. You know how many days a voyage to Japan takes, do you not, Captain Rankin?

NARRATOR: Less than six months later, on January 12, 1860, Captain Rankin received a telegraph from Washington, D.C., which read:

6TH VOICE: "Prepare to sail on 27th for extended tour of Far East, including China and Japan. Detailed orders following."

7TH VOICE: "Shanghai, China, May 11, 1862. To Captain Benjamin Rankin, aboard U.S.S. *Levant.* . . . Captain Chalmers of the *Ohio* will deliver into your hands the person of Philip Nolan. From past contact with him, you will know how to receive and handle his case."

RANKIN (*After a pause; in low voice*): You think the end is in sight, doctor?

DOCTOR: He's liable to go off any minute.

RANKIN: Would you leave me alone with him?

DOCTOR: Very well. If you need me, I'll be outside.

RANKIN (*Quietly*): Philip. Philip, it's Rankin.

NOLAN (*In weak voice*): Hello, Captain.

RANKIN: Is there anything you wish?

NOLAN: Just sit here and talk to me. (*Pause*) I know I'm dying. Perhaps now you will tell me what I want to know.

RANKIN: Anything you wish.

NOLAN (*Breathing heavily*): I want you to know that there is not a man on this ship—that there is not in America, God bless her!—a more loyal man than I.

RANKIN (*Kindly*): What would you like to hear?

NOLAN: Has our country grown since I saw it last?

RANKIN: A good many states have been added. Ohio, Kentucky, Michigan, Indiana, and Mississippi; and California and Texas and Oregon.

NOLAN: What of America's progress?

RANKIN: It has made tremendous strides, Philip. Our cotton manufacturing is the greatest in the world. We have made great improvements in the steam train.

NOLAN: Steam train? What is that?

RANKIN: A form of carriage propelled by steam. Then a Naval Academy has been established at Annapolis and a Military Academy at West Point in New York. A great piece of literature has been written by a woman named Stowe—*Uncle Tom's Cabin*.

NOLAN: Are we at peace?

RANKIN: There was a war with England in 1812.

NOLAN: Yes, I heard rumors of it at the time, I have also heard there is trouble between the North and the South. (*Hastily*) No! Don't tell me. I prefer not to know. Who is our President now?

RANKIN: A great man named Abraham Lincoln. He's from the state of Illinois, a man who worked his way up through the ranks.

NOLAN: Good for him.

RANKIN: The United States is fast growing into the greatest democracy in the world.

NOLAN (*Weakly*): That's wonderful news.

RANKIN (*Alarmed*): Philip, are you—

NOLAN: Better than I have ever been. You see that old flag against the wall?

RANKIN: Yes.

NOLAN: I want to be wrapped in it. Will you see to that?

RANKIN: Yes, I promise.

NOLAN: God bless you! (*Voice becomes weaker.*) On the table is a Bible.

RANKIN: I have it.

NOLAN: Open it. (*Pause*) Read what is written on the fly leaf.

RANKIN (*Slowly*): "Bury me in the sea. It has been my home, and I love it. But will not someone set up a stone for my memory somewhere on my native soil, that my disgrace may not be more than I ought to bear? Say on it: 'In memory of Philip Nolan, Lieutenant in the Army of the United States. He loved his country as no other man has loved her; but no man deserved less at her hands.'"

THE END

▣▣Treasure Island

by *Robert Louis Stevenson*
Adapted for round-the-table reading
by *Marjorie Ann York*

Characters

SAILOR
JIM HAWKINS
LONG JOHN SILVER
MORGAN
HANDS
DOCTOR LIVESEY
CAPTAIN SMOLLETT
SQUIRE TRELAWNEY
BEN GUNN
MEMBERS OF THE CREW

SAILOR (*Singing loudly*):
  Fifteen men on the dead man's chest,
  Yo-ho-ho, and a bottle of rum!
  Drink and the devil had done for the rest,
  (*Fading*) Yo-ho-ho, and a bottle of rum!
JIM: I'm Jim Hawkins, cabin boy aboard the *Hispaniola*, sailing
  from England to Treasure Island. (*Pause*) One day, not long
  ago, an old sea dog fell dead while staying at my family's inn.
  In his sea chest was a treasure map. It turns out the map first
  belonged to the bloody pirate, Captain Flint. I showed the

378

map to my friends, Doctor Livesey and Squire Trelawney, and soon after we resolved to find the treasure and split it three ways. So, we bought and outfitted this schooner, and as we were all landlubbers, we were lucky to find a fine sailor, Captain Smollett, to navigate the ship for us. Then we hired a crew. Oh, they work hard enough, but they're a rough lot, and Captain Smollett doesn't trust them. At first, our voyage had been very ordinary, until a few odd things began to happen. (*Mysteriously*) Our mate, Mr. Arrow, fell overboard one dark night. Then a few weeks later, I went down to get an apple from a barrel in the hold of the ship. Supplies were so low, I couldn't see into the barrel, so I climbed inside it to take my pick. Just as I got inside the barrel, I heard two of the crew, Hands and Morgan, coming toward me, along with Long John Silver, our one-legged cook . . .

SILVER (*Gruffly*): So what's ailing ye now, Morgan?

MORGAN (*Impatiently*): We're sick of holding off any longer.

SILVER: Ye'll be sicker of it afore I give the word to mutiny. (*Harshly*) Ye'll work proper, speak soft, and keep sober. When we get to the island, then we'll get the map—*and* the treasure.

HANDS (*Derisively*): D'ya think they're just gonna sit tight while we cut their throats and take the map?

MORGAN (*With bravado*): We took a vote. Didn't we, Hands?

SILVER (*Aghast*): Shiver me timbers? Ye voted in the Council?

HANDS (*Gruffly*): Aye, Silver. Them's pirate's rights. We know the rules.

SILVER (*Angrily*): I make the rules! First one goes agin' them, and I'll open him with me knife. We'll do as I said. Once at the island, we'll slit every honest throat aboard. Then the map is ours, and we'll take this ship home piled with treasure. I claim only one thing—Cap'n Smollett. An honest sea cap'n like him sticks in me gullet. (*Gleefully*) Why, I'll break his bones with me bare hands!

MORGAN (*Admiringly*): You're a real man, Long John. Good as Cap'n Flint.

SILVER: Aye. Flint's crew were always the roughest. The devil himself would have been afeard to go to sea with us. And Flint was the best of the lot. It'll be an honor to wrestle Flint's map with Cap'n Smollett, (*Evilly*) and take over where he left off.

SAILOR (*Calling*): Land ho! Land ho!

JIM (*After a pause*): They ran up the ladder. I climbed out of the barrel and ran forward to report to my friends. In the captain's quarters, I told the story to the doctor, the squire, and the captain. The doctor was the first to speak.

DOCTOR: What do you suggest, gentlemen?

JIM: We'll just have to give them the map, Doctor Livesey. (*Anxiously*) They'll slit our throats for it, won't they, Captain Smollett?

CAPTAIN: Indeed they will, lad. It goes against the grain to command a ship of pirate scum.

SQUIRE: I agree with you, Captain. Now that they know about the treasure—

DOCTOR (*Thoughtfully*): But they don't know where it is, Squire Trelawney.

JIM: Why not give them a *fake* map? By the time they figure it out, we could have the treasure and be gone.

DOCTOR (*Enthusiastically*): Capital idea, Jim! We could mark up our sailing chart showing the treasure on the opposite side of the island.

CAPTAIN (*Enthusiastically*): You've hit it! We'll be gone by the time they learn the difference.

SQUIRE: I'm for it. We've a few faithful hands aboard. We'll beat Silver's crew at their own trickery.

CAPTAIN: We may as well force the issue right now, gentlemen, and save our necks. (*Shouting*) Pipe all hands! (SAILOR *mimicks sound of bosun's pipe*) Now we'll go and face that bunch of villains. But stick close together, gentlemen, and don't turn your backs to the likes of them. (*Pauses, loudly*) My lads, this is the place we've been sailing for. You've done good duty aloft and below, and to show appreciation, I'm passing out double rations of grog.

SILVER: Double grog and more!

CAPTAIN (*Loudly*): What say you, Silver? Come up and speak out.

SILVER: We'll take the grog and the treasure, too.

CAPTAIN (*Feigning ignorance*): What treasure?

SILVER (*In sneering tone*): Don't fool with me, Cap'n. We know this is a treasure ship, and we want our share.

CAPTAIN (*In disgust*): Mutiny, eh? I'll have you in irons.

SILVER: Not so, Cap'n. The crew is with me.

CAPTAIN (*Uncomfortably*): Oh? Well, speak your mind.

SILVER (*Triumphantly*): I know ye have a map showing where the treasure is hid. We want it.

CAPTAIN (*Firmly*): I'll see you stretched from a yardarm first!

SILVER: Ye'll not live to see! (*Shouting*) Forward, lads!

DOCTOR: Wait! If we give you the map, will you take an oath you'll not harm us?

SILVER: The map first, Doctor Livesey. Then I'll promise.

DOCTOR: Give it to them, Captain.

CAPTAIN (*Balking*): Why I'd rather—(*Conceding*) well, if you say so, doctor. Before I hand it over to you, Silver, will you and your men promise not to harm anyone aboard?

SILVER (*Impatiently*): Aye! Hand it over.

CAPTAIN: And your men?

SILVER: Speak out, lads.

CREW (*Shouting*): Aye! Aye!

CAPTAIN: Well, here's your map! Much good it may do you.

HANDS (*Shouting*): We have the map! Now let's slit their throats!

SILVER (*Roughly*): Back, ye fool! I've a better plan. No doubt ye know, Cap'n Smollett, we were pirate Flint's crew. That being so, we do nothing that's not our right. That gold on the island is rightly ours. I'd let your blood for pleasure, but the gold is more important. We'll have that afore we slit yer throats.

CAPTAIN (*Furiously*): Stand back, I warn you!

SILVER: Ha! Ye've only a handful of men. I've nineteen on my side.

SQUIRE (*Angrily*): You'll hang, you scoundrel!

SILVER (*Scornfully*): I think not, ye landlubbing squire.

SQUIRE: You may win for now, but you'll hang later.

SILVER (*Slyly*): Not while I can make a trade.

CAPTAIN (*Suspiciously*): A trade? What's in your scurvy mind now?

SILVER: I'll trade the young 'un's life for mine.

DOCTOR (*Upset*): Jim? You wouldn't dare!

SILVER (*Laughing*): I'll not kill him, Doctor, at least not now. But any more of yer hanging talk, and I'll slit his throat for sure.

SQUIRE: Jim's only a boy!

SILVER: To me, he's a hostage. (*Pause*) Get over here, young lad.

DOCTOR (*Protectively*): Leave the boy alone!

SILVER (*Warningly*): He'll not be harmed unless he's slow getting here.

JIM (*With spirit*): I'm not afraid, Doctor Livesey.

SILVER: Yer a brainy lad, Hawkins.

CAPTAIN (*Sternly*): Heaven help you if harm comes to that boy, John Silver.

CREW (*Laughing and singing*):
Fifteen men on the dead man's chest,
Yo-ho-ho, and a bottle of rum! (*Etc.*)

JIM: We boarded the longboat with the pirates and we went ashore, landing near a thicket of trees. While Silver and his men beached the boat, I ran far into the woods. (*Laughs*) They didn't even miss me! Suddenly I ran into what looked like a great white shaggy animal, but it turned out to be a man. He called himself Ben Gunn, a buccaneer marooned years ago on the island by Long John Silver. When I told him my story, he said Silver was a villain and agreed to help us against the pirates. He wanted me to promise that we'd take him back to England with us. I couldn't speak for my friends, but I told him they were fair-minded men and we could probably use his help to sail the ship home. That made him happy, and we started toward his cave. As we walked, we heard gunfire. Ben Gunn said it was coming from Flint's stockade, which was still on the island. When Ben and I got to the stockade, there was the Union Jack waving in the breeze, and I saw Dr. Livesey, Captain Smollett, and the Squire, along with some honest crew members, defending the fort against the pirates. Ben decided to hide among the trees till I found out if my friends would take him in. We shook hands. Then I ran like mad toward the stockade. Doctor Livesey saw me coming and let me through the heavy gates.

DOCTOR (*In relief*): Praise heaven you're safe, Jim.

CAPTAIN: Good work, lad! How did you manage to escape Silver?

JIM (*Breathlessly*): I ran and hid as soon as we beached. Then I met a marooned buccaneer, named Ben Gunn. He knows a way to foil the pirates. Why, he used to sail with—

SILVER (*Calling*): Ahoy, stockade, ahoy!

CAPTAIN: It's that swine Silver!

DOCTOR: With a flag of truce!

CAPTAIN: Watch for trickery, men. Shoot if you spot a move.

SILVER (*Calling*): Flag o' truce. Cap'n Silver asks leave to come inside and make terms.

CAPTAIN (*Shouting*): Any treachery will be on your side, Silver. (*Pause*) Hold your fire, men. One of you help him over the stockade.

SILVER (*Calling*): As ye say, Cap'n Smollett. (*As if closer*) Morning, gentlemen, my respects. Well, Jim, we missed ye, lad.

DOCTOR: Enough of that! What do you want?

SILVER (*Angrily*): That was a nice trick sending me off with a fake map!

CAPTAIN (*Feigning ignorance*): Fake map?

SILVER (*Annoyed*): Don't act uppity. You've the stockade, but we have the ship. Just look yonder and see the skull and crossbones at the masthead. (*Pause*) Thought the sight of our Jolly Roger would make ye change yer ways. (*Laughs*) We not only have the ship, but the stores and the ammunition, too. And we aim to get the treasure.

CAPTAIN (*Grimly*): Along with our lives, no doubt.

SILVER (*With mock generosity*): No, we'll leave ye those. But we mean to have the treasure map. Ye'd best come aboard the *Hispaniola* until we have the treasure. Once it's loaded on the ship, I'll give ye my word of honor to clap you somewhere safe ashore.

CAPTAIN (*Wryly*): Naturally, you're to be trusted!

SILVER: If that's not to yer fancy, then ye can stay here. We'll divide stores with ye, man for man. I'll give ye my word to speak to the first ship I sight and send 'em to pick ye up. Ye'll not find a better bargain elsewhere, Cap'n.

CAPTAIN: Is that all?

SILVER: Every last word, by thunder! Refuse, and ye've seen the last of me but me musket balls.

CAPTAIN (*Tersely*): Very good. Now hear me. If you'll come up, one by one, unarmed, I'll engage to clap you all in irons and take you home to a fair trial in England.

SILVER (*Astonished*): Ye dare make terms!

CAPTAIN (*Vehemently*): I've flown my sovereign's colors, and I'll see you all with Davy Jones before I'll sail under the Jolly Roger. You can't find the treasure, and there's not a man among you fit to sail the ship. They're the last good words you'll get from me. I'll put a bullet in your back when next I meet you. Now, off with you, double quick!

SILVER: I'm going. (*Pause, then calling*) Just remember: Them that die'll be the lucky ones.

JIM (*After a pause*): They launched a furious attack on us, but we had the best shots inside the fort, so we beat the pirates off. Something had to be done fast, though. Somehow we had to reach the *Hispaniola* and beach it somewhere so the pirates couldn't find it. (*With resolve*) The more I thought about it, the more I figured I could do it. Ben Gunn had told me about a boat he'd made. With that I could reach the ship, cut her adrift and let her go ashore where she fancied. I decided to slip out without telling anyone my plan. (*After a pause*) I found Ben Gunn's boat hidden on the beach. The tide was with me, so I made it to the *Hispaniola* quickly. I cut her rope until the vessel drifted free. She turned on her keel, spinning across the current. (*Excitedly*) I was almost swamped. Then my little boat lurched and changed course. I was whirled along in the wake of the *Hispaniola*. The schooner turned twenty degrees and found a quiet bay. For hours I was showered by flying spray until a great weariness grew upon me. I lay in my sea-tossed bed and dreamed of home. (*Pause*) It was day when I awoke, tossing at the southwest end of Treasure Island. There was a great swell upon the ocean. But I was very near land. It made me bold, and I sat up and paddled. Then the sea mounted against me and pulled me toward the *Hispaniola*. Lapping alongside her, I crawled along the bowsprit and tumbled head first on the deck.

CREW (*Singing faintly*):
Fifteen men on the dead man's chest,
Yo-ho-ho, and a bottle of rum! (*Etc.*)

JIM: The few pirates aboard were all below. I struck down the Jolly Roger and hoisted the Union Jack. The ship was ours again! A few minutes later I had her sailing easily before the wind along the coast of Treasure Island. I headed her straight for the shore. She hit . . . staggered . . . and ground in the sand. I jumped clear and hurried to the stockade. It was very dark, but with the moon to help, I sighted the campfire. Surely that would be Ben Gunn. I ran joyfully toward it.

SILVER (*Calling*): Who goes?

JIM (*Whispering*): It was Silver! I tried to retreat and not even breathe.

SILVER (*Harshly*): Come here I say! Hands, go fetch him. (*Pause*) Ah, Hands bring yer prize to the firelight. Let's see what ye caught. (*Surprised*) Well, bless my bones—it's Jim Hawkins. (*Laughs*) Come to call, lad? Now that's right friendly. So ye come to join us now that we've got the real map.

JIM (*Alarmed*): The *real* map?

SILVER: Aye, lad. Ye sound like a parrot. Doctor Livesey did a bit of trucing.

JIM (*Defiantly*): He wouldn't trade with the likes of you!

SILVER (*Angrily*): Batten down yer hatches till yer spoken to! (*Calmly*) As I was saying, the doctor came to terms. Says he: "Cap'n Silver, let's bargain. We're beaten. You can have the map." (*Triumphantly*) Silver has beaten ye, lad!

JIM: Have you? Where's the *Hispaniola*? (*Boldly*) It's gone!

SILVER (*Roaring*): By thunder, you lie!

MORGAN: Enough of this! I'm for slitting Hawkins.

SILVER: Avast there, Morgan! Shiver me timbers! Where's the ship? Rough out there on the (*Breaks off, alarmed*)—why, I can't see it on the water.

JIM: You won't, either! The ship's lost. So's the treasure, and so are all of you. Marooned here with us. (*Proudly*) And I did it all.

SILVER (*Angrily*): Why, you—I'll take a cutlass to you, I will!

HANDS (*Gleefully*): Run the young 'un through.

SILVER: Avast, ye swabs, I say! Maybe ye all think you're cap'n here. I'll teach ye better. Take a cutlass, him that dares, and I'll see the color of his insides. I'm the best man here by a long sea mile—and I like the boy. He's more a man than any pair of rats of you.

MORGAN: Yer pardon, sir, but you're pretty free with the rules.

SILVER: Say yer piece, Morgan. Pipe up or lay to.

MORGAN: This crew's dissatisfied. We have rights. I say you be cap'n, but we claim our rights and demand a council.

CREW (*Shouting; ad lib*): Aye! Council! Morgan's right! (*Etc.*)

SILVER: Run, ye scurvy dogs! Council if ye like. Ye don't scare Long John. (*Whispering*) You're within a plank of death, lad, and so am I. They'll slip me the Black Spot for sure.

JIM (*Whispering*): The Black Spot?

SILVER (*Still whispering*): Aye. That's a summons. Means the cap'n has to do the crew's bidding. You're my last card, Jim Hawkins, and by the living thunder, I'm yours. I'll save my witness and ye'll save my neck.

JIM: You mean all's lost?

SILVER: Aye, by gum, I do. Ship's gone—neck's gone—that's it. I see no schooner. I'm tough, but I've given out. That lot at council are fools and cowards. I'll save yer life, but ye'll save Long John from swinging.

JIM (*Whispering*): I'll do what I can. Shh! They're coming.

SILVER (*Whispering*): Let 'em come, lad. I've still a shot in my locker. (*Normal voice*) Well, step up. Hand it over, lubber. I know the rules, I do. (*Pause*) The Black Spot! I thought so. (*Suspiciously*) Where'd you get the paper? (*Pause*) Ye fools! Ye fools! You've gone and cut this out of a Bible. What dog of ye cut a Bible? Answer me! Ye'll all swing for this.

HANDS (*Roughly*): Enough talk, John Silver. This crew tipped ye the Black Spot in full council. You're deposed.

SILVER: The Black Spot's not worth a biscuit! I have the map and the boy as hostage. I'm still cap'n.

HANDS: We want Flint's map. Then we find the treasure. And we're gonna dig for it now.

SILVER: So that's it, Hands. Well, shovels it is then. We'll find the treasure. Hawkins, here, will lead us to the ship, or he'll walk the plank for it. Are ye with me? (CREW *cheers.*)

JIM (*After a pause*): The pirates were now in good humor. Picking up shovels, we went treasure hunting. Silver led the way. They dragged me along as they struggled through the trees. But as we got near the treasure, the crew began to sing and leap to and fro. Morgan found the spot first. . . .

MORGAN (*Yelling angrily*): There's a hole here already! The treasure's gone. There's nothing here but a piece of old wood with Flint's name on it. We'll keelhaul ye for this, Silver, ye and Hawkins, too!

SILVER: Avast! First scum of ye makes a move to me'll be sorry. I'll split ye with me cutlass.

DOCTOR (*Calling*): Don't anyone make a move!

JIM (*Relieved*): Doctor Livesey! Am I glad to see you! And Ben Gunn.

SILVER: By thunder—Ben Gunn!

GUNN: Aye, Mister Silver. The same ye marooned so long ago.

DOCTOR: Are you all right, Jim?

JIM: I am now, sir.

SILVER: Aye, Doctor. Ye came in about the nick for me and Hawkins.

DOCTOR (*Dismissively*): No one addressed you, Silver. I'd not care if we found you dead.

SILVER: That's unkind, seeing that I saved the boy's life.

DOCTOR (*In disbelief*): Is that true, Jim?

JIM: It is, sir.

DOCTOR: So you double-crossed your crew, Silver.

SILVER (*Slyly*): No, I just like the lad.

DOCTOR: And especially your own neck, no doubt.

JIM: I promised to save him from swinging, Doctor.

DOCTOR: So that's it. Well, Silver, as much as I hate to say it, you might have saved your neck after all.

JIM (*Interrupting*): But how did you ever find me, Doctor?

DOCTOR: We've Ben Gunn to thank for that. He's been watching.

JIM: But the treasure's gone.

GUNN: Aye. I have it. 'Tis how I spent my time. Digging it up.

SILVER (*Astonished*): *You* have the treasure?

GUNN (*Proudly*): That I have—the doctor's seen it.

SILVER (*Sadly*): Ben, old shipmate, to think it's ye that beat me.

GUNN: Aye! And pretty well, too.

SILVER: But, Ben, old friend—

GUNN: I'm no friend to you, nor you to me. Jim and the doctor are me friends. I know ye not at all, Mister Silver.

JIM (*After a pause*): So we returned to the *Hispaniola*. My friends had found it and were standing guard. Captain Smollett wanted to put Silver in irons. I told them about my promise, but they didn't care. Doctor Livesey talked the captain and the squire into letting me keep my promise. For saving my life, Silver was let aboard as a free man. The captain just ignored him, but Squire Trelawney had to speak his mind.

SQUIRE: John Silver, you're a prodigious villain and a monstrous impostor. But I'm told I am not to prosecute you—well, then I will not.

SILVER: Thank ye kindly, sir.

SQUIRE (*Crossly*): Don't thank me! It is a gross dereliction of my duty. You should swing from a yardarm.

JIM: Those were the last words that anyone aboard the *Hispaniola* spoke to Long John Silver—(*Sheepishly*) except every now and again *I* spoke to him. After all, he did save my life. Well, anyway, three days later the gold, a huge fortune, was all loaded aboard. We weighed anchor and, before noon, to my great joy, we lost sight of Treasure Island. . . . In a few days, Long John Silver escaped in one of the boats, taking a sack of coins with him. But it was well worth it to get rid of him. We finally landed in Bristol. Ben Gunn spent his part of the treasure like there was no tomorrow. Captain Smollett retired from the sea. The Squire, Doctor, and I settled comfortably back into our lives. (*Eerily*) But at night when I hear the surf pounding on the coast, I sit upright in bed and hear far off the sound of Flint's men and their cutthroat song.

SAILOR (*Singing*):
Fifteen men on the dead man's chest,
Yo-ho-ho, and a bottle of rum! (*Etc.*)

THE END